INTRODUCTION TO FUNCTIONAL PROGRAMMING

Richard Bird

Programming Research Group,
Oxford University

Philip Wadler

Department of Computer Science,
University of Glasgow

PRENTICE HALL

NEW YORK   LONDON   TORONTO   SYDNEY   TOKYO   SINGAPORE

First published 1988 by
Prentice Hall International (UK) Ltd,
66 Wood Lane End, Hemel Hempstead,
Hertfordshire, HP2 4RG
A division of
Simon & Schuster International Group

© 1988 Richard Bird and Philip Wadler

Printed and bound in Great Britain by
BPCC Wheatons Ltd, Exeter.

Library of Congress Cataloging-in-Publication Data

Bird, R. J. (Richard J.)
 An introduction to functional programming.

 Bibliography: p.
 Includes index.
 1. Functional programming (Computer science)
I. Wadler, Philip, 1956–   II. Title.
QA76.6.B568   1988   005.1   87–36049
ISBN 0–13–484189–1

British Library Cataloguing in Publication Data

Bird, Richard, 1943–
 An introduction to functional programming. –
 (Prentice Hall international series in computer science).
 1. Electronic digital computers – Programming
I. Title   II. Wadler, Philip
 005.1   QA76.6
 ISBN 0–13–484189–1
 ISBN 0–13–484197-2 Pbk

---

3 4 5 6   93 92 91 90

Contents

CONTENTS

Preface

This is an introductory textbook on programming in general and functional programming in particular. No knowledge of computers or experience in writing programs is assumed. The book is therefore suitable for teaching a course in programming to first-year undergraduates, but it can also be used as an introduction to functional programming for students who are already experienced programmers.

In order to get the most out of the book, the student should know some mathematics, or at least possess a general appreciation of the principles of mathematical reasoning. Our primary aim in writing this book is to convey a view of programming as a mathematical activity, and mathematical reasoning lies at the heart of our subject. Functional programming involves notation and concepts of a kind which should be familiar to anyone with a little mathematical experience. For example, any student who has used the basic trigonometric functions to formulate problems in geometry, and has applied simple trigonometric laws and identities to derive solutions to these problems, will soon appreciate that a similar activity is being suggested for computational problems and their solution by functional programs. It follows that the kind of mathematical understanding required is not very complicated or specialised, just the general ability to follow manipulations of formulae through applying algebraic laws, and the appreciation of why such manipulations can be useful in the task of solving practical problems.

The order we have adopted for presenting material, as well as the particular topics covered, has a number of novel aspects. First of all, there is the gradually increasing emphasis on the idea of synthesising, or deriving, programs from their specifications. It is surprising how often a program can be calculated by simple equational reasoning from a mathematical description of what it is supposed to do. Many programs, particularly in the later part of the book, are derived from their specifications in this way. Others are left as exercises. Not all the programs in this book are constructed by calculation, for to do that would involve building detailed and special theories whose associated mathematics would take us beyond the scope of an introductory text. Such a task is a topic of active research and deserves a book of its own. Nevertheless, rather than deal with the subject of program synthesis, or derivation (or 'program transformation' as it is often called) in a separate chapter, we have decided to introduce the essential ideas gradually throughout the text.

Secondly, the subject of recursion is treated rather later on in the book (in Chapter 5) than an experienced reader might expect. However, there are two good reasons for introducing recursion later rather than earlier in a course on functional programming. First of all, we feel that the notion of a recursive function should be discussed at the same time as the notion of proof by mathematical induction. They are two sides of the same coin and one can best be understood only by referring to the other. Second, one can go a long way in solving problems by using a more-or-less fixed repertoire of functions, including a number of useful functions that operate on lists. By emphasising this collection of functions at the outset, we hope to foster a programming style which routinely deploys these functions as building blocks in the construction of larger ones.

Thirdly, we say very little about how functional programming languages are implemented. The major reason for this decision is that there now exist a number of excellent textbooks devoted primarily to the problem of interpreting and compiling functional languages.[1] Also, we feel that in the past too much emphasis has been given to this aspect of functional programming, and not enough to developing an appropriate style for constructing functional programs.

The fourth and final aspect of our presentation, and certainly one of the most important, concerns the decision to use mathematical notation, symbols and founts, rather than the concrete syntax of a particular programming language. It is not our intention in this book to promulgate a particular language, but only a particular style of programming. However, one does, of course, have to present some consistent notational framework and the knowledgeable reader will quickly recognise the similarity of the one we have chosen to that suggested by David Turner, of the University of Kent, in a succession of functional languages. These languages are SASL, KRC and, more recently, Miranda.[2] The last of these, Miranda, is very close to the kind of notation we are going to describe. The present book is *not* an introduction to Miranda, for we have found it convenient to differ in a few details (particularly in the names and precise definitions of the basic list processing functions), and many features of Miranda are not covered. Nevertheless, the book can be read with profit by someone who intends to use Miranda or, indeed, many other functional languages.

We should also acknowledge our debt to a number of other languages which propose some similar concepts and notations. These are ML (developed by Robin Milner at Edinburgh), Hope (Rod Burstall, Dave MacQueen and Don Sannella at Edinburgh), and Orwell (Philip Wadler at Oxford). The

---

[1] Including the recent *Implementation of Functional Programming Languages* by S.L. Peyton Jones, Prentice Hall, Hemel Hempstead, 1987.

[2] Miranda is a trademark of Research Software Limited.

proliferation of languages for functional programming is a testament to the vitality of the subject. On the other hand, we do not wish to add to this Tower of Babel. Hence we have attempted to avoid specific language details as much as possible.

Detailed organisation

In the first three chapters, we study basic notations for numbers, truth-values, tuples, functions and lists. Chapter 1 deals with fundamental concepts, reviews the definition of a mathematical function, and introduces sufficient notation to enable simple functions to be constructed. At the same time, we briefly introduce the fundamental idea of a specification as a mathematical description of the task a program is to perform. In Chapter 2 we introduce notation for basic kinds of data, and also say more about functions. We also discuss how one can achieve precise control over the layout of printed values.

Chapter 3 introduces lists, the most important data structure in functional programming. The names and informal meanings of a number of functions and operations on lists are presented, and some of the basic algebraic laws are described. Simple examples are given to help the student gain familiarity with these very useful tools for processing lists.

Chapter 4 deals with more substantial examples of list processing and is organised rather differently from preceding chapters. Each example is accompanied by exercises, projects, and various suggestions for possible improvements. An instructor can easily adapt these examples for use as classroom projects or student assignments. Some of the examples are not easy and require a fair amount of study.

In Chapter 5, we finally meet formally the notion of a recursive function and see the precise definitions of the operations discussed in previous chapters. At the same time we introduce the notion of an inductive proof and show how the algebraic laws and identities described in Chapter 3 can be proved. If the reader prefers, this chapter can be studied immediately after Chapter 3, or even in conjunction with it.

The emphasis in the first five chapters is on the expressive power of functional notation. The computer stays in the background and its role as a mechanism for evaluating expressions is touched upon only lightly. In Chapter 6 we turn to the subject of efficiency; for this we need to understand a little more about how a computer performs its task of evaluation. We discuss simple models of evaluation, and relate function definitions to how they utilise time and space resources when executed by a computer. We also discuss some general techniques of algorithm design which are useful in deriving efficient solutions to problems.

In Chapter 7 we introduce the notion of an infinite list, and show how such lists can be used to provide alternative solutions to some old problems, as well as being a useful framework in which to study new ones. In particular, we describe how infinite lists can be used in constructing programs that interact with the user.

In Chapters 8 and 9 we turn to new kinds of data structure and show how they can be represented in our programming notation. In particular, Chapter 9 is devoted to the study of trees and their applications. One of the advantages of an expression-based notation for programming is that the study of data structures can be presented in a direct and simple manner, and one can go much further in describing and deriving algorithms that manipulate general data structures than would be possible in a conventional programming language.

Advice to the instructor

We have used the material in this text as a basis for courses in functional programming to first-year Mathematics and Computation undergraduates at Oxford, to graduate students on an M.Sc. course, and on various industrial courses. Drafts of the book have also been used to teach undergraduates and graduates in the USA and The Netherlands. The sixteen lecture course which is typical at Oxford means that only a selection of topics can be presented in the time available. We have followed the order of the chapters, but concentrated on Chapters 2, 3, 4, 7 and part of Chapter 9. Chapter 5 on recursion and induction has usually been left to tutorial classes (another typical aspect of the Oxford system). The material in Chapter 5 is not really difficult and is probably better left to small classes or private study; too many induction proofs carried out at the blackboard have a distinctly soporific effect. On the other hand, Chapter 4, on examples, deserves a fair amount of attention. We have tried to choose applications that interest and stimulate the student and encourage them to try and find better solutions. Some of the examples have been set as practical projects with considerable success.

We judge that the whole book could be taught in a two-term (or two-semester) course. It can also be adapted for a course on Algorithm Design (emphasising the material in Chapter 6), and for a course on Data Structures (emphasising Chapter 9, in particular).

It is of course important that formal teaching should be supported by laboratory and practical work. At Oxford we have used the language Orwell as a vehicle for practical computing work, but Miranda is a suitable alternative. In fact, any higher-order functional language with non-strict semantics would do as well, particularly if based on an equational style of definition with patterns on the left-hand side of definitions.

Acknowledgements

This book has been rather a long time in the making. It has benefited enormously from the continued support, enthusiasm and constructive advice of colleagues and students, both at Oxford and other universities. The suggestions of colleagues in the Programming Research Group at Oxford have been particularly relevant, since they have been personally responsible for teaching the material to their tutorial students while a lecture course was in progress.

A special debt is owed to John Hughes, now at Glasgow, whose grasp of functional programming was a major influence on this book. We also owe a particular debt to David Turner who stimulated our interest in functional programming and provided a simple yet powerful notation, in KRC, for inspiring programmers to produce mathematical programs.

Several people have read earlier drafts of the book and identified numerous errors and omissions; in particular, we should like to thank Martin Filby, Simon Finn, Jeroen Fokker, Maarten Fokkinga, Iain Houston, Antony Simmins, Gerard Huet, Ursula Martin, Lambert Meertens, Simon Peyton Jones, Mark Ramaer, Hamilton Richards, Joe Stoy, Bernard Sufrin, and David Turner.

Finally, we should like to acknowledge the contribution of Tony Hoare who encouraged us to write this book and provided, through his leadership of the Programming Research Group, such a stimulating environment in which to work.

Oxford   Richard Bird
January 1988   Philip Wadler

Note on third printing
In this printing, about a dozen new errors have been identified and corrected. The authors would be pleased to hear of any more.

RB (bird@uk.ac.ox.prg)

Chapter 1

Fundamental Concepts

1.1 Functional programming

Programming in a functional language consists of building definitions and using the computer to evaluate expressions. The primary role of the programmer is to construct a function to solve a given problem. This function, which may involve a number of subsidiary functions, is expressed in notation that obeys normal mathematical principles. The primary role of the computer is to act as an evaluator or calculator: its job is to evaluate expressions and print the results. In this respect, the computer acts much like an ordinary pocket calculator. What distinguishes a functional calculator from the humbler variety is the programmer's ability to make definitions to increase its powers of calculation. Expressions which contain occurrences of the names of functions defined by the programmer are evaluated by using the given definitions as simplification (or 'reduction') rules for converting expressions to printable form.

A characteristic feature of functional programming is that if an expression possesses a well-defined value, then the order in which a computer may carry out the evaluation does not affect the outcome. In other words, the meaning of an expression is its value and the task of the computer is simply to obtain it. It follows that expressions in a functional language can be constructed, manipulated and reasoned about, like any other kind of mathematical expression, using more or less familiar algebraic laws. The result, as we hope to justify, is a conceptual framework for programming which is at once very simple, very concise, very flexible and very powerful.

1.1.1 Sessions and scripts

To illustrate the idea of using a computer as a calculator, imagine we are sitting at a terminal and the computer has indicated its willingness to evaluate an expression by displaying a prompt sign:

1

?

at the beginning of a blank line. We can then type an expression, followed by a newline character, and the computer will respond by printing the result of evaluating the expression, followed by a new prompt ? on a new line, indicating that the process can begin again with another expression.

One kind of expression we might type is a number:

? 42
42

Here, the computer's response is simply to redisplay the number we typed. The decimal numeral 42 is an expression in its simplest possible form and no further process of evaluation can be applied to it.

We might type a slightly more interesting kind of expression:

? 6 × 7
42

Here, the computer can simplify the expression by performing the multiplication. In this book, we shall adopt common mathematical notations for writing expressions. In particular, the multiplication operator will be denoted by the sign ×. It may or may not be the case that a particular keyboard contains this sign, but we shall not concern ourselves in the text with how to represent mathematical symbols in a restricted character set.

We will not elaborate here on the possible forms of numerical and other kinds of expression that can be submitted for evaluation. They will be dealt with thoroughly in the following chapters. The important point to absorb for the moment is that one can just type expressions and have them evaluated. This sequence of interactions between user and computer is called a 'session'.

Now let us illustrate the second, and intellectually more challenging, aspect of functional programming: building definitions. A list of definitions will be called a 'script'. Here is a simple example of a script:

$$
\begin{aligned}
square\ x &= x \times x \\
min\ x\ y &= x, \qquad \text{if } x \le y \\
&= y, \qquad \text{if } x > y
\end{aligned}
$$

In this script, two functions, named $square$ and min, have been defined. The function $square$ takes a value x as argument and returns the value of x multiplied by itself as its result. The function min takes two numbers, x and y, as arguments and returns the smaller value. For the present we will not discuss the exact syntax used for making definitions. Notice, however, that definitions are written as equations between certain kinds of expression; these expressions can contain variables, here denoted by the symbols x and y.

Having created a script, we can submit it to the computer and enter a session. For example, the following session is now possible:

? *square* (3 + 4)
49

? *min* 3 4
3

? *square* (*min* 3 4)
9

In effect, the purpose of a definition is to introduce a *binding* associating a given name with a given value. In the above script, the name *square* is associated with the function which squares its argument, and the name *min* is associated with the function which returns the smaller of its two arguments. A set of bindings is called an *environment* or *context*. Expressions are always evaluated within some context and can contain occurrences of the names found in that context. The evaluator will use the definitions associated with these names as rules for simplifying expressions.

Some expressions can be evaluated without the programmer having to provide a context. A number of operations may be given as primitive in that the rules of simplification are built into the evaluator. For example, we shall suppose the basic operations of arithmetic are provided as primitive. Other commonly useful operations may be provided in special libraries of predefined functions.

At any stage a programmer can return to the script in order to add or modify definitions. The new script can then be resubmitted to the computer to provide a new context and another session started.

For example, suppose we return to the script and add the definitions:

$$side \quad = \quad 12$$
$$area \quad = \quad square\ side$$

These equations introduce two numerical constants, *side* and *area*. Notice that the definition of *area* depends on the previously defined function *square*. Having resubmitted the script, we can enter a session and type, for example:

? *area*
144

? *min* (*area* + 4) 150
148

To summarise the important points made so far:

1. Scripts are collections of definitions supplied by the programmer.

2. Definitions are expressed as equations between certain kinds of expression and describe mathematical functions.

3. During a session, expressions are submitted for evaluation; these expressions can contain references to the functions defined in the script.

Exercises

1.1.1 Using the function *square*, design a function *quad* which raises its argument to the fourth power.

1.1.2 Define a function *max* which returns the greater of its two arguments.

1.1.3 Define a function for computing the area of a circle with given radius r (use $22/7$ as an approximation to π).

1.2 Expressions and values

As we have seen, the notion of an expression is central in functional programming. There are many kinds of mathematical expression, not all of which are permitted in the notation we shall describe, but all possess certain characteristics in common. The most important feature of mathematical notation is that an expression is used solely to describe (or *denote*) a *value*. In other words, the meaning of an expression *is* its value and there are no other effects, hidden or otherwise, in any procedure for actually obtaining it. Furthermore, the value of an expression depends only on the the values of its constituent expressions (if any) and these subexpressions may be replaced freely by others possessing the same value. An expression may contain certain 'names' which stand for unknown quantities, but it is normal in mathematical notation to presume that different occurrences of the same name refer to the same unknown quantity (within obvious syntactic limits). Such names are usually called 'variables', but every mathematician understands that variables do *not* vary: they always denote the same quantity, provided we remain within the same context of the definitions associated with them. The characteristic property of mathematical expressions described here is called *referential transparency*.

Among the kinds of value an expression may denote are included: numbers, truth-values, characters, tuples, functions, and lists. All of these will be described in due course. As we shall see later on in the book, it is also possible to introduce new kinds of value and define operations for generating and manipulating them.

1.2.1 Reduction

The computer evaluates an expression by reducing it to its 'simplest equivalent form' and printing the result. The terms *evaluation*, *simplification*, and *reduction* will be used interchangeably to describe this process. We can give a brief flavour of the essence of reduction by considering the evaluation of the expression *square* $(3 + 4)$. Suppose we let the sign $\Rightarrow$ mean 'reduces to'.

One possible reduction sequence is as follows:

$$\begin{aligned} square \ (3+4) \quad &\Rightarrow \quad square \ 7 \quad (+) \\ &\Rightarrow \quad 7 \times 7 \quad\ \ (square) \\ &\Rightarrow \quad 49 \qquad\ (\times) \end{aligned}$$

In this sequence, the label $(+)$ refers to a use of the built-in rule for addition, $(\times)$ refers to a similar rule for multiplication, and $(square)$ refers to a use of the rule:

$$square \ x \quad \Rightarrow \quad x \times x$$

which is associated with the definition of $square$ supplied by the programmer. The expression 49 cannot be further reduced, so that is the result printed by the computer.

The above sequence of reduction steps is not the only way to simplify the expression $square \ (3+4)$. Indeed, another sequence is as follows:

$$\begin{aligned} square \ (3+4) \quad &\Rightarrow \quad (3+4) \times (3+4) \quad (square) \\ &\Rightarrow \quad 7 \times (3+4) \qquad\quad (+) \\ &\Rightarrow \quad 7 \times 7 \qquad\qquad\ \ (+) \\ &\Rightarrow \quad 49 \qquad\qquad\qquad (\times) \end{aligned}$$

In this reduction sequence the rule for $square$ is applied first, but the final result is the same. A fuller account of reduction, including a discussion of different reduction strategies, will be given in Chapter 6. The point to grasp here is that expressions can be evaluated by a basically simple process of substitution and simplification, using both primitive rules and rules supplied by the programmer in the form of definitions.

It is important to be clear about the distinction between values and their representations by expressions. The simplest equivalent form of an expression, whatever that may be, is *not* a value but a representation of it. Somewhere, in outer space perhaps, one can imagine a universe of abstract values, but on earth they can only be recognised and manipulated by their representations. There are many representations for one and the same value. For example, the abstract number forty-nine can be represented by the decimal numeral 49, the roman numeral XLIX, the expression 7×7, as well as infinitely many others. Computers usually operate with the binary representation of numbers in which forty-nine may be represented by the pattern 0000000000110001 of 16 bits.

We shall say an expression is *canonical* (or in *normal form*) if it cannot be further reduced. A value is printed as its canonical representation. Notice that the notion of a canonical expression is dependent both on the syntax given for forming expressions and the precise definition of the permissible reduction rules. Some values have no canonical representations, others have no finite ones. For example, the number π has no finite decimal representation.

It is possible to get a computer to print out the decimal expansion of π digit by digit, but the process will never terminate.

Some expressions cannot be reduced at all. In other words, they do not denote well-defined values in the normal mathematical sense. For instance, supposing the operator / denotes numerical division, the expression 1/0 does not denote a well-defined number. A request to evaluate 1/0 may cause the evaluator to respond with an error message, such as 'attempt to divide by zero', or go into an infinitely long sequence of calculations without producing any result. In order that we can say that, without exception, every (well-formed) expression denotes a value, it is convenient to introduce a special symbol $\perp$, pronounced 'bottom', to stand for the undefined value. In particular, the value of 1/0 is $\perp$ and we can assert $1/0 = \perp$. The computer is not expected to be able to produce the value $\perp$. Confronted with an expression whose value is $\perp$, the computer may give an error message, or it may remain perpetually silent. Thus, $\perp$ is a special kind of value, rather like the special value ∞ in mathematical calculus. Like special values in other branches of mathematics, $\perp$ can be admitted to the universe of values only if we state precisely the properties it is required to have and its relationship with other values. We shall not go into the properties of $\perp$ for a while, but for now merely note the reasons for its existence and its special status.

Exercises

1.2.1 Count the number of different ways that:

$$square\,(square\,(3+7))$$

can be reduced to normal form.

1.2.2 Consider the definition:

$$three\;x = 3$$

In how many ways can *three* $(3 + 4)$ be reduced to normal form?

1.2.3 Imagine a language of expressions for representing integers defined by the syntax rules: (i) *zero* is an expression; (ii) if e is an expression, then so are $(succ\;e)$ and $(pred\;e)$. An evaluator reduces expressions in this language by applying the following rules repeatedly until no longer possible:

$$(succ\,(pred\;e)) \;\Rightarrow\; e \qquad (succ.1)$$
$$(pred\,(succ\;e)) \;\Rightarrow\; e \qquad (pred.1)$$

Simplify the expression

$$(succ\,(pred\,(succ\,(pred\,(pred\;zero)))))$$

In how many ways can the reduction rules be applied to this expression? Do they all lead to the same final result? Prove that the process of reduction must terminate for all given expressions. (*Hint:* Define an appropriate notion of expression size, and show that reduction does indeed reduce size.)

Suppose an extra syntactic rule is added to the language: (iii) if e_1 and e_2 are expressions, then so is $(add\, e_1\, e_2)$. The corresponding reduction rules are:

$$
\begin{aligned}
(add\ zero\ e_2) &\Rightarrow e_2 & (add.1)\\
(add\ (succ\ e_1)\ e_2) &\Rightarrow (succ\ (add\ e_1\ e_2)) & (add.2)\\
(add\ (pred\ e_1)\ e_2) &\Rightarrow (pred\ (add\ e_1\ e_2)) & (add.3)
\end{aligned}
$$

Simplify the expression:

$$(add\ (succ\ (pred\ zero))\ zero).$$

Count the number of different ways the reduction rules can be applied to the above expression. Do they always lead to the same final result? Prove that the the process of reduction must always terminate for any given initial expression. (*Hint:* Extend the notion of expression size.)

1.2.4 Imagine a language of finite sequences of 0 and 1. The rules for simplifying strings in this language are given by:

$$
\begin{aligned}
1??x &\Rightarrow x1101\\
0??x &\Rightarrow x00
\end{aligned}
$$

In these rules, the variable x denotes an arbitrary sequence of 0s and 1s and the sign '?' denotes a single 0 or 1. Reduce the following expressions to canonical form:

$$1110 \qquad 10 \qquad 1110100$$

Construct an expression for which the reduction process does not terminate. (Such a system of reduction rules is known as a *Post Normal System*; see Minsky [1] for further details. Although it is easy to construct strings that 'loop', it is an open problem whether or not there is an initial string on which the above system fails to terminate by producing an infinite number of successively larger strings.)

1.3 Types

In the notation we are going to describe, the universe of values is partitioned into organised collections, called *types*. Types can be divided into two kinds. Firstly, there are *basic* types whose values are given as primitive. For example, numbers constitute a basic type (the type *num*), as do truth-values (the type *bool*) and characters (the type *char*). Secondly, there are *compound* (or *derived*) types, whose values are constructed from those of other types. Examples of derived types include: $(num, char)$, the type of pairs of values, the first component of which is a number and the second a character; $(num \rightarrow num)$, the type of functions from numbers to numbers; and $[char]$, the type of lists of characters. Each type has associated with it certain operations which are not meaningful for other types. For instance, one cannot sensibly add a number to a character or multiply two functions together.

It is an important principle of the notation we are going to describe that every well-formed expression can be assigned a type that can be deduced from the constituents of the expression alone. In other words, just as the value of an expression depends only on the values of its component expressions, so does its type. This principle is called *strong-typing*.

The major consequence of the discipline imposed by strong-typing is that any expression which cannot be assigned a 'sensible' type is regarded as not being well-formed and is rejected by the computer before evaluation. Such expressions have *no* value: they are simply regarded as illegal.

Here is an example of a script which contains a definition that cannot be assigned a sensible type:

$$
\begin{aligned}
ay\ x &= \text{'A'} \\
bee\ x &= x + ay\ x
\end{aligned}
$$

The expression 'A' in this script denotes the character A. For any x, the value of $ay\ x$ is 'A' and so has type *char*. Since $+$ is reserved to denote the operation of numerical addition, the right-hand side of the definition of *bee* is not well-typed: one cannot add characters numerically. It follows that the function *bee* does not possess a sensible type, and the script is rejected by the computer. (On the other hand, the function *ay* does possess a sensible type; we shall see what it is in the next section.)

There are two stages of analysis when an expression is submitted for evaluation. The expression is first checked to see whether it conforms to the correct syntax laid down for expressions. If it does not, the computer signals a syntax error. This stage is called *syntax-analysis*. If it does, then the expression is analysed to see if it possesses a sensible type. This stage is called *type-analysis*. If the expression fails to pass this stage, the computer signals a type error. Only if the expression passes both stages can the process of evaluation begin. Similar remarks apply to definitions before a script is accepted.

Strong typing is important because adherence to the discipline can help in the design of clear and well-structured programs. What is more, a wide range of logical errors can be trapped by any computer which enforces it.

1.4   Functions and definitions

The most important kind of value in functional programming is a function value. Mathematically speaking, a function f is a rule of correspondence which associates with each element of a given type A a unique member of a second type B. The type A is called the *source* type, and B the *target* type of the function. We will express this information by writing:

$$f :: A \rightarrow B$$

This formula asserts that the type of f is $A \rightarrow B$. In other words, the type-expression $A \rightarrow B$ denotes a type whenever A and B do, and describes the type of functions from A to B.

A function $f :: A \rightarrow B$ is said to take *arguments* in A and return *results* in B. If x denotes an element of A, then we write $f(x)$, or just $f\,x$, to denote the result of *applying* the function f to x. This value is the unique element of B associated with x by the rule of correspondence for f. The former notation, $f(x)$, is the one normally employed in mathematics to denote functional application, but the brackets are not really necessary and we shall use the second form, $f\,x$, instead. However, when formal expressions are mixed in with running prose we shall often surround them with brackets to aid the eye. For example, we write $(f\,x)$ rather than $f\,x$.

We shall be careful never to confuse a function with its application to an argument. In some mathematics texts one often finds the phrase 'the function $f(x)$', when what is really meant is 'the function f'. In such texts, functions are rarely considered as values which may themselves be used as arguments to other functions and the usage causes no confusion. In functional programming, however, functions are values with exactly the same status as all other values; in particular, they can be passed as arguments to functions and returned as results. Accordingly, we cannot afford to be casual about the difference between a function and the result of applying it to an argument.

It is important to keep in mind the distinction between a function value and a particular definition of it. There are many possible definitions for one and the same function. For instance, we can define the function which doubles its argument in the following two ways:

$$
\begin{aligned}
double\ x &= x + x \\
double'\ x &= 2 \times x
\end{aligned}
$$

The two definitions describe different procedures for obtaining the correspondence, but *double* and *double'* denote the same function and we can assert $double = double'$ as a mathematical truth. Regarded as procedures for evaluation, one definition may be more or less 'efficient' than the other, in the sense that the evaluator may be able to reduce expressions of the form $(double\ x)$ more or less quickly than expressions of the form $(double'\ x)$. However, the notion of efficiency is not one which can be attached to function values themselves. Indeed, it depends on the given form of the definition and the precise characteristics of the mechanism that evaluates it.

1.4.1 Type information

When defining functions in a script, it is allowable to include type information
about the function. For example, we can define the function *square* in a script
by writing:

$$square \quad :: \quad num \to num$$
$$square \; x \quad = \quad x \times x$$

Although it is often good practice to include them, function definitions do
not have to be accompanied by type declarations. The type of the function
can be inferred from its defining equation alone. This is an instance of the
strong-typing discipline mentioned in the previous section. The operator $\times$ is
reserved exclusively for the multiplication of numeric quantities, so the type
assignment *square* $:: num \to num$ can be deduced mechanically.

Some functions have very general source and target types. Consider the
following definition:

$$id \; x \quad = \quad x$$

This equation defines the identity function: it maps every member of the
source type to itself. Its type is therefore $A \to A$ for some suitable type A.
But every type A is suitable, since no particular property of the elements
of A is required in the definition of *id*. The problem of giving a sensible
type to *id* is solved by introducing *type variables*. The type assigned to *id* is
$\alpha \to \alpha$. Here α denotes a type variable. We shall use greek letters $\alpha, \beta, \gamma, \ldots$,
and so on, to denote type variables. Like other kinds of variable, a type
variable can be instantiated to different types in different circumstances. For
instance, the expression $(id \; 3)$ is well-formed and has type *num* because
num can be substituted for α in the type of *id*, yielding a $(num \to num)$
version. Similarly, the expression $(id \; square)$ is well-formed and has type
$(num \to num)$ because $(num \to num)$ (the type of the function *square*)
can be substituted for α. Finally, the expression $(id \; id)$ is also well-formed
because the type $(\alpha \to \alpha)$ can itself be substituted for α. The type of $(id \; id)$
is therefore $(\alpha \to \alpha)$. And, of course, we have $id \; id = id$.

Here is another example of a valid definition whose associated type contains variables. Recall the definition of the function *ay* from the previous
section:

$$ay \; x = \text{`A'}$$

The type associated with *ay* is *ay* $:: \alpha \to char$. The source type of *ay* can
be any type at all.

We now have the beginnings of a language of expressions that denote
types. This language contains constant expressions, such as *num* or *char*,
variables, such as α and β, and operators, such as $\to$. If such an expression
does contain variables, then we say that it denotes a *polymorphic* type. In
particular, the functions *id* and *ay* have polymorphic types.

1.4.2 Forms of definition

In many situations we may want to define the value of a function by case analysis. Consider again the function *min* from Section 1.1:

$$min\ x\ y\ =\ x,\ \text{if } x \le y$$
$$=\ y,\ \text{if } x > y$$

This definition consists of two expressions, each of which is distinguished by boolean-valued expressions, called *guards*. A boolean-valued expression is an expression which evaluates to one of the truth-values *True* or *False*. The first alternative of the definition says that the value of $(min\ x\ y)$ is defined to be x, provided the expression $x \le y$ evaluates to *True*. The second alternative says that $(min\ x\ y)$ is defined to be y provided the expression $x > y$ evaluates to *True*. The two cases, $x \le y$ and $x > y$, exhaust all possibilities, so the value of *min* is defined for all numbers x and y. It does not matter in which order we write the alternatives because the two cases are disjoint.

Another way to define *min* is to write:

$$min\ x\ y\ =\ x,\ \text{if } x \le y$$
$$=\ y,\ \textbf{otherwise}$$

The special word 'otherwise' can be thought of as a convenient abbreviation for the condition which returns the value *True* when all previous guards return the value *False*.

The final piece of notation we shall introduce here is called a *local* definition. In mathematical descriptions one often finds an expression qualified by a phrase of the form 'where ...'. For instance, one might find '$f(x,y) = (a+1)(a+2)$, where $a = (x+y)/2$'. The same device can be used in a formal definition:

$$f(x,y)\ =\ (a+1) \times (a+2)$$
$$\textbf{where}\ a = (x+y)/2$$

Here, the special word 'where' is used to introduce a local definition whose context (or *scope*) is the expression on the right-hand side of the definition of f. Notice that the whole of the where-clause is indented to show it is part of this expression.

A local definition can be used in conjunction with a definition by case analysis. Consider the following:

$$f\ x\ y\ =\ x+a,\ \text{if } x > 10$$
$$=\ x-a,\ \textbf{otherwise}$$
$$\textbf{where}\ a = square\ (y+1)$$

In this definition, the where-clause qualifies *both* parts of the right-hand side. Although, for readability, there are two occurrences of the = sign in the case analysis for f, there is only one equation and the scope of the where-clause includes all of it.

1.4.3   Currying

Consider again the definition of *min*:

$$min\ x\ y\ =\ x,\ \ \textbf{if}\ x \leq y$$
$$=\ y,\ \ \textbf{if}\ x > y$$

Notice that the arguments to *min* are written without brackets and an intervening comma. We can, if we like, add brackets and write:

$$min'\,(x,y)\ =\ x,\ \ \textbf{if}\ x \leq y$$
$$=\ y,\ \ \textbf{otherwise}$$

The two functions, *min* and *min'*, are very closely related, but there is a subtle difference: they have different types. The function *min'* takes a single argument which is a structured value consisting of a *pair* of numbers; its type is given by:

$$min' :: (num, num) \rightarrow num$$

The function *min*, on the other hand, takes two arguments one at a time. Its type is given by:

$$min :: num \rightarrow (num \rightarrow num)$$

In other words, *min* is a function which takes a number and returns a function (from numbers to numbers). For each value of x the expression $(min\ x)$ denotes a function which takes an argument y and returns the minimum of x and y.

Here is another example. The function *add*, defined by:

$$add\ x\ y\ =\ x + y$$

also has type $num \rightarrow (num \rightarrow num)$. For each x, the function $(add\ x)$ 'adds x to things'. In particular, $(add\ 1)$ is the successor function which increments its argument by 1, and $(add\ 0)$ is the identity function on numbers.

This simple device for replacing structured arguments by a sequence of simple ones is known as 'currying', after the American logician H. B. Curry. One advantage of currying is that it reduces the number of brackets which have to be written in expressions (an aspect of the notation the reader will quickly grow to appreciate). For currying to work properly in a consistent manner, we require that the operation of functional application associates to the left. That is, $min\ x\ y$ means $(min\ x)\ y$ and not $min\,(x\ y)$. As an operator, functional application has a very 'quiet' notation, being represented by just a space. In formal expressions this quietness improves readability, and with currying we can exploit quietness to the full.

We have now said enough about functions, types and definitions to enable simple scripts to be written. Further material on functions will be found at the end of the next chapter.

Exercises

1.4.1 Describe one appropriate type for the definite integral function of mathematical analysis, as used in the phrase 'the integral of f from a to b'.

1.4.2 Give examples of functions with the following types:

$$(num \rightarrow num) \rightarrow num$$
$$num \rightarrow (num \rightarrow num)$$
$$(num \rightarrow num) \rightarrow (num \rightarrow num)$$

1.4.3 Give a definition of a function $sign :: num \rightarrow num$ which returns 1 if its argument is positive, -1 if its argument is negative, and 0 otherwise.

1.4.4 Suggest possible types for the following functions:

$$
\begin{aligned}
one\ x &= 1 \\
apply\ f\ x &= f\ x \\
compose\ f\ g\ x &= f\ (g\ x)
\end{aligned}
$$

1.5   Specifications and implementations

In computer programming, a *specification* is a mathematical description of the task a program is to perform, while an *implementation* is a program that satisfies the specification. Specifications and implementations are quite different in nature and serve different purposes. Specifications are expressions of the programmer's intent (or client's expectations) and their purpose is to be as brief and clear as possible; implementations are expressions for execution by computer and their purpose is to be efficient enough to execute within the time and space available. The link between the two is the requirement that the implementation satisfies, or meets, the specification, and the serious programmer is obliged to provide a *proof* that this is indeed the case.

A specification for a function value is some statement of the intended relationship between argument values and results. A simple example is given by the following specification of a function *increase* $:: num \rightarrow num$:

$$increase\ x > square\ x$$

for all $x \geq 0$. This just says that the result of *increase* should be greater than the square of its argument, whenever the argument is greater than or equal to zero.

Here is one possible implementation of *increase*:

$$increase\ x = square\ (x + 1)$$

This is a valid definition in our programming notation. The proof that this definition of *increase* satisfies the specification is as follows: assuming $x \geq 0$, we have:

$$
\begin{aligned}
increase\ x \ &= \ square\,(x+1) & &(increase) \\
&= \ (x+1) \times (x+1) & &(square) \\
&= \ x \times x + 2 \times x + 1 & &(\text{algebra}) \\
&> \ x \times x & &(\text{assumption: } x \geq 0) \\
&= \ square\ x & &(square)
\end{aligned}
$$

Here we have invented a definition of *increase* first, and afterwards verified that it meets the specification. Clearly, there are many other functions which will satisfy the specification and, since this is the only requirement, all are equally good.

One way of specifying a function is to state the rule of correspondence explicitly. The functional notation we shall describe can be very expressive, and it is often possible to write down a formal definition within the notation which will actually serve as the specification. This specification can then be executed directly. However, it may prove so grossly inefficient that the possibility of execution will be of theoretical interest only. Having written an executable specification, the programmer is not necessarily relieved of the burden (or pleasure) of producing an equivalent but acceptably efficient alternative.

The problem of showing that formal definitions meet their specifications can be tackled in a number of ways. One approach, illustrated above, is to design the definition first and afterwards verify that the necessary conditions are satisfied. Another approach, which can lead to clearer and simpler programs, is to systematically develop (or *synthesise*) the definition from the specification. For example, if we look at the specification of *increase* we may argue that since $x + 1 > x$ for all x, we have:

$$square\ x + 1 > square\ x$$

and so we can define:

$$increase\ x = square\ x + 1$$

In fact, the new definition of *increase* satisfies a stronger specification than required, since *increase* $x > square\ x$ for all possible values of x, including negative ones. This does not invalidate the definition because any implementation that gives more than is required is at least as good as one that does not. We shall see other, more convincing, examples of systematic program development as we progress.

This paradigm of software development – first write a clear specification, then develop an acceptably efficient implementation – is the focus of active research in computation and should not be taken as a cut-and-dried method,

applicable in all circumstances. Two potential sources of difficulty are that
the formal specification may not match our informal intentions, and the proof
that the implementation matches the specification may be so large or complicated that it cannot be guaranteed to be free of error. Nevertheless, by
trying to follow the approach whenever we can, the reliability of programs
can be greatly increased.

Exercises

1.5.1 Using any suitable notation, write down a specification of a function
isSquare that determines whether or not its argument is an integer which is
the square of another integer. Suppose the value of $(intsqrt\ x)$ is the largest
integer which is no greater than $\sqrt{x}$. Will the following definition meet your
specification?

$$isSquare\ x = (square\ (intsqrt\ x) = x)$$

1.5.2 Write down a precise specification of the function *intsqrt* mentioned
in the previous question.

Chapter 2

Basic Data Types

This chapter introduces the basic types of value out of which expressions are constructed. They include numbers, booleans, characters and tuples. We shall describe how the values of each type are represented and give some of the primitive operations for manipulating them. Along the way we shall discuss further features of our notation for functional programming, including: (i) the relationship between functions and operators; (ii) how to exercise precise control over the layout of results; and (iii) how to abbreviate the names of types.

2.1 Numbers

The data type *num* consists of whole numbers (or *integers*) and fractional numbers (also called *floating-point numbers*). A whole number is a number whose fractional part is zero. Numeric constants are represented in decimal notation, as the following examples show:

$$42 \quad -42 \quad 0 \quad 13.632 \quad -0.6 \quad 6.0$$

Although there are infinitely many numbers, computers have finite capacities and can only store a limited range. Even within a finite range there are infinitely many fractional numbers, so not all numbers can be stored exactly. It is wise to be aware that a limitation exists, especially since it can cause what appears to be a mathematically correct program to fail or return unexpected results. However, precise details of number representation and accuracy will vary from implementation to implementation and we shall not go into details.

We will use the operations of Table 2.1 for processing elements of *num*. Each of these is used as a *binary infix operator*; for example, we write $x + y$. The minus sign $(-)$ can also be used as a *unary prefix operator*, that is, we write $-x$ to denote the negation of x.

+	addition
−	subtraction
×	multiplication
/	division
^	exponentiation
div	integer division (see later)
mod	integer remainder (see later)

Table 2.1 Arithmetic operations

As the representation of an arbitrary number may not be exact, operations on fractional numbers may not produce the same answers as in ordinary arithmetic. For example, the values of $(x \times y)/y$ and x may not be equal. However, when the arguments and results of operations are whole numbers, and are within the range of permissible values prescribed by a particular implementation, then the arithmetic will be exact. In other words, all the basic operations except division / return exact integer results on integer arguments, provided the integers are in the permitted range.

Here are some simple examples of numerical expressions:

? 3 − 7 − 2
−6

? 3 × 7 + 4.1
25.1

? 3 × (7 + 4.1)
33.3

? *square* 3 × 4
36

? 3 ^ 4 × 2
162

It is clear from these examples that more than one operator may appear in an expression and that different operators have different binding powers. Moreover, when the same operator occurs twice in succession, as in the case $(3 − 7 − 2)$, a certain order of association is assumed. We deal with these matters, precedence and order of association, separately.

2.1.1 Precedence

When several operators appear together in an expression, certain rules of *precedence* are provided to resolve possible ambiguity. The precedence rules for the common arithmetic operators are absorbed in childhood without ever being stated formally. Their sole purpose in life is to allow one to reduce the number of brackets in an expression. The relative binding powers of the binary arithmetic operators can be summarised as follows (operators with a higher precedence appear above those with a lower precedence):

$$\widehat{} \qquad\qquad\qquad \text{exponentiation}$$
$$\times\ /\ \textbf{div mod} \qquad \text{the 'multiplying' operators}$$
$$+\ - \qquad\qquad\qquad \text{the 'addition' operators}$$

In addition, as functional application binds more tightly than any other operator, it goes above exponentiation in this list.

To illustrate these rules:

$$3\,\widehat{}\,4 \times 5 \qquad \text{means} \qquad (3\,\widehat{}\,4) \times 5$$
$$3 \times 7 + 4.1 \qquad \text{means} \qquad (3 \times 7) + 4.1$$
$$square\ 3 \times 4 \qquad \text{means} \qquad (square\ 3) \times 4$$

Of course, just as in normal mathematical notation, one can always use (round) brackets to force a different order of grouping. In particular, brackets will always be used to remove possible ambiguity from expressions involving unary minus, so unary minus is not assigned a precedence in the notation used in this book. For example, we shall write either $(-x)\,\widehat{}\,y$ or $-(x\,\widehat{}\,y)$, but never just $-x\,\widehat{}\,y$.

2.1.2   Order of association

The second device for reducing brackets is to provide an order of *association* for operators of equal binding power. Operators can associate either to the *left* or to the *right*. We have already encountered one example of declaring such a preference: functional application – the operator denoted by just a space – associates to the left in expressions. In arithmetic, operators on the same level of precedence are usually declared to associate to the left as well. Thus $5 - 4 - 2$ means $(5 - 4) - 2$ and not $5 - (4 - 2)$. However, exponentiation associates to the right, so $3\,\widehat{}\,4\,\widehat{}\,5$ means $3\,\widehat{}\,(4\,\widehat{}\,5)$ and not $(3\,\widehat{}\,4)\,\widehat{}\,5$. Another example of an operator which associates to the right is the function type operator $\rightarrow$: thus, $\alpha \rightarrow \beta \rightarrow \gamma$ means $\alpha \rightarrow (\beta \rightarrow \gamma)$ and not $(\alpha \rightarrow \beta) \rightarrow \gamma$. Of course, it is not necessary to insist that an order of association be prescribed for every operator. If no preference is indicated, then brackets must be used to avoid ambiguity.

A declaration of a specific order of association should not be confused with a different, though related, property of operators known as *associativity*. An operator $\oplus$ is said to be associative if:

$$(x \oplus y) \oplus z = x \oplus (y \oplus z)$$

for all values x, y and z of the appropriate type. For example, $+$ and $\times$ are associative operators, but $\hat{\ }$ is not. For an associative operator, the choice of the order of association has no effect on meaning.

2.1.3 div and mod

The operators **div** and **mod** perform integer division and remainder respectively. If x is an arbitrary integer and y is a *positive* integer, then $(x \text{ div } y)$ and $(x \text{ mod } y)$ are defined to be the unique integers q and r satisfying the condition:

$$x = q \times y + r \quad \text{and} \quad 0 \le r < y$$

In this book, we shall only use **div** and **mod** under the stated conditions on x and y. Here are some simple examples:

? 7 **div** 3
2

? (-7) **div** 3
-3

? 7 **mod** 3
1

? (-7) **mod** 3
2

2.1.4 Operators and sections

So far we have not said what the types of the arithmetic operators are. Unary negation has type $num \rightarrow num$, while the binary operators all have type $num \rightarrow num \rightarrow num$. Thus we can write:

$$(+) :: num \rightarrow num \rightarrow num$$
$$(\times) :: num \rightarrow num \rightarrow num$$

and so on. Notice that the operators in the above type declarations are enclosed in brackets. A bracketed operator is called a *section*. Enclosing an operator in brackets converts it to an ordinary prefix function which can be applied to its arguments like any other function. For example, we have:

$$(+)\, x\, y \;=\; x + y$$
$$(\times)\, x\, y \;=\; x \times y$$

These equations explain why the type assigned to each binary operator is that of a curried function which takes its arguments one at a time. Like any other name, a bracketed operator can be used in expressions and passed as an argument to a function. To give a brief illustration, if we define:

$$both\, f\, x \;=\; f\, x\, x$$

then we have:
$$both\,(+)\,3 = (+)\,3\,3 = 3 + 3 = 6$$
Note also that:
$$double = both\,(+)$$
where *double* is the function that doubles a number.

The notational device of enclosing a binary operator in brackets to convert it into a normal prefix function can be extended: an argument can also be enclosed along with the operator. If $\oplus$ denotes an arbitrary binary operator (not necessarily a numerical one), then $(\oplus x)$ and $(x\oplus)$ are functions with the definitions:

$$
\begin{aligned}
(x\oplus)\,y &= x \oplus y \\
(\oplus x)\,y &= y \oplus x
\end{aligned}
$$

These forms are also called sections. For example, we have:

$$
\begin{aligned}
(\times 2) \quad &\text{is the 'doubling' function,} \\
(1/) \quad &\text{is the 'reciprocal' function,} \\
(/2) \quad &\text{is the 'halving' function,} \\
(+1) \quad &\text{is the 'successor' function.}
\end{aligned}
$$

There is one exception to the rule for forming sections: $(-x)$ is interpreted as the unary operation of negation applied to x. If we want a function which subtracts x from things, then we have to define it explicitly:

$$subtract\,x\,y = y - x$$

Having defined *subtract* as a curried function, we can apply it to only one argument and obtain the function $(subtract\,x)$ which subtracts x from its argument.

2.1.5   Example: computing square roots

Let us now illustrate some of the basic arithmetic operations by constructing a definition of the function *sqrt* for computing the square root of a number. The mathematical specification of *sqrt* is that:

$$sqrt\,x \geq 0 \quad \textbf{and} \quad (sqrt\,x)\char`\^2 = x$$

whenever $x \geq 0$. In other words, $(sqrt\,x)$ must be defined for non-negative x, and its value is the non-negative square root of x.

There are two points worth noting about this specification. First of all, it does not provide, or even suggest, a method for computing square roots. Second, it is rather strong in that it does not make allowances for the limited precision of arithmetic operations on actual computers. For example, it requires that:

$$sqrt\,2 = 1.4142135623\ldots$$

be computed exactly. As we shall see in a later chapter, it is quite possible to design a function which returns an infinite list of digits, though the process of printing this list will never terminate. The programmer can then show that *sqrt* meets its specification by proving that the list of digits, if continued for long enough, will approximate the answer to any required degree of accuracy. However, for the purposes of the present example we shall weaken the specification to require only that:

$$sqrt\ x \geq 0 \quad \text{and} \quad abs\,((sqrt\ x)\,\hat{}\,2 - x) < eps$$

for a suitably small number $eps > 0$, chosen to take account of the limited precision of the basic arithmetic operations. Here, *abs* is the function:

$$\begin{aligned} abs\ x \quad &= \quad -x, \quad \textbf{if}\ x < 0 \\ &= \quad x, \qquad \textbf{otherwise} \end{aligned}$$

which returns the absolute value of a number.

To illustrate the revised specification, suppose we take $eps = 0.0001$ and $x = 2$. We require:

$$abs\,((sqrt\ 2)\,\hat{}\,2 - 2) < 0.0001$$

and since:

$$\begin{aligned} 1.4141 \times 1.4141 \quad &= \quad 1.99967881 \\ 1.4142 \times 1.4142 \quad &= \quad 1.99996164 \\ 1.4143 \times 1.4143 \quad &= \quad 2.00024449 \end{aligned}$$

the value:

$$sqrt\ 2 = 1.4142$$

is an acceptable answer.

In order to construct *sqrt* we shall use Newton's method for finding the roots of a given function. This is an iterative method which repeatedly improves approximations to the answer until the required degree of accuracy is achieved. In the case of square roots, Newton's method says that if y_n is an approximation to $\sqrt{x}$, then:

$$y_{n+1} = (y_n + x/y_n)/2$$

is a better approximation. For example, taking $x = 2$ and $y_0 = x$, we have:

$$\begin{aligned} y_0 \qquad\qquad\qquad\qquad\qquad &= \quad 2 \\ y_1 \quad = \quad (2 + 2/2)/2 \qquad\qquad &= \quad 1.5 \\ y_2 \quad = \quad (1.5 + 2/1.5)/2 \qquad &= \quad 1.4167 \\ y_3 \quad = \quad (1.4167 + 2/1.4167) \quad &= \quad 1.4142157 \end{aligned}$$

and so on. By iterating this process we can determine $\sqrt{2}$ to any required degree of accuracy, subject to the limitations of computer arithmetic.

There are three logically distinct components in the definition of *sqrt* by Newton's method. First, there is the function:

$$improve\ x\ y = (y + x/y)/2$$

which generates a new approximation (*improve x y*) from an approximation *y*. Second, there is the termination condition:

$$satis\ x\ y = abs\ (y\,\char`\^2 - x) < eps$$

which tests when an approximation is good enough. Finally, there is the general idea of repeatedly applying a function *f* to an initial value until some condition *p* becomes true. This idea can be expressed as a function *until*, defined as follows:

$$
\begin{aligned}
until\ p\ f\ x\ &=\ x, && \textbf{if } p\ x \\
&=\ until\ p\ f\ (f\ x), && \textbf{otherwise}
\end{aligned}
$$

The type of *until* is:

$$until :: (\alpha \rightarrow bool) \rightarrow (\alpha \rightarrow \alpha) \rightarrow \alpha \rightarrow \alpha$$

Thus, *until* takes a function $p :: \alpha \rightarrow bool$, a function $f :: \alpha \rightarrow \alpha$, and a value $x :: \alpha$ as arguments, and returns a value of type α. The function *until* is an example of a *recursive* function. If $p\ x = False$, then the value of $(until\ p\ f\ x)$ is defined in terms of another value of *until*. Recursive definitions will be studied in detail in Chapter 5.

Putting these functions together, we have:

$$sqrt\ x = until\ (satis\ x)\ (improve\ x)\ x$$

Since the functions *improve* and *satis* are specific to square roots, an alternative way of writing the above definition is:

$$
\begin{aligned}
sqrt\ x\ &=\ until\ satis\ improve\ x \\
\textbf{where}\ \ satis\ y\ &=\ abs\ (y\,\char`\^2 - x) < eps \\
improve\ y\ &=\ (y + x/y)/2
\end{aligned}
$$

In this version, the functions *satis* and *improve* are made local to the definition of *sqrt*. One advantage of local functions is that they can refer to the arguments of the main function directly. Thus, as local functions, *satis* and *improve* do not have to name *x* as an explicit argument.

The definition of *sqrt* is assembled from three component functions and is an example of a modular style of programming. In this style, definitions are constructed out of combinations of simpler functions. Such definitions are easy to understand and easy to modify. To illustrate this, let us formulate a more general statement of Newton's method. The full statement of Newton's method says that if y is an approximation to a root of a function f, then:

$$y - \frac{f(y)}{f'(y)}$$

is a better approximation, where $f'(y)$ is the derivative of f evaluated at y. For example, with $f(x) = x^2 - a$, we obtain $f'(x) = 2x$ and so:

$$y - \frac{f(y)}{f'(y)} = y - \frac{y^2 - a}{2y} = (y + a/y)/2$$

This is the specific approximation function for square roots used above.

We can define a function *deriv* for approximating the derivative of a function at a given point by:

$$deriv\ f\ x\ =\ (f\,(x + dx) - f\,x)/dx$$
$$\textbf{where}\ \ dx = 0.0001$$

Provided dx is sufficiently small, this gives a reasonable estimate of the derivative of f at x. We can now construct an alternative definition of *sqrt* as follows:

```
newton f   =   until satis improve
               where  satis y     =   abs (f y) < eps
                      improve y   =   y − (f y/deriv f y)
                      eps         =   0.0001
sqrt x     =   newton f x
               where f y = y^2 − x
```

This program is more general than the previous one. For example, we can define a cube root function *cubrt* by:

```
cubrt x   =   newton f x
              where f y = y^3 − x
```

Exercises

2.1.1 The operators $\times$ and **div** have the same binding power and associate to the left. What, therefore, is the value of the following expressions?

$$3\ \textbf{div}\ 1 \times 3$$
$$3 \times 7\ \textbf{div}\ 4$$
$$6\ \textbf{div}\ 2 \times 8\ \textbf{div}\ 4$$

2.1.2 Using the definition of **mod** given in Section 2.1.3, show that for all positive x, y and z:

$$(x + y)\ \textbf{mod}\ z\ =\ (x\ \textbf{mod}\ z + y\ \textbf{mod}\ z)\ \textbf{mod}\ z$$
$$x \times (y\ \textbf{mod}\ z)\ =\ (x \times y)\ \textbf{mod}\ (x \times z)$$

2.1.3 Assuming all the integers x, y and z are in range, prove that:

$$x \operatorname{div} 2 + (x+1) \operatorname{div} 2 \;=\; x$$
$$(x \times y) \operatorname{div} y \;=\; x$$
$$(x \operatorname{div} y) \operatorname{div} z \;=\; x \operatorname{div} (y \times z)$$

2.1.4 What function is $(+(-x))$?

2.1.5 For what arguments do the following functions return *True*?

$$(= 9) \cdot (2+) \cdot (7\times)$$
$$(3 >) \cdot (\operatorname{mod} 2)$$

2.1.6 Which of the following statements are true (if any)?

$$(\times) x \;=\; (\times x)$$
$$(+) x \;=\; (x+)$$
$$(-) x \;=\; (-x)$$

2.1.7 In Newton's method, the test for determining whether an approximation y to $\sqrt{x}$ is good enough was defined to be:

$$abs\,(y \,\hat{}\, 2 - x) < eps$$

Another test is:

$$abs\,(y \,\hat{}\, 2 - x) < eps \times x$$

Rewrite the *sqrt* function to use this test.

Yet another test for convergence is to stop when two successive approximations y and y' are sufficiently close:

$$abs\,(y - y') < eps \times abs\,y$$

Rewrite the definition of *sqrt* to use this new test. Give reasons why these new tests are likely to be superior in practice.

2.2   Booleans

Life would be fairly dull if *num* was the only available data type and the only operations were those described in the previous section. At the very least we would like to compare numbers and test whether two numerical expressions are equal. For this we need the truth-values. There are two canonical expressions for denoting truth-values, namely *True* and *False*. These two expressions constitute the data type *bool* of boolean values (named after the nineteenth century logician G. Boole). A function that returns boolean values is called a *predicate*.

Booleans are important because they are the results returned by the comparison operators, which are given as follows:

$$= \quad \text{equals}$$
$$\neq \quad \text{not equals}$$
$$< \quad \text{less than}$$
$$> \quad \text{greater than}$$
$$\leq \quad \text{less than or equals}$$
$$\geq \quad \text{greater than or equals}$$

Here are two simple examples of the use of the comparison operators:

? $2 = 3$
False

? $2 < 1 + 3$
True

All six comparison operators have the same level of precedence and, as the second example suggests, this is lower than that of the arithmetic operators.

The comparison operators are not confined to numbers only, but can take expressions of arbitrary type as arguments. The only restriction is that the two arguments must have the same type. If they do not, then the comparison causes a type violation and is rejected by the evaluator. Each comparison operator is therefore a polymorphic function with type:

$$\alpha \rightarrow \alpha \rightarrow bool$$

For example, we can evaluate:

? *False* = *True*
False

? *False* < *True*
True

Comparisons on boolean values are defined so that *False* is less than *True*.

2.2.1   Equality

It is important to bear in mind that an equality test on numbers may not return the correct result unless the numbers are integers within the permitted range. It follows that fractional numbers should only be compared up to a specified tolerance. To be specific, it is better to define a function:

$$within\ eps\ x\ y \quad = \quad abs\,(x - y) < eps$$

and use (*within eps*) instead of (=) as a more realistic equality test on fractional numbers.

In essence, the evaluator computes the result of an equality test of the form $e_1 = e_2$ by reducing the expressions e_1 and e_2 to their canonical form and testing whether the two results are identical. If the expressions do not have a canonical representation, then the result of the test is the undefined value $\bot$. In particular, function values have no canonical representation, so testing functions for equality always results in $\bot$. For example, suppose:

$$
\begin{aligned}
double\ x &= x + x \\
square\ x &= x \times x
\end{aligned}
$$

Then we have:

$$(double = square) = \bot$$

Note the crucial distinction between the equals sign $=$ as used in its normal mathematical (or *denotational*) sense and its use as a computable test for equality. In mathematics, the assertion *double = square* is a false statement. In computation, the result of *evaluating* the test *double = square* is $\bot$. Similarly, the assertion $\bot = \bot$ is a true statement of mathematics (since anything equals itself), but evaluating $\bot = \bot$ results in the value $\bot$. This is not to say that the evaluator is an unmathematical machine, just that its behaviour is described by a different set of mathematical rules, rules that are chosen to be executable mechanically.

2.2.2   The logical operators

Boolean values may also be combined using the following *logical* operators:

$$
\begin{aligned}
\lor \quad & \text{disjunction (logical 'or'),} \\
\land \quad & \text{conjunction (logical 'and'),} \\
\neg \quad & \text{negation (logical 'not').}
\end{aligned}
$$

Here are some examples:

$? \ 1 < 2 \land 2 < 3$
True

$? \ \neg(1 < 2)$
False

$? \ 3 < 2 \land (2 < 3 \lor 1 = 2)$
False

As for the rules of precedence, the operator $\land$ of conjunction binds more tightly than the disjunction operator $\lor$, and negation $\neg$ binds tightest of all. However, it is always good practice to put in brackets whenever there is the slightest doubt about the intended meaning of an expression, and such a course should always be adopted for the logical connectives.

2.2.3 Examples

Let us now give some examples involving boolean values. First, suppose we want function to determine whether a year is a leap year or not. In the Gregorian calendar, a leap year is a year that is divisible by 4, except that if it is divisible by 100, then it must also be divisible by 400. We can express this in a number of equivalent ways. One is to define:

$$leap\ y\ =\ (y \bmod 4 = 0) \wedge (y \bmod 100 \neq 0 \vee y \bmod 400 = 0)$$

Another is to use a definition by cases:

$$
\begin{aligned}
leap\ y\ &=\ (y \bmod 400 = 0), \quad \textbf{if}\ y \bmod 100 = 0 \\
&=\ (y \bmod 4 = 0), \qquad \textbf{otherwise}
\end{aligned}
$$

Next, suppose we want to construct a function, *analyse* say, which takes three positive numbers a, b and c in non-decreasing order, representing the lengths of the sides of a possible triangle. The function *analyse* is to return one of the numbers 0, 1, 2 or 3 depending on whether: (0) the sides do not form a proper triangle; (1) they form an equilateral triangle; or (2) an isosceles triangle; or (3) a scalene triangle.

Three sides form a proper triangle if and only if the length of the longest side c is less than the sum of the lengths of the other two sides, a and b. The triangle will be equilateral if all the lengths are equal, isosceles if just two of the lengths are equal, and scalene if all lengths are different. We can organise this information as follows:

$$
\begin{aligned}
analyse\ a\ b\ c\ &=\ 0, \quad \textbf{if}\ a + b \leq c \\
&=\ 1, \quad \textbf{if}\ a + b > c \wedge a = c \\
&=\ 2, \quad \textbf{if}\ a + b > c \wedge a \neq c \wedge (a = b \vee b = c) \\
&=\ 3, \quad \textbf{if}\ a + b > c \wedge a < b \wedge b < c
\end{aligned}
$$

Under the asumption that $0 < a \leq b \leq c$, all the guards are disjoint and, taken together, include all possible cases.

If no guard evaluates to *True*, then the result of a function defined by cases is the undefined value $\perp$. For example, the following function is defined for non-negative numbers only:

$$
\begin{aligned}
pred\ n\ &=\ 0, \qquad \textbf{if}\ n = 0 \\
&=\ n - 1, \quad \textbf{if}\ n > 0
\end{aligned}
$$

Finally, note that all the alternatives in a conditional definition must have the same type. Since numbers are not booleans, the following script is *illegal* and causes a type violation:

$$
\begin{aligned}
bad\ x\ &=\ 1, \qquad \textbf{if}\ x > 1 \\
&=\ \textit{False}, \quad \textbf{otherwise}
\end{aligned}
$$

Exercises

2.2.1 For each of the following expressions, say whether or not it is well-formed. If the expression is well-formed, then give its value; otherwise, say whether the error is a syntax-error, type-error, or some other kind:

$$(3 = - - 3) \wedge \mathit{True}$$
$$1 \wedge 1 = 2$$
$$(1 < x \wedge x < 100) \vee x = \mathit{True} \vee x = \mathit{False}$$
$$\mathit{False} = (1 < 3)$$

2.2.2 Define a function *sumsqrs* which takes three numbers and returns the sum of the squares of the larger two.

2.3   Characters and strings

Mathematicians would be happy if given just numbers and booleans to play with, but computer scientists prefer to fill their terminal screens with more interesting kinds of squiggles. The ASCII character set gives 128 characters, composed of both visible signs and control characters. These characters constitute the data type *char* and are provided as primitive. The denotation for characters is to enclose them in single quotation marks. Thus:

? 'a'
'a'

? '7'
'7'

? ' '
' '

It is important to understand that the character '7' is quite a different entity from the decimal number 7: the former is a character and is a member of the type *char*, while the latter denotes a number and is a member of the type *num*. As with the case of decimals, these primitive expressions cannot be further evaluated and are simply redisplayed by the evaluator. The third example shows one way of denoting the space character. For the purposes of this book, it is convenient to introduce special symbols for denoting the two most important non-visible control characters: space and newline. The newline character will be denoted by the sign '↲' and, whenever it is desirable for reasons of legibility, the space character will be denoted by the sign '␣'.

Two primitive functions are provided for processing characters, *code* and *decode*. The function *code* :: *char* → *num* converts a character to the integer corresponding to its ASCII code number, and *decode* :: *num* → *char* does the reverse. For example:

? *code* 'b'
98

? *decode* 98
'b'

? *decode* (*code* 'b' + 1)
'c'

? *code* '↓'
10

Characters can be compared and tested for equality, just as any other type, and the linear ordering on letters is, in part, just what one would expect. Thus:

? 'a' < 'z'
True

In ASCII, upper-case letters have a lower code number than lower-case letters, so:

? 'A' < 'a'
True

Using this information we can define simple functions on characters. For instance, here are three functions for determining whether a character is a digit, a lower-case letter, or an upper-case letter:

$$
\begin{aligned}
\textit{isdigit } x &= \text{ '0'} \leq x \wedge x \leq \text{'9'} \\
\textit{isupper } x &= \text{ 'A'} \leq x \wedge x \leq \text{'Z'} \\
\textit{islower } x &= \text{ 'a'} \leq x \wedge x \leq \text{'z'}
\end{aligned}
$$

Next, we can define a function for converting lower-case letters to upper-case:

$$
\begin{aligned}
\textit{capitalise} \quad &:: \quad \textit{char} \rightarrow \textit{char} \\
\textit{capitalise } x \quad &= \quad \textit{decode} \,(\textit{offset} + \textit{code } x), \quad \textbf{if } \textit{islower } x \\
&= \quad x, \qquad\qquad\qquad\qquad \textbf{otherwise} \\
&\quad \textbf{where } \textit{offset} = \textit{code} \text{ 'A'} - \textit{code} \text{ 'a'}
\end{aligned}
$$

This definition uses the fact that the lower- and upper-case letters have codes which are in numerical sequence, but does not depend on their actual values. In particular, we can calculate:

$$
\begin{aligned}
\textit{capitalise} \text{ 'a'} \quad &= \quad \textit{decode} \,(\textit{offset} + \textit{code} \text{ 'a'}) \\
&= \quad \textit{decode} \,((\textit{code} \text{ 'A'} - \textit{code} \text{ 'a'}) + \textit{code} \text{ 'a'}) \\
&= \quad \textit{decode} \,(\textit{code} \text{ 'A'}) \\
&= \quad \text{'A'}
\end{aligned}
$$

without knowing the ASCII codes for 'A' and 'a'.

2.3.1 Strings

A sequence of characters is called a *string*. Strings are denoted by using double quotation marks. The difference between 'a' and "a" is that the former is a character, while the latter is a list of characters which happens to contain only one element. Lists in general will be the topic of the next chapter.

Comparisons on strings follow the normal lexicographic ordering, so we have:

? "hello" < "hallo"
False

? "Jo" < "Joanna"
True

The most important feature of strings is how they are printed:

? "a"
a

? "Hello"
Hello

? "This sentence contains ↵a newline."
This sentence contains
a newline.

Unlike any other data type, strings are printed literally. This means: (i) the double quotation marks do not appear in the output; and (ii) special characters, such as '↵', are printed as the actual character they represent. This printing convention for strings gives complete control over the layout of results, as we shall now see.

2.3.2 Layout

Depending on the application, a programmer may want to produce tables of numbers, pictures of various kinds, or formatted text. Provided we assume the existence of one new primitive function, called *show*, the printing convention for strings described above gives us all the control we need. The function *show* takes an arbitrary value as argument and, provided the value is well-defined, converts it to a printable representation. The type of *show* is given by:

$$show :: \alpha \rightarrow string$$

Here, *string* is the type which consists of lists of characters. For example, the value of (*show n*) for a number *n* is the list of characters which make up the decimal representation of *n*, so we have:

$$show\ 42 = \text{“42”}$$

Similarly, $(show\ b)$ for a boolean b returns the string which prints as the representation of b, so:

$$show\ True\ =\ \text{“True”}$$

The function $show$ can also be applied to characters and strings. We have for instance that:

$$show\ \text{‘a’}\ =\ \text{“ ‘a’ ”}$$
$$show\ \text{“hello”}\ =\ \text{“ “hello” ”}$$

If the result of an evaluation is not a string, then the evaluator automatically applies the function $show$. If it is a string, then it is printed literally. Hence we have:

? “me how”
me how

? $show$ “me how”
“me how”

? $show$ (“me”, “how”) = “(me,how)”
False

? $show$ (“me”, “how”)
(“me”, “how”)

More interesting examples are possible if we make use of the operation $+\!\!+$ which concatenates lists together:

? “The year is␣” $+\!\!+$ $show$ (3×667)
The year is 2001

? $show$ 100 $+\!\!+$ “↲” $+\!\!+$ $show$ 101 $+\!\!+$ “↲” $+\!\!+$ $show$ 102
100
101
102

When printing strings it is sometimes useful to have control over just where on the line the value of an expression appears. Most usually we want the value to appear either on the left ('left-justified'), or on the right ('right-justified'), or in the centre ('centre-justified'). We define functions:

$$ljustify, cjustify, rjustify :: num \rightarrow string \rightarrow string$$

so that $(ljustify\ n\ x)$ is the string x padded with extra spaces on the right to make a string of total width n, $(cjustify\ n\ x)$ is the string x centred with spaces on both sides, and $(rjustify\ n\ x)$ is x with spaces on the left.

In order to define these functions, we shall suppose the existence of a function $width$ which returns the 'width' of a string when printed. This is a measure of the horizontal space occupied by the string. For a string of characters in a fixed-width fount, the function *width* just returns the number of characters in the string. We also need a function *space* so that (*space n*) returns a string of space characters whose width is n. Again, for fixed-width founts this will be just a string containing n spaces.

We can now define the layout functions as follows:

$$
\begin{aligned}
ljustify\ n\ x\ &=\ x \mathbin{+\!\!+} space\,(n-m), && \textbf{if } n \geq m \\
&\ \textbf{where }\ m = width\ x \\[6pt]
rjustify\ n\ x\ &=\ space\,(n-m) \mathbin{+\!\!+} x, && \textbf{if } n \geq m \\
&\ \textbf{where }\ m = width\ x \\[6pt]
cjustify\ n\ x\ &=\ space\ lm \mathbin{+\!\!+} x \mathbin{+\!\!+} space\ rm, && \textbf{if } n \geq m \\
&\ \textbf{where }\ m\ =\ width\ x \\
&\phantom{=\ \textbf{where }}\ lm\ =\ (n-m)\,\textbf{div}\,2 \\
&\phantom{=\ \textbf{where }}\ rm\ =\ (n-m)-lm
\end{aligned}
$$

All three functions are partial, returning $\bot$ if the string is too long to fit in the given width.

Exercises

2.3.1 Define a function *nextlet* which takes a letter of the alphabet and returns the letter coming immediately after it. Assume that letter A follows Z.

2.3.2 Define a function *digitval* which converts a digit character to its corresponding numerical value.

2.3.3 Put the following strings in ascending order: "McMillan", "Macmillan", and "MacMillan".

2.3.4 What are the values of the following expressions?

$$
\begin{aligned}
&show\,(show\ 42) \\
&show\ 42 \mathbin{+\!\!+} show\ 42 \\
&show\ \text{``}\text{\textdagger}\text{''}
\end{aligned}
$$

2.3.5 Define total versions of the justification functions of Section 2.3.2 so that, for example, (*cjustify n x*) returns x if its length is longer than n.

2.4   Tuples

One way of combining types to form new ones is by pairing them. For example, the type (*num, char*) consists of all pairs of values for which the first component is a number and the second a character. In particular, (3, 'a') and

(17.3, '+') are both values of type $(num, char)$. The type (α, β) corresponds to the cartesian product operation of set theory, where the notation $\alpha \times \beta$ is more often seen.

We can evaluate expressions involving pairs of values:

? $(4 + 2, \text{'a'})$
$(6, \text{'a'})$

? $(3, 4) = (4, 3)$
False

? $(3, 6) < (4, 2)$
True

? $(3, (\text{"a"}, \textit{False})) < (3, (\text{"a"}, \textit{True}))$
True

The ordering on pairs of values is given by the rule that $(x, y) < (u, v)$ if $x < u$, or if $x = u$ and $y < v$. This is called the lexicographic or 'dictionary' ordering. Thus, since *False* < *True*, we have $(\text{"a"}, \textit{False}) < (\text{"a"}, \textit{True})$, and so $(3, (\text{"a"}, \textit{False})) < (3, (\text{"a"}, \textit{True}))$.

As well as forming pairs of values, we can also form triples, quadruples and so on. (There is no concept of a one-tuple, so the use of brackets for grouping does not conflict with their use in tuple formation.) For example, $(num, char, bool)$, is the type of triples of values, each value consisting of a number, a character and a boolean in that order.

Each of the types $(\alpha, (\beta, \gamma))$, $((\alpha, \beta), \gamma)$ and (α, β, γ) is distinct: the first is a pair whose second component is also a pair, the second is a pair whose first component is a pair, and the third is a triple. Pairs, triples, quadruples, and so on, all belong to different types. One advantage of this system of tuples is that if, for example, one inadvertently writes a pair instead of a triple in an expression, then the strong typing discipline can pinpoint the error.

Here are some simple functions on tuples. First, we define the selection functions:

$$
\begin{array}{lll}
\textit{fst} & :: & (\alpha, \beta) \rightarrow \alpha \\
\textit{fst}\,(x, y) & = & x \\[4pt]
\textit{snd} & :: & (\alpha, \beta) \rightarrow \beta \\
\textit{snd}\,(x, y) & = & y
\end{array}
$$

Both *fst* and *snd* are polymorphic functions; they select the first and second component of the pair respectively. Neither function works on any other tuple-type. If we want to have selection functions for other kinds of tuple, then they have to be defined separately for each case. For example, we can define:

$$fst3\ (x, y, z)\ =\ x$$
$$snd3\ (x, y, z)\ =\ y$$
$$thd3\ (x, y, z)\ =\ z$$

Here is a function which returns the quotient and remainder of one number by another:

$$quotrem \qquad ::\ (num, num) \to (num, num)$$
$$quotrem\ (x, y)\ =\ (x\ \textbf{div}\ y, x\ \textbf{mod}\ y)$$

Finally, here is a function which computes the roots of a quadratic equation with coefficients (a, b, c):

$$roots \qquad ::\ (num, num, num) \to (num, num)$$
$$roots\ (a, b, c)\ =\ (r1, r2), \qquad\qquad\qquad \textbf{if}\ d \geq 0$$
$$\textbf{where}\ r1\ =\ (-b + r)/(2 \times a)$$
$$r2\ =\ (-b - r)/(2 \times a)$$
$$r\ =\ sqrt\ d$$
$$d\ =\ b\char`^2 - 4 \times a \times c$$

2.4.1   Example: rational arithmetic

A fraction or, more properly speaking, a *rational* number is a pair (x, y) of integers which represents the number x/y. For example, $(1, 7)$, $(3, 21)$ and $(168, 1176)$ all denote the fraction $1/7$. Only fractions (x, y) with $y \neq 0$ represent well-defined values. A fraction (x, y) is said to be in its lowest terms if x and y are relatively prime; in other words, if the greatest common divisor $(gcd\ x\ y)$ of x and y is 1. A negative fraction is represented by a pair (x, y) for which x alone is negative, and the number 0 is represented by $(0, 1)$.

We can restate these conditions in alternative terminology which we have used before. The *canonical* representation of a fraction is a pair (x, y) of integers such that $y > 0$ and $gcd\ (abs\ x)\ y\ =\ 1$. If fractions r and s have canonical representations (x, y) and (u, v), then $r = s$ if and only if $x = u$ and $y = v$, so two fractions are equal just when their canonical representations are identical.

Let us define functions to perform addition, subtraction, multiplication and division of fractions, ensuring that the results are in canonical form. The definitions below should be easy to follow:

$$radd\ (x, y)\ (u, v)\ =\ norm\ (x \times v + u \times y, y \times v)$$
$$rsub\ (x, y)\ (u, v)\ =\ norm\ (x \times v - u \times y, y \times v)$$
$$rmul\ (x, y)\ (u, v)\ =\ norm\ (x \times u, y \times v)$$
$$rdiv\ (x, y)\ (u, v)\ =\ norm\ (x \times v, y \times u)$$

where:

$$norm\,(x,y) \;=\; (u \text{ div } d, v \text{ div } d), \quad \text{if } y \neq 0$$
$$\text{where } u \;=\; (sign\,y) \times x$$
$$v \;=\; abs\,y$$
$$d \;=\; gcd\,(abs\,u)\,v$$

Function *abs* returns the absolute value of its argument, and *sign* returns 1,0 or −1 depending on whether its argument is positive, zero, or negative. The function *gcd* will be defined in the next chapter. Note that *rdiv* is a partial function which takes the value $\perp$ for the divisor $(0,1)$.

If we define:

$$compare\;op\,(x,y)\,(u,v) = op\,(x \times v)\,(y \times u)$$

then we can define comparison operations:

$$
\begin{aligned}
requals &\;=\; compare\,(=) \\
rless &\;=\; compare\,(<) \\
rgreater &\;=\; compare\,(>)
\end{aligned}
$$

and so on.

Finally, we give a simple function for printing fractions. The definition below uses the function *show* introduced in the previous section.

$$
\begin{aligned}
showrat\,(x,y) \;&=\; show\,u, &&\text{if } v = 1 \\
&=\; show\,u + \text{``/''} + show\,v, &&\text{otherwise} \\
&\quad \textbf{where } (u,v) = norm\,(x,y)
\end{aligned}
$$

For example, we can write:

? *showrat* $(55, 8)$
55/8

? *showrat* $(56, 8)$
7

Exercises

2.4.1 Suppose a date is represented by a triple (d, m, y) of three integers, where d is the day, m is the month, and y the year. Define a function *age* which takes two dates, the first being the birthdate of some individual P and the second the current date, and returns the age of P as a whole number of years.

2.4.2 For a given integer x, let (y, z) be a pair of integers such that: (i) $abs\,(y) \leq 5$; (ii) $x = y + 10 \times z$; and (iii) z is the number of smallest absolute value which satisfies (i) and (ii). Show that y and z are uniquely determined by these conditions, and define a function *split* so that *split* $x = (y, z)$.

2.5   Patterns

It is possible to define functions using patterns on the left-hand sides of
equations. A simple example, involving the boolean values *True* and *False*,
is given by the equations:

$$\begin{aligned}
cond\ True\ x\ y &= x \\
cond\ False\ x\ y &= y
\end{aligned}$$

These equations can be written in any order since the two patterns *True* and
False are distinct and cover all possible boolean values. The given definition
of *cond* is equivalent to:

$$\begin{aligned}
cond\ p\ x\ y &= x, \quad \textbf{if}\ p = True \\
&= y, \quad \textbf{if}\ p = False
\end{aligned}$$

As another example, we can define the logical connectives using patterns.
For instance:

$$\begin{aligned}
True \wedge x &= x \\
False \wedge x &= False \\
True \vee x &= True \\
False \vee x &= x
\end{aligned}$$

These equations define the operators $(\wedge)$ and $(\vee)$ using patterns for the first
argument. It is also possible to define versions using patterns for the second
argument, or indeed for both arguments simultaneously.

We can also define functions over the natural numbers (that is, the non-
negative integers) using patterns. A simple example is:

$$\begin{aligned}
permute\ 0 &= 1 \\
permute\ 1 &= 2 \\
permute\ 2 &= 0
\end{aligned}$$

These equations define a function *permute* which returns a well-defined result
only if its argument is one of the numbers 0, 1 or 2. The definition of *permute*
is equivalent to the following one:

$$\begin{aligned}
permute\ n &= 1, \quad \textbf{if}\ n = 0 \\
&= 2, \quad \textbf{if}\ n = 1 \\
&= 0, \quad \textbf{if}\ n = 2
\end{aligned}$$

We can also use patterns containing variables. For example, the following
definition describes a version of the predecessor function:

$$\begin{aligned}
pred\ 0 &= 0 \\
pred\ (n+1) &= n
\end{aligned}$$

In this definition, the pattern $(n + 1)$ can only be 'matched' by a value if n matches a natural number. Hence *pred* is defined for natural numbers only. Notice that the two patterns 0 and $(n + 1)$ are *exhaustive* in that they cover all natural numbers, and *disjoint* in that no natural number matches more than one pattern (since n itself must match a natural number). It therefore does not matter in which order we write the two equations defining *pred*.

Here is another example of a function defined by pattern matching:

$$
\begin{aligned}
count\ 0 \quad &= \ 0 \\
count\ 1 \quad &= \ 1 \\
count\ (n + 2) \ &= \ 2
\end{aligned}
$$

Like *pred*, the function *count* is defined for natural numbers only. It returns the values 0, 1 or 2, depending on whether its argument is 0, 1 or greater than 1. Since n must match a natural number, the three patterns 0, 1 and $(n + 2)$ are disjoint and exhaustive, and the equations can be written in any order.

Pattern matching is one of the cornerstones of an equational style of definition; more often than not it leads to a cleaner and more readily understandable definition than a style based on conditional equations. As we shall see, it also simplifies the process of reasoning formally about functions.

Exercises

2.5.1 Define versions of the functions $(\wedge)$ and $(\vee)$ using patterns for the second argument. Define versions which use patterns for both arguments. Draw up a table showing the values of *and* and *or* for each version.

2.5.2 Is the definition of *pred* given in the text equivalent to the following one?

$$
\begin{aligned}
pred\ n \ &= \ 0, \qquad \text{if } n = 0 \\
&= \ n - 1, \quad \text{if } n > 0
\end{aligned}
$$

2.6 Functions

As has been suggested by many of the foregoing examples, the source types and target types of functions are not restricted in any way: functions can take any kind of value as argument and return any kind of value as result. In particular, these values may themselves be functions. A function which takes a function as argument, or delivers one as result, is called a *higher-order* function. Notwithstanding the rather elevated terminology, the idea is very simple and not at all mysterious. The differential operator of calculus, for example, is a higher-order function which takes a function as argument and returns a function, the derivative, as result. The function $\log_b$ for varying b is another example. We automatically define a higher-order function when currying arguments, and examples of curried functions have already been seen. In this section we consider further aspects of functions.

2.6.1 Functional composition

The composition of two functions f and g is the function h such that $h\,x = f\,(g\,x)$. Functional composition is denoted by the operator $(\cdot)$. We have:

$$(f \cdot g)\,x \;=\; f\,(g\,x)$$

The type of $(\cdot)$ is given by:

$$(\cdot) :: (\beta \to \gamma) \to (\alpha \to \beta) \to (\alpha \to \gamma)$$

Functional composition takes a function of type $(\alpha \to \beta)$ on the right, a function of type $(\beta \to \gamma)$ on its left, and returns a function of type $(\alpha \to \gamma)$. Thus $(\cdot)$ is another example of a polymorphic function which can assume different instances in different expressions (and even within the same expression). The only restriction is that the source type of its left-hand argument must agree with the target type of its right-hand argument, and this is just what is expressed in the type declaration above.

Functional composition is an associative operation. We have:

$$(f \cdot g) \cdot h = f \cdot (g \cdot h)$$

for all functions f, g and h. Accordingly, there is no need to put in brackets when writing sequences of compositions.

One advantage of functional composition is that some definitions can be written more concisely. For example, rather than defining a function by a scheme of the form:

$$soln\ x \;=\; function1\ (function2\ (function3\ x))$$

we can write more simply:

$$soln \;=\; function1 \cdot function2 \cdot function3$$

2.6.2 Operators

As we have seen, a binary operator is just like a function, the only difference being that it is written between its two arguments rather than before them. We can also section operators to convert them to prefix form and pass them as arguments to other functions.

We can also define new operators. For example, consider the operations of rational arithmetic discussed in Section 2.4. Instead of defining:

$$radd\ (x,y)\,(u,v) \;=\; \dots$$

we can also define *radd* as an operator:

$$(x, y) \oplus (u, v) \;=\; \ldots$$

Similarly for the other functions. In this book, we shall denote all operators by special symbols, such as $\oplus$, $\otimes$, $\star$, and so on, or by writing their names in bold fount. (At a terminal with a restricted set of founts, operators can be denoted by some special convention, such as prefixing a name with the character \$.) To avoid fuss, we shall suppose all non-primitive operators have the same binding power and associate to the right; they can also be sectioned to convert them to prefix form (see Section 2.1).

One good test of whether to define a function as an operator is to see if the operation is associative. Since the rational addition operator $\oplus$ is associative, it is more pleasant to be able to write:

$$x \oplus y \oplus z$$

than to distinguish artificially between:

$$radd\,(radd\;x\;y)\,z \quad \text{and} \quad radd\;x\,(radd\;y\;z)$$

2.6.3   Inverse functions

Suppose $f :: A \to B$ has the property that distinct values in A are mapped to distinct values in B. Thus:

$$f\,x = f\,y \quad \text{if and only if} \quad x = y$$

for all x and y in A. Such a function is said to be *injective*. With every injective function f there corresponds a second function, called the *inverse* of f and denoted by f^{-1}, which satisfies the equation:

$$f^{-1}(f\,x) = x$$

for all x in A. For example, the function:

$$
\begin{aligned}
f \quad &:: \quad num \to (num, num) \\
f\,x \;&= \quad (sign\;x, abs\;x)
\end{aligned}
$$

is injective and has inverse:

$$f^{-1}(s, a) = s \times a$$

It is quite common in mathematical specifications to specify a function f by the requirement that it should be the inverse of a given function g known to be injective. For example, one way to specify the function *sqrt* is to say:

$$sqrt\,(square\;x) = x$$

for all $x \geq 0$. The function *square* is injective on the non-negative numbers.

The use of inverse functions as a method of specification gives no hint as to how an executable (or *constructive*) definition might be formulated. The task of a programmer is to synthesise a constructive definition which meets the specification. In later chapters we shall meet a number of instances of this idea. It will not in general be the case that an injective function $f :: A \rightarrow B$ has an inverse f^{-1} that satisfies the further equation

$$f(f^{-1}\, y) = y$$

for all y in B. This only happens when f has the additional property that for every y in B there exists some x in A such that $f\, x = y$. A function satisfying this condition is said to be *surjective*. If f is both injective and surjective, then f is said to be *bijective*.

If $f :: A \rightarrow B$ is surjective, but not necessarily bijective, then it is still possible to specify g by the requirement that:

$$f\, (g\, x) = x$$

for all x in B. In general, though, there will be more than one function g which satisfies the equation. For instance, taking $f\, (x, y) = x \times y$, we have that each of:

$$\begin{aligned} g1\, x &= (sign\, x, abs\, x) \\ g2\, x &= (x, 1) \\ g3\, x &= (2 \times x, x/2) \end{aligned}$$

is a possible definition of g. In the absence of any further constraints, each definition is perfectly satisfactory. We shall also meet examples of this kind of specification later on.

2.6.4 Strict and non-strict functions

So far we have seen some examples of polymorphic functions, but other kinds of value can be polymorphic too. In particular, the special value $\bot$ is polymorphic. In other words, $\bot$ is a value of every type. This means that any function f may, conceptually at least, be applied to $\bot$. If $f\bot = \bot$, then f is said to be a *strict* function; otherwise it is *non-strict*. Most of the common functions of arithmetic are strict functions and only return well-defined results for well-defined arguments.

The idea of a non-strict function may seem strange at first sight, since it seems to entail getting something for nothing. However, such functions are perfectly possible and can be very useful. Consider, for instance, the following definition:

$$\begin{aligned} three &\quad :: \quad num \rightarrow num \\ three\, x &\quad = \quad 3 \end{aligned}$$

Suppose we submit the above definition to the evaluator, enter a session and type *three* $(1/0)$. This is what would happen:

? *three* $(1/0)$
3

What has happened is that the evaluator does not require the value of the argument to *three* in order to determine the result, so it does not attempt to evaluate it. The value of $1/0$ is $\bot$, so *three* $\bot \neq \bot$ and the function is non-strict.

For a number of reasons, a non-strict semantics is preferable to a strict one. First, it makes reasoning about equality easier. For example, with a non-strict semantics we can reason that

$$2 + three\ x = 5$$

for all x, by straightforward substitution of the definition of *three* into the left-hand side. No qualification about x possessing a well-defined value is necessary. A non-strict semantics leads to a simpler and more uniform treatment of substitution, and hence to a simpler logical basis for reasoning about the correctness of functional programs.

There are other advantages too: we can define new control structures by defining new functions. To illustrate, we can define a function *cond*, with type $(bool \rightarrow \alpha \rightarrow \alpha \rightarrow \alpha)$, which exactly matches the control structure provided by conditional definitions:

$$
\begin{aligned}
cond\ p\ x\ y\ &=\ x,\ \textbf{if } p \\
&=\ y,\ \textbf{otherwise}
\end{aligned}
$$

For example, instead of defining:

$$
\begin{aligned}
recip\ x\ &=\ 0,\ \ \ \ \textbf{if } x = 0 \\
&=\ 1/x,\ \textbf{otherwise}
\end{aligned}
$$

we can write:

$$recip\ x\ =\ cond\ (x = 0)\ 0\ (1/x)$$

Under a non-strict semantics, the evaluation of $(cond\ True\ x\ y)$ does not require the value of y so it is not computed; similarly, the evaluation of $(cond\ False\ x\ y)$ does not require the value of x. The function *cond* is, of course, strict in its first argument since this value is needed to determine the answer. In particular, we have:

$$recip\ 0\ =\ cond\ (0 = 0)\ 0\ (1/0)\ =\ cond\ True\ 0\ \bot\ =\ 0$$

On the other hand, with a strict semantics we would have:

$$recip\ 0\ =\ cond\ (0 = 0)\ 0\ (1/0)\ =\ cond\ True\ 0\ \bot\ =\ \bot$$

Therefore, with a strict semantics, *cond* does not correspond to a conditional definition.

We have met other examples of non-strict functions in previous sections. For example, the pairing operation (x, y) is non-strict. The values $(\perp, \perp), (x, \perp)$ and $(\perp, y)$ are all distinct provided $x \neq \perp$ and $y \neq \perp$. Thus, the selection functions *fst* and *snd* are also non-strict. To illustrate:

? *fst* $(1 + 0, 1/0)$
1

? *snd* $(1/0, 1 + 0)$
1

The operational explanation of strict and non-strict functions is in terms of reduction strategies. For example, an evaluator may reduce expressions of the form $fst(x, y)$ in one of two ways: it may first try to reduce the expressions x and y to their simplest possible form, and only when this stage is complete go on to apply the rule for *fst* and so select the value of x. Alternatively, it may apply the rule for *fst* immediately. In this case, the expression y is not reduced, so it is irrelevant whether or not it has a well-defined value (of course, it must still be syntactically correct and possess a well-defined type). The first strategy is called *eager-evaluation*, while the second is called *lazy-evaluation*. Further details of how they work will be explained in Chapter 6.

Exercises

2.6.1 Suppose $h\, x\, y = f\, (g\, x\, y)$. Which of the following statements are true?

$$
\begin{aligned}
h &= f \cdot g \\
h\, x &= f \cdot (g\, x) \\
h\, x\, y &= (f \cdot g)\, x\, y
\end{aligned}
$$

2.6.2 Write down a definition of a function with type $(num \to num)$ which returns no well-defined values.

2.6.3 Consider the function $halve = (\mathbf{div}2)$. Is it possible to specify a function f by the requirement:

$$f\,(halve\, x) = x$$

for all natural numbers x? Give one function f that satisfies the equation:

$$halve\,(f\, x) = x$$

2.6.4 Show that the function $(f \cdot g)$ is strict if both f and g are strict.

2.6.5 Define the operators of logical conjunction and disjunction, using only the function *cond*. Draw up a table showing their values for all possible arguments, well-defined or otherwise.

2.7   Type synonyms

Although it is a good idea to declare the types of the functions we define, it is sometimes inconvenient, or at least unilluminating, to spell them out in terms of the basic types. A better method is to use *type synonyms*. A type synonym enables the programmer to introduce a new name for a given type. For example, suppose we want to define a function, *move* say, which takes a number, representing a distance, an angle and a pair consisting of a coordinate position, and moves to a new position as indicated by the angle and distance. We can introduce type synonyms for these values as follows:

$$
\begin{array}{rcl}
position & == & (num, num) \\
angle & == & num \\
distance & == & num
\end{array}
$$

Notice the special symbol == used in the declaration of type synonyms; this avoids confusion with a value definition.

Now we can declare the type and definition of *move* in the following way:

$$
\begin{array}{rcl}
move & :: & distance \to angle \to position \to position \\
move\ d\ a\ (x, y) & = & (x + d \times cos\ a, y + d \times sin\ a)
\end{array}
$$

This type declaration of *move* is both short and helpful in understanding what the function does.

In an earlier section we used the word *string* as a synonym for a list of characters. In fact we have:

$$string == [char]$$

which formalises the terminology (as we shall see in the next chapter, the type of lists of values of type α is denoted by $[\alpha]$).

Type synonyms cannot be recursive. Every synonym must be expressible in terms of existing types, and this would not be possible if synonyms were allowed to depend on one another.

Type synonyms can also be generic in that they can be parameterised by type variables. For example:

$$
\begin{array}{rcl}
pairs\ \alpha & == & (\alpha, \alpha) \\
automorph\ \alpha & == & \alpha \to \alpha
\end{array}
$$

are all valid synonym declarations.

2.8   Type inference

So far we have not given any details of how the evaluator deduces the types of expressions and definitions. Although it is not essential for the programmer to be aware of the precise mechanism, it is instructive to give the general idea by following the method through on some examples.

1. First let us consider functional composition, defined by the equation:

$$(\cdot)\, f\, g\, x = f\,(g\,x)$$

The process of type inference begins by assigning types to the argument names on the left-hand side, and a type to the result. Thus, we have:

$$
\begin{aligned}
f &\ ::\ t1 \\
g &\ ::\ t2 \\
x &\ ::\ t3 \\
f\,(g\,x) &\ ::\ t4
\end{aligned}
$$

where $t1$, $t2$, $t3$ and $t4$ are new type names. The type of $(\cdot)$ is therefore given by:

$$(\cdot) :: t1 \to t2 \to t3 \to t4$$

This does not complete the process since there are certain relationships between the new types that must be taken into account. In order to see what these relationships are, we must analyse the defining expression $f\,(g\,x)$.

To analyse an expression, we make use of the following three rules:

   (i) (*Application rule*) If $f\,x :: t$, then $x :: t'$ and $f :: t' \to t$ for some new type t';

  (ii) (*Equality rule*) If both the types $x :: t$ and $x :: t'$ can be deduced for a variable x, then $t = t'$;

 (iii) (*Function rule*) If $t \to u = t' \to u'$, then $t = t'$ and $u = u'$.

Using the application rule on $f\,(g\,x) :: t4$, we deduce that:

$$
\begin{aligned}
g\,x &\ ::\ t5 \\
f &\ ::\ t5 \to t4
\end{aligned}
$$

for some new type $t5$. Similarly, from $g\,x :: t5$ we deduce that:

$$
\begin{aligned}
x &\ ::\ t6 \\
g &\ ::\ t6 \to t5
\end{aligned}
$$

for some new type $t6$.

Using the equality rule, we can now obtain the following identities:

$$
\begin{aligned}
t1 &= t5 \to t4 \\
t2 &= t6 \to t5 \\
t3 &= t6
\end{aligned}
$$

This completes the type analysis for the present example. The type we can deduce for $(\cdot)$ is:

$$(\cdot) :: (t5 \to t4) \to (t6 \to t5) \to t6 \to t4$$

As a final step, we can replace the type names by generic type variables, giving:

$$(\cdot) :: (\beta \to \gamma) \to (\alpha \to \beta) \to \alpha \to \gamma$$

as the inferred type of functional composition.

2. Next, consider the definition:

$$f \; x \; y \;\; = \;\; fst \; x + fst \; y$$

This time, the right hand side contains occurrences of names which do not appear on the left, namely $(+)$ and fst. We suppose:

$$
\begin{aligned}
(+) & \quad :: \quad num \to num \to num \\
fst & \quad :: \quad (\alpha, \beta) \to \alpha
\end{aligned}
$$

As a necessary first step, we must take account of the fact that the two occurrences of the polymorphic function fst need not receive the same instantiations for the type variables α and β. After all, the expression:

$$fst \, (1, \textit{True}) + fst \, (1, 42)$$

is well-typed, even though the first occurrence of fst has type $(num, bool) \to num$, and the second has type $(num, num) \to num$. To deal with this point, we rewrite the definition of f in the form:

$$f \; x \; y \;\; = \;\; fst_1 \; x + fst_2 \; y$$

and assume two different instantiations:

$$
\begin{aligned}
fst_1 & \quad :: \quad (u1, u2) \to u1 \\
fst_2 & \quad :: \quad (v1, v2) \to v1
\end{aligned}
$$

of the general type of fst.

Now we proceed as in the first example, introducing the types:

$$
\begin{aligned}
x & \quad :: \quad t1 \\
y & \quad :: \quad t2 \\
fst_1 \; x + fst_2 \; y & \quad :: \quad t3
\end{aligned}
$$

so that f has type $t1 \to t2 \to t3$.

Writing the right-hand side of the definition of f in the form:

$$(+) \, (fst_1 \; x) \, (fst_2 \; y),$$

we can now use the application rule to deduce:

$$(fst_2\, y) \quad :: \quad t4$$
$$(+)\,(fst_1\, x) \quad :: \quad t4 \to t3$$

Further application of the rule gives:

$$y \quad :: \quad t5$$
$$fst_2 \quad :: \quad t5 \to t4$$

$$(fst_1\, x) \quad :: \quad t6$$
$$(+) \quad :: \quad t6 \to t4 \to t3$$

$$x \quad :: \quad t7$$
$$fst_1 \quad :: \quad t7 \to t6$$

Using the function rule and equality rule together, we derive:

$$t1 = t7$$
$$t2 = t5 = (v1, v2)$$
$$t3 = t4 = t6 = v1 = u1 = num$$
$$t7 = (u1, u2)$$

Hence the type derived for f is:

$$(num, u2) \to (num, v2) \to num$$

Finally, we replace the unconstrained type names by generic type variables to obtain:

$$f :: (num, \alpha) \to (num, \beta) \to num$$

as the inferred type for f.

3. Next, consider the definition:

$$fix\, f = f\,(fix\, f)$$

To deduce a type for fix, we proceed as before and introduce the types:

$$f \quad :: \quad t1$$
$$f\,(fix\, f) \quad :: \quad t2$$

so that $fix :: t1 \to t2$.

Analysing the expression $f\,(fix\, f)$ by the application rule, we obtain:

$$f \quad :: \quad t3 \to t2$$
$$fix\, f \quad :: \quad t3$$
$$fix \quad :: \quad t4 \to t3$$
$$f \quad :: \quad t4$$

Using the equality and function rules, we obtain the identities:

$$t1 = t4 = t3 \rightarrow t2$$
$$t2 = t3$$

so that $fix :: (t3 \rightarrow t3) \rightarrow t3$. Finally, replacing $t3$ by a generic type variable, we get:

$$fix :: (\alpha \rightarrow \alpha) \rightarrow \alpha$$

as the inferred type for fix.

4. Finally, let us consider an example where typing goes wrong. Suppose we define:

$$selfapply \; f = f \; f$$

Proceeding as before, we introduce new types:

$$f \;\; :: \;\; t1$$
$$f \; f \;\; :: \;\; t2$$

so that $selfapply :: t1 \rightarrow t2$. In this case, the application and equality rules give:

$$t1 = t1 \rightarrow t2$$

This equation does not possess a solution for $t1$ and the definition of $selfapply$ is rejected by the type analyser.

Exercises

2.8.1 Suppose the functions $const$, $subst$ and fix are defined by the equations:

$$const \; x \; y \;\; = \;\; x$$
$$subst \; f \; g \; x \;\; = \;\; f \; x \, (g \; x)$$
$$fix \; f \; x \;\; = \;\; f \, (fix \; f) \; x$$

Deduce their types.

2.8.2 Show that the identity function id is equal to $(subst \, const \, const)$, where $subst$ and $const$ are as defined in the previous question. The function $compose$ can also be expressed in terms of these functions. How?

2.8.3 Define the function $apply$ which applies its first argument to its second. What is its type? What is the relationship between $apply$ and id?

2.8.4 Suppose the function $query$ is defined by:

$$query \; f \; x \; g \;\; = \;\; g \; f \, (f \; x \; g)$$

Is there a sensible type which can be assigned to this function? If not, explain why.

Chapter 3

Lists

The next two chapters are about lists, their operations and their uses. Lists are as important in functional programming as sets are in many branches of mathematics. To enumerate a set is to produce a list of its members in some order, so the two concepts are closely related. Unlike a set, a particular value may occur more than once in a given list, and the order of the elements is significant.

There are many useful operations on lists. Lists can be taken apart, or rearranged and combined with other lists to form new lists; lists of numbers can be summed and multiplied; and lists of lists can be concatenated together to form one long list. Most of the present chapter will be concerned with introducing the more important list operations and giving simple examples of their use. The next chapter will be devoted to more substantial examples. We shall also mention some of the algebraic laws which govern the operations. For the moment, however, formal definitions and proofs will not be given. This will be done in Chapter 5 when we discuss recursive definitions and the formal basis for conducting reasoning about functions.

3.1 List notation

By definition, a *list* is a linearly ordered collection of values; one can talk about the first element of a list, the second element, and so on. Lists are also called *sequences*, a term more often found in other branches of mathematics, but there is no difference between the concepts and we shall use the two words interchangeably. Like sequences in mathematics, a list can contain an infinite number of elements. However, in the present chapter we shall concentrate exclusively on finite lists. Infinite lists will be dealt with in a later chapter.

An important property of lists is that all the elements of a given list must have the same type: one can have a list of numbers, a list of characters, even a list of lists (of values all of the same type), but one cannot mix values of different types in the same list.

A finite list is denoted using square brackets and commas. For example, $[1, 2, 3]$ is a list of three numbers and ["hallo", "goodbye"] is a list of two strings. The empty list is written as [] and a singleton list, containing just one element a, is written as $[a]$. In particular, [[ ]] is a singleton list, containing the empty list as its only member.

If the elements of a list all have type α, then the list itself will be assigned the type $[\alpha]$ (read as 'list of α'). For example:

$$
\begin{array}{rcl}
[1, 2, 3] & :: & [num] \\
['h', 'a', 'l', 'l', 'o'] & :: & [char] \\
[[1, 2], [3]] & :: & [[num]] \\
[(+), (\times)] & :: & [num \rightarrow num \rightarrow num]
\end{array}
$$

On the other hand, $[1, \text{"fine day"}]$ is not a well-formed list because its elements have different types.

Strings, introduced in the previous chapter, are just special kinds of lists, namely lists of characters. Thus, "hallo" is just a convenient built-in shorthand for the list ['h', 'a', 'l', 'l', 'o'] and has type $[char]$. Hence:

? ['h', 'a', 'l', 'l', 'o']
hallo

Every generic operation on lists is therefore also applicable to strings.

The empty list [] is empty of all conceivable values, so it is assigned the polymorphic type $[\alpha]$. In any particular expression, [] may have a more refined type. For instance, in the expression [[], [1]] the type of [] is $[num]$ since the second element [1] has this type; similarly, in the expression ["an", [], "list"] the type of [] is $[char]$ since that is the type of the other elements.

Unlike a set, a list may contain the same value more than once. For example, $[1, 1]$ is a list of two elements, both of which happen to be 1, and is distinct from the list [1] which contains only one element. Two lists are equal if and only if they contain the same values in the same order. Hence we have:

? $[1, 1] = [1]$
False

? $[1, 2, 3] = [3, 2, 1]$
False

The special form $[a .. b]$ is provided to denote the list of numbers in increasing order from a to b inclusive, going up in steps of 1. If $a > b$, then $[a .. b] = [\,]$. For example:

? $[1 .. 5]$
$[1, 2, 3, 4, 5]$

A second special form $[a, b .. c]$ is also provided; this denotes the arithmetic progression $a, a + d, a + 2 \times d, \ldots$, and so on, where $d = b - a$. For example:

```
? [2,4..10]
[2,4,6,8,10]
```

```
? [1..5] = [1,2..5]
True
```

```
? [4,3..1]
[4,3,2,1]
```

Exercises

3.1.1 Give an example of an expression which contains two occurrences of the empty list, the first occurrence having type $[num]$ and the second type $[char]$.

3.1.2 Determine the number of elements of $[a .. b]$ and $[a, b .. c]$ in terms of a, b and c.

3.2   List comprehensions

The final piece of special notation provided for lists is called a *list comprehension*. It employs a syntax adapted from conventional mathematics for describing sets. The syntax is:

$$[\langle expression \rangle \mid \langle qualifier \rangle; \ldots; \langle qualifier \rangle]$$

in which $\langle expression \rangle$ denotes an arbitrary expression, and a $\langle qualifier \rangle$ is either a boolean-valued expression or a *generator*. The forms for a generator we shall use are:

$$\langle variable \rangle \leftarrow \langle list \rangle$$
$$(\langle variable \rangle, \langle variable \rangle) \leftarrow \langle listofpairs \rangle$$
$$(\langle variable \rangle, \langle variable \rangle, \langle variable \rangle) \leftarrow \langle listoftriples \rangle$$

and so on.

The best way of explaining what list comprehensions do is to give some examples. A simple starting point is:

```
? [x × x | x ← [1..10]; even x]
[4,16,36,64,100]
```

This list comprehension reads: "the list of values $x \times x$, where x is drawn from the list $[1..10]$ and x is even". Notice that the order of the elements in the result is determined by the order of the elements in the generator. Notice also that x is a local or 'dummy' variable which can be replaced by any other variable name, and whose scope is confined to the list comprehension.

We can have more than one generator in a comprehension, in which case later generators vary more quickly than their predecessors. For example:

? $[(a, b) \mid a \leftarrow [1..3]; \; b \leftarrow [1..2]]$
$[(1,1),(1,2),(2,1),(2,2),(3,1),(3,2)]$

? $[(a, b) \mid b \leftarrow [1..2]; \; a \leftarrow [1..3]]$
$[(1,1),(2,1),(3,1),(1,2),(2,2),(3,2)]$

Furthermore, later generators can depend on the variables introduced by earlier ones:

? $[(i,j) \mid i \leftarrow [1..4]; \; j \leftarrow [i+1..4]]$
$[(1,2),(1,3),(1,4),(2,3),(2,4),(3,4)]$

We can freely intersperse generators with boolean-valued expressions:

? $[(i,j) \mid i \leftarrow [1..4]; \; even \; i; \; j \leftarrow [i+1..4]; \; odd \; j]$
$[(2,3)]$

To illustrate one of the other forms for generators, suppose we define

$$pairs \;\; = \;\; [(i,j) \mid i \leftarrow [1..2]; \; j \leftarrow [1..3]]$$

Then we have:

? $[i + j \mid (i,j) \leftarrow pairs]$
$[2,3,4,3,4,5]$

Finally, the main expression of a comprehension does not have to make use of the variable introduced by a generator:

? $[3 \mid j \leftarrow [1..4]]$
$[3,3,3,3]$

? $[x \mid x \leftarrow [1..3]; \; y \leftarrow [1,2]]$
$[1,1,2,2,3,3]$

We can use list comprehensions in definitions. For example:

$$spaces \; n \;\; = \;\; [\text{`}\sqcup\text{'} \mid j \leftarrow [1..n]]$$

The function *spaces* returns a list of n space characters.

Here is a function to list the divisors of a positive integer:

$$divisors \; n \;\; = \;\; [d \mid d \leftarrow [1..n]; \; n \bmod d = 0]$$

The function *divisors* can be used to define the greatest common divisor of two positive integers :

$$gcd \; a \; b \;\; = \;\; max \; [d \mid d \leftarrow divisors \; a; \; b \bmod d = 0]$$

Here, the function *max* takes a non-empty list of numbers and returns the largest number in the list. We shall see its definition presently. It is left as an exercise to modify the definition of *gcd* to allow zero arguments.

Using *divisors* we can determine whether a number is prime:

$$prime\ n\ =\ (divisors\ n = [1, n])$$

A number $n > 1$ is prime if the only divisors d in the range $1 \le d \le n$ are 1 and n itself; hence the above definition. Note that *divisors* $1 = [1]$, and since the lists $[1]$ and $[1, 1]$ are not the same, the above definition correctly determines that 1 is not a prime.

The given definition of *prime* is not particularly efficient, but it is less bad than one might suppose. Testing two lists for equality does not necessarily involve generating *all* the members of each list. As soon as two elements in corresponding positions are found not to be equal, the test can return *False* without generating any further elements. Nevertheless, in the case of primes there is a simple optimisation. If a number n has a proper divisor (i.e. a divisor d in the range $1 < d < n$), then it must also have one in the range $2 \le d \le \sqrt{n}$. The proof of this fact is left as a simple exercise. It means we can define:

$$prime\ n\ =\ n > 1 \wedge [d \mid d \leftarrow [2 \mathbin{..} intsqrt\ n];\ n \bmod d = 0] = [\,]$$

where (*intsqrt* n) returns the largest integer whose square is at most n.

Next, here is a program to list all Pythagorean triads in a given range. These are triples of numbers (x, y, z) such that $x^2 + y^2 = z^2$. We have:

$$triads\ n\ =\ [(x, y, z) \mid x \leftarrow [1 \mathbin{..} n];\ y \leftarrow [1 \mathbin{..} n];\ z \leftarrow [1 \mathbin{..} n]; \\ x\,\hat{}\,2 + y\,\hat{}\,2 = z\,\hat{}\,2]$$

For example:

```
? triads 5
[(3, 4, 5), (4, 3, 5)]
```

In the above definition of *triads*, we have not taken steps to ensure that each essentially distinct triad is printed only once. We can remedy this by defining:

$$triads\ n\ =\ [(x, y, z) \mid x \leftarrow [1 \mathbin{..} n];\ y \leftarrow [x \mathbin{..} n];\ z \leftarrow [y \mathbin{..} n]; \\ x\,\hat{}\,2 + y\,\hat{}\,2 = z\,\hat{}\,2]$$

In the new definition, the value of y is restricted to the range $x \le y \le n$, and the value of z to the range $y \le z \le n$. Since z must be at least as big as the larger of x and y, all triads will still be found.

Exercises

3.2.1 Evaluate the expression:

$$[j \mid i \leftarrow [1, -1, 2, -2]; \ i > 0; \ j \leftarrow [1 .. i]]$$

3.2.2 Under what conditions on xs and ys does the equation:

$$[x \mid x \leftarrow xs; \ y \leftarrow ys] = [x \mid y \leftarrow ys; \ x \leftarrow xs]$$

hold?

3.2.3 Using a list comprehension, define a function for counting the number of negative numbers in a list.

3.2.4 Define a function *intpairs* so that (*intpairs n*) is a list of all distinct pairs of integers $1 \leq x, y \leq n$.

3.2.5 Write a program to find all quadruples (a, b, c, d) in the range $0 < a, b, c, d \leq n$ such that $a^2 + b^2 = c^2 + d^2$.

3.2.6 Define x^n using a list comprehension.

3.2.7 Determine the value of (*divisors* 0), where:

$$divisors \ n \ = \ [d \mid d \leftarrow [1 .. n]; \ n \bmod d = 0]$$

3.2.8 Define a function *mindivisor* which returns the smallest divisor, greater than 1, of a given positive integer. Using *mindivisor*, construct a function for testing whether a number is prime.

3.2.9 Define *gcd* to allow for zero arguments.

3.2.10 Show that if n has a divisor in the range $1 < d < n$, then it has one in the range $1 < d \leq \sqrt{n}$.

3.3 Operations on lists

We now introduce a number of useful functions and operations on lists.

Concatenation. Two lists can be concatenated together to form one longer list. This function is denoted by the binary operator $+\!\!+$ (pronounced ' concatenate'). In a restricted character set, such as ASCII, the symbol $+\!\!+$ can be written as a double-plus sign **++**.

Here are two simple examples of concatenation:

? $[1, 2, 3] + [4, 5]$
$[1, 2, 3, 4, 5]$

? $[1, 2] + [\,] + [1]$
$[1, 2, 1]$

The type of $+$ is given by:

$$(+) \quad :: \quad [\alpha] \to [\alpha] \to [\alpha]$$

Concatenation takes two lists, both of the same type, and produces a third list, again of the same type. Hence the above type assignment.

Note that $+$ is an associative operation and has identity element $[\,]$. In other words, we have:

$$(xs + ys) + zs = xs + (ys + zs)$$
$$[\,] + xs = xs + [\,] = xs$$

for all lists xs, ys and zs.

Notice the names given to list variables. By convention, we shall use letters x, y, z, etc., to denote elements of lists, and identifiers xs, ys, zs, etc., to denote lists themselves. We shall also sometimes extend the convention, writing xss, yss, zss, etc., to denote lists whose elements are themselves lists.

Concatenation performs the same function for lists as the union operator $\cup$ does for sets. A companion function is *concat* which concatenates a list of lists into one long list. This function, which corresponds to the big-union operator $\bigcup$ for sets of sets, can be expressed using a list comprehension:

$$concat \quad :: \quad [[\alpha]] \to [\alpha]$$
$$concat\ xss \quad = \quad [x \mid xs \leftarrow xss;\ x \leftarrow xs]$$

For example:

? *concat* $[[1, 2], [\,], [3, 2, 1]]$
$[1, 2, 3, 2, 1]$

? *concat* ["We", " ", "like", " ", "lists."]
We like lists.

We shall give an alternative definition of *concat* in a later section.

Length. The length of a finite list is the number of elements it contains. This operation is denoted by the prefix operator $\#$. For example:

? $\#[1, 1, 2, 2, 3, 3]$
6

? $\#[\,]$
0

The type of length is given by:

$$(\#) :: [\alpha] \to num$$

The nature of the list elements is irrelevant when computing the length of a list; hence the type assignment.

A simple relationship between $\#$ and $+\!\!+$ is given by the equation:

$$\#(xs +\!\!+ ys) = \#xs + \#ys$$

for all finite lists xs and ys. We also have the law:

$$\#[e \mid x \leftarrow xs] = \#xs$$

for all expressions e and lists xs.

Head and tail. The function hd selects the first element of a list, and tl selects the remaining portion. Thus, hd and tl satisfy the equations:

$$
\begin{aligned}
hd\,([x] +\!\!+ xs) &= x \\
tl\,([x] +\!\!+ xs) &= xs
\end{aligned}
$$

for all lists xs and elements x.

Both functions are partial in that $hd\,[\,] = tl\,[\,] = \bot$. The types of hd and tl are:

$$
\begin{aligned}
hd &:: [\alpha] \to \alpha \\
tl &:: [\alpha] \to [\alpha]
\end{aligned}
$$

A simple relationship between hd and tl is given by the equation:

$$xs = [hd\ xs] +\!\!+ tl\ xs$$

for all non-empty lists xs.

Init and last. The functions *init* and *last* are similar to hd and tl except that they break a list at the end rather than the beginning. We have:

$$
\begin{aligned}
init\,(xs +\!\!+ [x]) &= xs \\
last\,(xs +\!\!+ [x]) &= x
\end{aligned}
$$

for all lists xs and elements x. Both functions are partial in that the values of *init* $[\,]$ and *last* $[\,]$ are $\bot$. The functions *init* and *last* are related by the equation:

$$xs = init\ xs +\!\!+ [last\ xs]$$

for all non-empty lists xs.

Take and drop. The functions *take* and *drop* each take a non-negative integer n and a list xs as arguments. The value of (*take* n xs) is the initial segment of xs of length n (or xs itself if $\#xs < n$). For example:

? *take* 3 [1 . . 10]
[1, 2, 3]

? *take* 3 [1 . . 2]
[1, 2]

The function *drop* can be specified by the equation

$$take \; n \; xs \mathbin{+\!\!+} drop \; n \; xs = xs$$

The value of (*drop n xs*) is therefore the list which remains when the first n elements are removed. In particular, we have:

$$
\begin{aligned}
take \; 0 \; xs &= [\,] \\
drop \; 0 \; xs &= xs
\end{aligned}
$$

We also have the laws:

$$
\begin{aligned}
take \; m \cdot drop \; n &= drop \; n \cdot take \; (m + n) \\
drop \; m \cdot drop \; n &= drop \; (m + n)
\end{aligned}
$$

where m and n are arbitrary natural numbers.

The functions *tl* and *init* satisfy the equations:

$$
\begin{aligned}
tl \; xs &= drop \; 1 \; xs \\
init \; xs &= take \; (\#xs - 1) \; xs
\end{aligned}
$$

for $xs \neq [\,]$.

Takewhile and dropwhile. The functions *takewhile* and *dropwhile* are similar to *take* and *drop* except that they both take a predicate as the first argument instead of a natural number. The value of (*takewhile p xs*) is the longest initial segment of xs all of whose elements satisfy the predicate p. For example:

? *takewhile even* [2, 4, 6, 1, 5, 6]
[2, 4, 6]

? *takewhile even* [1 . . 100]
[]

? *takewhile* (= 'a') "aardvark"
aa

The function *dropwhile* is similar, except that it 'drops' the longest initial segment whose elements satisfy p. The type assigned to *takewhile* and *dropwhile* is:

$$(\alpha \to bool) \to [\alpha] \to [\alpha]$$

The first argument is a predicate (of type $\alpha \to bool$), the second argument is a list of type $[\alpha]$, and the result is another list of type $[\alpha]$.

Reverse. The function *reverse* reverses the order of elements in a finite list. For example:

? *reverse* "Richard Bird"
driB drahciR

? *reverse* "Madam, I'm Adam."
.madA m'I ,madaM

We can use *reverse* to define *last* in terms of *hd*, and *init* in terms of *tl*:

$$last = hd \cdot reverse$$
$$init = reverse \cdot tl \cdot reverse$$

Zip. The function *zip* takes a pair of lists and returns a list of pairs of corresponding elements. Its type is given by:

$$zip :: ([\alpha], [\beta]) \rightarrow [(\alpha, \beta)]$$

For example:

? *zip* ([0..4], "hallo")
[(0, 'h'), (1, 'a'), (2, 'l'), (3, 'l'), (4, 'o')]

? *zip* ([0..1], "hallo")
[(0, 'h'), (1, 'a')]

As the second example shows, if the two lists do not have the same length, then the length of the zipped list is the shorter of the lengths of the two arguments.

The function *zip* has many uses. Here are some representative examples.

1. *Scalar product.* The scalar product of two vectors x and y is defined by:

$$\sum_{i=1}^{n} x_i \times y_i$$

The function *sp*, for computing scalar products, can be defined by:

$$sp(xs, ys) = sum [x \times y \mid (x, y) \leftarrow zip(xs, ys)]$$

In this definition, *sum* is a function which sums the elements of a list of numbers; we shall meet its definition presently. Notice the form of the generator in this list comprehension: a pair of values is drawn from a list of pairs.

An alternative definition of the function *sp* is given by:

$$sp = sum \cdot zipwith(\times)$$

where *zipwith* is defined by:

$$zipwith \, f(xs, ys) = [f \, x \, y \mid (x, y) \leftarrow zip(xs, ys)]$$

The second definition is shorter than the first, and *zipwith* is a useful function in its own right, but either style is acceptable.

2. *Non-decreasing sequences.* Suppose we want to define a function *nondec* which determines whether a sequence $[x_1, \ldots, x_n]$ is in non-decreasing order. Informally, we have that *nondec* $[x_1, x_2, \ldots, x_n]$ is true whenever:

$$x_1 \leq x_2 \wedge x_2 \leq x_3 \wedge \cdots \wedge x_{n-1} \leq x_n$$

This condition can be expressed as a list comprehension in the following way:

$$nondec\ xs\ =\ and\ [x \leq y \mid (x,y) \leftarrow zip\ (xs, tl\ xs)]$$

The function *and* takes a list of boolean values and returns *True* if all of the elements of the list are *True*, and *False* otherwise.

We would like to have *nondec* $[\,] = True$. The above definition gives:

$$
\begin{aligned}
nondec\ [\,]\ &=\ and\ [x \leq y \mid (x,y) \leftarrow zip\ ([\,], tl\ [\,])] \\
&=\ and\ [x \leq y \mid (x,y) \leftarrow zip\ ([\,], \bot)]
\end{aligned}
$$

and it is not immediately clear what the value of this expression is. In fact, $zip\ ([\,], \bot) = [\,]$, so the above expression reduces to *and* $[\,]$ and thus to the required value *True*. This property of *zip* will be discussed in more detail when we come to the formal definition of *zip* in Chapter 5.

3. *Position.* Consider a function *position* such that (*position xs x*) returns the position of the first occurrence of x in xs (counting from 0), and -1 if x does not appear in xs. Thus *position* has type:

$$position :: [\alpha] \rightarrow \alpha \rightarrow num$$

This is an instructive problem because the best way to tackle it is to solve a more general problem first:

$$positions\ xs\ x\ =\ [i \mid (i,y) \leftarrow zip\ ([0\mathinner{\ldotp\ldotp}\#xs - 1], xs);\ x = y]$$

The function *positions* specifies *all* positions at which x appears in xs. We can now define *position* by:

$$position\ xs\ x\ =\ hd\ (positions\ xs\ x \mathbin{+\!\!+} [-1])$$

It turns out that the simplicity of this definition is achieved at no increase in the cost of evaluation. In order to calculate the head of a list, it is not necessary to determine the value of every element of the list. These remarks will be amplified in Chapter 6 where the efficiency of computation is discussed in detail.

List indexing. A list can be indexed by a natural number n to find the value appearing at position n. This operation is denoted by the operator (!) with type:

$$(!) :: [\alpha] \to num \to \alpha$$

For example:

? $[2, 4, 6, 8] \,!\, 2$
6

? $[2, 4, 6, 8] \,!\, 0$
2

Observe that the index of the first element of the list is position number 0. For many applications this is a better choice than beginning at position 1, although there are occasions when base 1 indexing is simpler.

We can define (!) with the help of *zip* in the following way:

$$xs \,!\, n = hd \, [y \mid (i, y) \leftarrow zip \, ([0 \, .. \, \#xs - 1], xs); \; i = n]$$

This is similar to the definition of *position* above. The number of steps required to find the nth element is proportional to n.

The operator (!) corresponds to the mathematical device of using subscripts to indicate a specified element of a list, and seems a very natural function. For example, we can use (!) to give an alternative definition of the function *nondec*. A sequence of numbers $x_0, x_1, \ldots, x_{n-1}$ is in non-decreasing order if $x_k \leq x_{k+1}$ for all k in the range $0 \leq k < n - 1$. Hence we have:

$$nondec \; xs \;\; = \;\; and \, [xs \,!\, k \leq xs \,!\, (k+1) \mid k \leftarrow [0 \, .. \, \#xs - 2]]$$

As we have suggested, indexing a list is a fairly expensive operation in functional programming, taking about k steps to compute $xs \,!\, k$, and should be avoided when there is a simple alternative. For example, the number of steps required to evaluate ($nondec \; xs$) according to the definition above is proportional to n^2, where n is the length of xs. Our earlier definition in terms of *zip* takes time proportional to n, and is therefore to be preferred.

List-difference. The operator $(--)$ subtracts one list from another. It plays an analogous role for lists to that of set-difference for sets. The informal description of $(--)$ is that the value of ($xs -- ys$) is the list which results when, for each (not necessarily distinct) element y in ys, the first occurrence (if any) of y is removed from xs. For example:

? $[1, 2, 1, 3, 1, 3] -- [1, 3]$
$[2, 1, 1, 3]$

? (``angle''} -- \text{``l'') $+\!\!+$ ``l''
angel

Concatenation and list-difference are related by the equation:

$$(xs + \!\!\!+ \; ys) \; -\!\!- \; xs = ys$$

for all finite lists xs and ys.

We also have:

$$
\begin{aligned}
tl \; xs &= \; xs \; -\!\!- \; [hd \; xs] \\
drop \; n \; xs &= \; xs \; -\!\!- \; take \; n \; xs
\end{aligned}
$$

Using list-difference, we can define the condition that one list is a permutation of another list:

$$permutation \; xs \; ys \;\; = \;\; (xs \; -\!\!- \; ys = [\,]) \wedge (ys \; -\!\!- \; xs = [\,])$$

A list xs is a permutation of a list ys if, for all x, the number of occurrences of x in xs is the same as the number of occurrences of x in ys. The former number is no greater than the latter if $xs \; -\!\!- \; ys = [\,]$, and no smaller if $ys \; -\!\!- \; xs = [\,]$. Hence the definition.

Exercises

3.3.1 Express $\#[e \mid x \leftarrow xs; \; y \leftarrow ys]$ in terms of $\#xs$ and $\#ys$.

3.3.2 Which of the following equations are true and which are false?

$$
\begin{aligned}
[[\,]] + \!\!\!+ \; xs &= \; xs \\
[[\,]] + \!\!\!+ \; xs &= \; [xs] \\
[[\,]] + \!\!\!+ \; xs &= \; [[\,], xs] \\
[[\,]] + \!\!\!+ \; [xs] &= \; [[\,], xs] \\
[xs] + \!\!\!+ \; [\,] &= \; [xs] \\
[xs] + \!\!\!+ \; [xs] &= \; [xs, xs]
\end{aligned}
$$

3.3.3 Give an informal characterisation of those finite lists xs and ys which satisfy:

$$xs + \!\!\!+ \; ys = ys + \!\!\!+ \; xs$$

3.3.4 What is the value of $[hd \; xs] + \!\!\!+ \; tl \; xs$ when $xs = [\,]$?

3.3.5 Show, using an informal argument, that if p is the minimum of m and n, then:

$$take \; m \cdot take \; n = take \; p$$

3.3.6 Verify or disprove the assertion that:

$$(drop \; n \; xs) \, ! \, m = xs \, ! \, (n + m)$$

for all finite lists xs and natural numbers n and m.

3.3.7 Is *zip* associative in the sense that:

$$zip\,(xs, zip\,(ys, zs)) = zip\,(zip\,(xs, ys), zs)$$

for all *xs*, *ys* and *zs*?

3.3.8 Using *zip* define the function *zip4* which converts a 4-tuple of lists into a list of 4-tuples.

3.3.9 Define a function *trips* so that *trips xs* returns a list of all adjacent triples of elements of *xs*.

3.3.10 Suppose a list *xs* of integers contains an equal number of odd and even numbers. Define a function *riffle* so that (*riffle xs*) is some rearrangement of *xs* in which odd and even numbers alternate.

3.3.11 Find *xs* and *ys* such that:

$$(xs +\!\!+ ys) -\!\!- ys \neq xs$$

3.3.12 In a version of the game Mastermind, one player thinks of an *n*-digit number, while the other player repeatedly tries to guess it. After each guess, player 1 scores the guess by stating the number of bulls and cows. A bull is a correct digit in the correct place. A cow is a digit appearing in the secret number, but not in the correct place. No digit is scored more than once. For example, if the secret code is 2113, then:

$$\begin{array}{lll} 1234 & scores & 03 \\ 1111 & scores & 20 \\ 1212 & scores & 12 \end{array}$$

Using $(-\!\!-)$, construct a function *score* which takes a code and a guess and returns the number of bulls and cows.

3.4 Map and filter

Two useful higher-order functions, closely related to list comprehensions, are *map* and *filter*. The function *map* applies a function to each element of a list. The type of *map* and its definition as a list comprehension are as follows:

$$\begin{array}{lll} map & :: & (\alpha \rightarrow \beta) \rightarrow [\alpha] \rightarrow [\beta] \\ map\,f\,xs & = & [f\,x \mid x \leftarrow xs] \end{array}$$

For example, we have:

? *map square* [9, 3]
[81, 9]

? *sum* (*map square* [1 .. 100])
338700

The use of *map* is nicely illustrated by the last example: the English phrase
"the sum of the squares of the first 100 positive integers" is converted into a
formal expression in a very simple and direct manner. One could also define:

$$sigma\ f\ m\ n\ =\ sum\ (map\ f\ [m\mathrel{..}n])$$
$$sumsquares\ =\ sigma\ square\ 1\ 100$$

and so capture a common mathematical notation as a generic function *sigma*.

There are a number of useful algebraic identities concerning *map*. For
instance:

$$map\ (f\cdot g)\ =\ (map\ f)\cdot(map\ g)$$

This identity says that if we apply g to every element of a list, and then apply
f to each element of the result, then the same effect is obtained by applying
$(f\cdot g)$ to the original list. In other words, *map* distributes through functional
composition. One consequence of the rule is that if f has an inverse f^{-1},
then:

$$(map\ f)^{-1} = map\ f^{-1}$$

The proof is left as an exercise for the reader.

Two further laws about *map* are:

$$map\ f\ (xs\mathbin{+\!\!+}ys)\ =\ (map\ f\ xs)\mathbin{+\!\!+}(map\ f\ ys)$$
$$map\ f\cdot concat\ =\ concat\cdot map\ (map\ f)$$

The first law says that $(map f)$ distributes through concatenation. The second
is a generalisation of the first: it says that applying f to each element of a
concatenated list of lists is the same as applying $(map f)$ to each component
list and concatenating the results.

Equalities such as the above are important for reasoning about the properties of functions. We shall see how to prove them in Chapter 5.

Filter.   The second function *filter* takes a predicate p and a list xs and
returns the sublist of xs whose elements satisfy p. Like *map* it can be defined
by a list comprehension:

$$filter\quad ::\quad (\alpha\rightarrow bool)\rightarrow[\alpha]\rightarrow[\alpha]$$
$$filter\ p\ xs\ =\ [x\mid x\leftarrow xs;\ p\ x]$$

For example, we have:

? *filter even* $[1,2,4,5,32]$
$[2,4,32]$

? $(sum\cdot map\ square\cdot filter\ even)\,[1\mathrel{..}10]$
220

Observe in the last example how the phrase "the sums of the squares of the even numbers in the range 1 to 10" is translated directly into a formal expression in our programming notation. Observe also that the type of *filter* is the same as *takewhile* and *dropwhile*, two of the functions we introduced in a previous section.

Like *map*, there are a number of useful identities concerning *filter*. We have, in particular, that:

$$filter\ p\ (xs \mathbin{+\!\!\!+} ys) \;=\; filter\ p\ xs \mathbin{+\!\!\!+} filter\ p\ ys$$
$$filter\ p \cdot concat \;=\; concat \cdot map\ (filter\ p)$$
$$filter\ p \cdot filter\ q \;=\; filter\ q \cdot filter\ p$$

The first law says that *filter* distributes through concatenation. The second law generalises this distributive property to lists of lists. Finally, the third law says that filters can be applied in any order. The third law is only valid if $p\ x \neq \bot$ and $q\ x \neq \bot$ for $x \neq \bot$.

Translating comprehensions. There is a close relationship between the functions *map* and *filter* and the notation of list comprehensions. We have defined *map* and *filter* in terms of list comprehensions, but it is also possible to go in the other direction and translate list comprehensions into combinations of *map*, *filter* and the function *concat* (which was also defined earlier as a comprehension). There are just four basic rules for carrying out the conversion:

(1) $[x \mid x \leftarrow xs]$ $\qquad\qquad\quad = \quad xs$
(2) $[f\ x \mid x \leftarrow xs]$ $\qquad\qquad = \quad map\ f\ xs$
(3) $[e \mid x \leftarrow xs;\ p\ x;\ \cdots]$ $\quad = \quad [e \mid x \leftarrow filter\ p\ xs;\ \cdots]$
(4) $[e \mid x \leftarrow xs;\ y \leftarrow ys;\ \cdots] \; = \; concat\,[[e \mid y \leftarrow ys;\ \cdots] \mid x \leftarrow xs]$

This set of rules is sufficient to translate any comprehension provided it begins with a generator. Note that Rule (1) is a special case of Rule (2), namely when $f = id$. In order to apply Rules (2) and (3) it may be necessary to introduce subsidiary functions. For example, in order to translate the comprehension:

$$[1 \mid x \leftarrow xs]$$

it is necessary to introduce a function *const*, defined by:

$$const\ k\ x = k$$

Now we have:

$$
\begin{aligned}
[1 \mid x \leftarrow xs] \;&=\; [const\ 1\ x \mid x \leftarrow xs] \quad (const.1)\\
&=\; map\ (const\ 1)\ xs \qquad\ \ (\text{Rule 2})
\end{aligned}
$$

Similarly, in order to translate:

$$[x \mid x \leftarrow xs;\ x = min\ xs]$$

we introduce the function:

$$minof\ xs\ x = (x = min\ xs)$$

Now we can write:

$$
\begin{aligned}
& [x \mid x \leftarrow xs;\ x = min\ xs] \\
& = \quad [x \mid x \leftarrow xs;\ minof\ xs\ x] \quad\quad (minof.1) \\
& = \quad [x \mid x \leftarrow filter\ (minof\ xs)\ xs] \quad (\text{Rule 3}) \\
& = \quad filter\ (minof\ xs)\ xs \quad\quad\quad\quad (\text{Rule 1})
\end{aligned}
$$

Here are three further examples of translating comprehensions:

(a) We have:

$$
\begin{aligned}
& [x \times x \mid x \leftarrow xs;\ even\ x] \\
& = \quad [x \times x \mid x \leftarrow filter\ even\ xs] \quad\quad (\text{Rule 3}) \\
& = \quad [square\ x \mid x \leftarrow filter\ even\ xs] \quad (square) \\
& = \quad map\ square\ (filter\ even\ xs) \quad\quad\quad (\text{Rule 2})
\end{aligned}
$$

(b) We have:

$$
\begin{aligned}
& [x \mid xs \leftarrow xss;\ x \leftarrow xs] \\
& = \quad concat\ [[x \mid x \leftarrow xs] \mid xs \leftarrow xss] \quad (\text{Rule 4}) \\
& = \quad concat\ [xs \mid xs \leftarrow xss] \quad\quad\quad\quad (\text{Rule 1}) \\
& = \quad concat\ xss \quad\quad\quad\quad\quad\quad\quad\quad (\text{Rule 1})
\end{aligned}
$$

(c) We have:

$$
\begin{aligned}
& [(i,j) \mid i \leftarrow [1 .. n];\ j \leftarrow [i+1 .. n]] \\
& = \quad concat\ [[(i,j) \mid j \leftarrow [i+1 .. n]] \mid i \leftarrow [1 .. n]] \quad (\text{Rule 4}) \\
& = \quad concat\ [map\ (pair\ i)\ [i+1 .. n] \mid i \leftarrow [1 .. n]] \quad (\text{Rule 2}) \\
& = \quad concat\ (map\ mpair\ [1 .. n]) \quad\quad\quad\quad\quad\quad\quad (\text{Rule 2})
\end{aligned}
$$

Here we have used the definitions:

$$
\begin{aligned}
pair\ i\ j\ & = \ (i,j) \\
mpair\ i\ & = \ map\ (pair\ i)\ [i+1 .. n]
\end{aligned}
$$

The choice as to whether to write a program using *concat*, *map* and *filter*, or to use comprehensions, is a matter of style. Sometimes one is more clear, sometimes the other and sometimes both are equally good (or bad). One advantage of the higher-order functions is that it is easier to state algebraic properties and use these properties in the manipulation of expressions. On the other hand, list comprehensions are clear and simple to understand. Moreover, there is no need to invent special names for the subsidiary functions which arise when *map* and *filter* are used.

Exercises

3.4.1 The function *filter* can be defined in terms of *concat* and *map*:

$$filter\ p\ =\ concat \cdot map\ box$$
$$\textbf{where}\ \ box\ x = \ldots$$

Give the definition of *box*.

3.4.2 What is the type of $(map\ map)$?

3.4.3 Using the rules given in Section 3.4, convert the following expressions into combinations of *map*, *filter* and *concat*:

$$[x \mid xs \leftarrow xss;\ x \leftarrow xs;\ odd\ x]$$
$$[(x, y) \mid x \leftarrow xs;\ p\ x;\ y \leftarrow ys]$$

3.4.4 Consider the following two expressions:

$$[(x, y) \mid x \leftarrow xs;\ p\ x;\ y \leftarrow ys]$$
$$[(x, y) \mid x \leftarrow xs;\ y \leftarrow ys;\ p\ x]$$

Are they equivalent? Supposing $\#xs = 1000$, $\#(filter\ p\ xs) = 10$ and $\#ys = 100$, compare the costs of evaluating the two expressions. What conclusions do you draw?

3.5 The fold operators

Most of the operations we have seen so far return lists as results. The fold operators are more general in that they can convert lists into other kinds of value as well. The fold operators come in two flavours, *foldr* and *foldl*. We will begin by considering *foldr*. Its informal definition is as follows:

$$foldr\ f\ a\ [x_1, x_2, \ldots, x_n] = f\ x_1\ (f\ x_2\ (\ \cdots\ (f\ x_n\ a)\cdots))$$

An equivalent formulation, possibly easier to read, is:

$$foldr\ (\oplus)\ a\ [x_1, x_2, \ldots, x_n] = x_1 \oplus (x_2 \oplus (\ \cdots\ (x_n \oplus a)\cdots))$$

Here $(\oplus)$, like f, is just a variable that is bound to a function of two arguments. The equivalence of the two definitions can be seen by recalling that $x \oplus y$ is equivalent to $(\oplus)\ x\ y$.

In particular, we have:

$$
\begin{aligned}
foldr\ (\oplus)\ a\ [\,] &= a \\
foldr\ (\oplus)\ a\ [x_1] &= x_1 \oplus a \\
foldr\ (\oplus)\ a\ [x_1, x_2] &= x_1 \oplus (x_2 \oplus a) \\
foldr\ (\oplus)\ a\ [x_1, x_2, x_3] &= x_1 \oplus (x_2 \oplus (x_3 \oplus a))
\end{aligned}
$$

and so on. The brackets always group to the right; this explains the name *foldr*, which stands for 'fold right'.

From the informal definition we can infer that the second argument of $\oplus$ must have the same type as the result of $\oplus$, but that, in general, the first argument may have a different type. Thus, the most general type for *foldr* is:

$$foldr :: (\alpha \to \beta \to \beta) \to \beta \to [\alpha] \to \beta$$

Often α and β will be instantiated to the same type; this will happen, for example, if $\oplus$ denotes an associative operation.

Using *foldr* we can define:

$$
\begin{aligned}
sum &= foldr\,(+)\,0 \\
product &= foldr\,(\times)\,1 \\
concat &= foldr\,(+\!\!+)\,[\,] \\
and &= foldr\,(\wedge)\,True \\
or &= foldr\,(\vee)\,False
\end{aligned}
$$

The function *sum* adds the elements of a list of numbers, while *product* multiplies them. We have met *concat* in Section 3.3 where it was defined by a list comprehension. The functions *and* and *or* both take a list of booleans as argument: *and* returns *True* if every element of the list equals *True*, while *or* returns *True* if at least one element of the list equals *True*. We have already met *and* in a previous section.

All of the above examples share an important property: in the expression (*foldr* ($\oplus$) *a*) the function $\oplus$ is associative and has identity element *a*. In other words, we have for all x, y, and z that:

$$
\begin{aligned}
x \oplus (y \oplus z) &= (x \oplus y) \oplus z \\
x \oplus a &= x = a \oplus x
\end{aligned}
$$

We will abbreviate this by saying that $\oplus$ and *a* form a *monoid*. The reader should verify that each of the five definitions above has this property. If $\oplus$ and *a* form a monoid, then:

$$
\begin{aligned}
foldr\,(\oplus)\,a\,[\,] &= a \\
foldr\,(\oplus)\,a\,[x_1, x_2, \ldots, x_n] &= x_1 \oplus x_2 \oplus \cdots \oplus x_n
\end{aligned}
$$

because the disposition of brackets has no effect on meaning.

Here are some examples where the arguments to *foldr* do not form a monoid. First, consider:

$$
\begin{aligned}
(\#) &= foldr\ oneplus\ 0 \\
&\mathbf{where}\ \ oneplus\ x\ n = 1 + n
\end{aligned}
$$

This defines the length of a list by counting one for each element. Note that *oneplus* ignores its first argument. The type of *oneplus* is:

$$oneplus :: \alpha \to num \to num$$

and so it cannot be associative.

Second, here are two examples of definitions of functions which we have already met informally:

$$reverse \quad = \quad foldr \; postfix \; [\,]$$
$$\textbf{where} \; postfix \; x \; xs = xs \; \mathbin{+\!\!+} \; [x]$$

$$takewhile \; p \quad = \quad foldr \; (\oplus) \; [\,]$$
$$\textbf{where} \; x \oplus xs \quad = \quad [x] \mathbin{+\!\!+} xs, \quad \textbf{if} \; p \; x$$
$$= \quad [\,], \qquad \textbf{otherwise}$$

The first function reverses a list $[x_1, x_2, \ldots, x_n]$ by appending $x_n, x_{n-1}, \ldots, x_1$ in succession to the end of an initially empty list. To check the definition of $takewhile \; p$, consider the expression $takewhile \; (< 3) \, [1 \mathbin{..} 4]$. We have:

$$takewhile \; (< 3) \, [1 \mathbin{..} 4] \quad = \quad 1 \oplus (2 \oplus (3 \oplus (4 \oplus [\,])))$$
$$= \quad [1] \mathbin{+\!\!+} ([2] \mathbin{+\!\!+} ([\,]))$$
$$= \quad [1, 2]$$

as required.

Fold left. We now consider $foldl$, the other flavour of the fold operator. Informally, it is defined by:

$$foldl \; (\oplus) \; a \; [x_1, x_2, \ldots, x_n] = (\cdots((a \oplus x_1) \oplus x_2) \cdots) \oplus x_n$$

In particular, we have:

$$foldl \; (\oplus) \; a \; [\,] \quad = \quad a$$
$$foldl \; (\oplus) \; a \; [x_1] \quad = \quad a \oplus x_1$$
$$foldl \; (\oplus) \; a \; [x_1, x_2] \quad = \quad (a \oplus x_1) \oplus x_2$$
$$foldl \; (\oplus) \; a \; [x_1, x_2, x_3] \quad = \quad ((a \oplus x_1) \oplus x_2) \oplus x_3$$

and so on. Here the brackets group to the left, so $foldl$ stands for "fold left". The type of $foldl$ is:

$$foldl :: (\beta \to \alpha \to \beta) \to \beta \to [\alpha] \to \beta$$

This is almost identical to the type of $foldr$, except that in $foldr$ the first argument has type $(\alpha \to \beta \to \beta)$. When $\oplus$ is associative, both α and β are instantiated to the same type, and so $foldr$ and $foldl$ have the same type in such a case.

Clearly, $foldr$ and $foldl$ are closely related functions differing only in the way the operations are grouped. One example of the use of $foldl$ is given by:

$$pack \; xs \quad = \quad foldl \; (\oplus) \; 0 \; xs$$
$$\textbf{where} \; n \oplus x = 10 \times n + x$$

This codes a sequence of digits as a single number, assuming the most significant digit comes first. Thus we have:

$$pack \; [x_{n-1}, x_{n-2}, \ldots, x_0] = \sum_{k=0}^{n-1} x_k 10^k$$

3.5.1 Laws

There are a number of important laws concerning *foldr* and *foldl*. The first
three are called *duality theorems*.

The *first duality theorem* states that:

$$foldr\ (\oplus)\ a\ xs = foldl\ (\oplus)\ a\ xs$$

whenever $\oplus$ and a form a monoid and xs is a finite list. Thus, *foldr* and
foldl define the same function over monoids. However, as we shall see in
Chapter 6, it is sometimes more efficient to define a function using *foldr* and
sometimes more efficient to use *foldl*. For example, we could have defined
sum and *product* using *foldl* instead of *foldr*, and we shall see that using *foldl*
is indeed more efficient. On the other hand, we shall also see that *concat*,
and, and *or* are better defined using *foldr*.

The *second duality theorem* is a generalisation of the first. Suppose $\oplus$ and $\otimes$
and a are such that for all x, y, and z we have:

$$x \oplus (y \otimes z) = (x \oplus y) \otimes z$$
$$x \oplus a = a \otimes x$$

In other words, $\oplus$ and $\otimes$ associate with each other, and a on the right of $\oplus$
is equivalent to a on the left of $\otimes$. Under these conditions we have:

$$foldr\ (\oplus)\ a\ xs = foldl\ (\otimes)\ a\ xs$$

for any finite list xs.

The second duality theorem has the first duality theorem as a special
case, namely when $(\oplus) = (\otimes)$.

To illustrate the second duality theorem, here are the definitions of $(\#)$
and *reverse* in terms of *foldl*:

$$
\begin{aligned}
(\#) \quad &= \quad foldl\ plusone\ 0 \\
&\textbf{where}\ \ plusone\ n\ x = n + 1 \\[2mm]
reverse \quad &= \quad foldl\ prefix\ [\,] \\
&\textbf{where}\ \ prefix\ xs\ x = [x] \mathbin{+\!\!+} xs
\end{aligned}
$$

It follows from the second duality theorem that these definitions are equivalent to the previous ones that used *foldr*. Later on, we shall see that these
new definitions are in fact more efficient. The reader should verify that
oneplus, *plusone* and 0 meet the conditions of the second duality theorem,
as do *postfix*, *prefix*, and [].

The *third duality theorem* states that:

$$foldr\ (\oplus)\ a\ xs = foldl\ (\tilde{\oplus})\ a\ (reverse\ xs)$$

for any finite list xs, where $\widetilde{\oplus}$ is defined by:

$$x \mathbin{\widetilde{\oplus}} y = y \oplus x$$

so that $\widetilde{\oplus}$ is $\oplus$ with the arguments reversed.

For example, reversing the arguments of *prefix* gives a function *cons* defined by:

$$cons\ x\ xs\ \ =\ \ [x] +\!\!+\ xs$$

Moreover, we have that:

$$xs = foldr\ cons\ [\,]\ xs$$

for all lists xs. Now, from the third duality theorem we have:

$$foldr\ cons\ [\,]\ xs = foldl\ prefix\ [\,]\ (reverse\ xs)$$

and so:

$$xs = reverse\ (reverse\ xs)$$

for any finite list xs, just as we would expect.

There are many other useful identities concerning *foldr* and *foldl*. For example, if $\oplus$ and a form a monoid, then:

$$foldr\ (\oplus)\ a\ (xs +\!\!+ ys) = (foldr\ (\oplus)\ a\ xs) \oplus (foldr\ (\oplus)\ a\ ys)$$

for all lists xs and ys. A similar identity holds for *foldl*.

We also have, for arbitrary f and a, that:

$$
\begin{aligned}
foldl\ f\ a\ (xs +\!\!+ ys)\ &=\ \ foldl\ f\ (foldl\ f\ a\ xs)\ ys \\
foldr\ f\ a\ (xs +\!\!+ ys)\ &=\ \ foldr\ f\ (foldr\ f\ a\ ys)\ xs
\end{aligned}
$$

for all lists xs and ys.

3.5.2 Fold over non-empty lists

Say we wish to find the maximum element of a list. We would like to do this by defining:

$$max\ \ =\ \ foldl\ (\mathbf{max})\ a$$

where $(\mathbf{max})$ is a binary operator that returns the greater of its two arguments. But what should we choose as the value of a? Since $(\mathbf{max})$ is associative, we would have a monoid if a were chosen to be the identity element for $(\mathbf{max})$; that is:

$$x\ \mathbf{max}\ a = x = a\ \mathbf{max}\ x$$

for all x. If we know that the list contains only non-negative numbers, then choosing a to be 0 gives the desired property, and we can define:

$$maxnaturals \ = \ foldl \, (\mathbf{max}) \, 0$$

Unfortunately there is no value of a with the desired property in the general case of arbitrary numbers.

We will solve this problem by introducing two new functions $foldl1$ and $foldr1$ which are variants of $foldl$ and $foldr$. Informally, $foldl1$ and $foldr1$ are defined by:

$$foldl1 \ (\oplus) \, [x_1, x_2, \ldots, x_n] \ = \ (\cdots((x_1 \oplus x_2) \oplus x_3) \cdots) \oplus x_n$$
$$foldr1 \ (\oplus) \, [x_1, x_2, \ldots, x_n] \ = \ (x_1 \oplus (x_2 \oplus \cdots (x_{n-1} \oplus x_n) \cdots))$$

In particular, we have:

$$foldl1 \ (\oplus) \, [x_1] \ = \ x_1$$
$$foldl1 \ (\oplus) \, [x_1, x_2] \ = \ x_1 \oplus x_2$$
$$foldl1 \ (\oplus) \, [x_1, x_2, x_3] \ = \ (x_1 \oplus x_2) \oplus x_3$$

and so on. The difference between $foldl1$ and $foldr1$ is only apparent for lists of length 3 or more. We have:

$$foldr1 \ (\oplus) \, [x_1, x_2, x_3] \ = \ x_1 \oplus (x_2 \oplus x_3)$$

in which the brackets group the other way. Both functions are undefined on the empty list. The type of $foldl1$ and $foldr1$ is:

$$foldl1, foldr1 :: (\alpha \to \alpha \to \alpha) \to [\alpha] \to \alpha$$

The reader should compare this with the types of $foldl$ and $foldr$; here, there is only one type variable (α) instead of two (α and β).

Now we can solve our problem by defining:

$$max \ = \ foldl1 \, (\mathbf{max})$$

We could, of course, have used $foldr1$ instead. Further, it is easy to define $foldl1$ in terms of $foldl$:

$$foldl1 \ (\oplus) \, xs \ = \ foldl \, (\oplus) \, (hd \ xs) \, (tl \ xs)$$

The definition of $foldr1$ is left as an exercise for the reader.

3.5.3 Scan

Sometimes it is convenient to apply a fold left operation to every initial segment of a list. This is done by the function $scan$, which can be defined informally in the following way:

$$scan \ (\oplus) \, a \, [x_1, x_2, \ldots,] = [a, a \oplus x_1, (a \oplus x_1) \oplus x_2, \ldots]$$

In particular:

$$scan \, (\oplus) \, a \, [x_1, x_2, x_3]$$
$$= \, [a, (a \oplus x_1), ((a \oplus x_1) \oplus x_2), (((a \oplus x_1) \oplus x_2) \oplus x_3)]$$

It follows that the last element of the list $(scan \, (\oplus) \, a \, xs)$ is just the value of $(foldl \, (\oplus) \, a \, xs)$. Hence:

$$foldl \, (\oplus) \, a = last \cdot scan \, (\oplus) \, a$$

Notice that each element in a *scan* can be computed in terms of the preceding element using just one extra $\oplus$ operation. More precisely, if $x \oplus y$ can be computed in a constant number of steps, and the list xs has length n, then $(scan \, (\oplus) \, a \, xs)$ can be computed in a number of steps proportional to n.

For example, *scan* can be used to compute running sums or running products:

$$scan \, (+) \, 0 \, [1,2,3,4,5] \; = \; [0,1,3,6,10,15]$$
$$scan \, (\times) \, 1 \, [1,2,3,4,5] \; = \; [1,1,2,6,24,120]$$

The last expression is equal to *map fact* $[0 \mathinner{.\,.} 5]$, where:

$$fact \; n \; = \; product \, [1 \mathinner{.\,.} n]$$

is a definition of the factorial function. However, this second definition of the list of factorial numbers is *less* efficient since each term is computed independently. In fact, $(map \, fact \, [0 \mathinner{.\,.} n])$ requires about n^2 multiplications.

As a related example, we have:

$$scan \, (/) \, 1 \, [1 \mathinner{.\,.} n] = [1/0!, 1/1!, \ldots, 1/n!]$$

where $n!$ is the conventional notation for $(fact \, n)$.

Exercises

3.5.1 Consider the function *all* which takes a predicate p and a list xs and returns *True* if all elements of xs satisfy p, and *False* otherwise. Give a formal definition of *all* which uses *foldr*.

3.5.2 Which, if any, of the following equations are true?

$$foldl \, (-) \, x \, xs \; = \; x - sum \, xs$$
$$foldr \, (-) \, x \, xs \; = \; x - sum \, xs$$

3.5.3 Verify the equation:

$$foldl \, (\oplus) \, a \, (xs \mathbin{+\!\!+} ys) = foldl \, (\oplus) \, (foldl \, (\oplus) \, a \, xs) \, ys$$

Using the fact that:

$$reverse \, (xs \mathbin{+\!\!+} ys) = reverse \, ys \mathbin{+\!\!+} reverse \, xs$$

and one of the duality laws, derive a similar equation for $foldr \, (\oplus) \, a \, (xs \mathbin{+\!\!+} ys)$.

3.5.4 Consider the following definition of a function *insert*:

$$insert\ x\ xs\ =\ takewhile\ (\leq x)\ xs \mathbin{+\!\!+} [x] \mathbin{+\!\!+} dropwhile\ (\leq x)\ xs$$

Show that if *xs* is a list in non-decreasing order, then so is (*insert x xs*). Using *insert*, define a function *isort* for sorting a list into non-decreasing order.

3.5.5 The function *remdups* removes adjacent duplicates from a list. For example, *remdups* $[1,2,2,3,3,3,1,1] = [1,2,3,1]$. Define *remdups* using either *foldl* or *foldr*.

3.5.6 Given a list $xs = [x_1, x_2, \ldots, x_n]$ of numbers, the sequence of successive maxima (*ssm xs*) is the longest subsequence $[x_{j_1}, x_{j_2}, \ldots, x_{j_m}]$ such that $j_1 = 1$ and $x_j < x_{j_k}$ for $j < j_k$. For example, the sequence of successive maxima of $[3,1,3,4,9,2,10,7]$ is $[3,4,9,10]$. Define *ssm* in terms of *foldl*.

3.5.7 The following law relates *foldl* and *map*:

$$foldl\ (\oplus)\ a \cdot map\ f = foldl\ (\otimes)\ a$$

where $x \otimes y = x \oplus f\ y$. Derive this law from the corresponding law relating *foldr* and *map*, using the fact that:

$$map\ f \cdot reverse = reverse \cdot map\ f$$

and one of the duality theorems.

3.5.8 Define the functions *foldr1* and *scan1* that relate to *foldr* and *scan* analogously to the way that *foldl1* relates to *foldl*.

3.5.9 The mathematical constant *e* is defined by:

$$e = \sum_{n \geq 0} \frac{1}{n!}$$

Write down an expression that can be used to evaluate *e* to some reasonable measure of accuracy.

3.6 List patterns

When introducing the basic types of the previous chapter we showed how to define functions by pattern matching. Pattern matching with list arguments is also possible. To explain how it works it is necessary to introduce one final operator which plays a special role with lists. The operator is denoted by the sign (:) (pronounced 'cons') and inserts a value as a new first element of a list. (In fact, (:) has already appeared in Section 3.5.1 with the name *cons*.) The type of (:) is given by:

$$(:) :: \alpha \to [\alpha] \to [\alpha]$$

For example, we have:

? 1 : []
[1]

? 1 : 2 : [3, 4]
[1, 2, 3, 4]

? 'h' : 'e' : 'l' : 'l' : 'o' : []
hello

By convention, (:) associates to the right, so $1 : 2 : [3,4]$ means $1 : (2 : [3,4])$.

Every list can be constructed by inserting its elements one by one into the empty list (hence the reason for the name 'cons', which is an abbreviation for the word 'construct'). In fact, we can regard an enumerated list:

$$[x_1, x_2, \ldots, x_n]$$

as shorthand for the expression:

$$x_1 : x_2 : \ldots : x_n : []$$

Cons is related to concatenation in that we have:

$$x : xs = [x] \mathbin{+\!\!+} xs$$

for all x and xs.

One important distinction between $(\mathbin{+\!\!+})$ and (:) is that every list can be expressed in terms of [] and (:) in *exactly one way*. This is not true for concatenation because it is an associative operation. For example, the list $[1, 2, 3]$ can be expressed as $[1] \mathbin{+\!\!+} [2, 3]$, or as $[1, 2] \mathbin{+\!\!+} [3]$. This special property of (:) means we can do pattern matching with [] and (:). For example, we can define *hd* and *tl* formally by the equations:

$$
\begin{aligned}
hd\,(x : xs) &= x \\
tl\,(x : xs) &= xs
\end{aligned}
$$

Similarly, we can define a test *null* for determining whether a list is empty by:

$$
\begin{aligned}
null\,[] &= True \\
null\,(x : xs) &= False
\end{aligned}
$$

Finally, we can define a function *single* for determining whether a list contains a single element by the equations:

$$
\begin{aligned}
single\,[] &= False \\
single\,[x] &= True \\
single\,(x : y : xs) &= False
\end{aligned}
$$

Here, the pattern $[x]$ is used as an abbreviation for $x : []$. Note that the three cases described by the above patterns are exhaustive and disjoint. An

arbitrary list is either empty, in which case it matches the pattern [ ], or it
is a singleton list, in which case it matches the pattern $x : [\ ]$, or it is of the
form $x : y : xs$.

Further examples of definition by list patterns will be given in the next
two chapters.

Exercises

3.6.1 In how many ways can $[1 .. n]$ be expressed as the concatenation of
two non-empty lists?

3.6.2 Which of the following equations are true?

$$
\begin{aligned}
[\ ] : xs &= xs \\
[\ ] : xs &= [[\ ], xs] \\
xs : [\ ] &= xs \\
xs : [\ ] &= [xs] \\
x : y &= [x, y] \\
(x : xs) \mathbin{+\!\!+} ys &= x : (xs \mathbin{+\!\!+} ys)
\end{aligned}
$$

3.6.3 Using pattern matching with (:), define a function $rev2$ that reverses
all lists of length 2, but leaves others unchanged. Ensure that the patterns
are exhaustive and disjoint.

3.6.4 Consider the function $insert$ of Exercise 3.5.4. Another way to define
$insert$ is in terms of a function $swap$:

$$ insert\ x = foldr\ swap\ [x] $$

The function $(swap\ x)$ applied to a non-empty list xs adds x as either the
first or second element. Using pattern matching, give a definition of $swap$.
Estimate the cost of sorting by this method.

Chapter 4

Examples

The examples of list processing dealt with in the present chapter come from a variety of sources and cover both numeric and symbolic applications. In particular, we shall build a simple package for doing arithmetic with arbitrary precision integers, design some useful functions for handling text, and show how to construct pictures of different kinds. Each application is accompanied by a number of exercises in which the reader is invited to check relationships, explore possible extensions and suggest improvements.

We begin with a simple problem, involving both numeric and symbolic aspects, in which the operation of list indexing plays a central role.

4.1 Converting numbers to words

Sometimes we need to write numbers in words. For instance, to fill out a cheque or cash transfer correctly, not only must the amount appear in figures, it must also be written in words. Suppose, for simplicity, that the given number is an integer greater than zero but less than one million. We want to design a function *convert* so that, provided n is in the stated range, the value of (*convert* n) is the list of characters corresponding to the usual English formulation of the whole number n.

The informal specification above assumes we know exactly what 'the usual English formulation' of a number is. In fact, different rules and conventions are adopted in different places. The rules we shall follow are illustrated by the following examples:

? *convert* 308000
three hundred and eight thousand

? *convert* 369027
three hundred and sixty-nine thousand and twenty-seven

? *convert* 369401
three hundred and sixty-nine thousand four hundred and one

Notice the dash in the phrases "twenty-seven" and "sixty-nine", and the connecting word "and" which appears: (i) after the word "hundred" if the tens part is non-zero; and (ii) after the word "thousand" if the hundreds part is zero (but the tens part is not).

A good way to tackle such problems is to consider a simpler problem first. There is, of course, no guarantee that solutions obtained for simpler problems can be used directly in the problem which inspired them; they may only serve to familiarise the solver with some of the features and difficulties involved. Even so, the work is not wasted; familiarity with a problem is one of our most important tools for solving it. And often we will be able to use the solution directly or by adapting it.

An obvious place to begin is to suppose that the number n belongs to a smaller interval, say $0 < n < 100$. In this case n has one or two digits. These digits are going to be needed, so we start with the definition:

$$
\begin{aligned}
convert2\ n &= combine2\ (digits2\ n) \\
digits2\ n &= (n \ \mathbf{div}\ 10, n \ \mathbf{mod}\ 10)
\end{aligned}
$$

In order to define the function $combine2$, we shall need the English names for the simplest numbers. These can be given as lists of strings:

$$
\begin{aligned}
units &= \quad [\text{"one"}, \text{"two"}, \text{"three"}, \text{"four"}, \text{"five"}, \\
&\qquad \text{"six"}, \text{"seven"}, \text{"eight"}, \text{"nine"}] \\
teens &= \quad [\text{"ten"}, \text{"eleven"}, \text{"twelve"}, \text{"thirteen"}, \text{"fourteen"}, \\
&\qquad \text{"fifteen"}, \text{"sixteen"}, \text{"seventeen"}, \text{"eighteen"}, \text{"nineteen"}] \\
tens &= \quad [\text{"twenty"}, \text{"thirty"}, \text{"forty"}, \text{"fifty"}, \\
&\qquad \text{"sixty"}, \text{"seventy"}, \text{"eighty"}, \text{"ninety"}]
\end{aligned}
$$

The definition of $combine2$ uses these lists by indexing into them at the appropriate places. The definition is as follows:

$$
\begin{aligned}
combine2\ (0, u+1) &= units\ !\ u \\
combine2\ (1, u) &= teens\ !\ u \\
combine2\ (t+2, 0) &= tens\ !\ t \\
combine2\ (t+2, u+1) &= tens\ !\ t \ \text{+++}\ \text{"-"} \ \text{+++}\ units\ !\ u
\end{aligned}
$$

Recall that list indexing with the operator (!) begins at 0, not 1. The patterns on the left are mutually disjoint, so the order of the equations is not important. However, no value is specified for the pattern $(0, 0)$.

The case $0 < n < 100$ yielded easily enough, so now let us try the range $0 < n < 1000$ when n can have up to three digits. Taking account of the structure of our first solution, we begin with:

$$
\begin{aligned}
convert3\ n &= combine3\ (digits3\ n) \\
digits3\ n &= (n \ \mathbf{div}\ 100, n \ \mathbf{mod}\ 100)
\end{aligned}
$$

Here, (*digits3 n*) returns a pair (h, t) where h is the hundreds part of n (so $0 \le h < 10$), and t the part less than 100. For example, *digits3* $(427) =$ $(4, 27)$. We can now define:

$$
\begin{aligned}
\textit{combine3}\;(0, t+1) \quad &= \quad \textit{convert2}\;(t+1) \\
\textit{combine3}\;(h+1, 0) \quad &= \quad \textit{units}\;!\;h \;\text{\text#}\; \text{``\textvisiblespace hundred''} \\
\textit{combine3}\;(h+1, t+1) \quad &= \quad \textit{units}\;!\;h \;\text{\text#}\; \text{``\textvisiblespace hundred and\textvisiblespace''} \\
&\qquad \text{\text#}\, \textit{convert2}\;(t+1)
\end{aligned}
$$

This step is the crucial one as far as the design of the overall algorithm is concerned. We split n into digits in two stages: first into a hundreds part h and a part t less than a hundred; and then, in the definition of *convert2*, split t into a tens part and a part less than ten.

Now we are ready to tackle the next and final step in which n lies in the range $0 < n < 1000000$ and so can have up to 6 digits. In a similar spirit to before, we split n into two numbers m and h, where m is the thousands part and h is the part less than a thousand. We can therefore write:

$$
\begin{aligned}
\textit{convert6}\;n \quad &= \quad \textit{combine6}\;(\textit{digits6}\;n) \\
\textit{digits6}\;n \quad &= \quad (n\;\mathbf{div}\;1000, n\;\mathbf{mod}\;1000)
\end{aligned}
$$

There will be a connecting "and" between the words for m and h only in the case that $m > 0 \wedge 0 < h < 100$. The function *combine6* can thus be defined in the following way:

$$
\begin{aligned}
\textit{combine6}\;(0, h+1) \quad &= \quad \textit{convert3}\;(h+1) \\
\textit{combine6}\;(m+1, 0) \quad &= \quad \textit{convert3}\;(m+1) \;\text{\text#}\; \text{``\textvisiblespace thousand''} \\
\textit{combine6}\;(m+1, h+1) \quad &= \quad \textit{convert3}\;(m+1) \;\text{\text#}\; \text{``\textvisiblespace thousand''} \\
&\qquad \text{\text#}\, \textit{link}\;(h+1) \;\text{\text#}\; \textit{convert3}\;(h+1)
\end{aligned}
$$

The subsidiary function *link* is defined by:

$$
\begin{aligned}
\textit{link}\;h \quad &= \quad \text{``\textvisiblespace and\textvisiblespace''}, \quad \textbf{if}\; h < 100 \\
&= \quad \text{``\textvisiblespace''}, \qquad\quad\; \textbf{otherwise}
\end{aligned}
$$

The required function *convert* is just the function *convert6*, so we are done.

As well as being a good illustration of the use of ($\text{\text#}$) and (!), this example also demonstrates the advantages of pattern matching over conditional equations. Each case is expressed clearly and concisely, and it is easier to check that all cases are covered.

Exercises

4.1.1 Modify the solution so that a full-stop character is printed after a number.

4.1.2 Generalise the solution to handle positive numbers up to one billion.

4.1.3 Show how the solution can be adapted to handle negative numbers.

4.1.4 Write a similar program to convert a whole number of pence into words. For example, the number 3649 should convert to "thirty-six pounds and forty-nine pence".

4.1.5 As a more difficult exercise, write a program which will do the inverse of *convert*. In other words, the input is the English formulation of a number and the output is the corresponding decimal representation.

4.2   Variable-length arithmetic

We saw in Chapter 2 that the built-in operations of arithmetic can only handle integers in some restricted range. For numbers outside this range the operations are not well-defined. One way round the problem is to construct our own package of functions for computing with integers of arbitrary size. In this section we shall define the basic arithmetic operations for variable-length integers.

As a first step we consider only non-negative integers. A non-negative integer x can be represented as a non-empty list of 'digits' in some given base b. To avoid ambiguity, these digits will be referred to as 'bigits' (short for 'b-digits'). Each bigit x will lie in the range:

$$0 \leq x < b$$

where the value of b is yet to be determined. It is useful to introduce the type synonyms:

$$vint \;\; == \;\; [bigit]$$
$$bigit \;\; == \;\; num$$

Thus, an element of *vint* (a variable-length integer) is a sequence of *bigit* values, where a *bigit* is an element of *num*.

We shall suppose that numbers are represented with the most significant bigit first. This representation is the one used with ordinary decimals and, in the absence of a good reason to the contrary, is the sensible one to adopt for our arithmetic package. Thus, an integer x is represented by a sequence $[x_{n-1}, x_{n-2}, \ldots x_0]$, where:

$$x = \sum_{k=0}^{n-1} x_k b^k$$

The major criterion which influences the choice of base is that we require:

$$b\char`\^2 \leq maxint$$

where *maxint* denotes the maximum integer that can be handled by the built-in operations. This condition ensures that 'bigit-by-bigit' multiplications can be performed by the built-in operation ($\times$) of multiplication without danger of going out of range. For concreteness, if we take:

$$b \;=\; 10000$$

then it is assumed that all numbers up to 10^8 lie within the permitted range of the primitive operations. To illustrate this particular choice of b, the number 123456789 can be represented by the list $[1, 2345, 6789]$, and 100020003 can be represented by $[1, 2, 3]$. The number 0 can be represented by the list $[0]$. These representations are not unique since an arbitrary number of leading zeros can be added to an integer without changing its value. We can 'standardize' a representation by applying the function *strep* to remove non-significant zeros. The definition is:

$$
\begin{aligned}
strep\ xs \;=\; & [0], \quad \textbf{if } ys = [\,] \\
& ys, \quad \textbf{otherwise} \\
& \textbf{where } ys = dropwhile\ (= 0)\ xs
\end{aligned}
$$

The definition of *strep* ensures that 0 will have the standard representation $[0]$.

4.2.1   Comparison operations

Thanks to our choice of representation, which has the most significant bigit first, the comparison operations on *vint* can be based on the primitive lexicographic ordering on lists. We have, of course, to align the two numbers before performing the comparison, so we define:

$$
\begin{aligned}
align\ xs\ ys \;=\; & (copy\ 0\ n \,\mathbin{+\!\!+}\, xs,\, ys), \quad &&\textbf{if } n > 0 \\
\;=\; & (xs,\, copy\ 0\ (-n) \,\mathbin{+\!\!+}\, ys), \quad &&\textbf{otherwise} \\
& \textbf{where } n = \#ys - \#xs
\end{aligned}
$$

The function *copy* can be defined by:

$$copy\ x\ n \;=\; [\,x \mid j \leftarrow [1 .. n]\,]$$

If we now define:

$$vcompare\ op\ xs\ ys \;=\; op\ us\ vs \quad \textbf{where } (us, vs) = align\ xs\ ys$$

then we have:

$$
\begin{aligned}
veq \;&=\; vcompare\ (=) \\
vleq \;&=\; vcompare\ (\le) \\
vless \;&=\; vcompare\ (<)
\end{aligned}
$$

and so on.

4.2.2 Addition and subtraction

The functions *vadd* and *vsub* for doing variable-length addition and subtraction are easily defined. We align the two numbers, do the operation bigit by bigit, and then 'normalise' the result. Normalisation involves reducing the result of each operation to a bigit in the required range. For example, suppose we want to add the numbers:

$$[7, 3, 7]$$
$$[4, 6, 9]$$

where we suppose that $b = 10$. The bigit-by-bigit addition of these numbers is:

$$[11, 9, 16]$$

and the normalised result, namely:

$$[1, 2, 0, 6]$$

is obtained by reducing each bigit modulo b after adding in the carry from the previous normalisation step. More precisely, suppose we define:

$$
\begin{aligned}
carry && :: && bigit \rightarrow [bigit] \rightarrow [bigit] \\
carry\ x\ (c : xs) &&=&& (x + c)\ \textbf{div}\ b : (x + c)\ \textbf{mod}\ b : xs
\end{aligned}
$$

The carry bigit c at each step of the normalisation process is the leading element of the list of bigits being normalised. Now, to normalise the list $[x_1, x_2, \ldots, x_n]$, we compute:

$$carry\ x_1\ (carry\ x_2 \cdots (carry\ x_n\ [0]))$$

and then convert the result to standard form. The term $[0]$ ensures that the process is started with an initial carry of 0. The expression above is just:

$$foldr\ carry\ [0]\ [x_1, x_2, \ldots, x_n]$$

so we can define the normalisation function *norm* by:

$$norm\ =\ strep \cdot foldr\ carry\ [0]$$

The addition and subtraction operations can now be defined by the equations:

$$
\begin{aligned}
vadd\ xs\ ys &= norm\ (zipwith\ (+)\ (align\ xs\ ys)) \\
vsub\ xs\ ys &= norm\ (zipwith\ (-)\ (align\ xs\ ys))
\end{aligned}
$$

The interesting point about the function *vsub* is what happens when the second argument is greater than the first, so the answer is a negative number. For example, again supposing $b = 10$, we have:

? *vsub* $[1, 0, 6]$ $[3, 7, 5]$
$[-1, 7, 3, 1]$

A negative result is indicated by a leading bigit of -1. The remaining bigits represent the value of the number in what is known as 'complement' form. Subtracting $[3, 7, 5]$ from $[1, 0, 6]$ yields first the unnormalised value $[-2, -7, 1]$ and then the normalised result $[-1, 7, 3, 1]$. This list of digits represents the number $106 - 375 = -269$. The absolute value of a negative number can be obtained by negating all the bigits in the representation (including the 'sign' bigit -1) and normalising. So, negating and normalising $[-1, 7, 3, 1]$ gives $[2, 6, 9]$. It follows that we can define the predicate *negative*, which tests whether the result of subtraction is negative, and the function *negate* for negating a number by:

$$
\begin{aligned}
negative\ xs &= (hd\ xs < 0) \\
negate &= norm \cdot map\ neg \\
neg\ x &= -x
\end{aligned}
$$

The behaviour of *vsub* suggests one possible representation for negative integers, namely signed-complement notation. In signed-complement notation, there is a leading sign-bigit of -1 for negative numbers and the remaining digits are in complement form. As we have seen, signed-complement representation is convenient for addition and subtraction since no special measures have to be taken for negative arguments and results. Another possible representation is the one normally used with decimal calculations done by hand. This is called signed-magnitude notation. Here, a number is denoted by its *absolute* value, together with an indication of whether the number is positive or negative.

4.2.3   Multiplication

Next, we need to define the function *vmul* which multiplies two variable-length integers. The most straightforward definition is a translation of the school book method, whereby the multiplicand *xs* is multiplied by each bigit *y* of the multiplier *ys* and the partial sums are added together, shifting appropriately. The list of partial sums, in decreasing order of significance, is given by (*psums xs ys*), where:

$$
\begin{aligned}
psums\ xs\ ys &= map\ (bmul\ xs)\ ys \\
bmul\ xs\ y &= norm\ (map\ (\times y)\ xs)
\end{aligned}
$$

To do the shifting and adding, let $\oplus$ be defined by:

$$
xs \oplus ys = vadd\ (xs \mathbin{+\!\!+} [0])\ ys
$$

The operator $\oplus$ shifts *xs* by appending a zero on the right, and then adds the result to *ys* with the function *vadd*.

If the list of partial sums is $[ps_1, ps_2, \ldots, ps_n]$, then its sum is:

$$(((ps_1 \oplus ps_2) \oplus ps_3) \oplus \cdots \oplus ps_n)$$

This pattern of computation can be expressed with the function *foldl1* of the previous chapter. Hence we can define:

$$vmul\ xs\ ys\ =\ foldl1\ (\oplus)\ (psums\ xs\ ys)$$

4.2.4   Quotient and remainder

Finally, we turn to the problem of division. As every schoolchild knows, division is the hardest of the arithmetic operations to get right since it involves a certain amount of guesswork. The framework of the conventional division algorithm for finding the quotient and remainder consists of a repeated sequence of steps. At each step, a single bigit of the quotient is computed and the remainder is calculated for the next step. The result is a sequence of pairs:

$$[(q_0, rs_0), (q_1, rs_1), \ldots, (q_n, rs_n)]$$

where $q_0 q_1 \ldots q_n$ is the final quotient and rs_n the final remainder. A pair (q_k, rs_k) is determined, by a function *dstep* say, from the previous pair, the given divisor, and the kth digit of the dividend.

We can implement this scheme using the function *scan* introduced in Section 3.5.3:

$$divalg\ xs\ ys\ =\ scan\ (dstep\ ys)\ (0, take\ m\ xs)\ (drop\ m\ xs)$$
$$\mathbf{where}\ m = \#ys - 1$$

The starting value $(0, take\ m\ xs)$ of *scan* is the quotient and remainder for the first step of the division algorithm. The process begins with the remaining bigits $(drop\ m\ xs)$ of the dividend. The value returned by *divalg* is a list of pairs, the first components of which are the bigits forming the quotient. The second component of the last element of the result of *divalg* is the required remainder. To illustrate:

$$divalg\ [1, 7, 8, 4]\ [6, 2] = [(0, [1]), (0, [1, 7]), (2, [5, 4]), (8, [4, 8])]$$

The quotient bigits are therefore $[0, 0, 2, 8]$ and the remainder is $[4, 8]$.

To define *dstep*, we need to distinguish three cases: the dividend xs for the current step has length less than, equal to, or greater than the length of the divisor ys. In fact, since the remainder rs from the previous step has length at most $\#ys$ and $xs = rs \mathbin{+\!\!+} [x]$ for some bigit x, we always have $\#xs \leq \#ys + 1$. We therefore define

$$
\begin{aligned}
dstep\ ys\ (q, rs)\ x\ &=\ astep\ xs\ ys, \quad \mathbf{if}\ \#xs < \#ys \\
&=\ bstep\ xs\ ys, \quad \mathbf{if}\ \#xs = \#ys \\
&=\ cstep\ xs\ ys, \quad \mathbf{if}\ \#xs = \#ys + 1 \\
&\quad \mathbf{where}\ xs = rs \mathbin{+\!\!+} [x]
\end{aligned}
$$

The definition of *astep* is easy: if $\#xs < \#ys$, then the new quotient is 0 and the new remainder is xs. Hence:

$$astep\ xs\ ys\ =\ (0, xs)$$

Next, consider *bstep*. If $\#xs = \#ys$, then the new quotient q might be any value in the range $0 \leq q < b$. However, we shall see that when *divalg* is applied in the final version of the algorithm, it will be a condition on the divisor ys that its first bigit is at least $(b\ \mathbf{div}\ 2)$. This means that if $\#xs = \#ys$, then there can be a quotient of at most 1. Therefore we can define *bstep* in the following way:

$$
\begin{aligned}
bstep\ xs\ ys\ &=\ (0, xs), && \textbf{if } negative\ zs \\
&=\ (1, zs), && \textbf{otherwise} \\
&\quad \textbf{where } zs = vsub\ xs\ ys
\end{aligned}
$$

Finally, we deal with *cstep*, the most complicated case. In order to implement *cstep* we make use of the following result from Knuth([2]:Section 4.3.1). Suppose $x = x_0 x_1 \ldots x_n$ and $y = y_1 y_2 \ldots y_n$ are non-negative integers in base b notation such that $x/y < b$. Define:

$$\hat{q} = ((x_0 \times b + x_1)\ \mathbf{div}\ y_1)\ \min\ (b - 1)$$

The result we need says that if $y_1 \geq b\ \mathbf{div}\ 2$, then:

$$\hat{q} - 2 \leq q \leq \hat{q}$$

where $q = x\ \mathbf{div}\ y$ is the true quotient. In other words, if y_1 is sufficiently large, then the guess $\hat{q}$ overestimates the true quotient q by at most 2.

This guess is used in the definition of *cstep*. If it turns out to be too big, then the result is corrected by further subtractions as necessary. The definition of *cstep* is

$$
\begin{aligned}
cstep\ xs\ ys\ &=\ (q, rs0), && \textbf{if } vless\ rs0\ ys \\
&=\ (q + 1, rs1), && \textbf{if } vless\ rs1\ ys \\
&=\ (q + 2, rs2), && \textbf{otherwise} \\
&\quad \textbf{where } rs0 &&=\ vsub\ xs\ (bmul\ ys\ q) \\
&\qquad\quad\ rs1 &&=\ vsub\ rs0\ ys \\
&\qquad\quad\ rs2 &&=\ vsub\ rs1\ ys \\
&\qquad\quad\ q &&=\ (guess\ xs\ ys) - 2
\end{aligned}
$$

The function *guess* is defined by:

$$
\begin{aligned}
guess\ (x0 : x1 : xs)\ (y1 : ys)\ &=\ b - 1, && \textbf{if } x0 \geq y1 \\
&=\ (x0 \times b + x1)\ \mathbf{div}\ y1, && \textbf{otherwise}
\end{aligned}
$$

Now we are in a position to define the function *vqrm* which returns the quotient and remainder on dividing one number by another. To ensure that the leading bigit $y1$ of the divisor ys is sufficiently large, we first multiply both divisor and dividend by a suitable scale factor d. The definition of $vqrm$ is:

$$
\begin{aligned}
vqrm\ xs\ ys\ &=\ (strep\ qs, strep\ rs)\\
\textbf{where}\ qs\ &=\ map\ fst\ ds\\
rs\ &=\ bdiv\ (snd\ (last\ ds))\ d\\
ds\ &=\ divalg\ (bmul\ xs\ d)\ (bmul\ ys\ d)\\
d\ &=\ b\ \textbf{div}\ (hd\ ys + 1)
\end{aligned}
$$

The remaining task is to define the function $bdiv$ for dividing a number by a single bigit. This is an important special case which arises frequently in practical calculations, so it merits individual attention. Suppose $x = x_1 x_2 \ldots x_n$ is the dividend and d the single bigit divisor. The elements of the quotient $q = q_1 q_2 \ldots q_n$ can be computed by the scheme:

$$q_i = r_i\ \textbf{div}\ d$$

where $r_1 = x_1$ and, in general:

$$r_{i+1} = b \times (r_i\ \textbf{mod}\ d) + x_{i+1}$$

Moreover, the single bigit remainder r is given by $r = r_n\ \textbf{mod}\ d$. We can implement this scheme using the function $scan$:

$$
\begin{aligned}
bqrm\ (x:xs)\ d\ &\\
=\ (strep\ qs, &(last\ rs)\ \textbf{mod}\ d)\\
\textbf{where}\ qs\ &=\ map\ (\textbf{div}d)\ rs\\
rs\ &=\ scan\ (\oplus)\ x\ xs\\
r \oplus x\ &=\ b \times (r\ \textbf{mod}\ d) + x
\end{aligned}
$$

In particular, if the dividend is also a single bigit, so that $xs = [\,]$ in the above definition, then we have:

$$bqrm\ [x]\ d = ([x\ \textbf{div}\ d], x\ \textbf{mod}\ d)$$

as required. We can now define:

$$
\begin{aligned}
bdiv\ xs\ d\ &=\ fst\ (bqrm\ xs\ d)\\
bmod\ xs\ d\ &=\ snd\ (bqrm\ xs\ d)
\end{aligned}
$$

This completes our package of arithmetic operations for variable-length integers. Notice, in particular, how $foldr$, $foldl$ and $scan$ can be used to capture certain patterns of computation, patterns that arise time and again in the development of algorithms.

Exercises

4.2.1 Define a function *absint* so that if number x is represented by the list of bigits xs, then:

$$x = absint \ xs$$

Check that

$$absint \ ([0] + xs) = absint \ xs$$

Hence justify the equation:

$$absint \ (strep \ xs) = absint \ xs$$

where *strep* returns the standard representation of a number.

4.2.2 Justify the equation:

$$vless \ xs \ ys = (absint \ xs < absint \ ys)$$

4.2.3 Is it the case that $negate = vsub \ [0]$?

4.2.4 Suggest a possible representation for signed-magnitude numbers. Redefine *vadd* and *vsub* to work with this representation.

4.2.5 Suppose *inv* is a function which converts a string of digit characters to an element of *vint*. We can define *inv* by:

$$inv = pack \cdot map \ digit$$

where *digit* converts a digit character to a decimal digit, and *pack* converts a list of decimal digits to an element of *vint*. Define *digit*. Using *foldl* and *vadd*, define *pack*.

4.2.6 Consider *outv*, the inverse function to *inv* of the previous exercise. Under what conditions on xs (if any) should the equation:

$$outv \ (inv \ xs) = xs$$

hold? Assuming $b = 10000$, construct a definition of *outv*.

4.2.7 Can *foldl* be used instead of *foldl1* in the definition of *vmul*?

4.2.8 Is $\oplus$, where:

$$xs \oplus ys = vadd \ (xs + [0]) \ ys$$

an associative operator? Can *foldl1* be replaced by *foldr1* in the definition of *vmul*?

4.2.9 Define *vmul* to work with negative as well as positive arguments, assuming signed-magnitude representation.

4.2.10 What simple modification to *dstep* in the definition of division avoids the recalculation of #*ys* at each stage?

4.2.11 Suppose y and b are integers with $1 \leq y < b$. Prove that

$$b \operatorname{div} 2 \leq y \times (b \operatorname{div} (y+1)) < b$$

4.2.12 Modify the definition of *vqrm* so that it works for arbitrary numbers, negative as well as positive.

4.2.13 Define functions *vdiv* and *vmod* which return the quotient and remainder on division.

4.2.14 The definition of *vqrm* given in the text can be tuned in a number of ways. In particular, it is possible to improve the guess for q (see Knuth [2]) and a number of length calculations can be avoided by using versions of addition and subtraction which produce $(n+1)$-bit results from n-bit arguments. Show how to make *vqrm* more efficient.

4.3   Text processing

Now let us turn to something completely different. In this section we shall investigate the mathematics of an interesting non-numerical application which deals with the general problem of processing text.

A text can be viewed in many different ways. The 'atomic' view is that a text is just a list of characters, so we introduce the type synonym:

$$text \;\; == \;\; [char]$$

However, for certain problems it may be more convenient to view a text as a sequence of words, or perhaps as a sequence of lines, or even as a sequence of paragraphs. In this section we shall develop functions for converting from one view of texts to another.

4.3.1   Texts as lines

Consider first the problem of converting a text, viewed as a list of characters, to a sequence of lines. A *line* is a list of characters not containing the newline character '↲'. We therefore introduce the synonym:

$$line \;\; == \;\; [char]$$

Let the required function be called *lines*. Its type is given by:

$$lines :: text \to [line]$$

For example, we want to have:

? *lines* "This is a ↱text↱"
["This is a", "text", ""]

? *lines* "This is a↱↱text↱"
["This is a", "", "text", ""]

? *lines* "This is a text"
["This is a text"]

As these examples illustrate, any sequence of characters between two successive newline characters constitutes a line, as does the sequence of characters from the beginning of the text up to the first newline (if any), and the sequence of characters from the last newline to the end of the text. Note that the sequence of characters after the last newline may be empty. The decision to break a text up in this way reflects the view that a newline is a *separator* character between lines rather than a *terminator* character to signal the end of a line. In particular, it implies that the number of lines in a text is always one more than the number of newline characters.

The function *lines* can be specified formally as the inverse of another function, *unlines* say, which inserts a newline character between adjacent lines and then concatenates the result. The definition of *unlines* uses *foldr1*:

$$
\begin{aligned}
unlines \quad &:: \quad [line] \rightarrow text \\
unlines \quad &= \quad foldr1\ (\oplus) \\
xs \oplus ys \quad &= \quad xs + ['↱'] + ys
\end{aligned}
$$

The operator $\oplus$ is associative but does not possess an identity element, so the value of (*unlines* []) is not defined. Hence a definition by either *foldr1* or *foldl1* is appropriate. The former is more efficient (see Chapter 6).

We can now specify *lines* by requiring:

$$
lines\ (unlines\ xss) \quad = \quad xss \qquad \text{(spec.)}
$$

for all non-empty sequences of lines *xss*. In other words, *lines* is specified as the inverse of *unlines*.

In order to construct an executable definition of *lines*, we shall look for a definition of the form:

$$
lines \quad = \quad foldr\ (\otimes)\ a
$$

for a suitable choice of $\otimes$ and initial value a. Since *unlines* uses the function *foldr* (actually, *foldr1*), it seems plausible to see if a definition of *lines* can be based on *foldr* too.

We are going to discover a and $\otimes$ simply by a process of calculation. To do this we shall make use of the following facts about *foldr1* and *foldr*:

$$
\begin{aligned}
foldr1\ f\ [x] \quad &= \quad x \\
foldr1\ f\ ([x] + xs) \quad &= \quad f\ x\ (foldr1\ f\ xs) \qquad \text{(provided } xs \neq []) \\
foldr\ f\ a\ [] \quad &= \quad a \\
foldr\ f\ a\ ([x] + xs) \quad &= \quad f\ x\ (foldr\ f\ a\ xs)
\end{aligned}
$$

(In fact, suitably rewritten, these equations constitute the formal recursive definitions of these functions, as we shall see in the next chapter.) For the moment, each equation can be justified by appeal to the informal definitions of *foldr1* and *foldr*. We can use the equations to derive the following facts about *lines* and *unlines*:

$$unlines\,[xs] \;=\; xs \qquad\qquad (unlines.1)$$
$$unlines\,([xs] + xss) \;=\; xs \oplus unlines\,xss \qquad (unlines.2)$$

$$lines\,[\,] \;=\; a \qquad\qquad (lines.1)$$
$$lines\,([x] + xs) \;=\; x \otimes lines\,xs \qquad (lines.2)$$

The first two equations follow from the equations for *foldr1*, and the second two from the equations for *foldr* and the putative form for *lines*.

Now, to calculate a, we reason as follows:

$$
\begin{aligned}
a \;&=\; lines\,[\,] &&(lines.1)\\
&=\; lines\,(unlines\,[[\,]]) &&(unlines.1,\text{ with } xs = [\,])\\
&=\; [[\,]] &&(\text{spec.})
\end{aligned}
$$

The last equality uses the specification of *lines* as the inverse of *unlines*. So we have succeeded, fairly quickly, in calculating a.

Next, let us tackle $\otimes$. We have:

$$
\begin{aligned}
x \otimes xss \;&=\; x \otimes lines\,(unlines\,xss) &&(\text{spec.})\\
&=\; lines\,([x] + unlines\,xss) &&(lines.2)
\end{aligned}
$$

To continue, we need to distinguish the cases $x = {}$ 'Y' and $x \neq {}$ 'Y'.

Case $x = {}$ 'Y'. We have:

$$
\begin{aligned}
lines\,(['\mathsf{Y}'] &+ unlines\,xss)\\
&=\; lines\,([\,] + ['\mathsf{Y}'] + unlines\,xss) &&(+)\\
&=\; lines\,([\,] \oplus unlines\,xss) &&(\oplus.1)\\
&=\; lines\,(unlines\,([[\,]] + xss)) &&(unlines.2)\\
&=\; [[\,]] + xss &&(\text{spec.})
\end{aligned}
$$

It follows that:

$$'\mathsf{Y}' \otimes xss = [[\,]] + xss$$

Case $x \neq {}$ 'Y'. Writing $xss = [ys] + yss$ (which is acceptable as $\otimes$ is applied only to non-empty lists), we have:

$$
\begin{aligned}
lines\,([x] &+ unlines\,([ys] + yss))\\
&=\; lines\,([x] + (ys + ['\mathsf{Y}'] + unlines\,yss)) &&(unlines.2)\\
&=\; lines\,(([x] + ys) + ['\mathsf{Y}'] + unlines\,yss) &&(+\text{ assoc.})\\
&=\; lines\,(([x] + ys) \oplus unlines\,yss) &&(\oplus.1)\\
&=\; lines\,(unlines\,([[x] + ys] + yss)) &&(unlines.2)\\
&=\; [[x] + ys] + yss &&(\text{spec.})
\end{aligned}
$$

Hence it follows that

$$x \otimes xss = [[x] + hd\ xss] + tl\ xss$$

Putting the above results together, we have:

$$
\begin{aligned}
lines &= foldr\ (\otimes)\ [[\,]] \\
x \otimes xss &= [[\,]] + xss, && \text{if } x = \text{'\textbackslash'} \\
&= [[x] + hd\ xss] + tl\ xss, && \text{otherwise}
\end{aligned}
$$

This is the desired constructive definition of *lines*.

What we have just done is a fairly sophisticated example of program synthesis. Starting from a precise but non-executable specification, and using only simple equational reasoning, we have derived an executable definition of the required function. Moreover, the technique is a familiar one in many areas of mathematics: first a form for the solution is guessed, and then the unknowns in the form are calculated.

4.3.2 Lines as words

It is instructive to develop this example a little further to show how other text processing functions can be synthesised. Define a *word* to be a non-empty sequence of characters not containing the newline or space characters. We introduce the synonym:

$$word \ \ == \ \ [char]$$

In a similar spirit to before, we can seek a constructive definition of a function *words* for breaking a line into words. The type of *words* is therefore:

$$words :: line \rightarrow [word]$$

For example:

? *words* "This␣␣␣is␣a␣line"
["This", "is", "a", "line"]

? *words* "line"
["line"]

The function *unwords* defined by:

$$
\begin{aligned}
unwords &= foldr1\ (\oplus) \\
xs \oplus ys &= xs + [\text{'␣'}] + ys
\end{aligned}
$$

takes a sequence of words and concatenates them after inserting a single space between adjacent words. We can (almost) define *words* as the inverse of *unwords* and so derive a constructive definition in exactly the same way as before. The only difference is that, by definition, a word is a *non-empty* sequence of characters: lines can be empty, but words cannot be. Putting it another way, if two newline characters are adjacent, there is an empty line between them; but if two space characters are adjacent, there is no word between them. The resolution of this problem is simple: define the inverse of *unwords* in the same way as we did for *lines*, but then filter out the 'empty' words. We therefore obtain:

$$words \ = \ filter \ (\neq []) \cdot foldr \ (\otimes) \ [[\,]]$$

where $\otimes$ is as previously defined, except that '↲' is replaced by '␣'.

Note that, although *words·unwords* is the identity function on non-empty sequences of words, the function *unwords · words* is not the identity function on lines. Indeed, it is not even a total function. When it is defined, redundant spaces are removed between words.

4.3.3   Lines into paragraphs

Finally, to complete a logical trio of functions, we can define a *paragraph* to be a non-empty sequence of non-empty lines and seek a definition of a function *paras* which breaks a sequence of lines into paragraphs. If we introduce the type synonym:

$$para == [line]$$

then the type of *paras* is given by:

$$paras :: [line] \rightarrow [para]$$

This time, the inverse function *unparas* takes a sequence of paragraphs and converts it to a sequence of lines by inserting a single empty line between adjacent paragraphs and concatenating the result. It can be defined by:

$$
\begin{aligned}
unparas \ &= \ foldr1 \ (\oplus) \\
xs \oplus ys \ &= \ xs +\!\!+ [[\,]] +\!\!+ ys
\end{aligned}
$$

Just as in the case of words, we can construct the inverse of *unparas* and then filter out the empty sequences to obtain the definition of *paras*.

4.3.4   The basic package

Let us now summarise the above results by writing out the complete definitions of the functions we have described (and choosing more suitable names for the operators). Our basic text processing package is contained in the following script:

$$
\begin{aligned}
\textit{unlines} &= \textit{foldr1 (insert `$\downarrow$')} \\
\textit{unwords} &= \textit{foldr1 (insert `$\sqcup$')} \\
\textit{unparas} &= \textit{foldr1 (insert [ ])}
\end{aligned}
$$

$$\textit{insert a xs ys} = \textit{xs} +\!\!+ [a] +\!\!+ \textit{ys}$$

$$
\begin{aligned}
\textit{lines} &= \textit{foldr (breakon `$\downarrow$') [[ ]]} \\
\textit{words} &= \textit{filter ($\neq$ [ ]) $\cdot$ foldr (breakon `$\sqcup$') [[ ]]} \\
\textit{paras} &= \textit{filter ($\neq$ [ ]) $\cdot$ foldr (breakon [ ]) [[ ]]}
\end{aligned}
$$

$$
\begin{aligned}
\textit{breakon a x xss} &= \textit{[[ ]]} +\!\!+ \textit{xss}, & &\textbf{if } x = a \\
&= \textit{[[x]} +\!\!+ \textit{hd xss]} +\!\!+ \textit{tl xss}, & &\textbf{otherwise}
\end{aligned}
$$

These six functions have a variety of uses. We give just two. The number of lines, words and paragraphs in a text can be counted by:

$$
\begin{aligned}
\textit{countlines} &= \textit{($\#$) $\cdot$ lines} \\
\textit{countwords} &= \textit{($\#$) $\cdot$ concat $\cdot$ map words $\cdot$ lines} \\
\textit{countparas} &= \textit{($\#$) $\cdot$ paras $\cdot$ lines}
\end{aligned}
$$

Second, we can "normalise" a text by removing redundant empty lines between paragraphs and spaces between words. We have:

$$
\begin{aligned}
\textit{normalise} &:: \textit{text} \rightarrow \textit{text} \\
\textit{normalise} &= \textit{unparse $\cdot$ parse} \\[4pt]
\textit{parse} &:: \textit{text} \rightarrow \textit{[[[word]]]} \\
\textit{parse} &= \textit{map (map words) $\cdot$ paras $\cdot$ lines} \\[4pt]
\textit{unparse} &:: \textit{[[[word]]]} \rightarrow \textit{text} \\
\textit{unparse} &= \textit{unlines $\cdot$ unparas $\cdot$ map (map unwords)}
\end{aligned}
$$

To *parse* a text here means to break it into lines, paragraphs and words.

4.3.5 Filling paragraphs

The function *normalise* does not change the number of words on a line, but merely removes redundant spaces. A more useful function is "filling". To fill a paragraph is to arrange the words of the paragraph into a sequence of lines in such a way that (i) the length of each line does not exceed a certain fixed column width; and (ii) the sequence as a whole minimises some notion of waste. For example, we may want the number of lines to be as small as possible. One simple algorithm for filling paragraphs is "greedy" in nature: at each stage the algorithm chooses the longest sequence of words which will fit on a line. For this algorithm to work (indeed, for the filling problem to have a solution at all) it is necessary to suppose that the column width is enough to accommodate the longest possible word. It can be shown that the greedy algorithm minimises the number of lines.

We can define the greedy algorithm in the following way:

$$
\begin{aligned}
\textit{fill} \quad &:: \quad num \rightarrow [word] \rightarrow [[word]] \\
\textit{fill } m \textit{ ws} \;=\; &[\,], \qquad\qquad\qquad\qquad\quad \textbf{if } ws = [\,] \\
=\; &[\textit{fstline}] + \textit{fill } m \textit{ restwds}, \quad \textbf{otherwise} \\
&\textbf{where } \textit{fstline} \;=\; \textit{take } n \textit{ ws} \\
&\qquad\quad\;\; \textit{restwds} \;=\; \textit{drop } n \textit{ ws} \\
&\qquad\quad\;\; n \;=\; \textit{greedy } m \textit{ ws}
\end{aligned}
$$

In this algorithm, the value of ($greedy\ m\ ws$) is the length of the longest initial segment of ws which will fit on a line of given column width m. One way of defining $greedy$ is to write:

$$
greedy\ m\ ws \;=\; max\ [\#us \mid us \leftarrow inits\ ws;\ \#unwords\ us \leq m]
$$

Here, ($inits\,ws$) is a list of all non-empty initial segments of ws. This definition of $greedy$ is not very efficient because the value of $unwords$ is recomputed for each value us. A more efficient version is as follows:

$$
\begin{aligned}
greedy\ m\ ws \;=\; &\#takewhile\ (\leq m)\ (scan\ (\oplus)\ (-1)\ ws) - 1 \\
&\textbf{where } n \oplus word = n + \#word + 1
\end{aligned}
$$

The operator $\oplus$ is defined so that:

$$
scan\ (\oplus)\ (-1)\ ws = [-1] + [\#unwords\ us \mid us \leftarrow inits\ ws]
$$

If this list is truncated by applying the function $takewhile\ (\leq m)$, then the length of the result will be one greater (because of the starting value -1) than the length of the longest initial segment us of ws for which $\#unwords\,us \leq m$. But this is just the definition of ($greedy\ m\ ws$). The new definition is more efficient because not all initial segments of ws need to be examined, and also because lengthy recalculations of $unwords$ are avoided.

Using $fill$ we can left-justify a text within a specified column width m by the function $filltext$ defined as follows:

$$
\begin{aligned}
filltext\ m \;&=\; unparse \cdot map\ (fill\ m) \cdot textparas \\
textparas \;&=\; map\ linewords \cdot paras \cdot lines \\
linewords \;&=\; concat \cdot map\ words
\end{aligned}
$$

This function converts a text to a list of paragraphs, each paragraph being converted to a list of words, fills each paragraph, and reconstitutes the text leaving one space between words, and one blank line between paragraphs.

4.3.6 Summary

We have covered a good deal of ground with this example and it is worthwhile to identify the main landmarks. First, just as in the treatment of variable-length arithmetic, there is the consistent use of higher-order functions to express common patterns of computation in a concise manner. Our basic text processing package is only eight lines long, but it is remarkably powerful.

Second, we see the technique of specifying functions of interest as the inverses of functions which we know how to compute. These specifications are not executable but they capture in the clearest possible way just what we want to achieve.

Third, there is the systematic use of equational reasoning to derive constructive definitions of some functions from their specifications. In essence, we have derived these programs by a process of *manipulating* formulae: a process very much in the spirit of normal mathematical traditions.

Exercises

4.3.1 Justify the claim that the operator $\oplus$ used in the definition of *unlines* is associative but does not possess an identity element.

4.3.2 Verify the following equations:

$$
\begin{aligned}
\textit{unlines } [xs] &= xs & (\textit{unlines}.1) \\
\textit{unlines } ([xs] \mathbin{+\!\!+} xss) &= xs \oplus \textit{unlines } xss & (\textit{unlines}.2) \\
\\
\textit{lines } [\,] &= a & (\textit{lines}.1) \\
\textit{lines } ([x] \mathbin{+\!\!+} xs) &= x \otimes \textit{lines } xs & (\textit{lines}.2)
\end{aligned}
$$

4.3.3 Suppose we adopt the convention that a newline character is a terminator for lines, rather than a separator. Redefine *unlines* to take account of this decision and repeat the derivation of the new version of *lines*.

4.3.4 Give an example to show that *unwords · words* is a partial function.

4.3.5 Show that the greedy algorithm minimises the number of lines. As a fairly difficult additional exercise, show that the greedy algorithm also minimises the function *waste*, where

$$\textit{waste } m \textit{ lines} = \textit{sum } [m - \#\textit{unwords } ws \mid ws \leftarrow \textit{lines}]$$

4.3.6 Check that

$$\textit{scan } (\oplus)\, (-1)\, ws = [-1] \mathbin{+\!\!+} [\#\textit{unwords } us \mid us \leftarrow \textit{inits } ws]$$

4.3.7 Extend the problem of filling text by developing an algorithm for inserting sufficient spaces between words so that the text is justified to the right boundary.

4.4 Turtle graphics

The next example is fun since it involves drawing pictures. It will also demand more hard work on the part of the reader, since much of the material is presented in the way of exercises.

Consider a device (called a 'turtle') which can move around a potentially infinite rectangular grid. At any one moment, the turtle is at some grid point and is oriented in one of four directions: North, East, South or West. The turtle is equipped with a pen which can be either in the 'up' or 'down' position. When the pen is down, each grid point that the turtle passes over is marked; when the pen is up the turtle moves without leaving a trail.

The commands which can be issued to the turtle are of three kinds:

1. To turn, either one direction to the *left* or to the *right*.

2. To *move* one step along the grid in the direction currently indicated.

3. To put the pen *up* or *down*.

Given an initial state and a sequence of commands, the turtle will trace out a certain pattern over the grid. The object of this section is to define functions for moving the turtle and drawing the resulting trail.

A turtle *state* consists of a current direction, a pen position and a point on the grid. A turtle *command* is a function from states to states. The following type synonyms can therefore be introduced:

$$
\begin{aligned}
state &== (direction, pen, point) \\
direction &== num \\
pen &== bool \\
point &== (num, num) \\
command &== state \rightarrow state
\end{aligned}
$$

It is convenient to represent the coordinate system of the grid with the x-axis going from North to South, and the y-axis going from West to East (i.e. the standard system but turned 90 degrees clockwise). Directions can be coded as the numbers 0 (North), 1 (East), 2 (South), and 3 (West). The pen-up position can be represented by the value *False*, and pen-down by the value *True*.

The function *move* can be defined by the following equations:

$$
\begin{aligned}
move &\ ::\ command \\
move\,(0, p, (x, y)) &= (0, p, (x - 1, y)) \\
move\,(1, p, (x, y)) &= (1, p, (x, y + 1)) \\
move\,(2, p, (x, y)) &= (2, p, (x + 1, y)) \\
move\,(3, p, (x, y)) &= (3, p, (x, y - 1))
\end{aligned}
$$

The function *right* for turning 90 degrees right is given by:

$$right \qquad :: \quad command$$
$$right\,(d, p, (x, y)) \;=\; ((d + 1)\,\textbf{mod}\,4, p, (x, y))$$

The functions *left, up* and *down* are left as exercises for the reader.

For example, wherever the turtle happens to be initially, the following sequence of commands causes it to trace the perimeter of a square of side k and return to its starting point:

$$square\,k \;=\; [down] + \!\!+ \; concat\,(copy\,4\,side) + \!\!+ [up]$$
$$\textbf{where}\;\; side = copy\,move\,k + \!\!+ [right]$$

The function *turtle* takes a sequence of commands and returns a sequence of states. Assume the turtle always starts off at the origin facing North with its pen in the up position. We then have:

$$turtle \qquad :: \quad [command] \rightarrow [state]$$
$$turtle \qquad = \quad scan\,applyto\,(0, False, (0, 0))$$
$$applyto\,x\,f \;\;= \quad f\,x$$

The remaining task is to define a function for drawing a turtle trail. A trail is a list of those coordinate points visited by the turtle while the pen was down. We define:

$$display \quad :: \quad [command] \rightarrow [char]$$
$$display \quad = \quad layout \cdot picture \cdot trail \cdot turtle$$

Here, *trail* produces a list of points, *picture* converts this list into a two-dimensional picture (a value of type [[char]]), and *layout* flattens the picture into a list of characters by inserting newlines between rows and concatenating the results. We shall leave the definitions of *trail* and *layout* as exercises for the reader.

One way to convert a trail into a picture is to first build a boolean array (called, say, a "bitmap") and then represent the boolean values by strings of suitable characters. This factorisation allows easy modification to the visible form of the picture. We can define:

$$picture \quad :: \quad [point] \rightarrow [[char]]$$
$$picture \quad = \quad symbolise \cdot bitmap$$

$$bitmap\,ps \;=\; [[(x, y)\,\textbf{in}\,ps \mid y \leftarrow yran] \mid x \leftarrow xran]$$
$$\textbf{where}\; xran \;\;= \quad range\,(map\,fst\,ps)$$
$$yran \;\;= \quad range\,(map\,snd\,ps)$$
$$range\,xs \;\;= \quad [min\,xs \,.. \, max\,xs]$$

Here, the test $(x\,\textbf{in}\,xs)$ returns *True* if x is an element of xs, and *False* otherwise. We can define it in the following way:

$$x\,\textbf{in}\,xs \;\;= \quad or\,(map\,(= x)\,xs)$$

In the worst case, the test for list membership requires n steps, where n is the length of xs.

Since a turtle trail may mark the same point many times, one sensible optimisation is to remove duplicates from the list of points. In fact, if we first sort the points, then duplicate values will be brought together and it is only necessary to remove *adjacent* duplicates. Assuming the existence of a function *sort* which will sort points in increasing order of x-coordinate (and for equal x-coordinates, in increasing order of y-coordinate), we have:

$$sortpoints \ = \ remdups \cdot sort$$

where *remdups* is a function for removing adjacent duplicates. Its definition is left as an exercise.

The above method for computing *bitmap* is inefficient. A faster method can be based on the assumption that the points are sorted in increasing order, first on x-coordinate and then on y-coordinate. First, divide the list of points ps into sublists, one for each value x in $xran$. The sublist corresponding to x is the (possibly empty) list of original points whose first coordinate is x. Each sublist will be sorted in increasing order of y-coordinate. Next, divide each of these sublists into sub-sublists, one for each value of y in $yran$. The sub-sublist corresponding to y will be those points of the sublist whose second coordinate is y. The sub-sublist (for y), of the sublist (for x), will either be empty, in the case (x, y) is not a marked point, or consist of just a single element (x, y). In this way it is possible to determine the correct "bit" value of (x, y). The corresponding definition is:

$$
\begin{aligned}
fastbitmap \ ps \ &= \ [[ps2 \neq [\,] \mid ps2 \leftarrow splitwith \ snd \ yran \ ps1] \\
&\qquad \mid ps1 \leftarrow splitwith \ fst \ xran \ ps] \\
\textbf{where} \ xran \ &= \ range \ (map \ fst \ ps) \\
yran \ &= \ range \ (map \ snd \ ps)
\end{aligned}
$$

The function *splitwith* is given by the equations:

$$
\begin{aligned}
splitwith \ f \ xs \ ys \ &= \ split \ (map \ (equals \ f) \ xs) \ ys \\
equals \ f \ x \ y \ &= \ (f \ y = x)
\end{aligned}
$$

$$
\begin{aligned}
split \ &:: \ [\alpha \rightarrow bool] \rightarrow [\alpha] \rightarrow [[\alpha]] \\
split \ [\,] \ xs \ &= \ [\,] \\
split \ (p : ps) \ xs \ &= \ [takewhile \ p \ xs] \ +\!\!+ \ split \ ps \ (dropwhile \ p \ xs)
\end{aligned}
$$

The function *split* takes a sequence of predicates $[p_1, p_2, \ldots, p_n]$ and a list xs, and partitions xs into a sequence of lists $[xs_1, xs_2, \ldots, xs_n]$, where xs_1 is the longest initial segment of xs all of whose elements satisfy p_1, and xs_2 is the longest initial segment of the remaining list, all of whose elements satisfy p_2, and so on. The function *splitwith* is an optimised version of:

$$splitwith \ f \ xs \ ys \ = \ [[y \mid y \leftarrow ys; f \ y = x] \mid x \leftarrow xs]$$

under the assumption that *xs* is strictly increasing, and (*map f ys*) is a non-decreasing sequence of elements from *xs*.

Exercises

4.4.1 Define the commands *left*, for making a left-turn, and *up* and *down* for putting the pen up and down.

4.4.2 Define a function (*block k*) which causes the turtle to trace a solid square of side *k*.

4.4.3 Define *trail* and *layout*.

4.4.4 Assuming there are *n* points, representing a continuous trail, estimate the worst case time complexity of *bitmap* as a function of *n* (i.e. say whether the number of steps required is proportional to n, n^2, n^3, or whatever). (*Hint:* Think of a simple trail for which the algorithm is at its worst and hence put bounds on the lengths of *xran* and *yran*.)

4.4.5 Define a function *boolstr* which converts each truth-value to a suitable string of characters, and hence define *symbolise*.

4.4.6 Bearing in mind that duplicate values in a sorted list are adjacent, construct a definition of *remdups* for removing duplicate elements. (*Hint:* Use a list comprehension in conjunction with the standard function *zip*.) For what kind of turtle trails would it be sensible to apply *remdups* before, as well as after, sorting?

4.4.7 Estimate the increase in efficiency by using *fastbitmap* rather than *bitmap*.

4.4.8 It is possible to derive *fastbitmap* (using the unoptimised definition of *splitwith*) from the original definition of *bitmap*. The derivation uses only equational reasoning and a small number of laws about list comprehensions. As a challenging exercise, find the rules and produce the derivation.

4.4.9 Define some interesting turtle trails and draw them using the functions introduced above.

4.5   Printing a calendar

As a final example in the use of list processing techniques, we shall design a program for printing a calendar. Given a year, the program will display a 4×3 array of calendar months. The format for printing a month is illustrated in Figure 4.1.

The right way to tackle problems of this kind, as we have seen in some earlier examples, is to try and separate the construction phase from the

```
┌─────────────────────────────────────────┐
│ OCTOBER 1988                              │
│                                          │
│ Sun      2    9   16   23   30           │
│ Mon      3   10   17   24   31           │
│ Tue      4   11   18   25                │
│ Wed      5   12   19   26                │
│ Thu      6   13   20   27                │
│ Fri      7   14   21   28                │
│ Sat   1  8   15   22   29                │
└─────────────────────────────────────────┘
```

Figure 4.1 A calendar month.

printing phase as much as possible. As logically independent tasks, we can consider how to provide the necessary information to build an "abstract" calendar and how to print it in the required format. If we succeed in this separation of concerns, modifications to the program, such as printing the calendar in a different format or printing only part of the calendar, will be easier to carry out.

4.5.1 Pictures

Let us consider the printing phase first. Essentially, this means we have to build a *picture* of the calendar. However, unlike the pictures of turtle trails in the previous section (which were generated from lists of points in the plane), we now have to build pictures out of smaller pictures by means of appropriate combinators.

A picture can be represented by a list of lists of characters in which each element list has the same length. The *height* of a picture is the number of element lists, and the *width* is their common length. Thus:

$$
\begin{aligned}
height\ p &= \#p \\
width\ p &= \#(hd\ p)
\end{aligned}
$$

Note that p must be a non-empty list for it to have a well-defined width, so $height\ p \geq 1$.

We can build pictures either directly or in terms of component pictures by means of picture operators. Here are two simple picture operators:

$$
\begin{aligned}
p\ \textbf{above}\ q &= p \mathbin{+\!\!+} q, & &\text{if } width\ p = width\ q \\
p\ \textbf{beside}\ q &= zipwith\ (+\!\!+)\ (p, q), & &\text{if } height\ p = height\ q
\end{aligned}
$$

The operation (p **above** q) places picture p directly above picture q, and (p **beside** q) places p to the left of q. In the first operation, the widths of the two pictures must be the same and, in the latter, the two heights.

These operations can be generalised to functions *stack* and *spread* in the same way that (+) can be generalised to *concat*:

$$stack \quad = \quad foldr1 \text{ (\textbf{above})}$$
$$spread \quad = \quad foldr1 \text{ (\textbf{beside})}$$

Both *stack* and *spread* take a list of pictures; *stack* stacks them vertically, and *spread* spreads them horizontally. Although the operators (**above**) and (**beside**) are associative, neither has an identity element, so a definition by *foldr1* is appropriate. Any identity element would have to have the same height and width as every picture and this is clearly not possible.

On the other hand, it is possible to define an empty picture of a specified height and width; this is just a picture filled with spaces:

$$empty\,(h, w) \quad = \quad copy\,h\,(copy\,w\,\text{`}\llcorner\text{'}), \quad \text{if } h > 0 \wedge w > 0$$

This defines $empty\,(h, w)$ to be a list (of length $h > 0$) of lists (each of length $w > 0$) of space characters.

The function (*block n*) defined by:

$$block\,n \quad = \quad stack \cdot map\,spread \cdot group\,n$$

takes a list of pictures, all of which must have the same height and width, assembles them into groups of n, turns each group into a spread, and finally stacks the results above one another. The subsidary function (*group n*) takes a list of length $m \times n$ and returns m lists of length n. One definition of (*group n*) is:

$$group\,n\,xs \quad = \quad [take\,n\,(drop\,j\,xs) \mid j \leftarrow [0, n\,..\,(\#xs - n)]]$$

The effect of *block* 3 on the twelve pictures $p_1, p_2, \ldots, p_{12}$ would be to transform them into the picture:

$$
\begin{array}{ccc}
p_1 & p_2 & p_3 \\
p_4 & p_5 & p_6 \\
p_7 & p_8 & p_9 \\
p_{10} & p_{11} & p_{12}
\end{array}
$$

On the other hand, the function (*blockT n*) defined by:

$$blockT\,n \quad = \quad spread \cdot map\,stack \cdot group\,n$$

would convert the same list of pictures into the picture:

$$
\begin{array}{cccc}
p_1 & p_4 & p_7 & p_{10} \\
p_2 & p_5 & p_8 & p_{11} \\
p_3 & p_6 & p_9 & p_{12}
\end{array}
$$

Thus $(blockT\ n)$ flips the result of applying $(block\ n)$ about the left–right downwards diagonal. We shall use these two functions below.

We can turn a picture into a larger one by framing it. For example, suppose we want to frame a picture p in the top left-hand corner of a larger picture of height m and width n. This can be done by the function $lframe$:

$$lframe\ (m, n)\ p\ =\ (p\ \textbf{beside}\ empty\ (h, n - w))\ \textbf{above}\ empty\ (m - h, n)$$
$$\textbf{where}\ h\ =\ height\ p$$
$$w\ =\ width\ p$$

It is left as an exercise for the reader to modify the definition of $lframe$ so that it also works in the case $m = height\ p$ or $n = width\ p$. In a similar fashion we can centre a picture in a larger one, or place it in the top right-hand corner.

Finally, we can display a picture by the function $display$ where:

$$display\ =\ unlines$$

This is just a renaming of the function $unlines$ considered in Section 4.3.

Given the above functions, the printing phase of the calendar problem is straightforward:

$$calendar\ =\ display \cdot block\ 3 \cdot map\ picture \cdot months$$

In the definition of $calendar$, the function $months$ takes a year number and turns it into a list of length 12 with one entry for each month. The function $picture$ turns this information into a picture for a month, ($block\ 3$) arranges the results as a 4×3 picture, and $display$ converts it to printable form. This leaves only the functions $months$ and $picture$ to be defined.

Exactly what information do we need to build a calendar for a particular month? Well, we need the month name and the year. This will enable us to print a title for each month. We also need to know the day of the week on which the first day of each month falls and the number of days in the month. These two numbers will enable us to fill a table with the entries for a month.

Let us suppose, therefore, that the function $months$ returns a list of 4-tuples (mn, yr, fd, ml), where mn is the name of the month, yr the year, fd the first day of the month and ml the length of the month. We shall postpone the definition of $months$ until we have considered how to define $picture$.

4.5.2 Picturing a calendar

We can start the definition of $picture$ as follows:

$$picture\ (mn, yr, fd, ml)\ =\ (title\ mn\ yr)\ \textbf{above}\ (table\ fd\ ml)$$

Assuming each month is converted to a picture of width 25 (so that 3 months will fit side-by-side on a normal terminal screen), we can define the picture for a title by:

$$\textit{title mn yr} \;=\; \textit{lframe}\,(2,25)\,[\textit{mn} \mathbin{+\!\!+} \text{``$\sqcup$''} \mathbin{+\!\!+} \textit{show yr}]$$

This frames the title in a 2 × 25 picture, leaving a blank line between the heading and the table.

In a similar way, we can define the table:

$$
\begin{aligned}
\textit{table fd ml} \;&=\; \textit{lframe}\,(8,25)\,(\textit{daynames}\ \textbf{beside}\,(\textit{entries fd ml}))\\
\textit{daynames} \;&=\; [\text{``Sun''},\text{``Mon''},\text{``Tue''},\text{``Wed''},\text{``Thu''},\text{``Fri''},\text{``Sat''}]
\end{aligned}
$$

This places the 7 × 3 picture of the days beside the entries for a month and converts the result into a 8 × 25 picture. One blank line is left at the bottom of the picture to separate it from the month below.

In order to define $\textit{entries}$ we need to assign numbers to the days of the week. It is convenient to say Sunday is day 0, Monday is day 1, and so on up to Saturday, which is day 6. Suppose first we can define a table of consecutive numbers (reading downwards) arranged so that the first day of the month occupies its rightful place. For example, with $fd = 6$ we get:

$$
\begin{array}{rrrrrr}
-5 & 2 & 9 & 16 & 23 & 30\\
-4 & 3 & 10 & 17 & 24 & 31\\
-3 & 4 & 11 & 18 & 25 & 32\\
-2 & 5 & 12 & 19 & 26 & 33\\
-1 & 6 & 13 & 20 & 27 & 34\\
0 & 7 & 14 & 21 & 28 & 35\\
1 & 8 & 15 & 22 & 29 & 36
\end{array}
$$

Each of these numbers can be converted to simple 1 × 3 pictures of digits, or empty pictures if the number corresponds to an impossible date. This collection of pictures can be assembled into a table by using the function $blockT$:

$$
\begin{aligned}
\textit{entries fd ml} \;&=\; \textit{blockT}\ 7\,(\textit{dates fd ml})\\
\textit{dates fd ml} \;&=\; \textit{map}\,(\textit{date ml})\,[1 - fd\mathbin{..}42 - fd]\\
\textit{date ml d} \;&=\; [\textit{rjustify}\ 3\ \text{``$\sqcup$''}], \qquad \textbf{if}\ d < 1 \lor ml < d\\
&=\; [\textit{rjustify}\ 3\,(\textit{show d})], \quad \textbf{otherwise}
\end{aligned}
$$

4.5.3 Building a calendar

The remaining task is to define the function $\textit{months}$. This function can be defined with the help of a function $\textit{zip4}$ which takes a 4-tuple of lists into a list of 4-tuples. We shall leave its definition in terms of $\textit{zip}$ as an exercise. First of all, we define:

$$\textit{months yr} \;=\; \textit{zip4}\,(\textit{mnames},\textit{copy}\ 12\ \textit{yr},\textit{fstdays yr},\textit{mlengths yr})$$

The month names are given by a simple list:

$mnames$ = ["JANUARY", "FEBRUARY", "MARCH", "APRIL",
            "MAY", "JUNE", "JULY", "AUGUST", "SEPTEMBER",
            "OCTOBER", "NOVEMBER", "DECEMBER"]

and so are the lengths of the months:

$$mlengths\ yr = [31, feb, 31, 30, 31, 30, 31, 31, 30, 31, 30, 31]$$
$$\textbf{where}\ feb = 29,\ \textbf{if}\ leap\ yr$$
$$= 28,\ \textbf{otherwise}$$

The definition of ($leap\ yr$) is based on the well-known formula for determining whether the year is a leap year or not:

$$leap\ yr = (yr\ \textbf{mod}\ 400 = 0),\ \textbf{if}\ yr\ \textbf{mod}\ 100 = 0$$
$$= (yr\ \textbf{mod}\ 4 = 0),\qquad \textbf{otherwise}$$

We also need one more formula from 'Calendar Theory', namely how to calculate the day of the week for January 1. Calling this value $jan1$ we have:

$$jan1\ yr = (yr + (yr - 1)\ \textbf{div}\ 4 - (yr - 1)\ \textbf{div}\ 100$$
$$+ (yr - 1)\ \textbf{div}\ 400)\ \textbf{mod}\ 7$$

This works because in the Gregorian calendar January 1 in the year 0 was a Sunday, and $(365\ \textbf{mod}\ 7) = 1$. (Recall, day numbers were chosen to be the range 0 to 6.) From this value we can calculate the first days of all other months. We have:

$$fstdays\ yr = take\ 12\ (map\ (\textbf{mod}7)\ (scan\ (+)\ (jan1\ yr)\ (mlengths\ yr)))$$

This computes the accumulated sums of the month lengths (using $scan$), starting at January 1, reduces them modulo 7 to find the day of the week for the first days of each month, and finally takes just the initial 12 values to give the required answer.

This completes our description of the calendar problem.

Exercises

4.5.1 Show that:

$$lframe\ (m, n)\ p = \bot$$

if $m = height\ p$ or $n = width\ p$. Redesign $lframe$ so that these cases are allowed.

4.5.2 Define the function $rframe\ (m, n)$ which places a picture in the top right hand corner of a larger picture of height m and width n. Similarly, define $cframe\ (m, n)$ which places a picture in the centre of a larger one.

4.5.3 Define a function which given a year and a month prints out the calendar for the given month.

4.5.4 Define a version of the calendar problem which prints a month with the days across the top of the table rather than down the left-hand side.

4.5.5 Define a version of the calendar problem which prints a month with the days of the week beginning with Monday rather than Sunday.

4.5.6 Define a function which takes a date and returns the day of the week on which the date falls.

4.5.7 Define the function *zip4* in terms of *zip*.

Chapter 5

Recursion and Induction

This chapter introduces the important ideas of definition by recursion and proof by induction. We begin by seeing how they work in the case of natural numbers, and then go on to apply them to lists. In particular, recursion can be used to define the functions introduced in Chapter 3, and induction can be used to prove the many laws and identities encountered there.

5.1 Recursion and induction over natural numbers

Let us begin by examining recursion and induction at work in a familiar context: the definition of exponentiation. Recall that $x \char`^ n$ means x raised to the nth power. We will restrict our attention to the important case where n is a natural number.

In a mathematics textbook, $x \char`^ n$ is usually written x^n. There one might see the following recursive definition of exponentiation:

$$
\begin{aligned}
x^0 &= 1 \\
x^{(n+1)} &= x \times (x^n)
\end{aligned}
$$

In our notation, this is rewritten simply as:

$$
\begin{aligned}
x \char`^ 0 &= 1 \\
x \char`^ (n+1) &= x \times (x \char`^ n)
\end{aligned}
$$

This definition uses pattern matching with the natural numbers, introduced in Section 2.5.

The above definition can be rewritten in a form that does not employ pattern matching:

$$
\begin{aligned}
x \char`^ n &= 1, & \text{if } n = 0 \\
&= x \times x \char`^ (n-1), & \text{if } n > 0
\end{aligned}
$$

However, the definition using 0 and $(n+1)$ is preferred, because it is clearer and it is closer to normal mathematical practice.

It should be clear that these equations define $x \char`^ n$ for any natural number n. If n is zero then the first equation applies, while if n is greater than zero then the second equation applies. Thus:

$$
\begin{aligned}
5\char`^3 &= 5 \times (5\char`^2) & (\char`^.2) \\
&= 5 \times (5 \times (5\char`^1)) & (\char`^.2) \\
&= 5 \times (5 \times (5 \times (5\char`^0))) & (\char`^.2) \\
&= 5 \times (5 \times (5 \times 1))) & (\char`^.1) \\
&= 125
\end{aligned}
$$

The comment "$(\char`^.2)$" at the end of a line means that the equality on that line is justified by the second equation defining $(\char`^)$, and similarly for "$(\char`^.1)$". In general, we will refer to the ith equation of the definition of a function f by writing $(f.i)$.

Notice that the pattern $(n+1)$ matches the argument 3 by binding n to 2. The pattern $(n+1)$ cannot match 0, because n must be bound to a natural number. Thus, for every natural number n the term $x \char`^ n$ will match either the first equation or the second equation defining $(\char`^)$, but never both equations. If n is not a natural number, as in $x \char`^ (-3)$ or $x \char`^ 2.5$ or $x \char`^ \bot$, then neither equation matches, so $x \char`^ n = \bot$. (Here we are referring to the recursive definition above. Of course, $x \char`^ y$ is actually well-defined for any real number y, but we are ignoring that for now.)

It may seem that there is something magical about defining $x \char`^ (n+1)$ in terms of $x \char`^ n$. Is such as step valid? It is easy to convince ourselves that it is. Clearly, $x \char`^ 0$ has a value, because this is given by equation $(\char`^.1)$. By equation $(\char`^.2)$, we know that if $x \char`^ n$ has a value then so will $x \char`^ (n+1)$. So since $x \char`^ 0$ has a value, so does $x \char`^ 1$; and then since $x \char`^ 1$ has a value, so does $x \char`^ 2$; and so on. So $x \char`^ n$ has a value for every natural number n, as required.

In practice, this reasoning may also be applied backwards. (Indeed, the word 'recurse' comes from the Latin for 'to go back'.) Given a value for x and n the value of $x \char`^ n$ is found by finding the value of $x \char`^ (n-1)$, and this is found by finding the value of $x \char`^ (n-2)$, and so on, until eventually $x \char`^ 0$ must be reached.

This argument, whether you think of it forward or backwards, is an example of a proof by *mathematical induction*. In general, to prove by induction that a proposition $P(n)$ holds for any natural number n one must show two things:

Case 0. That $P(0)$ holds; and

Case $(n+1)$. That if $P(n)$ holds, then $P(n+1)$ holds also.

This is valid for exactly the same reason that recursive definitions are valid. We know by the first case that $P(0)$ holds; and so we know by the second case that $P(1)$ holds also; and so we know again by the second case that $P(2)$ holds also; and so on. So $P(n)$ must hold for *every* natural number n.

As an example, let us prove the well-known law:

$$x \,\hat{} \, (m + n) = (x \,\hat{} \, m) \times (x \,\hat{} \, n)$$

for all x and all natural numbers m and n.

Proof. The proof is by induction on m.

Case 0. We have:

$$
\begin{aligned}
x \,\hat{} \, (0 + n) &= x \,\hat{} \, n & \text{(law of +)} \\
&= 1 \times (x \,\hat{} \, n) & \text{(law of ×)} \\
&= (x \,\hat{} \, 0) \times (x \,\hat{} \, n) & (\hat{}.1)
\end{aligned}
$$

which establishes the case.

Case $(m + 1)$. Assume that $x \,\hat{} \, (m + n) = (x \,\hat{} \, m) \times (x \,\hat{} \, n)$; this is called the *induction hypothesis*. Then we have:

$$
\begin{aligned}
x \,\hat{} \, ((m + 1) + n) &= x \,\hat{} \, ((m + n) + 1) & \text{(laws of +)} \\
&= x \times (x \,\hat{} \, (m + n)) & (\hat{}.2) \\
&= x \times ((x \,\hat{} \, m) \times (x \,\hat{} \, n)) & \text{(hypothesis)} \\
&= (x \times (x \,\hat{} \, m)) \times (x \,\hat{} \, n) & \text{(law of ×)} \\
&= (x \,\hat{} \, (m + 1)) \times (x \,\hat{} \, n) & (\hat{}.2)
\end{aligned}
$$

which establishes the case. □

This example shows the style we will use for inductive proofs, laying out each case separately and using a "□" to mark the end.

As a second example of a recursive definition, consider the Fibonacci numbers. In a mathematics textbook, these might be defined by the following recurrence relationship:

$$
\begin{aligned}
F_0 &= 0 \\
F_1 &= 1 \\
F_{k+2} &= F_k + F_{k+1}
\end{aligned}
$$

Thus, F_0 through F_9 are:

$$0, 1, 1, 2, 3, 5, 8, 13, 21, 34$$

where each number in the sequence is the sum of the two preceding it.

In our notation we will write F_k as $fib\,k$, and the above definition becomes:

$$
\begin{aligned}
fib\,0 &= 0 \\
fib\,1 &= 1 \\
fib\,(k + 2) &= fib\,k + fib\,(k + 1)
\end{aligned}
$$

Recall that $(k + 2)$ is a legal pattern, just like $(n + 1)$. The pattern $(k + 2)$ cannot match 0 or 1, since k must be a natural number, so for any k the value of *fib k* is defined by exactly one of the above equations.

The Fibonacci numbers satisfy an astounding number of laws, many of which are conveniently proved by induction. We will prove only one here. For others, the reader should consult the exercises, or Knuth [3], or the *Fibonacci Quarterly* journal.

Let ϕ and $\hat{\phi}$ be the roots of the equation $x^2 - x - 1 = 0$, that is:

$$\phi = \frac{1 + \sqrt{5}}{2} \quad \text{and} \quad \hat{\phi} = \frac{1 - \sqrt{5}}{2}$$

So $\phi^2 = \phi + 1$ and $\hat{\phi}^2 = \hat{\phi} + 1$. Then we have:

$$F_k = \frac{1}{\sqrt{5}}(\phi^k - \hat{\phi}^k)$$

for all natural numbers k. (Here we are using traditional mathematical notation, rather than the programming notation. The two notations may be mixed freely, as convenient, so long as no confusion arises.)

Proof. The proof is by induction on k. Let $c = 1/\sqrt{5}$.

Case 0. By simple calculation, we have: $F_0 = 0 = c(\phi^0 - \hat{\phi}^0)$, which establishes the case.

Case 1. Again by simple calculation, we have that $F_1 = 1 = c(\phi^1 - \hat{\phi}^1)$, which establishes the case.

Case $(k + 2)$. Assume that $F_k = c(\phi^k - \hat{\phi}^k)$ and $F_{k+1} = c(\phi^{k+1} - \hat{\phi}^{k+1})$; these are the induction hypotheses. Then we have that

$$
\begin{aligned}
F_{k+2} &= F_k + F_{k+1} & (F.3)\\
&= c(\phi^k - \hat{\phi}^k) + c(\phi^{k+1} - \hat{\phi}^{k+1}) & \text{(hypothesis)}\\
&= c(\phi^k(1 + \phi) - \hat{\phi}^k(1 + \hat{\phi})) & \text{(arithmetic)}\\
&= c(\phi^{k+2} - \hat{\phi}^{k+2}) & (\phi^2 = \phi + 1, \hat{\phi}^2 = \hat{\phi} + 1)
\end{aligned}
$$

which establishes the case. $\square$

The induction principle used this time is a little different from the one used previously. Here, in order to show $P(n)$ we show three things:

Case 0. That $P(0)$ holds; and

Case 1. That $P(1)$ holds; and

Case $(n + 2)$. That if $P(n)$ and $P(n + 1)$ hold, then $P(n + 2)$ holds also.

This principle is valid by an argument similar to the one given previously.

Recursion and induction are a sufficient basis on which to formulate a large proportion of mathematics, including most of the mathematics that we need for writing computer programs. For present purposes we are taking operations like addition and multiplication as primitives. But if need be, we could actually define them using recursion, taking only the forms 0 and $(n + 1)$ as primitives:

$$
\begin{aligned}
0 + n &= n \\
(m + 1) + n &= (m + n) + 1 \\[6pt]
0 \times n &= 0 \\
(m + 1) \times n &= (m \times n) + n
\end{aligned}
$$

Using these definitions and induction, one could prove all the familiar properties of arithmetic, such as that addition and multiplication are associative and commutative, and that multiplication distributes over addition.

This concludes our review of recursive definition and inductive proof over the natural numbers. Recursive definitions and proof by induction both rely on the same case analysis, observing that each natural number must either be 0 or else have the form $(n + 1)$. They are two sides of the same coin, and, to mix the metaphor, they fit together like a hand into a glove. In the following sections, we shall use recursion to define many useful functions, and induction to prove laws satisfied by the functions so defined.

Exercises

5.1.1 Using the recursive definitions of addition and multiplication of natural numbers given in Section 5.1, prove all or some of the following familiar properties of arithmetic:

$$
\begin{aligned}
0 + n &= n &&= n + 0 && \text{(+ has identity 0)} \\
1 \times n &= n &&= n \times 1 && \text{(× has identity 1)} \\
m + n &= n + m && && \text{(+ commutative)} \\
k + (m + n) &= (k + m) + n && && \text{(+ associative)} \\
m \times n &= n \times m && && \text{(× commutative)} \\
k \times (m \times n) &= (k \times m) \times n && && \text{(× associative)} \\
k \times (m + n) &= (k \times m) + (k \times n) && && \text{(+ distributes through ×)}
\end{aligned}
$$

for all natural numbers k, m, and n.

5.1.2 Prove that:

$$
\begin{aligned}
F_{n+1}F_{n-1} - (F_n)^2 &= (-1)^n \\
F_{n+m} &= F_n F_{m+1} + F_{n-1}F_m
\end{aligned}
$$

for all natural numbers $n \geq 1$ and $m \geq 0$, where F_m is the mth Fibonacci number.

5.1.3 The *binomial coefficient* $\binom{n}{k}$ denotes the number of ways of choosing k objects from a collection of n objects. Here is a table of the values of $\binom{n}{k}$ for $0 \le n, k \le 4$:

$n \backslash k$	0	1	2	3	4
0	1	0	0	0	0
1	1	1	0	0	0
2	1	2	1	0	0
3	1	3	3	1	0
4	1	4	6	4	1

Observe that this table is essentially Pascal's Triangle shifted to the left and padded with zeros. Each element in the table (except for the edges) is the sum of the element immediately above it and the element above it and to the left. In the programming notation, we will write *binom n k* for $\binom{n}{k}$.

   a. Give a recursive definition of *binom*.

   b. Prove that if $k > n$ then $\binom{n}{k} = 0$.

   c. Rewrite the equation:

$$\sum_{0 \le k \le n} \binom{n}{k} = 2^n$$

    in our programming notation. Prove that the equation is true for all natural numbers n.

5.2   Recursion and induction over lists

The principles of recursion and induction may be applied to lists as well as to natural numbers. For natural numbers, recursion and induction are based on two cases: every natural number is either 0 or else has the form $(n + 1)$ for some n. Similarly, recursion and induction on lists are also based on two cases: every list either is the empty list $[\,]$ or else has the form $(x : xs)$ for some x and xs.

    Recall from Section 3.6 that $(:)$ adds an element to the front of a list, so $1 : 2 : 3 : [\,]$ is equivalent to $[1, 2, 3]$. Every list either is $[\,]$ or must have the form $(x : xs)$ for some value x and some list xs.

    Here is an example of a recursive definition over lists. The operator $(\#)$, which finds the length of a list, can be defined by:

$$\begin{aligned} \#[\,] &= 0 \\ \#(x : xs) &= 1 + (\#xs) \end{aligned}$$

Just as 0 and $(n + 1)$ were used as patterns in definitions before, now we are using $[\,]$ and $(x : xs)$ as patterns. Indeed, the notation was designed to allow such patterns precisely because they make it easy to write recursive definitions.

We can use these two equations to compute the length of the list $[1,2,3]$ as follows:

$$
\begin{aligned}
\#[1,2,3] \;&=\; 1 + (\#[2,3]) &&(\#.2)\\
&=\; 1 + (1 + (\#[3])) &&(\#.2)\\
&=\; 1 + (1 + (1 + (\#[\,]))) &&(\#.2)\\
&=\; 1 + (1 + (1 + 0)) &&(\#.1)\\
&=\; 3
\end{aligned}
$$

As a second example, here is the recursive definition of concatenation:

$$
\begin{aligned}
[\,] \mathbin{+\!\!+} ys \;&=\; ys\\
(x : xs) \mathbin{+\!\!+} ys \;&=\; x : (xs \mathbin{+\!\!+} ys)
\end{aligned}
$$

For example:

$$
\begin{aligned}
[1,2] \mathbin{+\!\!+} [3,4] \;&=\; 1 : ([2] \mathbin{+\!\!+} [3,4]) &&(+\!\!+.2)\\
&=\; 1 : (2 : ([\,] \mathbin{+\!\!+} [3,4])) &&(+\!\!+.2)\\
&=\; 1 : (2 : [3,4]) &&(+\!\!+.1)\\
&=\; [1,2,3,4]
\end{aligned}
$$

Induction adapts to lists as easily as recursion does. The principle of induction over lists is as follows. To prove by induction that $P(xs)$ holds for any finite list xs one must show two things:

Case $[\,]$. That $P([\,])$ holds; and

Case $(x : xs)$. That if $P(xs)$ holds, then $P(x : xs)$ holds for every x.

This is valid by an argument similar to the one we used for natural numbers. We know by the first case that $P([\,])$ holds; and so we know by the second case that $P([x])$ also holds for every x (since $[x]$ is $x : [\,]$); and so we know again by the second case that $P([y,x])$ also holds for every y and x (since $[y,x]$ is $y : [x]$); and so on. Thus $P(xs)$ holds for every finite list xs. It is easy to formalise this proof by inducting on the length of the list xs, so the principle of induction over lists is actually just a consequence of the principle of induction over natural numbers.

In Chapter 3 we stated a number of laws without giving any proofs. Let us finally prove some of them.

The first law we saw states that concatenation is associative, that is:

$$
xs \mathbin{+\!\!+} (ys \mathbin{+\!\!+} zs) = (xs \mathbin{+\!\!+} ys) \mathbin{+\!\!+} zs
$$

for every finite list xs, ys, and zs.

Proof. The proof is by induction on xs.

Case $[\,]$. We have:

$$
\begin{aligned}
[\,] \mathbin{+\!\!+} (ys \mathbin{+\!\!+} zs) \;&=\; ys \mathbin{+\!\!+} zs &&(+\!\!+.1)\\
&=\; ([\,] \mathbin{+\!\!+} ys) \mathbin{+\!\!+} zs &&(+\!\!+.1)
\end{aligned}
$$

which establishes the case.

Case $(x : xs)$. We have:

$$
\begin{aligned}
(x : xs) +\!\!\!+ (ys +\!\!\!+ zs) &= x : (xs +\!\!\!+ (ys +\!\!\!+ zs)) & (+\!\!\!+.2) \\
&= x : ((xs +\!\!\!+ ys) +\!\!\!+ zs) & \text{(hypothesis)} \\
&= (x : (xs +\!\!\!+ ys)) +\!\!\!+ zs & (+\!\!\!+.2) \\
&= ((x : xs) +\!\!\!+ ys) +\!\!\!+ zs & (+\!\!\!+.2)
\end{aligned}
$$

which establishes the case. $\square$

The reader should consider why the induction in this proof is on xs, and not ys or zs.

The next law we saw states that the identity element for concatenation is $[\,]$, that is:

$$[\,] +\!\!\!+ xs = xs +\!\!\!+ [\,] = xs$$

for every finite list xs. The first half of this law is part of the recursive definition of concatenation. The second half is an easy proof by induction on xs, and the pleasure of this proof will be left to the reader.

To drive the idea of induction home, we will do one more proof. The next law we saw relates length and concatenation, namely:

$$\#(xs +\!\!\!+ ys) = (\#xs) + (\#ys)$$

for every finite list xs and ys.

Proof. The proof is by induction on xs.

Case $[\,]$. We have:

$$
\begin{aligned}
\#([\,] +\!\!\!+ ys) &= \#ys & (+\!\!\!+.1) \\
&= 0 + (\#ys) & \text{(arithmetic)} \\
&= (\#[\,]) + (\#ys) & (\#.1)
\end{aligned}
$$

which establishes the case.

Case $(x : xs)$. We have:

$$
\begin{aligned}
\#((x : xs) +\!\!\!+ ys) &= \#(x : (xs +\!\!\!+ ys)) & (+\!\!\!+.2) \\
&= 1 + (\#(xs +\!\!\!+ ys)) & (\#.2) \\
&= 1 + (\#xs) + (\#ys) & \text{(hypothesis)} \\
&= (\#(x : xs)) + (\#ys) & (\#.2)
\end{aligned}
$$

which establishes the case. $\square$

In mathematics, one writes down a proof in the way that looks most elegant, not the way one first discovers it. Both of the proofs above were discovered by a technique that can reduce many proofs to a simple exercise in calculation. Here is how the technique was applied to the $(x : xs)$ case in the proof that concatenation is associative. What we wish to show is that:

$$(x : xs) +\!\!\!+ (ys +\!\!\!+ zs) = ((x : xs) +\!\!\!+ ys) +\!\!\!+ zs$$

This can be done as follows. First, we start with the left-hand side, and simplify it as much as possible:

$$
\begin{aligned}
(x : xs) \mathbin{+\!\!+} (ys \mathbin{+\!\!+} zs) &= x : (xs \mathbin{+\!\!+} (ys \mathbin{+\!\!+} zs)) \quad (\mathbin{+\!\!+}.2) \\
&= x : ((xs \mathbin{+\!\!+} ys) \mathbin{+\!\!+} zs) \quad \text{(hypothesis)}
\end{aligned}
$$

Here "simplify" means that whenever the left-hand side of a definition (or of the induction hypothesis) matches a term or a part of a term, then it is replaced by the corresponding right-hand side. Second, we do the same thing to the right-hand side:

$$
\begin{aligned}
((x : xs) \mathbin{+\!\!+} ys) \mathbin{+\!\!+} zs &= (x : (xs \mathbin{+\!\!+} ys)) \mathbin{+\!\!+} zs \quad (\mathbin{+\!\!+}.2) \\
&= x : ((xs \mathbin{+\!\!+} ys) \mathbin{+\!\!+} zs) \quad (\mathbin{+\!\!+}.2)
\end{aligned}
$$

Since the two results are the same, we have demonstrated the desired equality. The proof above was obtained by copying the first group of equations followed by writing the second group of equations in the reverse order.

Thus, many proofs just require a proper choice of induction variable followed by an exercise in simplification. This process is so simple that one might think it could be automated – and indeed it has been. A great deal of work has been done on automatic or machine-aided generation of proofs, and most of the systems for this have simplification of the sort described here at their core. The interested reader should consult Boyer and Moore [4], Gordon *et al* [5], or Paulson [6] for examples. On the other hand, as we shall see, many proofs require insight and ingenuity for their completion.

5.3 Operations on lists

In this section we show how some of the list operations introduced in Chapter 3 can be defined formally by using recursion, and how some of the related laws can be proved using induction. The operators discussed are chosen in order to illustrate variations on the basic principles introduced in the preceding sections. Formal definitions of the remaining operators are left as exercises.

5.3.1 Zip

Recall that *zip* takes a pair of lists and returns a list of pairs. Here is its recursive definition:

$$
\begin{aligned}
zip\,([\,], ys) &= [\,] \\
zip\,(x : xs, [\,]) &= [\,] \\
zip\,(x : xs, y : ys) &= (x, y) : zip\,(xs, ys)
\end{aligned}
$$

This definition obviously covers every possible combination of the two argument lists. Either:

Case [ ]**,** *ys*. The first is empty; or

Case $(x : xs)$, $[]$. The first is non-empty and the second is empty; or

Case $(x : xs)$, $(y : ys)$. The first is non-empty and the second is non-empty.

Thus, for every possible pair of lists, exactly one of the equations defining *zip* applies.

This definition applies in just the way one would expect. For example:

$$
\begin{aligned}
zip\,(\text{``ab''}, [1,2,3]) &= (\text{`a'}, 1) : zip\,(\text{``b''}, [2,3]) &(zip.3)\\
&= (\text{`a'}, 1) : (\text{`b'}, 2) : zip\,(\text{``''}, [3]) &(zip.3)\\
&= (\text{`a'}, 1) : (\text{`b'}, 2) : [] &(zip.2)\\
&= [(\text{`a'}, 1), (\text{`b'}, 2)]
\end{aligned}
$$

Here "ab" is equivalent to ['a', 'b'] which is equivalent to ('a' : ('b' : [])). Notice the result list has the same length as the shorter of the two argument lists.

It is easy to adapt our style of inductive proof to work with such patterns. We will demonstrate this by showing that:

$$
\#zip\,(xs, ys) = (\#xs)\,\textbf{min}\,(\#ys)
$$

for every finite list xs and ys.

Proof. The proof is by induction on both xs and ys.

Case $[]$, ys. We have:

$$
\begin{aligned}
\#zip\,([], ys) &= \#[] &(zip.1)\\
&= 0 &(\#.1)\\
&= 0\,\textbf{min}\,(\#ys)
\end{aligned}
$$

since $0\,\textbf{min}\,n = 0$ for every natural number n. This establishes the case.

Case $(x : xs)$, $[]$. We have:

$$
\begin{aligned}
\#zip\,(x : xs, []) &= \#[] &(zip.2)\\
&= 0 &(\#.1)\\
&= \#(x : xs)\,\textbf{min}\,0
\end{aligned}
$$

since $n\,\textbf{min}\,0 = 0$ for every natural number n. This establishes the case.

Case $(x : xs)$, $(y : ys)$. We have:

$$
\begin{aligned}
\#zip\,(x : xs, y : ys)&\\
&= \#((x, y) : zip\,(xs, ys)) &(zip.3)\\
&= 1 + \#zip\,(xs, ys) &(\#.2)\\
&= 1 + (\#xs\,\textbf{min}\,\#ys) &\text{(hypothesis)}\\
&= (1 + \#xs)\,\textbf{min}\,(1 + \#ys) &\text{($+$ distributes through \textbf{min})}\\
&= \#(x : xs)\,\textbf{min}\,\#(y : ys) &(\#.2)
\end{aligned}
$$

which establishes the case. $\square$

This inductive proof is valid because, as was observed before, the three cases
$([\,],ys)$, $(x:xs,[\,])$, and $(x:xs,y:ys)$ cover every possible combination of
two lists. Formally, one can justify this sort of "double induction" as two
nested inductions. Here the outer induction is on xs, and the inner induction
is on ys.

Rather than the definition above, one might be tempted to give the following definition of zip instead:

$$
\begin{aligned}
zip\,([\,],ys) &= [\,]\\
zip\,(xs,[\,]) &= [\,]\\
zip\,(x:xs,y:ys) &= (x,y):zip\,(xs,ys)
\end{aligned}
$$

However, this definition is *illegal* in the notation used in this book, because
it is ambiguous. Given the term $zip\,([\,],[\,])$, either the first equation or the
second equation might apply. In this case both equations happen to yield
the same result, $[\,]$, but we cannot guarantee this for all definitions. So it is
required that in every definition at most one equation must apply for every
possible choice of arguments.

Perhaps the reader thinks the second, illegal, definition is better, because
it is more symmetric. In fact the function zip is *not* symmetric. On any
sequential computer, evaluating $zip\,(xs,ys)$ will require examining either xs
first or ys first. A fundamental law of computation is that any process that
examines the value $\bot$ must return the value $\bot$. It is clear from the legal
definition that evaluation of $zip\,(xs,ys)$ examines xs first, and if xs is $[\,]$ then
ys is not examined. Thus, the term $zip\,(\bot,[\,])$ has the value $\bot$, since no
equation in the legal definition applies, while the term $zip\,([\,],\bot)$ has the
value $[\,]$, by equation $(zip.1)$. For the illegal definition to be valid, both
$zip\,(\bot,[\,])$ and $zip\,([\,],\bot)$ would have to return the value $[\,]$, but it is not
possible to obtain this behaviour using sequential computation. This is why
it was chosen to make the second definition illegal.

5.3.2   Take and drop

Recall that *take* and *drop* each take a natural number n and a list xs as
arguments. The value of $(take\ n\ xs)$ is the first n elements of xs (or all of
xs if $n > \#xs$), and the value of $(drop\ n\ xs)$ is xs with the first n elements
removed, (or $[\,]$ if $n > \#xs$). These functions can be defined recursively as
follows:

$$
\begin{aligned}
take\ 0\ xs &= [\,]\\
take\,(n+1)\,[\,] &= [\,]\\
take\,(n+1)\,(x:xs) &= x:take\ n\ xs\\[6pt]
drop\ 0\ xs &= xs\\
drop\,(n+1)\,[\,] &= [\,]\\
drop\,(n+1)\,(x:xs) &= drop\ n\ xs
\end{aligned}
$$

Again, these definitions cover every possible combination of the two arguments.

An important law relating *take* and *drop* is that:

$$take\ n\ xs \mathbin{+\!\!+} drop\ n\ xs = xs$$

for every natural number n and finite list xs. Using the methods developed so far, the following proof is straightforward.

Proof. The proof is by induction on n and xs.

Case 0, xs. We have:

$$
\begin{aligned}
take\ 0\ xs \mathbin{+\!\!+} drop\ 0\ xs &= [\,] \mathbin{+\!\!+} xs \quad (take.1, drop.1) \\
&= xs \quad\quad\ (+\!\!+.1)
\end{aligned}
$$

which establishes the case.

Case $(n+1)$, $[\,]$. We have:

$$
\begin{aligned}
take\ (n+1)\ [\,] \mathbin{+\!\!+} drop\ (n+1)\ [\,] &= [\,] \mathbin{+\!\!+} [\,] \quad (take.2, drop.2) \\
&= [\,] \quad\quad\ (+\!\!+.1)
\end{aligned}
$$

which establishes the case.

Case $(n+1)$, $(x : xs)$. We have:

$$
\begin{aligned}
take\ (n+1)\ (x:xs) &\mathbin{+\!\!+} drop\ (n+1)\ (x:xs) \\
&= (x : take\ n\ xs) \mathbin{+\!\!+} drop\ n\ xs \quad (take.3, drop.3) \\
&= x : (take\ n\ xs \mathbin{+\!\!+} drop\ n\ xs) \quad (+\!\!+.2) \\
&= x : xs \quad\quad\quad\quad\quad\quad\quad\quad\quad (\text{hypothesis})
\end{aligned}
$$

which establishes the case. $\square$

Observe that $take\ 0\ \bot = [\,]$ by $(take.1)$, whereas $take\ \bot\ [\,] = \bot$ since no equation applies; and similarly for *drop*. In particular, we have:

$$take\ \bot\ [\,] \mathbin{+\!\!+} drop\ \bot\ [\,] = \bot \mathbin{+\!\!+} \bot = \bot$$

which does *not* satisfy the law proved above. When we use induction to prove a law "for every natural number n" this does not cover the possibility that n is $\bot$. If we wish to cover this possibility, it must be included in the proof as an additional case. Similarly, the case that a list variable may be $\bot$ must also be treated separately; and we shall see examples of this in Chapter 7 when we discuss how to prove properties of infinite lists.

5.3.3   Head and tail

The function hd selects the first element of a list, and tl selects the remaining portion. These can be defined by a simple case analysis, without any need to resort to recursion, as follows:

$$
\begin{aligned}
hd\,(x:xs) &= x \\
tl\,(x:xs) &= xs
\end{aligned}
$$

No equation is provided defining $hd\,[\,]$ or $tl\,[\,]$, so these both take the value $\bot$.

We have already seen the law:

$$[hd\ xs] \mathbin{+\!\!+} tl\ xs = xs$$

for every non-empty finite list xs.

Proof. The proof is by case analysis on xs.

Case $(x:xs)$. We have:

$$
\begin{aligned}
[hd\,(x:xs)] \mathbin{+\!\!+} tl\,(x:xs) &= [x] \mathbin{+\!\!+} xs & (hd.1, tl.1) \\
&= x:xs & (+\!\!+.2, +\!\!+.1)
\end{aligned}
$$

which establishes the case. $\square$

The case for $[\,]$ was not included because it is given that xs is non-empty. This simple proof requires only a trivial case analysis, but no induction.

5.3.4   Init and last

These functions are similar to head and tail, but they select the initial segment of the list and its last element. We can define these using recursion, as follows:

$$
\begin{aligned}
init\,[x] &= [\,] \\
init\,(x:x':xs) &= x:init\,(x':xs) \\[4pt]
last\,[x] &= x \\
last\,(x:x':xs) &= last\,(x':xs)
\end{aligned}
$$

Here the two cases cover the possibility that the argument list has length one or the argument list has length two or greater.

The initial segment of a list can be formed by taking the first $n-1$ elements of the list, where n is its length; that is:

$$init\ xs = take\,(\#xs - 1)\ xs$$

for every non-empty finite list xs.

Proof. The proof is by induction on xs. The two cases considered are $[x]$ and $(x : x' : xs)$. This case analysis is valid, since every non-empty list must have one of these two forms.

Case $[x]$. We have that:

$$
\begin{aligned}
init\,[x] \;&=\; [] & (init.1)\\
&=\; take\;0\,[x] & (take.1)\\
&=\; take\,(\#[x]-1)\,[x] & (\#.1, \#.2)
\end{aligned}
$$

which establishes the case.

Case $(x : x' : xs)$. For the induction hypothesis, assume that:

$$ init\,(x' : xs) = take\,(\#(x' : xs) - 1)\,(x' : xs) $$

This is valid, since the list $(x' : xs)$ is shorter than the list $(x : x' : xs)$. Then we have:

$$
\begin{aligned}
init\,(x : (x' : xs)) \;&=\; x : init\,(x' : xs) & (init.2)\\
&=\; x : take\,(\#(x' : xs) - 1)\,(x' : xs) & \text{(hypothesis)}\\
&=\; x : take\,(\#xs)\,(x' : xs) & (\#.2)\\
&=\; take\,(\#xs + 1)\,(x : x' : xs) & (take.3)\\
&=\; take\,(\#(x : x' : xs) - 1)\,(x : x' : xs) & (\#.2)
\end{aligned}
$$

which establishes the case. $\square$

Again, the reader may be tempted to write:

$$
\begin{aligned}
init\,[x] \;&=\; []\\
init\,(x : xs) \;&=\; x : init\,xs
\end{aligned}
$$

for the definition of $init$. And, again, this is *illegal* in the notation used in this book. In particular, $init\,[x]$ can be reduced in two ways: it reduces to $[]$ by the first equation, and reduces to $x : init\,[]$ by the second equation (since $[x]$ is $(x : [])$).

5.3.5   Map and filter

The function *map* applies a function to each element of a list, and the function *filter* removes elements of a list that do not satisfy a predicate. They may be defined recursively as follows:

$$
\begin{aligned}
map\,f\,[] \;&=\; []\\
map\,f\,(x : xs) \;&=\; f\,x : map\,f\,xs
\end{aligned}
$$

$$
\begin{aligned}
filter\,p\,[] \;&=\; []\\
filter\,p\,(x : xs) \;&=\; x : filter\,p\,xs, & \textbf{if } p\,x\\
&=\; filter\,p\,xs, & \textbf{otherwise}
\end{aligned}
$$

The new elements we have here are higher-order functions and conditionals in a recursive function definition.

For example, we have:

$$
\begin{aligned}
&filter\ odd\ (map\ square\ [2,3]) \\
&= \ filter\ odd\ (4:map\ square\ [3]) &&(map.2) \\
&= \ filter\ odd\ (map\ square\ [3]) &&(filter.3) \\
&= \ filter\ odd\ (9:map\ square\ [\,]) &&(map.2) \\
&= \ 9:filter\ odd\ (map\ square\ [\,]) &&(filter.2) \\
&= \ 9:filter\ odd\ [\,] &&(map.1) \\
&= \ 9:[\,] &&(filter.1) \\
&= \ [9]
\end{aligned}
$$

One law satisfied by *map* and *filter* is:

$$filter\ p\ (map\ f\ xs) = map\ f\ (filter\ (p \cdot f)\ xs)$$

for any function f, total predicate p, and finite list xs. (A predicate p is *total* if for every x the value of $p\ x$ is always *True* or *False* and never $\bot$.)

Proof. The proof is by induction on xs. The two cases are $[\,]$ and $(x:xs)$. In the latter case, we will be interested in whether $(p\,(f\,x))$ is *True* or *False*, so we consider these cases separately.

Case $[\,]$. We have:

$$
\begin{aligned}
filter\ p\ (map\ f\ [\,]) &= \ filter\ p\ [\,] &&(map.1) \\
&= \ [\,] &&(filter.1) \\
&= \ map\ f\ [\,] &&(map.1) \\
&= \ map\ f\ (filter\ (p \cdot f)\ [\,]) &&(filter.1)
\end{aligned}
$$

which establishes the case.

Case $(x:xs)$, $(p\,(f\,x)) = True$. We have:

$$
\begin{aligned}
filter\ p\ (map\ f\ (x:xs)) &= \ filter\ p\ (f\ x:map\ f\ xs) &&(map.2) \\
&= \ f\ x:filter\ p\ (map\ f\ xs) &&(filter.2) \\
&= \ f\ x:map\ f\ (filter\ (p \cdot f)\ xs) &&(hypothesis) \\
&= \ map\ f\ (x:filter\ (p \cdot f)\ xs) &&(map.2) \\
&= \ map\ f\ (filter\ (p \cdot f)\ (x:xs)) &&(filter.2)
\end{aligned}
$$

which establishes the case.

Case $(x:xs)$, $(p\,(f\,x)) = False$. We have:

$$
\begin{aligned}
filter\ p\ (map\ f\ (x:xs)) &= \ filter\ p\ (f\ x:map\ f\ xs) &&(map.2) \\
&= \ filter\ p\ (map\ f\ xs) &&(filter.3) \\
&= \ map\ f\ (filter\ (p \cdot f)\ xs) &&(hypothesis) \\
&= \ map\ f\ (filter\ (p \cdot f)\ (x:xs)) &&(filter.3)
\end{aligned}
$$

which establishes the case. □

The above proof considered two possibilities for the value of $(p(f\,x))$, namely that it is *True* or *False*. This suffices if the predicate p is total. Otherwise, we must consider one additional case, namely, $(p(f\,x)) = \bot$. This case is left as an exercise.

5.3.6 Interval

The special form $[m\mathinner{\ldotp\ldotp}n]$ denotes the list of numbers from m to n. We can give a recursive definition of the function *interval*, where:

$$interval\ m\ n = [m\mathinner{\ldotp\ldotp}n]$$

in the following way:

$$
\begin{aligned}
interval\ m\ n\ &=\ [\,], &&\text{if } m > n\\
&=\ m : interval\,(m+1)\,n, &&\textbf{otherwise}
\end{aligned}
$$

Here, the two cases are distinguished by testing the condition $m > n$, rather than by the use of pattern matching. The value $(interval\ m\ n)$ is well defined for all m and n because the quantity $n - m$ decreases at each recursive call.

Reasoning about *interval* requires the following principle of induction. We may prove that a proposition $P(m, n)$ holds for every integer m and n by showing two things:

Case $m > n$. That $P(m, n)$ holds when $m > n$; and

Case $m \le n$. That if $P(m+1, n)$ holds, then $P(m, n)$ holds when $m \le n$.

This principle may be justified by induction (over natural numbers) on the quantity $n - m + 1$. Because of this, we will refer to this method of proof as induction on the difference between n and m.

We can now prove the useful law:

$$map\,(k+)\,(interval\ m\ n) = interval\,(k+m)\,(k+n)$$

for every integer k, m, and n.

Proof. The proof is by induction on the difference between m and n. Both cases make use of the fact that $k + m > k + n$ if and only if $m > n$.

Case $m > n$. We have:

$$
\begin{aligned}
&map\,(k+)\,(interval\ m\ n)\\
=\ &map\,(k+)\,[\,] &&(interval.1)\\
=\ &[\,] &&(map.1)\\
=\ &interval\,(k+m)\,(k+n) &&(interval.1)
\end{aligned}
$$

which establishes the case.

Case $m \leq n$. We have:

$$
\begin{aligned}
& map\,(k+)\,(interval\;m\;n) \\
=\;& map\,(k+)\,(m : interval\,(m + 1)\,n) && (interval.2) \\
=\;& k + m : map\,(k+)\,(interval\,(m + 1)\,n) && (map.2) \\
=\;& k + m : interval\,(k + m + 1)\,(k + n) && \text{(hypothesis)} \\
=\;& interval\,(k + m)\,(k + n) && (interval.2)
\end{aligned}
$$

which establishes the case. $\square$

We can generalise the induction principle above to apply when m and n are any numbers, not just integers, and for an arbitrary increment i. Namely, for any positive number i we may prove that $P(m, n)$ holds for any numbers m and n by showing:

Case $m > n$. That $P(m, n)$ holds when $m > n$; and

Case $m \leq n$. That if $P(m + i, n)$ holds, then $P(m, n)$ holds when $m \leq n$.

This principle may be justified by induction (over natural numbers) on the quantity $\lfloor (n - m)/i \rfloor$, where $\lfloor x \rfloor$ is the largest integer j such that $j \leq x$. Applying this principle shows that the law above holds for any numbers k, m, and n, not just integers.

Exercises

5.3.1 Give a recursive definition of the index operation $(xs\,!\,i)$.

5.3.2 Give recursive definitions of *takewhile* and *dropwhile*.

5.3.3 Prove the laws

$$
\begin{aligned}
init\,(xs + \!\!+ [x]) &= xs \\
last\,(xs + \!\!+ [x]) &= x \\
xs &= init\;xs + \!\!+ [last\;xs]
\end{aligned}
$$

for every x and every (non-empty) finite list xs.

5.3.4 Prove the laws:

$$
\begin{aligned}
take\;m\,(drop\;n\;xs) &= drop\;n\,(take\,(m + n)\,xs) \\
drop\;m\,(drop\;n\;xs) &= drop\,(m + n)\,xs
\end{aligned}
$$

for every natural number m and n and every finite list xs.

5.3.5 Prove the laws:

$$
\begin{aligned}
map\,(f \cdot g)\;xs &= map\;f\,(map\;g\;xs) \\
map\;f\,(concat\;xss) &= concat\,(map\,(map\;f)\;xss)
\end{aligned}
$$

for every function f and g, finite list xs, and finite list of finite lists xss.

5.3.6 Prove the law:

$$takewhile \ p \ xs \ +\!\!\!+ \ dropwhile \ p \ xs \ = \ xs$$

for every total predicate p and finite list xs.

5.3.7 Prove the laws:

$$
\begin{aligned}
(xs +\!\!\!+ ys) \, ! \, i &= xs \, ! \, i, & \textbf{if } i < \#xs \\
(xs +\!\!\!+ ys) \, ! \, i &= ys \, ! \, (i - \#xs), & \textbf{if } i \geq \#xs
\end{aligned}
$$

for every finite list xs and ys and every natural number i. (*Hint:* The second law will be easier to prove if it is rewritten in terms of j, where $j = i - \#xs$.)

5.3.8 Let *interval1* stand for the special form $[1 .. n]$. Show that the definition:

$$
\begin{aligned}
interval1 \ 0 &= [\,] \\
interval1 \ (n+1) &= 1 : map \ (+1) \ (interval1 \ n)
\end{aligned}
$$

follows from the definition of *interval* and the law given in the text.

5.3.9 Prove that if $k \leq m \leq n$ then:

$$interval \ k \ m \ +\!\!\!+ \ interval \ (m+1) \ n = interval \ k \ n$$

for every integer k, m, and n. Is the same law valid if k, m, and n are not restricted to integers? Explain why. [*Hint:* An obvious decomposition is to use the cases $k > m$ and $k \leq m$. This turns out not to be helpful, since we are given that $k \leq m$ in the statement of the law. Use the cases $k + 1 > m$ and $k + 1 \leq m$ instead.]

5.3.10 Let (*interval3 a b c*) stand for the special form $[a, b .. c]$. Give a recursive definition of *interval3*.

5.4 Auxiliaries and generalisation

Sometimes, instead of defining a function or proving a theorem directly, it is convenient or necessary to first define some other function or prove some other result. In other words, we may need to consider *auxiliary* definitions or theorems. In other situations, we can sometimes make our task easier by trying to define a more general function or prove a more general result. In other words, we may need to *generalise* definitions or theorems. In this section we shall look at some examples of these techniques.

5.4.1　List difference

The value of $xs -\!- ys$ is the list that results when, for each element y in ys, the first occurrence (if any) of y is removed from xs. A recursive definition of list difference is:

$$
\begin{aligned}
xs -\!- [\,] \quad &= \quad xs \\
xs -\!- (y : ys) \quad &= \quad remove\ xs\ y -\!- ys \\[1em]
remove\ [\,]\ y \quad &= \quad [\,] \\
remove\ (x : xs)\ y \quad &= \quad xs, \qquad\qquad\quad \textbf{if } x = y \\
&= \quad x : remove\ xs\ y, \quad \textbf{otherwise}
\end{aligned}
$$

Here it is convenient to define $(-\!-)$ using an auxiliary function, *remove*. The value of *remove xs y* is the result when the first occurrence (if any) of y is removed from xs. Thus, *remove* corresponds exactly to one phrase in the English language description of $xs -\!- ys$ given above.

An important law about list difference is that:

$$(xs +\!\!+ ys) -\!- xs = ys$$

for every finite list xs and ys. The proof of this law is straightforward using the techniques described in the previous sections, and is left as an exercise.

5.4.2　Reverse

One way to define the function that reverses the elements of a list is as follows:

$$
\begin{aligned}
reverse\ [\,] \quad &= \quad [\,] \\
reverse\ (x : xs) \quad &= \quad reverse\ xs +\!\!+ [x]
\end{aligned}
$$

Let us now prove that:

$$reverse\ (reverse\ xs) = xs$$

for every finite list xs.

Proof. The proof requires an auxiliary result, namely that:

$$reverse\ (ys +\!\!+ [x]) = x : reverse\ ys$$

for every x and every finite list ys. We will first prove the auxiliary result, and then prove the main result. The auxiliary is proved by induction on ys.

Case $[\,]$. We have:

$$reverse\ ([\,] +\!\!+ [x]) = [x] = x : reverse\ [\,]$$

which establishes the case.

Case $(y : ys)$. We have:

$$
\begin{aligned}
reverse\,(y : ys \mathbin{+\!\!+} [x]) &= reverse\,(ys \mathbin{+\!\!+} [x]) \mathbin{+\!\!+} [y] && (reverse.2) \\
&= x : reverse\ ys \mathbin{+\!\!+} [y] && (\text{hypothesis}) \\
&= x : reverse\,(y : ys) && (reverse.2)
\end{aligned}
$$

which establishes the case.

Here we have simplified the proof a little. For example, we have written $(y : ys \mathbin{+\!\!+} [x])$ for both $((y : ys) \mathbin{+\!\!+} [x])$ and $(y : (ys \mathbin{+\!\!+} [x]))$, which is valid by $(\mathbin{+\!\!+}.2)$. By now the reader should be familiar with the basic proof techniques, so that this simplification causes no confusion.

Having proved the auxiliary, we now turn to the proof of the main result. The proof is by induction on xs.

Case $[\,]$. We have:

$$reverse\,(reverse\,[\,]) = reverse\,[\,] = [\,]$$

which establishes the case.

Case $(x : xs)$. We have:

$$
\begin{aligned}
reverse\,(reverse\,(x : xs)) &= reverse\,(reverse\ xs \mathbin{+\!\!+} [x]) && (reverse.2) \\
&= x : reverse\,(reverse\ xs) && (\text{auxiliary}) \\
&= x : xs && (\text{hypothesis})
\end{aligned}
$$

which establishes the case, and completes the proof. $\square$

In the main proof, the only place that the auxiliary result was used was to demonstrate that:

$$reverse\,(reverse\ xs \mathbin{+\!\!+} [x]) = x : reverse\,(reverse\ xs)$$

Trying to prove this result directly does not work, as the reader may verify. This is where generalisation comes in. By replacing the subexpression *reverse xs* with a new variable ys we get a *more general* result, which is *easier* to prove. Indeed, as we saw above, the proof of the generalised result is now straightforward.

How does one decide when an auxiliary result is needed, and how to strengthen a potential auxiliary result? There are no hard and fast answers to these questions, which is why constructing programs and proofs can be an interesting and challenging task. However, the suggestions that follow may be useful.

One way to discover the auxiliary result is by intuition. Since $(x : xs)$ is equivalent to $([x] \mathbin{+\!\!+} xs)$ we might choose to rewrite (*reverse.2*) in the form:

$$reverse\,([x] \mathbin{+\!\!+} xs) = reverse\ xs \mathbin{+\!\!+} [x]$$

in order to emphasise the similarity. From here it is a small leap to conjecture that:

$$reverse\ (xs \mathbin{+\mkern-8mu+} [x]) = [x] \mathbin{+\mkern-8mu+} reverse\ xs$$

and this is the required auxiliary result.

We can also discover this result in a different way, by extending the method of discovering a proof described in Section 5.2. There we saw that a proof can be constructed by a combination of induction and simplification. We start with the equation:

$$reverse\ (reverse\ xs) = xs$$

and apply this technique. First, replace xs by $(x : xs)$. Next, simplify the left-hand side by applying $(reverse.2)$ and the right-hand side by applying the induction hypothesis. This yields:

$$reverse\ (reverse\ xs \mathbin{+\mkern-8mu+} [x]) = x : reverse\ (reverse\ xs)$$

which is our potential auxiliary result. As mentioned above, it is difficult to prove this result directly, so it needs to be strengthened. A standard method of generalisation is to look for a sub-expression that appears on both sides of the equation and replace it by a variable. A sub-expression that appears on both sides of the above is $reverse\ xs$, and we have already seen that replacing this by the variable y gives the equation:

$$reverse\ (ys \mathbin{+\mkern-8mu+} [x]) = x : reverse\ ys$$

which is just what is wanted. This method of simplification followed by generalisation is used by some automated theorem proving systems (see, for example, Boyer and Moore [4]).

5.4.3   Second duality theorem

Recall that the informal definitions of fold left and fold right were as follows:

$$foldr\ (\oplus)\ a\ [x_1, x_2, \ldots, x_n] = x_1 \oplus (x_2 \oplus (\cdots (x_n \oplus a) \cdots))$$
$$foldl\ (\oplus)\ a\ [x_1, x_2, \ldots, x_n] = (\cdots ((a \oplus x_1) \oplus x_2) \cdots) \oplus x_n$$

The equivalent formal definitions are:

$$foldr\ (\oplus)\ a\ [\,] = a$$
$$foldr\ (\oplus)\ a\ (x : xs) = x \oplus (foldr\ (\oplus)\ a\ xs)$$

$$foldl\ (\oplus)\ a\ [\,] = a$$
$$foldl\ (\oplus)\ a\ (x : xs) = foldl\ (\oplus)\ (a \oplus x)\ xs$$

The reader should take a moment to check that the formal definitions do indeed correspond to the informal definitions.

The second duality theorem (see Section 3.5.1) is as follows: let $(\oplus)$ and $(\otimes)$ be two binary operators and a a value such that:

$$
\begin{aligned}
x \oplus (y \otimes z) &= (x \oplus y) \otimes z \quad \text{(i)} \\
x \oplus a &= a \otimes x \quad \text{(ii)}
\end{aligned}
$$

for every x, y, and z. Then:

$$foldr\,(\oplus)\,a\,xs = foldl\,(\otimes)\,a\,xs$$

for every finite list xs.

Proof. The proof requires an auxiliary result, namely that:

$$x \oplus foldl\,(\otimes)\,y\,xs = foldl\,(\otimes)\,(x \oplus y)\,xs$$

for every x and y and every finite list xs. We will first prove the auxiliary result, and then prove the main result. The auxiliary is proved by induction on xs.

Case [ ]. We have:

$$
\begin{aligned}
x \oplus foldl\,(\otimes)\,y\,[\,] &= x \oplus y & (foldl.1) \\
&= foldl\,(\otimes)\,(x \oplus y)\,[\,] & (foldl.1)
\end{aligned}
$$

which establishes the case.

Case $(x' : xs)$. (To avoid confusion with the variable x that is already part of the formula, we replace xs by $(x' : xs)$ instead of $(x : xs)$.) We have:

$$
\begin{aligned}
x \oplus foldl\,(\otimes)\,y\,(x' : xs) &= x \oplus foldl\,(\otimes)\,(y \otimes x')\,xs & (foldl.2) \\
&= foldl\,(\otimes)\,(x \oplus (y \otimes x'))\,xs & \text{(hypothesis)} \\
&= foldl\,(\otimes)\,((x \oplus y) \otimes x')\,xs & \text{(i)} \\
&= foldl\,(\otimes)\,(x \oplus y)\,(x' : xs) & (foldl.2)
\end{aligned}
$$

which establishes the case. Note that the hypothesis applies here because it holds for *any* y; in this case, y matches the term $(y \otimes x')$.

Having proved the auxiliary, we now turn to the proof of the main result. The proof is by induction on xs.

Case [ ]. We have:

$$foldr\,(\oplus)\,a\,[\,] = a = foldr\,(\otimes)\,a\,[\,]$$

by $(foldl.1, foldr.1)$, which establishes the case.

Case $(x : xs)$. We have:

$$
\begin{aligned}
foldr \,(\oplus)\, a \,(x : xs) &= x \oplus foldr \,(\oplus)\, a \; xs & (foldr.2) \\
&= x \oplus foldl \,(\otimes)\, a \; xs & \text{(hypothesis)} \\
&= foldl \,(\otimes)\, (x \oplus a) \; xs & \text{(auxiliary)} \\
&= foldl \,(\otimes)\, (a \otimes x) \; xs & \text{(ii)} \\
&= foldl \,(\otimes)\, a \,(x : xs) & (foldl.2)
\end{aligned}
$$

which establishes the case, and completes the proof. $\Box$

In the main proof, the only place that the auxiliary result was used was to demonstrate that:

$$ x \oplus foldl \,(\otimes)\, a \; xs = foldl \,(\otimes)\, (x \oplus a) \; xs $$

This was generalised by replacing the value a by the variable y. One might expect that this would make the proof *harder*, because there is a property of a that might be used in the proof (namely, it satisfies law (ii) above) but y has no special properties. But in fact it makes the proof *easier* because it makes the induction hypothesis more widely applicable. In the proof of the auxiliary result given above, the induction hypothesis was invoked with y replaced by $(y \otimes x')$, and this was possible exactly because we had generalised the auxiliary.

5.4.4 Fast reverse

The next example again involves the reverse function, and is motivated by considerations of efficiency.

We can think of a computation as consisting of a number of *reduction steps*, where each reduction step consists of applying one equation in the definition of a function. For example, computing $[3, 2] +\!\!+ [1]$ requires three reduction steps:

$$
\begin{aligned}
{[3, 2]} +\!\!+ [1] &= 3 : ([2] +\!\!+ [1]) & (+\!\!+.2) \\
&= 3 : (2 : ([\,] +\!\!+ [1])) & (+\!\!+.2) \\
&= 3 : (2 : [1]) & (+\!\!+.1) \\
&= [3, 2, 1]
\end{aligned}
$$

The last line is *not* a reduction step; it is just a different way of writing down exactly the same structure. (Inside the computer, both $3 : (2 : [1])$ and $[3, 2, 1]$ are represented as $3 : (2 : (1 : [\,]))$.) In general, if xs has length n then computing $xs +\!\!+ ys$ will require n reductions by $(+\!\!+.2)$ followed by a single reduction of $(+\!\!+.1)$; so the number of reduction is roughly proportional to n.

Similarly, computation of *reverse* [1, 2, 3] requires ten reduction steps:

$$
\begin{aligned}
\textit{reverse}\ [1,2,3] \quad &= \quad \textit{reverse}\ [2,3] \mathbin{+\!\!+} [1] & (\textit{reverse}.2)\\
&= \quad (\textit{reverse}\ [3] \mathbin{+\!\!+} [2]) \mathbin{+\!\!+} [1] & (\textit{reverse}.2)\\
&= \quad ((\textit{reverse}\ [\,] \mathbin{+\!\!+} [3]) \mathbin{+\!\!+} [2]) \mathbin{+\!\!+} [1] & (\textit{reverse}.2)\\
&= \quad (([\,] \mathbin{+\!\!+} [3]) \mathbin{+\!\!+} [2]) \mathbin{+\!\!+} [1] & (\textit{reverse}.1)\\
&= \quad ([3] \mathbin{+\!\!+} [2]) \mathbin{+\!\!+} [1] & (\mathbin{+\!\!+}.1)\\
&= \quad [3,2] \mathbin{+\!\!+} [1] & (\mathbin{+\!\!+}.2, \mathbin{+\!\!+}.1)\\
&= \quad [3,2,1] & (\mathbin{+\!\!+}.2, \mathbin{+\!\!+}.2, \mathbin{+\!\!+}.1)
\end{aligned}
$$

In general, if xs has length n then computing *reverse* xs will require n reductions by (*reverse*.2), followed by one reduction by (*reverse*.1), followed by:

$$
1 + 2 + \cdots + n = \frac{n(n-1)}{2}
$$

reduction steps to perform the concatenations, so the number of reduction steps is roughly proportional to n^2.

It would be better to be able to compute *reverse* xs with a number of reduction steps that is proportional to n rather than to n^2. The following program has this performance:

$$
\begin{aligned}
\textit{rev}\ xs \qquad\qquad\ &= \quad \textit{shunt}\ [\,]\ xs\\[4pt]
\textit{shunt}\ ys\ [\,] \qquad &= \quad ys\\
\textit{shunt}\ ys\ (x:xs) &= \quad \textit{shunt}\ (x:ys)\ xs
\end{aligned}
$$

The definition uses an auxiliary function *shunt*. This definition is equivalent to the previous one. That is, we can prove that:

$$
\textit{rev}\ xs = \textit{reverse}\ xs
$$

for every list xs. In order to prove this, we will need to prove an auxiliary result about the auxiliary function, namely that:

$$
\textit{shunt}\ ys\ xs = \textit{reverse}\ xs \mathbin{+\!\!+} ys
$$

for every finite list xs and ys. The proof is a straightforward induction on xs and is left to the reader.

For example, *rev* [1, 2, 3] is computed as follows:

$$
\begin{aligned}
\textit{rev}\ [1,2,3] \quad &= \quad \textit{shunt}\ [\,]\ [1,2,3] & (\textit{rev}.1)\\
&= \quad \textit{shunt}\ [1]\ [2,3] & (\textit{shunt}.2)\\
&= \quad \textit{shunt}\ [2,1]\ [3] & (\textit{shunt}.2)\\
&= \quad \textit{shunt}\ [3,2,1]\ [\,] & (\textit{shunt}.2)\\
&= \quad [3,2,1] & (\textit{shunt}.1)
\end{aligned}
$$

It is easy to see that computing *rev* xs requires $n + 2$ reduction steps, where n is the length of xs.

The key to the improvement in performance is to solve a harder problem. The auxiliary function call *shunt ys xs* doesn't just reverse the list *xs*, it also concatenates it to the list *ys*. This is a useful thing to do because in the original definition, *reverse* $(x : xs)$ reduces to *reverse xs* $+\!\!+ [x]$. Combining the reverse operation with concatenation is what allows for the greater efficiency.

5.4.5   Fast Fibonacci

Again motivated by efficiency concerns, we now consider an efficient way of computing Fibonacci numbers.

The function *fib n*, which returns the nth Fibonacci number, was defined previously as follows:

$$
\begin{aligned}
\textit{fib } 0 \quad\quad &= \quad 0 \\
\textit{fib } 1 \quad\quad &= \quad 1 \\
\textit{fib } (n+2) \quad &= \quad \textit{fib } n + \textit{fib } (n+1)
\end{aligned}
$$

How many reduction steps does it take to compute *fib n*? If we write $T(n)$ for the number of reduction steps to compute *fib n* (the T stands for "time"), then the above definition implies the following:

$$
\begin{aligned}
T(0) \quad &= \quad 1 \\
T(1) \quad &= \quad 1 \\
T(n+2) \quad &= \quad T(n) + T(n+1) + 1
\end{aligned}
$$

The first two equations state that computing *fib* 0 or *fib* 1 requires a single reduction step, and the third equation states that computing *fib* $(n + 2)$ requires the steps to compute *fib n* and the steps to compute *fib* $(n + 1)$ and one more step (to apply the rule (*fib*.3) initially). Solving these equations gives $T(n) = 2 \times \textit{fib } (n + 1) - 1$, which is easy to verify by induction. Thus, the number of reduction steps to compute *fib n* is roughly proportional to the value of *fib n*.

It is preferable to compute *fib n* in only n steps. The following definition does so:

$$
\begin{aligned}
\textit{fastfib } n \quad\quad\quad &= \quad \textit{fst } (\textit{twofib } n) \\[4pt]
\textit{twofib } 0 \quad\quad\quad &= \quad (0, 1) \\
\textit{twofib } (n+1) \quad &= \quad (b, a + b) \\
&\quad\ \ \mathbf{where}\ \ (a, b) = \textit{twofib } n
\end{aligned}
$$

The key to understanding this definition is the fact:

$$
\textit{twofib } n = (\textit{fib } n, \textit{fib } (n + 1))
$$

which is easy to prove by induction, and from which it follows immediately that *fastfib n* = *fib n* for every natural number n. Here the key to efficiency is again to solve a harder problem. Rather than just compute *fib n*, it is more efficient to compute *fib n* and *fib* $(n + 1)$ at the same time.

Exercises

5.4.1 Prove that:
$$(xs \mathbin{+\!\!+} ys) -- xs = ys$$
for every finite list xs and ys.

5.4.2 Prove that:
$$reverse \, (xs \mathbin{+\!\!+} ys) = reverse \, ys \mathbin{+\!\!+} reverse \, xs$$
for every finite list xs and ys.

5.4.3 Prove that:
$$foldr \, f \, a \, (xs \mathbin{+\!\!+} ys) = foldr \, f \, (foldr \, f \, a \, ys) \, xs$$
for every function f, value a, and finite list xs and ys.

5.4.4 Prove that if $\tilde{f} \, x \, y = f \, y \, x$ for every x and y, then:
$$foldr \, f \, a \, xs = foldl \, \tilde{f} \, a \, (reverse \, xs)$$
for every function f, value a, and finite list xs.

5.4.5 Let $\oplus$ be associative with identity a, and define h by:
$$h = foldr \, (\oplus) \, a$$
Prove that:
$$
\begin{aligned}
h \, (xs \mathbin{+\!\!+} ys) &= (h \, xs) \oplus (h \, ys) \\
h \, (concat \, xss) &= h \, (map \, h \, xss)
\end{aligned}
$$
for every finite list xs and ys and every finite list of finite lists xss.

5.5 Program synthesis

In program proof, we begin by giving a program, and then demonstrate that it satisfies some property. In program synthesis, we begin by giving a specification, and then synthesise a program that satisfies it. Since a specification is simply a property we require a program to satisfy, these activities are clearly related.

Both methods require essentially the same reasoning. Often a proof can be converted into a synthesis just by changing the order of a few steps, and vice versa. But in program proof we must, as it were, create appropriate definitions out of thin air, whereas in program synthesis the definition is constructed in a systematic way. Thus synthesis is preferable when it can be

used. Here, we show how two of the inductive proofs considered previously
can be recast as syntheses of recursive definitions.

Initial segment.   In Section 5.3.4, we saw a recursive definition of *init*,
which was followed by a proof of the law that:

$$init\ xs = take\ (\#xs - 1)\ xs$$

for every non-empty finite list *xs*. We will now turn things around, and show
how the recursive definition can be synthesised, taking the above equation as
a specification.

The synthesis is by instantiation of *xs*. The two cases considered are [*x*]
and (*x* : *x'* : *xs*). This is valid since every non-empty list must have one of
these two forms.

Case [*x*]. We have:

$$
\begin{aligned}
init\ [x] &= take\ (\#[x] - 1)\ [x] &&(\text{instantiation})\\
&= [\,] &&(\#, take)
\end{aligned}
$$

which gives the first equation.

Case (*x* : *x'* : *xs*). We have:

$$
\begin{aligned}
init\ (x &: x' : xs)\\
&= take\ (\#(x : x' : xs) - 1)\ (x : x' : xs) &&(\text{instantiation})\\
&= take\ (\#xs + 1)\ (x : x' : xs) &&(\#.2, \text{arithmetic})\\
&= x : take\ (\#xs)\ (x' : xs) &&(take.3)\\
&= x : take\ (\#(x' : xs) - 1)\ (x' : xs) &&(\#.2, \text{arithmetic})\\
&= x : init\ (x' : xs) &&(\text{hypothesis})
\end{aligned}
$$

which gives the second equation.

Collecting the equations together we have:

$$
\begin{aligned}
init\ [x] &= [\,]\\
init\ (x : x' : xs) &= x : init\ (x' : xs)
\end{aligned}
$$

which is, of course, the same definition given previously.

There are many similarities between the proof given in Section 5.3.4 and
the synthesis given here. Both use the same case analysis, and examination
shows that the same equations with (essentially) the same justifications appear in both, though in a different order. Furthermore, both are equally
hard – or easy – to construct. This makes the synthesis something of a bar-
gain, since instead of requiring us to specify the recursive definition of *init*
in advance, it yields the definition as the result of systematic reasoning.

Also, note that (with one exception) each line of the above synthesis is
derived by simplifying the previous line. The exception is the second to

last line, where $(\#xs)$ is changed to $(\#(x' : xs) - 1)$, in order to provide a better "fit" against the given specification. Thus, as with many proofs, many syntheses consist of a proper choice of case analysis, followed (mainly) by simplification.

Fast Fibonacci. In Section 5.4.5, we saw a definition that can be used to compute $fib\ n$, the nth Fibonacci number, in about n steps, whereas the traditional definition requires about $fib\ n$ steps. The key idea was to define a function $twofib$ such that:

$$twofib\ n = (fib\ n, fib\ (n+1))$$

This allows for improved efficiency because one has available the value of two successive Fibonacci numbers when calculating the next one.

Previously the definition of $twofib$ was given and it was asserted that it was easy to prove the above equation from the definition. Clearly, it would be better to start with the equation, and then synthesise a definition of $twofib$ that satisfies it. That is what we shall do now.

The synthesis is by instantiation of n.

Case 0. We have:

$$
\begin{aligned}
twofib\ 0 \ &= \ (fib\ 0, fib\ 1) \quad \text{(instantiation)} \\
&= \ (0,1) \qquad\quad (fib.1, fib.2)
\end{aligned}
$$

which gives the first equation.

Case $(n+1)$. We have:

$$
\begin{aligned}
twofib\ (n+1) \ &= \ (fib\ (n+1), fib\ (n+2)) &&\text{(instantiation)} \\
&= \ (fib\ (n+1), fib\ n + fib\ (n+1)) &&(fib.3) \\
&= \ (b, a+b) &&\text{(rearrangement)} \\
&\quad \textbf{where}\ (a,b) = (fib\ n, fib\ (n+1)) \\
&= \ (b, a+b) &&\text{(hypothesis)} \\
&\quad \textbf{where}\ (a,b) = twofib\ n
\end{aligned}
$$

which gives the second equation.

Gathering the two equations together with the definition of $fastfib$, we have:

$$
\begin{aligned}
fastfib\ n \quad &= \quad fst\ (twofib\ n) \\[4pt]
twofib\ 0 \quad &= \quad (0,1) \\
twofib\ (n+1) \quad &= \quad (b, a+b) \\
&\qquad \textbf{where}\ (a,b) = twofib\ n
\end{aligned}
$$

just as before. It follows immediately from the initial law that $fastfib\ n = fib\ n$, as required.

Exercises

5.5.1 Synthesise the recursive definition of concatenate from the specification:

$$xs \mathbin{+\!\!+} ys = foldr \; (:) \; ys \; xs$$

for every finite list xs and ys.

5.5.2 Synthesise the recursive definition of length from the specification:

$$\#xs = sum \; (map \; (const \; 1) \; xs)$$

for every finite list xs. Do this once taking $sum = foldr(+)0$, and again taking $sum = foldl \; (+) \; 0$. (*Hint:* The second case requires an auxiliary function.)

5.5.3 The association list function $assoc$ is defined as follows:

$$assoc \; xys \; x \;\; = \;\; hd \; [y \mid (x',y) \leftarrow xys; \; x' = x]$$

Synthesise a recursive definition of $assoc$. (*Hint:* First translate the list comprehension in the definition of $assoc$ to be in terms of map and $filter$, using the method in Section 3.4.)

5.5.4 Synthesise the recursive definitions of list subtraction and $remove$ from the specification:

$$
\begin{aligned}
xs \mathbin{-\!\!-} ys \;\; &= \;\; foldl \; remove \; xs \; ys \\
remove \; xs \; y \;\; &= \;\; takewhile \; (\neq y) \; xs \mathbin{+\!\!+} drop \; 1 \; (dropwhile \; (\neq y) \; xs)
\end{aligned}
$$

for every y and every finite list xs and ys.

5.5.5 Synthesise the recursive definitions of $take$ and $drop$ from the specification:

$$take \; n \; xs \mathbin{+\!\!+} drop \; n \; xs = xs$$
$$\#(take \; n \; xs) = n \min (\#xs)$$

for every natural number n and every finite list xs.

5.6 Combinatorial functions

Many interesting problems are *combinatorial* in nature, that is, they involve selecting or permuting elements of a list in some desired manner. This section describes several combinatorial functions of widespread utility.

Initial segments. The function *inits* returns the list of all initial segments of a list, in order of increasing length. For example:

? *inits* "era"
["", "e", "er", "era"]

? *map sum* (*inits* [1 .. 5])
[0, 1, 3, 6, 10, 15]

Notice that:

$$scan\ f\ a\ xs = map\ (foldl\ f\ a)\ (inits\ xs)$$

provides one way to define the scan operation. If xs has length n, then $inits\,xs$ will have length $n + 1$.

A recursive definition of $inits$ is:

$$
\begin{aligned}
inits\ [\,] \quad &= \quad [[\,]] \\
inits\ (x : xs) \quad &= \quad [[\,]] + \!\!+ \ map\ (x\ :) (inits\ xs)
\end{aligned}
$$

The empty list has only one initial segment, namely itself; hence the first equation. A non-empty list $(x : xs)$ will still have the empty list as an initial segment, and its other initial segments will begin with an x and be followed by an initial segment of xs; hence the second equation.

Subsequences. The function $subs$ returns a list of all subsequences of a list. For example:

? $subs$ "era"
["", "a", "r", "ra", "e", "ea", "er", "era"]

The ordering of this list is a consequence of the particular definition of $subs$ given below. If xs has length n, then $subs\ xs$ has length 2^n. This can be seen by noting that each of the n elements in xs might be either present or absent in a subsequence, so there are $2 \times \cdots \times 2$ (n times) possibilities.

A recursive definition of $subs$ is:

$$
\begin{aligned}
subs\ [\,] \quad &= \quad [[\,]] \\
subs\ (x : xs) \quad &= \quad subs\ xs + \!\!+ \ map\ (x\ :) (subs\ xs)
\end{aligned}
$$

That is, the empty list has one subsequence, namely itself. A non-empty list $(x : xs)$ has as subsequences all the subsequences of xs, together with those sequences formed by following x with each possible subsequence of xs. Notice that this definition differs from that of $inits$ in only one place, but has a considerably different meaning.

Interleave. The term $interleave\ x\ ys$ returns a list of all possible ways of inserting the element x into the list ys. For example:

? $interleave$ 'e' "ar"
["ear", "aer", "are"]

If ys has length n, then $interleave\ x\ ys$ has length $n + 1$.

A recursive definition of $interleave$ is:

$$
\begin{aligned}
interleave\ x\ [\,] \quad &= \quad [[x]] \\
interleave\ x\ (y : ys) \quad &= \quad [x : y : ys] + \!\!+ \ map\ (y\ :) (interleave\ x\ ys)
\end{aligned}
$$

That is, there is only one way of interleaving x into an empty list, namely the list containing just x. The ways of interleaving x into a non-empty list

$(y : ys)$ are either to begin the list with x and follow it with $(y : ys)$, or to begin the list with y and follow it with an interleaving of x into ys.

Alternatively, a non-recursive definition is given by:

$$interleave\ x\ ys\ =\ [take\ i\ ys \mathbin{+\!\!+} [x] \mathbin{+\!\!+} drop\ i\ ys \mid i \leftarrow [0 \mathbin{..} \#ys]]$$

It is an interesting exercise to synthesize the recursive definition from the non-recursive one.

Permutations. The function *perms* returns a list of all permutations of a list. For example:

? *perms* "era"
["era", "rea", "rae", "ear", "aer", "are"]

If xs has length n, then *perm* xs has length $n! = n \times (n-1) \times \cdots \times 1$. This can be seen by noting that any of the n elements of xs may appear in the first position, and then any of the remaining $n-1$ elements may appear in the second position, and so on, until finally there is only one element that may appear in the last position.

A recursive definition of *perms* can be made using the function *interleave* defined in the previous section:

$$\begin{aligned} perms\ [] \quad &= \quad [[]] \\ perms\ (x : xs) \quad &= \quad concat\ (map\ (interleave\ x)\ (perms\ xs)) \end{aligned}$$

That is, there is only one permutation of the empty list, namely itself. The permutations of the non-empty list $(x : xs)$ are all ways of interleaving x into a permutation of xs.

The use of *concat* in the above definition is essential. This can be seen by considering types. The types of *perms* and *interleave* are:

$$\begin{aligned} perms \quad &:: \quad [\alpha] \rightarrow [[\alpha]] \\ interleave \quad &:: \quad \alpha \rightarrow [\alpha] \rightarrow [[\alpha]] \end{aligned}$$

Assuming $x :: \alpha$ and $xs :: [\alpha]$, we have:

$$(map\ (interleave\ x)\ (perms\ xs)) \quad :: \quad [[[\alpha]]]$$

So we must apply *concat* to the result of the map, to turn the value of type $[[[\alpha]]]$ into a value of type $[[\alpha]]$.

The second equation defining *perms* can also be written with a list comprehension:

$$perms\ (x : xs)\ =\ [zs \mid ys \leftarrow perms\ xs;\ zs \leftarrow interleave\ x\ ys]$$

The method in Section 3.4 can be used to translate this into the equation given previously.

One recipe for sorting a list is to examine all permutations of it and choose the first that is sorted in non-decreasing order:

$$sort \; xs \quad = \quad hd \; [ys \mid ys \leftarrow perms \; xs; \; nondec \; xs]$$
$$nondec \; xs \quad = \quad and \; [x \leq y \mid (x, y) \leftarrow zip \; (xs, tl \; xs)]$$

This definition of sorting, although correct, is extremely inefficient.

Partitions. A list of lists xss is a *partition* of a list xs if:

$$concat \; xss = xs$$

For example, ["era"] and ["e", "ra"] and ["e", "", "r", "", "a"] are all partitions of "era". In general, the partition of a list can be arbitrarily long, since it may contain any number of empty lists. We say that xss is a *proper partition* of xs if it is a partition and it contains no empty lists.

The function *parts* returns a list of all proper partitions of a list. For example:

? *parts* "era"
[["era"], ["er", "a"], ["e", "ra"], ["e", "r", "a"]]

If xs has length n then *parts* xs has length 2^{n-1}. This can be seen by noting that there are $n - 1$ places where a break might occur (between each element of the list xs) and for each place there are two possibilities (either a break occurs there or it does not).

A recursive definition of *parts* is given by:

$$
\begin{aligned}
parts \; [\,] \quad &= \quad [[\,]] \\
parts \; [x] \quad &= \quad [[[x]]] \\
parts \; (x : (x' : xs)) \quad &= \quad map \; (glue \; x) \; (parts \; (x' : xs)) \\
&\quad \mathbin{+\!\!+} \; map \; ([x] \; :) \; (parts \; (x' : xs)) \\
\\
glue \; x \; xss \quad &= \quad (x : hd \; xss) : tl \; xss
\end{aligned}
$$

The empty sequence has one partition, namely [], consisting of an empty sequence of sublists. A sequence of length one, [x], has exactly one partition, namely [[x]], and the list containing this one partition is [[[x]]]. A sequence of length two or more, $(x : (x' : xs))$, may have its partitions formed in two ways. Namely, if yss is a partition of $(x' : xs)$, then $glue \; x \; yss$ and [x] : yss will both be partitions of the original list. Notice that we can guarantee that $glue \; x \; yss$ exists since $(x' : xs)$ has at least length one so yss is non-empty. Further, every element in the partition yss must be non-empty, so in particular the first element is non-empty and therefore $glue \; x \; yss$ must be a different partition than [x] : yss.

A completely different way of generating the partitions of a list is as follows. Above we noted that if xs is a list of length n, then each partition of xs can be generated by choosing whether or not to break at each of the $n-1$ places between elements of xs. We can represent this choice by a list containing only numbers in the range 0 to $n-1$ and sorted in ascending order. For example, the list $[1,4]$ corresponds to the partition $[\text{“a”}, \text{“bcd”}, \text{“ef”}]$ of the list "abcdef".

Based on this idea, we have the following definition of partitions:

$$
\begin{aligned}
parts\ xs \quad &= \quad [break\ ks\ xs \mid ks \leftarrow subs\,[1\,..\,n-1]] \\
&\textbf{where}\ n \ = \ \#xs \\
break\ ks\ xs \quad &= \quad [sublist\ i\ j\ xs \mid (i,j) \leftarrow zip\,([0] +\!\!+ ks, ks +\!\!+ [n])] \\
&\textbf{where}\ n \ = \ \#xs \\
sublist\ i\ j\ xs \quad &= \quad drop\ i\,(take\ j\ xs)
\end{aligned}
$$

Here $sublist\ i\ j\ xs$ returns elements $i+1$ through j of xs, for example, ($sublist\ 1\ 4$ "abcdef") returns "bcd". The term ($break\ ks\ xs$) returns the partition of xs corresponding to ks, for example, ($break\ [1,4]$ "abcdef") returns $[\text{“a”}, \text{“bcd”}, \text{“ef”}]$, which are the $(0,1)$, $(1,4)$ and $(4,6)$ sublists of "abcdef".

We noted previously that $subs\ xs$ has length 2^n when xs has length n, so the alternative definition of $parts$ confirms the result that $parts\ xs$ has length 2^{n-1} when xs has length n. It is left to the exercises to prove that the two different definitions of $parts$ are indeed equivalent.

Exercises

5.6.1 The function $segs\ xs$ returns a list of all contiguous segments in a list. For example:

? $segs$ "list"
[“”, “t”, “s”, “st”, “i”, “is”, “ist”, “l”, “li”, “lis”, “list”]

Give a recursive definition of $segs$. If xs has length n, what is the length of $segs\ xs$?

5.6.2 The function $choose\ k\ xs$ returns a list of all subsequences of xs whose length is exactly k. For example:

? $choose\ 3$ "list"
[“ist”, “lst”, “lit”, “lis”]

Give a recursive definition of $choose$. Show that if xs has length n then $choose\ k\ xs$ has length nk (see Exercise 5.1.3).

5.6.3 Prove that:

$$
subs\,(map\ f\ xs) \quad = \quad map\,(map\ f)\,(subs\ xs)
$$

for every function f and finite list xs. What are the corresponding laws for $inits$, $perms$, and $parts$?

5.6.4 Derive the recursive definition of *interleave* from the definition in terms of list comprehensions. (*Hint:* Use the result of Exercise 5.3.8, modified to give a recursive definition of $[0 .. n]$.)

5.6.5 Prove that the two definitions of *parts* given in Section 5.6 are equivalent. (*Hint:* First, synthesise the following recursive definition of *breaks*:

$$
\begin{aligned}
breaks \, [\,] \, xs \quad &= \quad [xs] \\
breaks \, (k : ks) \, xs \quad &= \quad take \, k \, xs : \\
&\qquad breaks \, (map \, (+(-k)) \, ks) \, (drop \, k \, xs)
\end{aligned}
$$

Next, use this definition to prove the following two lemmas:

$$
\begin{aligned}
break \, (map \, (+1) \, ks) \, (x : xs) \quad &= \quad glue \, x \, (break \, ks \, xs) \\
break \, (1 : map \, (+1) \, ks) \, (x : xs) \quad &= \quad [x] : break \, ks \, xs
\end{aligned}
$$

Then use Exercises 5.3.8 and 5.6.3 to prove the final result.)

Chapter 6

Efficiency

So far, we have concentrated mainly on developing an expressive language, on proving properties of programs, and on deriving programs from specifications. Only occasionally have we considered the question of how efficiently such programs run. The time has come to focus on this important issue. This chapter describes some fundamental techniques used to model the efficiency of programs, discusses the efficiency of some common patterns of computation, and presents two important techniques for writing efficient programs.

6.1 Asymptotic behaviour

We have already seen several examples of programs that perform the same task but have different efficiencies. For instance, Sections 5.4.2 and 5.4.4 described two programs for reversing lists. If the list xs has length n, then *reverse xs* requires a number of steps proportional to n^2 to compute the reversed list, while *rev xs* only requires a number of steps proportional to n.

The awkward phrase 'number of steps proportional to' has appeared in this book wherever efficiency is discussed. Fortunately, a less cumbersome mathematical notation exists. First, we adopt the convention that $T_f(x)$ stands for the number of reduction steps to compute $(f x)$, that is, the number of steps required to reduce $(f\ x)$ to canonical form. The 'T' is short for 'time', since the number of reduction steps is generally proportional to the time required to perform a computation. The number of reduction steps is measured with respect to the graph reduction model of computation, which is discussed in more detail in the next section.

Second, we use the O-notation, which allows us to write the two statements above as follows:

$$
\begin{aligned}
T_{reverse}(xs) &= O(n^2) \\
T_{rev}(xs) &= O(n)
\end{aligned}
$$

where n is the length of xs. The 'O' is short for 'order of at most', and a precise explanation of its meaning follows.

If $g(n)$ is some function of n, then whenever we write:

$$g(n) = O(h(n))$$

this means that there exists some constant M such that:

$$|g(n)| \leq M|h(n)|$$

for every positive n. This does not define $g(n)$ precisely, but does say that $g(n)$ is bounded by a function that is proportional to $h(n)$.

Here $|g(n)|$ denotes the absolute value of $g(n)$. For our purposes, $g(n)$ will usually be positive, since it represents the time resources used by a program with input of size n. However, the definition above is traditional in mathematics, and makes some manipulations of O-notation easier.

As an example, say that $g(n)$ is a polynomial of degree m:

$$g(n) \;=\; a_0 + a_1 n + \cdots + a_m n^m$$

Then we have:

$$g(n) \;=\; O(n^m)$$

A suitable M in this case is given by $M = |a_0| + |a_1| + \cdots + |a_m|$. It is left as an exercise to show for this value of M that $|g(n)| \leq M n^m$ for every $n > 0$. The definition of O-notation is careful to guarantee the inequality only for positive n, so that the case $n = 0$ causes no problems.

Note that the O-notation must be used with some care. For example, if $f(n) = O(h(n))$ and $g(n) = O(h(n))$, this does *not* imply that $f(n) = g(n)$. By convention, we always write equations containing O-notation so that the left-hand side of an equation is never less precise than the right-hand side. For example, it is fine to write $n^2 + n = O(n^2)$, but we never write $O(n^2) = n^2 + n$. Otherwise, since $2n^2 = O(n^2)$, we could come to the absurd conclusion that $2n^2 = n^2 + n$ for every n.

To return to our example, the statements:

$$\begin{aligned} T_{reverse}(xs) &= O(n^2) \\ T_{rev}(xs) &= O(n) \end{aligned}$$

mean that there exist constants M_1 and M_2 such that for every list xs of length n, where $n > 0$, the number of steps to compute *reverse* xs is bounded by $M_1 n^2$, and the number of steps to compute *rev* xs is bounded by $M_2 n$.

Nothing is said about the relative values of M_1 and M_2. However, even if M_1 is much less than M_2, the second program is still the faster one in almost all cases. For example, say that M_1 is 2 and M_2 is 20. Then for short lists the first program is indeed better: applying *reverse* to a list of length 5 will require at most 50 steps (2×5^2), while applying *rev* requires up to 100 steps (20×5). But for longer lists the second program will be better: applying *reverse* to a list of length 20 requires up to 800 steps, while applying *rev* requires at most 400. As the lists get longer and longer, the advantage of *rev* becomes more and more pronounced.

Estimating the performance of a program using just O-notation is called *asymptotic analysis*, and the estimate is called the *order of magnitude*. For example, *reverse* has a quadratic order of magnitude, and *rev* has a linear one. In geometry, an asymptote is the limit of a curve as it approaches infinity. Similarly, asymptotic analysis describes the behaviour of a program as it 'approaches infinity', that is, as it processes larger and larger data items.

For many purposes an asymptotic analysis is sufficient. Generally, the time required to compute a value is proportional to the number of reduction steps required, regardless of the particular implementation used. If one program has a smaller order of magnitude than another, it will generally run faster under all implementations for sufficiently large input. Thus, asymptotic analyses yield information that is implementation independent.

On the other hand, sometimes more detailed information is necessary. For instance, we may need to compare two programs that have the same order of magnitude of reduction steps. Also, when the data are not large an asymptotic analysis may be less relevant and we may wish to know the size of the constants of proportionality. In such cases, an exact count of the number of reduction steps may be useful. Another useful method is testing: to run each program on a range of data values with a stopwatch in one hand – or the computerised equivalent. Generally, at least some testing will be desirable to confirm that the model is a reasonable predictor of actual behaviour. As in any engineering discipline, one must decide on the appropriate mixture between simple models (such as asymptotic analysis), more detailed models (such as counting the exact number of reduction steps), and testing (such as timing the program in a particular implementation).

Exercises

6.1.1 Use the T and O-notations to give computation times for the following functions: *hd*, *last*, (#), *fib*, and *fastfib*.

6.1.2 If $g(n) = O(n^2) - O(n^2)$ may we conclude that $g(n) = 0$? What should the right-hand side of the second equation be?

6.1.3 Prove that if:

$$g(n) = a_0 + a_1 n + \cdots + a_m n^m$$

then both of the statements:

$$g(n) = O(n^m)$$
$$g(n) = a_m n^m + O(n^{m-1})$$

are valid.

6.2   Models of reduction

As noted, the phrase 'number of reduction steps' has appeared several times in this book. The purpose of this section is to give a more precise definition of its meaning.

Say that we have defined:

$$
\begin{aligned}
pyth\ x\ y &= sqr\ x + sqr\ y \\
sqr\ x &= x \times x
\end{aligned}
$$

Then the term $pyth\ 3\ 4$ can be evaluated in six reduction steps:

$$
\begin{aligned}
pyth\ 3\ 4 &\Rightarrow sqr\ 3 + sqr\ 4 & (pyth) \\
&\Rightarrow (3 \times 3) + sqr\ 4 & (sqr) \\
&\Rightarrow 9 + sqr\ 4 & (\times) \\
&\Rightarrow 9 + (4 \times 4) & (sqr) \\
&\Rightarrow 9 + 16 & (\times) \\
&\Rightarrow 25 & (+)
\end{aligned}
$$

Each reduction step replaces a subterm – called a *redex* – by an equivalent term ('redex' is short for 'reducible expression'). In each step, either the redex matches the left-hand side of an equation (like $sqr\ 3$) and is replaced by the corresponding right-hand side (3×3), or the redex is a primitive application (like 3×3) and is replaced by its value (9).

The number of steps may depend on the order in which redexes are reduced. Say that:

$$
fst\ (x, y) = x
$$

as usual, and we wish to evaluate $fst\ (sqr\ 4, sqr\ 2)$. One possible reduction sequence is:

$$
\begin{aligned}
fst\ (sqr\ 4, sqr\ 2) &\Rightarrow fst\ (4 \times 4, sqr\ 2) & (sqr) \\
&\Rightarrow fst\ (16, sqr\ 2) & (\times) \\
&\Rightarrow fst\ (16, 2 \times 2) & (sqr) \\
&\Rightarrow fst\ (16, 4) & (\times) \\
&\Rightarrow 16 & (fst)
\end{aligned}
$$

which requires five steps. A second possibility is:

$$
\begin{aligned}
fst\ (sqr\ 4, sqr\ 2) &\Rightarrow sqr\ 4 & (fst) \\
&\Rightarrow 4 \times 4 & (sqr) \\
&\Rightarrow 16 & (\times)
\end{aligned}
$$

which requires only three.

These two reduction sequences illustrate two reduction policies, called *innermost reduction* and *outermost reduction*, respectively. In the first, each step reduces an *innermost* redex, that is, one that contains no other redex. In the second, each step reduces an *outermost* redex, that is, one that is contained in no other redex.

6.2.1 Termination

Some reduction orders may fail to terminate. Say we have defined:

$$answer = fst\,(42, loop)$$
$$loop = tl\,loop$$

and *fst* and *sqr* are as defined above. Evaluating *answer* by innermost reduction we have:

$$
\begin{aligned}
answer &\Rightarrow fst\,(42, loop) & (answer)\\
&\Rightarrow fst\,(42, tl\,loop) & (loop)\\
&\Rightarrow fst\,(42, tl\,(tl\,loop)) & (loop)\\
&\Rightarrow \ldots
\end{aligned}
$$

which does not terminate. But using outermost reduction we have:

$$
\begin{aligned}
answer &\Rightarrow fst\,(42, loop) & (answer)\\
&\Rightarrow 42 & (fst)
\end{aligned}
$$

which requires only two steps.

Thus, sometimes outermost reduction will yield an answer when innermost reduction fails to terminate. However, when both reduction methods terminate then they will both yield the same answer. Further, outermost reduction has the important property that, for every term, if there exists *any* reduction order that terminates, then there is an outermost reduction that terminates.

Outermost reduction is also called *normal order reduction*, because it is capable of reducing a term to normal (canonical) form whenever the term has such a form; and it is also called *lazy evaluation*, because it does not reduce a term unless it is essential for finding the answer. By contrast, innermost reduction is also called *applicative order reduction* and *eager evaluation*.

Recall that a function is *strict* if it is undefined whenever its argument is undefined. For example, multiplication is strict in its first and second argument, since $\perp \times x = \perp$ and $x \times \perp = \perp$. On the other hand, the tuple constructing function is not strict, since $(\perp, x) \neq \perp$ and $(x, \perp) \neq \perp$.

Outermost reduction is essential for evaluating non-strict functions, as the *answer* example shows. Some functional languages (unlike the notation described in this book) allow only strict functions. For such languages, innermost reduction may be used instead of outermost. This is because innermost and outermost reduction are equivalent when only strict functions are involved, that is, both will terminate for exactly the same terms.

6.2.2 Graph reduction

In the examples above, outermost reduction always requires no more reduction steps than innermost reduction, and often requires fewer. Thus, simply on efficiency grounds it seems preferable. Indeed, the termination problems of innermost reduction are simply an extreme case of this, where innermost reduction requires infinitely more steps than outermost.

However, it is not always true that outermost reduction, as defined above, requires fewer steps than innermost. Consider simplifying the expression $sqr\,(4+2)$. Using innermost reduction we have:

$$
\begin{aligned}
sqr\,(4+2) &\Rightarrow\ sqr\,6 \quad (+) \\
&\Rightarrow\ 6\times 6 \quad (sqr) \\
&\Rightarrow\ 36 \quad\ \ (\times)
\end{aligned}
$$

which requires three steps, while using outermost reduction we have:

$$
\begin{aligned}
sqr\,(4+2) &\Rightarrow\ (4+2)\times(4+2) \quad (sqr) \\
&\Rightarrow\ 6\times(4+2) \quad\quad\ \ (+) \\
&\Rightarrow\ 6\times 6 \quad\quad\quad\quad\ (+) \\
&\Rightarrow\ 36 \quad\quad\quad\quad\quad (\times)
\end{aligned}
$$

which requires four. The problem here is that the term $(4+2)$ is duplicated by the reduction of sqr, and so must be reduced twice. Although the number of steps required differs only by one, the difference could be made arbitrarily large by replacing the term $(4+2)$ by a term that requires more steps to reduce. Further, the problem is not limited to sqr; it arises for any definition where a variable on the left-hand side appears more than once on the right-hand side.

This problem can be solved by representing terms by *graphs* that indicate shared subterms. For example, the graph:

$$
(\bullet \times \bullet) \qquad (4+2)
$$

represents the term $(4+2)\times(4+2)$. Each instance of the subterm $4+2$ is represented by an arrow – called a *pointer* – to that term. Now, using (outermost) *graph reduction* we have:

$$
\begin{aligned}
sqr\,(4+2) &\Rightarrow\ (\bullet \times \bullet) \quad (4+2) \quad (sqr) \\
&\Rightarrow\ (\bullet \times \bullet) \quad 6 \quad\quad\ (+) \\
&\Rightarrow\ 36 \quad\quad\quad\quad\quad (\times)
\end{aligned}
$$

which requires only three steps. Thus, the use of graphs avoids the problem of duplicated subterms. With graph reduction, outermost reduction never performs more reduction steps than innermost.

Shared subterms in a graph may also be introduced by where clauses. For
instance, given the definition:

$$roots\ a\ b\ c\ =\ ((-b-d)/e, (-b+d)/e)$$
$$\textbf{where}\ d\ =\ sqrt\,(sqr\ b - 4 \times a \times c)$$
$$e\ =\ 2 \times a$$

the term *roots* 1 5 3 reduces (in a single step) to:

$$((-5 - \bullet)/\bullet, (-5 + \bullet)/\bullet) \qquad sqrt\,(sqr\ 5 - 4 \times 1 \times 3) \qquad (2 \times 1)$$

and this term can then be reduced in the same way as before. In Section 7.6
we shall see how where clauses may also be used to introduce *cyclic* graphs.

Arrows have no meaning except to indicate sharing. Both:

$$(sqr\ \bullet) \qquad (4 + 2)$$

and *sqr* $(4 + 2)$ are equivalent ways of writing the same term.

We will use the total number of arguments as a measure of the size of a
term or graph. For example, the term:

$$sqr\ 3 + sqr\ 4$$

has size four (each application of *sqr* has one argument, and $+$ has two
arguments) and the graph:

$$(\bullet \times \bullet) \qquad (4 + 2)$$

also has size four ($\times$ and $+$ each have two arguments).

6.2.3 Head normal form

Sometimes we need to reduce a subterm, but not all the way to normal form.
Consider the outermost reduction:

$$hd\,(map\ sqr\ [1..7])$$
$$\Rightarrow\quad hd\,(map\ sqr\ (1 : [2..7]))$$
$$\Rightarrow\quad hd\,(sqr\ 1 : map\ sqr\ [2..7])$$
$$\Rightarrow\quad sqr\ 1$$
$$\Rightarrow\quad 1 \times 1$$
$$\Rightarrow\quad 1$$

Here we needed to reduce $(map\ sqr\ [1..7])$, but not all the way to the normal
form $[1, 4, 9, 16, 25, 36, 49]$. This in turn required reducing $[1..7]$, but not all
the way to the normal form $[1, 2, 3, 4, 5, 6, 7]$.

However, any term that is reduced must be reduced to *head normal form*. By definition, a term is in head normal form if it is not a redex, and it cannot become a redex by reducing any of its subterms. Every term in normal form is in head normal form, but not vice versa. In particular, any term of the form $(e_1 : e_2)$ is in head normal form, because regardless of how far e_1 and e_2 are reduced there is no reduction rule that applies to this term. However, $(e_1 : e_2)$ is in normal form only when e_1 and e_2 are both in normal form. Similarly, any term of the form (e_1, e_2) is in head normal form, but is in normal form only when e_1 and e_2 are.

Whether a term needs to be reduced further than head normal form depends on the context in which it appears. In the example above, the subterm *map sqr* $[1 .. 7]$ only needed to be reduced to its head normal form, *sqr* 1 : *map sqr* $[2 .. 7]$. On the other hand, to print *map sqr* $[1 .. 7]$, first it would be reduced to head normal form, then *sqr* 1 would be reduced to its normal form, 1, then *map sqr* $[2 .. 7]$ would be reduced to head normal form, and so on.

6.2.4 Pattern matching

For rules involving pattern matching, the outermost reduction strategy is, by itself, not sufficient to guarantee that a terminating reduction sequence will be found if one exists. For an example, recall the definition of *zip*:

$$
\begin{aligned}
zip\,([\,],ys) &= [\,] \\
zip\,(x : xs, [\,]) &= [\,] \\
zip\,(x : xs, y : ys) &= (x, y) : zip\,(xs, ys)
\end{aligned}
$$

Now consider the reduction:

$$
\begin{aligned}
&zip\,(map\;sqr\,[\,], loop) \\
\Rightarrow\;&zip\,([\,], loop) \\
\Rightarrow\;&[\,]
\end{aligned}
$$

This is an outermost reduction, since $(map\;sqr\,[\,])$ appears inside no other redex. But the non-terminating reduction:

$$
\begin{aligned}
&zip\,(map\;sqr\,[\,], loop) \\
\Rightarrow\;&zip\,(map\;sqr\,[\,], tl\;loop) \\
\Rightarrow\;&zip\,(map\;sqr\,[\,], tl\,(tl\;loop)) \\
&\vdots
\end{aligned}
$$

is also outermost, since in each case $(tl\;loop)$ appears inside no other redex.

When a function application involves pattern matching, we allow a subterm to be reduced only if it is required by the pattern. Thus, given the above term:

$$
zip\,(map\;sqr\,[\,], loop)
$$

we must determine whether the first subterm matches $[\,]$ or $(x : xs)$ in the definition of *zip*. Hence, the next outermost reduction step must be to reduce $(map\ sqr\ [\,])$. We do not allow the second subterm, *loop*, to be reduced, because its value may not be needed (and, indeed, is not). On the other hand, given the term:

$$zip\ (1 : map\ sqr\ [2, 3], map\ sqr\ [4, 5, 6])$$

the first subterm matches $(x : xs)$, and so we must next determine whether the second subterm matches $[\,]$ or $(y : ys)$. Hence, the next outermost reduction step must be to reduce $(map\ sqr\ [4, 5, 6])$.

Although this constraint on the reduction order seems quite natural, a precise definition is surprisingly difficult and beyond the scope of this text. For a discussion of some of the issues, see Peyton Jones and Wadler [7]. In particular, readers should note that all of the definitions given in this book are *uniform* in the sense described in [7].

6.2.5   Models and implementations

We shall adopt *outermost graph reduction* as our model of computation, because it has two desirable properties: (i) it terminates whenever any reduction order terminates, and (ii) it requires no more (and possibly fewer) steps than innermost order reduction.

To be precise, the time and space required to evaluate a term e_0 are modelled as follows. Let:

$$e_0 \Rightarrow e_1 \Rightarrow e_2 \Rightarrow \cdots \Rightarrow e_n$$

be a sequence of outermost graph reduction steps yielding the normal (canonical) form e_n. Then the time required to reduce e_0 to normal form is taken to be the number of reduction steps, namely, n. Further, the space required is taken to be the size of the largest graph in the reduction sequence, namely, the maximum of the sizes of $e_0, \ldots, e_n$.

The implementation methods used in practice for functional languages usually correspond more or less closely to graph reduction, so that the graph reduction model is generally a good predictor of the behaviour of an actual implementation. As mentioned before, one must choose judiciously the proper mixture of modelling and testing when evaluating the efficiency of a program.

Some of the most efficient techniques for implementing functional languages are based directly on graph reduction. Of these, the most notable are the G-machine, devised by Thomas Johnsson and Lennart Augustsson, and the SKI-reducer, devised by David Turner. For further information, the reader is referred to Peyton Jones' textbook [8]. Another important implementation technique is the SECD machine, developed by Peter Landin. Originally it was designed for innermost reduction, but an adaptation for outermost reduction is described in Henderson's textbook [9].

Exercises

6.2.1 Give innermost, outermost, and outermost graph reduction sequences for each of the following terms:

$$cube \, (cube \, 3)$$
$$map \, (1+) \, (map \, (2\times) \, [1, 2, 3])$$
$$hd \, ([1, 2, 3] +\!\!+ loop)$$

Count the number of reduction steps in each sequence (if it terminates).

6.2.2 Give outermost reduction sequences for each of the following terms:

$$zip \, (map \, sqr \, [1 .. 3], map \, sqr \, [4 .. 6])$$
$$take \, (1 + 1) \, (drop \, (3 - 1) \, [1 .. 4])$$
$$take \, (42 - 6 \times 7) \, (map \, sqr \, [1234567 .. 7654321])$$

Indicate all outermost redexes that are not reduced because of the restrictions imposed by pattern matching.

6.2.3 Section 5.6 defined a function *subs* that returns all subsequences of a list:

$$subs \, [\,] \quad = \quad [[\,]]$$
$$subs \, (x : xs) \quad = \quad subs \, xs +\!\!+ map \, (x :) \, (subs \, xs)$$

An equivalent definition is:

$$subs' \, [\,] \quad = \quad [[\,]]$$
$$subs' \, (x : xs) \quad = \quad yss +\!\!+ map \, (x :) \, yss$$
$$\textbf{where} \; yss = subs' \, xs$$

Show the graph reduction steps in computing $subs \, [1, 2, 3]$ and $subs' \, [1, 2, 3]$. Use the O-notation to give formulae for the time and space required to compute $subs \, [1 .. n]$ and $subs' \, [1 .. n]$.

6.3 Reduction order and space

Outermost graph reduction is always at least as good as innermost, in the sense that it uses no more (and possibly fewer) reduction steps. However, sometimes using a combination of outermost and innermost reduction can save on the amount of space used. In this section, we introduce a special function, *strict*, and show how it can be used to control reduction order and save space. The main example involves the *foldl* function, and we conclude by considering the trade-offs between *foldl* and *foldr*.

As we know, *sum* can be defined using either *foldl* or *foldr*. For the time being, let's assume it is defined using *foldl*:

$$sum \quad = \quad foldl \, (+) \, 0$$

(We will shortly turn to the question of whether, in general, it is preferable to use *foldl* or *foldr* in such a definition.)

Consider reduction of the term $sum\,[1..1000]$:

$$sum\,[1..1000]$$
$$\Rightarrow\;foldl\,(+)\,0\,[1..1000]$$
$$\Rightarrow\;foldl\,(+)\,(0+1)\,[2..1000]$$
$$\Rightarrow\;foldl\,(+)\,((0+1)+2)\,[3..1000]$$
$$\vdots$$
$$\Rightarrow\;foldl\,(+)\,(\cdots((0+1)+2)+\cdots+1000)\,[\,]$$
$$\Rightarrow\;(\cdots((0+1)+2)+\cdots+1000)$$
$$\Rightarrow\;500500$$

Notice that in computing $sum\,[1..n]$ by outermost order reduction, the reduction terms grow in size proportional to n. On the other hand, if we use a judicious mixture of outermost and innermost reduction order, then we have the following reduction sequence:

$$sum\,[1..1000]$$
$$\Rightarrow\;foldl\,(+)\,0\,[1..1000]$$
$$\Rightarrow\;foldl\,(+)\,(0+1)\,[2..1000]$$
$$\Rightarrow\;foldl\,(+)\,1\,[2..1000]$$
$$\Rightarrow\;foldl\,(+)\,(1+2)\,[3..1000]$$
$$\Rightarrow\;foldl\,(+)\,3\,[3..1000]$$
$$\vdots$$
$$\Rightarrow\;foldl\,(+)\,500500\,[\,]$$
$$\Rightarrow\;500500$$

Now the maximum size of any term in the reduction sequence is bounded by a constant. In short, reducing $sum\,[1..n]$ to normal form by purely outermost reduction requires $O(n)$ space, while a combination of innermost and outermost reduction requires only $O(1)$ space.

This suggests that it would be useful to have a way of controlling reduction order, and we now introduce a special function, *strict*, that allows us to do so.

6.3.1 Controlling reduction order

Reduction order may be controlled by use of the special function *strict*. A term of the form *strict f e* is reduced by first reducing *e* to head normal form, and then applying *f*. The term *e* will itself be reduced by outermost reduction, except, of course, if further calls of *strict* appear while reducing *e*.

As a simple example, if we define:

$$incr\,x\;=\;x+1$$

then:

$$incr\,(incr\,(8 \times 5))$$
$$\Rightarrow\quad incr\,(8 \times 5)+1$$
$$\Rightarrow\quad ((8 \times 5)+1)+1$$
$$\Rightarrow\quad (40+1)+1$$
$$\Rightarrow\quad 41+1$$
$$\Rightarrow\quad 42$$

but:

$$strict\;incr\,(strict\;incr\,(8 \times 5))$$
$$\Rightarrow\quad strict\;incr\,(strict\;incr\,40)$$
$$\Rightarrow\quad strict\;incr\,(incr\,40)$$
$$\Rightarrow\quad strict\;incr\,(40+1)$$
$$\Rightarrow\quad strict\;incr\,41$$
$$\Rightarrow\quad incr\,41$$
$$\Rightarrow\quad 41+1$$
$$\Rightarrow\quad 42$$

Both cases perform the same reduction steps, but in a different order.

Currying applies to *strict* as to anything else. From this it follows that if f is a function of three arguments, writing $strict\,(f\,e_1)\,e_2\,e_3$ causes the second argument to be reduced early, but not the first or third.

Given this, we can rewrite the definition of *foldl* as follows:

$$foldl'\,(\oplus)\,a\,[\,]\quad\;\; =\quad a$$
$$foldl'\,(\oplus)\,a\,(x:xs)\quad =\quad strict\,(foldl'\,(\oplus))\,(a \oplus x)\,xs$$

We now have:

$$sum\,[1 .. 1000]$$
$$\Rightarrow\quad foldl'\,(+)\,0\,[1 .. 1000]$$
$$\Rightarrow\quad strict\,(foldl'\,(+))\,(0+1)\,[2 .. 1000]$$
$$\Rightarrow\quad foldl'\,(+)\,1\,[2 .. 1000]$$
$$\Rightarrow\quad strict\,(foldl'\,(+))\,(1+2)\,[3 .. 1000]$$
$$\Rightarrow\quad foldl'\,(+)\,3\,[3 .. 1000]$$
$$\vdots$$
$$\Rightarrow\quad foldl'\,(+)\,500500\,[\,]$$
$$\Rightarrow\quad 500500$$

which has the desired space behaviour. Here we have assumed it is valid to replace *foldl* by *foldl'* in the definition of *sum*. We will prove this shortly.

The function *strict* should be used sparingly. The definition of *foldl'* is one of the very few places where we recommend its use.

6.3.2   Strictness

The operational definition of *strict* given in the previous section may be
re-expressed in the following way:

$$
\begin{aligned}
strict\, f\, x \;&=\; \bot, \quad \textbf{if } x = \bot \\
&=\; f\, x, \quad \textbf{otherwise}
\end{aligned}
$$

Although this equation characterises the properties of *strict*, it is *not* a valid
definition in our notation since $x = \bot$ is not a computable boolean expression.

Recall that a function f is said to be strict if $f \bot = \bot$. It follows from the
above equation that $f = strict\, f$ if and only if f is a strict function. (To see
this, just consider the values of $(f\, x)$ and $(strict\, f\, x)$ in the two cases $x = \bot$
and $x \neq \bot$.) This explains the name *strict*.

Furthermore, if f is strict, but not everywhere $\bot$, and $e \neq \bot$, then reduction of $f\, e$ eventually entails reduction of e. Thus, if f is strict, evaluation
of $f\, e$ and $strict\, f\, e$ perform the same reduction steps, though possibly in a
different order. In other words, when f is strict, replacing it by $strict\, f$ does
not change the meaning or the time required to apply it, although it may
change the space required by the computation.

It is an easy exercise to show that if $\bot \oplus x = \bot$ for every x, then
$fold\,(\oplus)\,\bot\, xs = \bot$ for every finite list xs. In other words, if $(\oplus)$ is strict in its
left argument, then $foldl\,(\oplus)$ is strict, and so equivalent to $strict\,(foldl\,(\oplus))$,
and hence also equivalent to $foldl'\,(\oplus)$. It follows that replacing $foldl$ by $foldl'$
in the definition of *sum* is valid, and the same replacement is valid whenever
$foldl$ is applied to a binary operation that is strict in its first argument.

6.3.3   Fold revisited

The first duality theorem, stated in Section 3.5.1, states that if $(\oplus)$ is associative with identity a (that is, if $(\oplus)$ and a form a monoid), then:

$$
foldr\,(\oplus)\, a\, xs \;=\; foldl\,(\oplus)\, a\, xs
$$

for every finite list xs. We now consider the relative costs of computing the
terms on each side of this equation. Whether $foldr$ or $foldl$ is more efficient
will depend on the properties of $(\oplus)$.

A common case is that $(\oplus)$ is strict in both arguments, and can be computed in $O(1)$ time and $O(1)$ space. Examples that fall into this category
are $(+)$ and $(\times)$. In this case it is not hard to verify that $foldr\,(\oplus)\, a\, xs$ and
$foldl\,(\oplus)\, a\, xs$ both require $O(n)$ time and $O(n)$ space to compute. So there
is little to choose between $foldr$ and $foldl$. However, the same argument used
for *sum* generalises to show that in this case $foldl$ may safely be replaced by
$foldl'$, and that while $foldl'\,(\oplus)\, a\, xs$ still requires $O(n)$ time, it only requires
$O(1)$ space to compute. So in this case, $foldl'$ is the clear winner.

If ($\oplus$) does not satisfy the above properties, then choosing a winner may not be so easy. A good rule of thumb, though, is that if ($\oplus$) is non-strict in either argument then *foldr* is usually more efficient than *foldl*. We give two examples.

For the first example, consider the ($\land$) operation. Recall that ($\land$) is strict in its first argument, but non-strict in its second. In particular, *False* $\land$ *x* returns *False* without evaluating *x*. Assume we are given a list:

$$xs = [x_1, x_2, \ldots, x_n]$$

and that some element x_i of this list is *False*. Then

$$foldr \ (\land) \ True \ xs$$

requires $O(i)$ steps for its evaluation, while:

$$foldl \ (\land) \ True \ xs$$

requires $O(n)$ steps. Clearly, in this case *foldr* is a better choice.

For the second example, consider concatenation. Recall that the concatenation of two lists, $xs \mathbin{+\!\!+} ys$, requires time $O(n)$ to compute, where n is the length of xs. Let $xss = [xs_1, xs_2, \ldots, xs_m]$ be a sequence of m lists of lengths $n_1, \ldots, n_m$, respectively. We consider the times to compute $foldl \ (+\!\!+) \ [\,] \ xss$ and $foldr \ (+\!\!+) \ [\,] \ xss$.

If we use *foldl*, then $[\,]$ is concatenated to xs_1, requiring time $O(1)$; and xs_1 is concatenated to xs_2, requiring time $O(n_1)$; and $(xs_1 \mathbin{+\!\!+} xs_2)$ is concatenated to xs_3, requiring time $O(n_1 + n_2)$; and so on; and finally $(xs_1 \mathbin{+\!\!+} \cdots \mathbin{+\!\!+} xs_{m-1})$ is concatenated to xs_m, requiring time $O(n_1 + \cdots + n_{m-1})$. The total time required is:

$$O(n_1) + O(n_1 + n_2) + \cdots + O(n_1 + n_2 + \cdots + n_{m-1})$$
$$= \ O((m-1)n_1 + (m-2)n_2 + \cdots + n_{m-1})$$

On the other hand, if we use *foldr*, then xs_1 is concatenated to $(xs_2 \mathbin{+\!\!+} xs_3 \mathbin{+\!\!+} \cdots \mathbin{+\!\!+} xs_n)$, requiring time $O(xs_1)$; and xs_2 is concatenated to $(xs_3 \mathbin{+\!\!+} \cdots \mathbin{+\!\!+} xs_n)$, requiring time $O(xs_2)$; and so on; and finally xs_m is concatenated to $[\,]$, requiring time $O(xs_m)$. The total time required is:

$$O(n_1) + O(n_2) + \cdots + O(n_m) \ = \ O(n_1 + n_2 + \cdots + n_m)$$

Thus *foldr* computes its result more rapidly than *foldl* in almost all situations (but not if the final list, xs_m, is sufficiently long). It may be easier to understand this result if we make the simplifying assumption that all of the lists $xs_1, \ldots, xs_m$ have the same length $n = n_1 = \cdots = n_m$. Then using *foldl* requires time $O(m^2 n)$, while using *foldr* requires only time $O(mn)$.

To summarise: for functions, such as ($+$) or ($\times$), that are strict in both arguments and can be computed in constant time and space, *foldl'* is more efficient. But for functions, such as ($\land$) or ($+\!\!+$), that are non-strict in some argument, *foldr* is often more efficient.

Exercises

6.3.1 Prove that if $\bot \oplus x = \bot$ for every x, then $foldl\,(\oplus)\,\bot\,xs = \bot$ for every finite list xs.

6.3.2 We previously defined:

$$maximum \;=\; foldl1\,(\mathbf{min})$$

Apply the results of this section to this definition.

6.3.3 Give the time and space required to compute each of:

$$foldr\,(\vee)\,False\,(copy\;n\;True)$$
$$foldr\,(+\!\!+)\,[\,]\,(copy\;m\;(copy\;n\;{}'\mathrm{X}'))$$

What is the time and space when *foldr* is replaced by *foldl*?

6.4 Divide and conquer

One useful technique for designing efficient algorithms is known as "divide and conquer". The general idea is to solve a problem P by dividing it into subproblems – each an instance of P but on inputs of smaller size – in such a way that the solution of the original problem can be assembled from the solutions to the subproblems. In this section we shall give three applications of the divide and conquer technique, and show why it can lead to efficient solutions for certain kinds of problem.

6.4.1 Sorting

Let us start by considering the problem of sorting. We have already encountered one sorting method (in Exercise 3.5.4), namely *insertion sort*:

$$
\begin{aligned}
isort &= foldr\ insert\ [\,]\\
insert\ x\ xs &= takewhile\,(\le x)\,xs +\!\!+ [x] +\!\!+ dropwhile\,(\le x)\,xs
\end{aligned}
$$

Let $T_{insert}(n)$ denote the time to insert an element into a list of length n using *insert*, and let $T_{isort}(n)$ denote the time to sort a list of length n using *isort*. Since the evaluations of $takewhile\,(\le x)\,xs$ and $dropwhile\,(\le x)\,xs$ each require $O(n)$ steps, where $n = \#xs$, we have:

$$T_{insert}(n) = O(n)$$

It follows that:

$$T_{isort}(n) \;=\; T_{insert}(0) + T_{insert}(1) + \cdots + T_{insert}(n) \;=\; O(n^2)$$

So, insertion sort never requires more than quadratic time to sort its argument. Since it does require quadratic time in the worst case (for example, when the input list is in descending order), the above bound is tight.

Using methods we have described previously, it is a simple exercise to synthesise the following, equivalent, version of *insert*:

$$
\begin{aligned}
insert\ x\ [\,] \quad &= \quad [x] \\
insert\ x\ (y:ys) \quad &= \quad x:y:ys, \qquad \text{if } x \leq y \\
&= \quad y:insert\ x\ ys, \quad \textbf{otherwise}
\end{aligned}
$$

Evaluating $(insert\ x\ xs)$ with the new definition requires about three times fewer reduction steps than before, but the new version of *isort* still possesses a quadratic bound: if the length of the input list increases by a factor of 10, the time to sort it may increase by a factor of 100.

Insertion sort works by dividing the list into two parts – the first element and the remainder. It sorts the remainder, and then inserts the first element into the sorted list. A variation on this idea is to divide the list into two parts of roughly equal size, sort each part, and then merge the resulting lists. This approach yields the following divide and conquer algorithm, called *merge sort*:

$$
\begin{aligned}
msort\ xs \quad &= \quad xs, \qquad\qquad\qquad\qquad\qquad\; \text{if } n \leq 1 \\
&= \quad merge\ (msort\ us)\ (msort\ vs), \quad \textbf{otherwise} \\
&\quad\ \textbf{where } n \;=\; \#xs \\
&\qquad\qquad\ us \;=\; take\ (n\ \textbf{div}\ 2)\ xs \\
&\qquad\qquad\ vs \;=\; drop\ (n\ \textbf{div}\ 2)\ xs
\end{aligned}
$$

The function *merge* is defined by the equations:

$$
\begin{aligned}
merge\ [\,]\ ys \qquad\qquad\ &= \quad ys \\
merge\ (x:xs)\ [\,] \qquad\ &= \quad x:xs \\
merge\ (x:xs)\ (y:ys) \quad &= \quad x:merge\ xs\ (y:ys), \quad \text{if } x \leq y \\
&= \quad y:merge\ (x:xs)\ ys, \quad \textbf{otherwise}
\end{aligned}
$$

To analyse the performance of merge sort, let $T_{merge}(n)$ denote the time to merge two lists of combined length n, and let $T_{msort}(n)$ denote the time to sort a list of length n using *msort*. It is easy to check that $T_{merge}(n) = O(n)$ since each reduction step produces at least one more element of the result. To calculate $T_{msort}(n)$ for $n > 1$, observe that $O(n)$ steps are required to split the argument list into two sublists, approximately $T_{msort}(n\ \textbf{div}\ 2)$ steps are required to sort each sublist and, as we have seen, another $O(n)$ steps are required to merge the results. Hence:

$$
\begin{aligned}
T_{msort}(n) \quad &= \quad O(1), \qquad\qquad\qquad\qquad\quad\ \text{if } n \leq 1 \\
&= \quad 2\,T_{msort}(n\ \textbf{div}\ 2) + O(n), \quad \textbf{otherwise}
\end{aligned}
$$

Recurrence relations of this form arise frequently in the analysis of divide and conquer algorithms. To solve it, suppose we define T by:

$$\begin{aligned} T(n) &= d, & \textbf{if } n = 1 \\ &= 2T(n \textbf{ div } 2) + cn, & \textbf{if } n > 1 \end{aligned}$$

A proof by induction establishes that:

$$T(n) \leq cn \log_2 n + d$$

for all $n \geq 1$. It follows that:

$$T_{msort}(n) = O(n \log_2 n)$$

Thus, merge sort is considerably faster than insertion sort. If the length of the input list increases by a factor of 10, then insertion sort will require 100 times longer, while merge sort will only take 33 times longer ($33 = 10 \log_2 10$). For every factor of 10 in the length of the input, merge sort gains another factor of 3 over insertion sort. Hence, the difference between the two versions of insertion sort is insignificant when compared with the difference between insertion sort and merge sort. This demonstrates why we are mainly concerned with asymptotic analysis rather than constant factors.

Quicksort.   There is a second way we can apply the idea of divide and conquer to the problem of sorting. In merge sort most of the effort goes into combining the solutions to the subproblems (the *merge* function), while finding the subproblems is relatively easy (the input list is simply chopped in two). In the following algorithm, called *quicksort*, the effort is apportioned in a different manner:

$$\begin{aligned} qsort\,[\,] \quad &= \quad [\,] \\ qsort\,(x : xs) \quad &= \quad qsort\,[u \mid u \leftarrow xs;\ u < x] \mathbin{+\!\!+} [x] \mathbin{+\!\!+} \\ &\qquad qsort\,[u \mid u \leftarrow xs;\ u \geq x] \end{aligned}$$

The essential point about quicksort is that the input list (apart from its first element x) is divided into two sublists in such a way that no element of the first sublist is greater than any element of the second. This means that, after sorting, the two sublists can be combined by straightforward concatenation.

Both merge sort and quicksort divide the problem into two halves. In merge sort, the two subproblems are guaranteed, by the way they are generated, to be half the size of the original problem. There is no such guarantee for quicksort since the relative size of the sublists depends upon the value of the first element x of the original list. In particular, if x is the minimum value, then the first sublist will be empty, while the other list will contain everything except x. If the original list is already sorted, then the same phenomenon will arise at every division stage of the algorithm. Hence, in the worst case, quicksort requires quadratic time and we therefore have:

$$T_{qsort}(n) = O(n^2)$$

However, the expected performance of quicksort is better than quadratic. On the average, we can expect that, at every division stage, each sublist will be about half as long as the original list. If we let $T^A_{qsort}(n)$ denote the average case performance (under a suitable formalisation of what constitutes an average case), then we have:

$$T^A_{qsort}(n) = O(n \log_2 n)$$

For a thorough discussion of average case analysis, and the proof that the above claim holds, the reader should consult Knuth [10].

From the preceding discussion we see that it is desirable, when designing a divide and conquer algorithm, to ensure that the subproblems are roughly equal in size. Even more important, it is vital to guarantee that the subproblems are smaller than the original problem. If the subproblem has the same size as the original problem, then no progress will be made, and the algorithm will enter an infinite loop. Both merge sort and quicksort ensure that the subproblems are indeed smaller than the original. In merge sort, this happens since n **div** $2 < n$ whenever $n > 1$. In quicksort, this happens since the first element is removed from consideration each time.

6.4.2 Multiplication

As a second application of divide and conquer, consider the problem of multiplying two positive integers x and y, each represented as a list of n digits. We considered essentially this problem in Section 4.2.3 where a straightforward $O(n^2)$ algorithm was given. This consisted of forming a list of n partial sums, each sum being the result of multiplying x by a single digit of y, and then adding the partial sums together, shifting appropriately. Since each partial sum is a list of n or $(n + 1)$ digits, adding them all together requires $O(n^2)$ steps.

Suppose that, instead of multiplying by a single digit, we split x and y into equal-length halves:

$$\begin{aligned} x &= x_1 10^{n/2} + x_0 \\ y &= y_1 10^{n/2} + y_0 \end{aligned}$$

where, for simplicity, we assume that $n > 1$ is an exact power of two. We have:

$$\begin{aligned} x \times y &= z_2 10^n + z_1 10^{n/2} + z_0 \\ \textbf{where } z_2 &= x_1 \times y_1 \\ z_1 &= x_1 \times y_0 + x_0 \times y_1 \\ z_0 &= x_0 \times y_0 \end{aligned}$$

This equation shows that the problem of multiplying two n-digit numbers can be solved in terms of four multiplications of two $n/2$-digit numbers. Now, multiplying a number by a power of 10 means shifting its representation by adding an appropriate number of zero digits, an operation that takes linear time. Furthermore, adding two n-digit numbers also requires $O(n)$ steps. Thus the time $T(n)$ for performing multiplication by this divide and conquer approach satisfies:

$$
\begin{aligned}
T(n) &= O(1), && \text{if } n = 1 \\
&= 4T(n/2) + O(n), && \text{if } n > 1
\end{aligned}
$$

The reader should compare this recurrence relation with the one for merge sort. Here there are four subproblems of size $n/2$, while in the sorting problem there were only two. The recurrence can be solved by use of the following general result (whose proof is omitted):

Suppose T satisfies:

$$
\begin{aligned}
T(n) &= O(1), && \text{if } n \leq 1 \\
&= aT(n/b) + O(n), && \text{if } n > 1
\end{aligned}
$$

for positive integers a and b. Then we have:

$$
\begin{aligned}
T(n) &= O(n), && \text{if } a < b \\
&= O(n \log n), && \text{if } a = b \\
&= O(n^{\log_b a}), && \text{if } a > b
\end{aligned}
$$

With merge sort we have $a = b = 2$, so $T_{msort}(n) = O(n \log n)$. With multiplication we have $a = 4$ and $b = 2$ and, as $\log_2 4 = 2$, we have $T(n) = O(n^2)$. Thus the time required by the divide and conquer algorithm is asymptotically no better than the naive method of multiplication, and we appear to have gained nothing.

However, there is a small improvement to the algorithm that leads to a dramatic improvement in efficiency: replace the definition of z_1 in the above equation for $x \times y$ by the equivalent alternative:

$$
z_1 = (x_1 + x_0) \times (y_1 + y_0) - z_2 - z_0
$$

With this revision there are now only *three* multiplications of $n/2$-digit numbers. The price paid for removing one multiplication is that there is one more addition and two new subtractions. But since adding or subtracting two n-digit numbers requires $O(n)$ steps, we now have:

$$
T(n) = 3T(n/2) + O(n)
$$

in the case $n > 1$. Since $\log_2 3 = 1.59..$, we obtain:

$$
T(n) = O(n^{\log_2 3}) = O(n^{1.59})
$$

The new version of the divide and conquer algorithm is therefore asymptotically superior by a factor of $n^{0.4}$.

So, if the new method is substantially faster, why is it not taught in schools? The answer, as we said in Section 6.1, is that asymptotic analysis describes the behaviour of an algorithm only in the limit. The constants of proportionality are such that the naive method performs much better than the divide and conquer algorithm for small values of n. Although computers may be required to multiply 100-digit numbers, children rarely are, and, for them and us, the simple algorithm is best.

6.4.3   Binary search

Our last example of a divide and conquer algorithm concerns searching. In its simplest form, the problem of searching can be expressed in the following way: given integers a and b and a (total) predicate p, find the smallest x in the interval $[a \mathbin{..} b]$ such that $(p\,x)$ holds. We can translate this informal specification directly into an executable definition:

$$find\ p\ a\ b \;=\; min\,[x \mid x \leftarrow [a \mathbin{..} b];\ p\,x]$$

Although it expresses what is wanted in the clearest possible way, this definition does not lead to the most efficient algorithm. The reason for this is that the function min is strict, demanding complete evaluation of its argument, and so $(p\,x)$ is evaluated for every x in the range $a \leq x \leq b$. Setting $n = \#[a \mathbin{..} b]$, we therefore have that $(find\ p\ a\ b)$ requires n evaluations of p.

A superior algorithm is obtained just by replacing min with hd in the above definition. This step is justified by the fact that the first satisfactory value encountered is the smallest one existing in the given range. The new version of $find$ requires between 1 and n evaluations of p, depending on the precise values of a and b.

It is possible to do even better if p is known to be a monotonic predicate. We say p is *monotonic* if:

$$(p\,x = True \wedge x < y) \quad \text{implies} \quad p\,y = True$$

for all x and y. In other words, once p becomes true for a value x it remains true for all values greater than x.

Let us combine the idea of searching with a monotonic predicate with a divide and conquer approach. Suppose we split the interval $[a \mathbin{..} b]$, where $a < b$, into two equal halves $[a \mathbin{..} m]$ and $[m+1 \mathbin{..} b]$, where $m = (a+b)\,\mathbf{div}\,2$. The reader should check that if $a < b$, then each of these intervals has a length strictly smaller than $\#[a \mathbin{..} b]$. Now, either $p\,m = True$ or $p\,m = False$ (since p is assumed to be total). In the first case, the search for the smallest value satisfying p can be confined to the interval $[a \mathbin{..} m]$. Furthermore, if p is monotonic and $p\,m = False$, then there are *no* values in the range $[a \mathbin{..} m]$ that satisfy p. This means that, in the second case, the subsequent search can be confined to the interval $[m + 1 \mathbin{..} b]$. In either case, we can continue searching in an interval of roughly half the size of the original.

algorithm	subproblems	size	complexity
Binary search	1	$n/2$	$O(\log n)$
Mergesort	2	$n/2$	$O(n \log n)$
Quicksort	2	variable	$O(n^2)$
Multiplication	3	$n/2$	$O(n^{1.59})$
Multiplication	4	$n/2$	$O(n^2)$

Table 6.1 Divide and conquer algorithms.

Here is the modified definition of *find*:

$$
\begin{aligned}
\textit{find } p\ a\ b \ &=\ a, & \textbf{if } a = b \wedge p\,a \\
&=\ \textit{find } p\ a\ m, & \textbf{if } a < b \wedge p\,m \\
&=\ \textit{find } p\ (m+1)\ b, & \textbf{if } a < b \wedge \neg p\,m \\
&\textbf{where } m = (a+b)\,\textbf{div}\,2
\end{aligned}
$$

Note that, as with the earlier definitions, (*find p a b*) returns $\bot$ if there is no value in the range $[a\mathinner{.\,.}b]$ satisfying p.

The running time $T(n)$ of the new algorithm satisfies:

$$
\begin{aligned}
T(n) \ &=\ O(1), & \textbf{if } n = 1 \\
&=\ T(n/2) + O(1), & \textbf{if } n > 1
\end{aligned}
$$

This recurrence relation can be solved to give:

$$T(n) = O(\log n)$$

In other words, the divide and conquer technique leads to a logarithmic time algorithm for searching with a monotonic predicate.

Summary. We have discussed five divide and conquer algorithms and their properties are summarised in Table 6.1. With the exception of quicksort and the first multiplication algorithm, the divide and conquer technique leads to solutions that were asymptotically more efficient than the first solutions given for the problems. Quicksort is also more efficient than insertion sort, but only on the average.

Exercises

6.4.1 Suppose we define:

$$minimum = hd \cdot isort$$

Show that (*minimum xs*) requires $O(n)$ reduction steps, where $n = \#xs$. Now consider defining *minimum* by:

$$minimum = hd \cdot msort$$

Does this also give an $O(n)$ algorithm?

6.4.2 Yet another definition of the function *insert* in insertion sort is as follows:

$$
\begin{aligned}
insert\ x &= foldr\ swap\ [x] \\
swap\ x\ (y:ys) &= x:y:ys, &&\text{if } x \leq y \\
&= y:x:ys, &&\textbf{otherwise}
\end{aligned}
$$

Prove by structural induction that:

$$sorted\ xs \quad \text{implies} \quad sorted\ (insert\ x\ xs)$$

where (*sorted xs*) is the condition that *xs* is in non-decreasing order.

Suppose $C_{insert}(n)$ denotes the number of comparison operations required by *insert* on a list of length n. Show that:

$$C_{insert}(n) = n$$

Hence calculate $C_{isort}(n)$.

6.4.3 Let $C_{merge}(m, n)$ denote the number of comparison operations required by *merge* to merge two sorted lists of length m and n. Calculate an upper bound for $C_{merge}(m, n)$.

6.4.4 What is wrong with the following definition of *msort*?

$$
\begin{aligned}
msort\ xs &= xs, &&\text{if } n = 0 \\
&= merge\ (msort\ us)\ (msort\ vs), &&\textbf{otherwise} \\
&\textbf{where}\ n = \#xs \\
&\qquad\quad us = take\ (n\ \textbf{div}\ 2)\ xs \\
&\qquad\quad vs = drop\ (n\ \textbf{div}\ 2)\ xs
\end{aligned}
$$

6.4.5 Consider the function *rank* defined by:

$$rank\ xs\ k = (sort\ xs)\ !\ k$$

In other words, (*rank xs k*) is the kth element of *xs* in order of size. By replacing *sort* by *qsort* in this definition, synthesise a new definition of *rank* and estimate its time complexity.

6.4.6 As one practical application of sorting, consider the KWIC (Keyword in Context) problem. Given is a text that consists of a list of titles, one per line. For example:

Citizen Kane
Charlie Bubbles
Duck Soup
Casablanca

Required as output is an alphabetised list of titles sorted on each word. For example:

Bubbles. Charlie
Casablanca.
Charlie Bubbles.
Citizen Kane.
Duck Soup.
Kane. Citizen
Soup. Duck

Note the insertion of a full-stop character on each line to permit recovery of the original title. The procedure for solving the KWIC problem is

1. Break the text into lines – giving a list of titles;
2. Break each title into a list of words;
3. Generate the list of all rotations of all titles;
4. Sort this list on first words;
5. Output the result, one title per line.

Using the functions *words*, *lines* and *unparse* designed in Section 4.3, and a suitably generalised sorting function, design a function *kwic* that solves the problem. Modify your solution so that *kwic* takes an extra argument – a list *ws* of "inconsequential" words (such as "and", "of", and "the") – and produces only that sublist of rotated titles whose first word is not in *ws*.

6.4.7 Using a divide and conquer approach, show that the maximum and minimum values in a list of n elements can together be determined in no more than $3n/2$ comparison operations.

6.4.8 The product of two complex numbers $a + ib$ and $c + id$ is given by $(ac - bd) + i(ad + bc)$. This involves four ordinary multiplications. Find another method which uses only three multiplications.

6.4.9 Consider the following variant of the basic search problem: given an integer a and a total predicate p, find the smallest x, with $a \leq x$, such that $(p\ x)$ holds. The difference here is that the search is not confined to a bounded interval. Using infinite lists (which will be discussed in the next chapter), one solution can be formulated in the following way:

$$\textit{find p a} \quad = \quad \textit{hd}\,[x \mid x \leftarrow [a\,..]; \, p\,x]$$

If *find p a* $= a + n$, then $O(n)$ evaluations of p will be required to discover the answer.

If p is monotonic, then the number of evaluations of p can be reduced to $O(\log n)$ steps. How? (*Hint:* Consider a search that tries the values

$a, 2a, 4a, \ldots, 2^k a, \ldots$ until some value $b = 2^t a$ is found satisfying p (assume $a > 0$).)

6.4.10 Suppose *minout xs*, where *xs* is a list of distinct natural numbers, returns the smallest number not in *xs*. Using a divide and conquer approach, show how to compute *minout* in linear time.

6.5 Search and enumeration

In the previous section we considered the simple problem of searching an interval. The more general problem of *combinatorial* search involves searching for combinations of objects that satisfy a given property. Two such problems, both well-known puzzles, are treated in this section. In particular, we show how the traditional method of 'backtracking', often used to solve such problems, can be implemented by a technique known as 'list of successes'. We also explore how variations in the approach can affect efficiency.

6.5.1 Eight queens

Our first puzzle is the Eight Queens problem. Given a chessboard and eight queens, one must place the queens on the board so that no two queens hold each other in check; that is, no two queens may lie in the same row, column, or diagonal. A solution to this problem is shown in Figure 6.1.

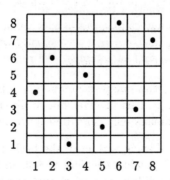

Figure 6.1 A solution to the Eight Queens problem.

A moment's thought reveals that each column (and each row) must contain exactly one queen, so one way to find a solution is as follows. Place a queen in the first column: any position will do. Then place a queen in the second column: any position not held in check by the first queen will do. Then place a queen in the third column: any position not held in check by the first two queens will do. Continue in this way until all eight queens have been placed. If at any point it is impossible to place a queen in column $m+1$ (because all positions are in check), then 'backtrack': reapply the method to find a different legal position for the queens in the first m columns, and try again.

To formalise this solution, we need a way to represent a board containing queens in the first m columns. We do so by a list of length m, giving for each column the row in which its queen appears. For example, the list:

$$[4,6,1,5,2,8,3,7]$$

represents the solution in Figure 6.1. We will also write (i,j) to stand for a queen located in column i and row j. Thus, the list above represents queens at coordinates $(1,4)$, $(2,6)$, $(3,1)$, and so on.

To extend a placement p by adding a queen in row n we simply write $p \mathbin{+\!\!+} [n]$; this places the new queen in column $(\#p+1)$. This extension is safe if no queen in the placement p puts the new queen in check:

$$safe\ p\ n\ =\ and\ [\neg check\,(i,j)\,(m,n) \mid (i,j) \leftarrow zip\,([1\mathinner{.\,.}\#p],p)]$$
$$\textbf{where}\ \ m = \#p + 1$$

Two queens at coordinates (i,j) and (m,n) will hold each other in check if they are in the same row or either of two diagonals:

$$check\,(i,j)\,(m,n)\ =\ (j=n) \vee (i+j=m+n) \vee (i-j=m-n)$$

We do not need to test whether two queens are in the same column, because our representation guarantees that this cannot occur.

Because of 'backtracking' we may need to consider several different ways of placing queens in the first m columns. We represent this by designing a function $queens\ m$ that returns all placements queens in the first m columns such that no two queens are in check:

$$queens\ 0\ \ \ \ \ =\ [[\,]]$$
$$queens\,(m+1)\ =\ [p \mathbin{+\!\!+} [n] \mid p \leftarrow queens\ m;\ n \leftarrow [1\mathinner{.\,.}8];\ safe\ p\ n]$$

In words, there is exactly one placement of no queens, represented by the empty list. Each placement of $(m+1)$ queens consists of a placement p of m queens, plus a new queen placed in some row n from 1 to 8, such that the new queen is safe from check by any queen in p.

If we want to find just one solution to the Eight Queens problem, then the first will do as well as any other:

? $hd\,(queens\ 8)$
$[1,5,8,6,3,7,2,4]$

If we prefer to find all solutions, then just typing $queens\ 8$ does the trick. As it happens, there is a total of 92 solutions. Because of the way $queens$ is written, these solutions are produced in lexical order: all solutions beginning with 1 are printed before all solutions beginning with 2, and so on.

Note that the concept of 'backtracking' has disappeared from the final program. Instead of thinking in a dynamic way of generating one solution and then another, we think in a static way of generating a list of all possible solutions. The name 'list of successes' has been coined to describe this technique. Because outermost reduction is used, only those parts of the lists that are actually needed will be computed. Thus, printing just the first solution requires less work than printing all the solutions. (For a particular run on an actual system, computing the first solution $hd\ (queens\ 8)$ required only 6 per cent of the time to compute all solutions $queens\ 8$.)

6.5.2   Search order

We now consider two ways of changing the order in which solutions are searched: switching the order of generators in the list comprehension, and permuting the order in which solutions are enumerated. The first dramatically increases the time required to find the first solution, while the second may dramatically reduce it. In both cases, the time to find all solutions remains virtually unchanged.

Generator order. An obvious variation of the previous program is:

$$
\begin{aligned}
sneeuq\ 0 \quad &=\quad [[\,]] \\
sneeuq\ (m+1) \quad &=\quad [p \mathbin{+\!\!+} [n] \mid n \leftarrow [1\mathinner{\ldotp\ldotp}8];\ p \leftarrow ps;\ safe\ p\ n] \\
&\quad\ \textbf{where}\ ps = sneeuq\ m
\end{aligned}
$$

This reverses the order of the two generators in the list comprehension. The call of $sneeuq\ m$ has been brought out into a where clause, since otherwise it would be recomputed once for each value of n.

Clearly, $sneeuq$ finds the same solutions as $queens$, but it finds them in a different order. The first solution it finds is:

? $sneeuq$ 8
$[4, 2, 7, 3, 6, 8, 5, 1]$

This is exactly the reverse of the first solution found by $queens$. It is not hard to see why: whereas $queens$ first considers all solutions beginning with 1, then beginning with 2, and so on, $sneeuq$ first considers all solutions *ending* with 1, then ending with 2, and so on. Symmetry guarantees that the reverse of every solution is itself a valid solution. In general, we have that:

$$queens\ m \quad = \quad map\ reverse\ (sneeuq\ m)$$

for every m from 0 to 8.

Which is faster, $queens$ or $sneeuq$? If we want to find all solutions, then it is not hard to see that both must perform essentially the same computations, and hence require essentially the same amount of time. (This is confirmed by a run on an actual system, which shows that the two times are within 3 per cent of each other.)

On the other hand, if we want to find only the first solution, then it is not immediately clear what their relative speeds will be. Since cleverness fails us, let us try a run on an actual system – lo and behold, it turns out that *queens* is more than ten times faster than *sneeuq*! Since both take equally long to find all solutions, this means that *sneeuq* takes a long time to find the first solution and then finds the remaining solutions relatively quickly, while *queens* divides the work more evenly. In particular, the actual runs reveal that *sneeuq* takes 80 per cent of its time to find the first solution, as compared to only 6 per cent for *queens*.

This behaviour is due purely to the reversal in generator order. To compute *sneeuq* $(m + 1)$, for each n from 1 to 8, the list *sneeuq m* is scanned for a placement p such that *safe p n* is true. Now, the first element of *sneeuq* 8 is

$$[4, 2, 7, 3, 6, 8, 5, 1]$$

This ends in a 1, so it must have been found on the first scan of *sneeuq* 7. How far did the list *sneeuq* 7 have to be scanned? Well, the element of *sneeuq* 7 that was found is:

$$[4, 2, 7, 3, 6, 8, 5]$$

This ends in a 5, so it must have been found on the fifth scan of *sneeuq* 6. Further, all solutions ending in a 1, 2, 3, or 4 must appear before this solution in the list *sneeuq* 7. So, to find the *first* element of the list *sneeuq* 8 required generating *over half* of the list *sneeuq* 7, and generating *all* of the list *sneeuq* 6. Once the lists *sneeuq* 7 and *sneeuq* 6 are generated they are saved (by the where clause), so this explains why proportionately so much of the work goes into finding the first solution.

In contrast, to compute *queens* $(m + 1)$, for each p in the list *queens m*, each n from 1 to 8 is tested to see if *safe p n* is true. Only a small fraction of the list *queens* 7 needs to be examined before the first solution is found, and this in turn requires examining only a small fraction of the list *queens* 6. So the work of finding the first solution is a relatively small proportion of the work of finding all solutions.

Enumeration order. As noted, *queens* 8 first returns all solutions beginning with 1, then all solutions beginning with 2, and so on. As it turns out, there are many more solutions beginning with a 4 than there are solutions beginning with a 1. Therefore, if we only want to find one solution, it may be better to enumerate solutions starting from row 4 rather than row 1. We can modify *queens* to accomplish this as follows:

$$queens4\ 0\qquad\quad =\quad [[\,]]$$
$$queens4\ (m + 1)\quad =\quad [p +\!\!+ [n] \mid p \leftarrow queens4\ m;\ n \leftarrow ns;\ safe\ p\ n]$$
$$\textbf{where}\ ns = [4\mathinner{\ldotp\ldotp}8] +\!\!+ [1\mathinner{\ldotp\ldotp}3]$$

A run confirms that this finds the first solution in only 14% of the time required by *queens*.

It was possible to find the first solution faster simply because the part of the solution space enumerated first (that is, solutions with the first queen in column 4) contains more solutions. Moral: if one is searching for a needle in a haystack, look in the part of the haystack that contains more needles.

Of course, this does no good if one wants to find all the needles in the haystack, and indeed, *queens4* is no faster than *queens* if one wants to find all solutions to the Eight Queens problem.

6.5.3 Instant insanity

Our second puzzle is marketed under the name 'Instant Insanity'. It consists of four cubes, with faces coloured blue, green, red, or white. The problem is to arrange the cubes in a vertical pile such that each visible column of faces contains four distinct colours. Like Eight Queens, we may solve this puzzle via backtracking.

We will represent a cube by listing the colours of its six faces in the following order: up, front, right, back, left, down. Each colour is indicated by a letter: blue ('B'), green ('G'), red ('R'), and white ('W'). Hence, each cube is represented by a string of six letters. The four cubes in the marketed puzzle are represented by:

$$cubes \; = \; [\text{``BGWGBR''}, \text{``WGBWRR''}, \text{``GWRBRR''}, \text{``BRGGWW''}]$$

Thus, the first cube is blue on top, green in front, and so on.

A cube must be oriented before placing it in the pile. The orientation of a cube can be changed by rotating it (through 90 degrees, leaving up and down in place); twisting it (about an axis extending from the up/front/right corner to the back/left/down corner); or flipping it (exchanging up and down, front and left, back and right).

$$rot \, [u, f, r, b, l, d] \; = \; [u, r, b, l, f, d]$$
$$twist \, [u, f, r, b, l, d] \; = \; [f, r, u, l, d, b]$$
$$flip \, [u, f, r, b, l, d] \; = \; [d, l, b, r, f, u]$$

Rotating a cube four times brings it back to its original position, as does twisting it three times, or flipping it twice. Hence there are $24 = 4 \times 3 \times 2$ different ways to orient a cube:

$$orientations \, c \; = \; [c''' \mid c' \; \leftarrow \; [c, rot \, c, rot \, (rot \, c), rot \, (rot \, (rot \, c))];$$
$$c'' \; \leftarrow \; [c', twist \, c', twist \, (twist \, c')];$$
$$c''' \; \leftarrow \; [c'', flip \, c'']]$$

Once a cube is placed in a pile, only its sides (front, right, back, left) will be visible:

$$visible \, [u, f, r, b, l, d] \; = \; [f, r, b, l]$$

Two cubes are compatible if they have different colours on every visible side:

$$compatible \; c \; c' \;\; = \;\; and \, [x \neq x' \mid (x, x') \leftarrow zip \, (visible \, c, visible \, c')]$$

It is allowed to add a cube c to a pile of cubes cs if it is compatible with every cube in the pile:

$$allowed \; c \; cs \;\; = \;\; and \, [compatible \, c \, c' \mid c' \leftarrow cs]$$

Since we are using the 'list of successes' method, we will design a function *solutions cs* that returns a list of all ways of orienting each cube in cs so that no side of the pile has two faces the same.

$$
\begin{aligned}
solutions \, [\,] \quad &= \quad [[\,]] \\
solutions \, (c : cs) \quad &= \quad [c' : cs' \mid cs' \leftarrow solutions \, cs; \\
&\qquad\qquad c' \; \leftarrow orientations \, c; \\
&\qquad\qquad allowed \, c' \, cs']
\end{aligned}
$$

In words, there is only one solution for an empty pile of cubes, namely the empty pile itself. Each solution for a pile $(c : cs)$ consists of a solution for the pile cs, and an orientation of the cube c that is an allowed extension of this pile.

Summary. We have presented programs that use backtracking search to find solutions to two well-known combinatorial puzzles. The backtracking algorithms have been implemented using a technique called 'list of successes'. Although this technique returns a list of all solutions to the problem, outermost reduction enables the first solution to be computed in a fraction of the time required to compute all solutions. Altering the search order can make a dramatic difference in the time to find the first solution, though the time to find all solutions remains unchanged. We will see additional applications of the 'list of successes' technique in Chapter 9.

Exercises

6.5.1 Because no two queens may appear in the same row, *safe p n* returns false if n appears in the list p. Therefore, it is safe to draw n from the list $[1 \,.\,.\, 8]$ with elements appearing in p removed. Modify the definitions of *queens*, *safe*, and *check* to take advantage of this observation.

6.5.2 Could the modification suggested by the previous exercise also be applied to *sneeuq*?

6.5.3 Every solution to the Eight Queens problem remains a solution after reflection through a vertical, horizontal, or diagonal line through the middle of the board; or after the board is rotated about its middle by 90 degrees. Write functions to convert a placement p into the placements corresponding to each of these transformations.

6.5.4 Use reflection through a horizontal line to write a program that finds all solutions to the Eight Queens problem twice as quickly as *queens*. Would it be as easy to use reflection through a vertical line in this way?

6.5.5 Use backtracking to write a program that finds all solutions to the Eight Queens problem that are symmetric around a diagonal.

6.5.6 The following program computes the length of (*queens i*) for each *i* from 0 to 8:
$$[\#(queens\ i)\ |\ i \leftarrow [0\mathbin{..}8]]$$
This program is wasteful, because the computation of, say, (*queens* 8) will re-compute (*queens* 7), which has already been computed. Write a more efficient program to compute the same result.

6.5.7 Why might one suspect that there would be more solutions to the Eight Queens problem that have the first queen in row 4 than have the first queen in row 1?

6.5.8 We can further explore the advantages of different search orders, using a function *rowqueens nss* that takes a list of lists specifying for each column the order in which its rows should be tried. For example, the search order used by *queens4* is duplicated by:
$$rowqueens\ (copy\ 8\ ([4\mathbin{..}8] \mathbin{+\!\!+} [1\mathbin{..}3]))$$
A search that tries row 4 first for column 1, and tries the rows in the order [1..8] otherwise, is specified by:
$$rowqueens\ (([4\mathbin{..}8] \mathbin{+\!\!+} [1\mathbin{..}3]) : copy\ 7\ [1\mathbin{..}8])$$
Write *rowqueens*.

6.5.9 The program *solutions* finds each solution to the Instant Insanity problem four times, each time rotated through 90 degrees. Modify *solutions* to find each solution only once.

6.5.10 Write a function that takes a pile of cubes *cs* and returns a list of the faces visible on each of the four sides of the pile.

6.5.11 A Magic Square of size n consists of the numbers from 1 to n^2 arranged in a square array such that the sum of any row, column, and diagonal is the same. Here is a Magic Square of size 3, the sum of each row, column, and diagonal being 15:

6	7	2
1	5	9
8	3	4

Design a program that finds Magic Squares.

6.5.12 There is a (unique) 9-digit number x with the following properties: (i) each of the digits 1 to 9 appears exactly once in x; (ii) For $1 \leq n \leq 9$ the number formed by taking the first n digits of x is exactly divisible by n. With pen and paper and a little intelligence, it is fairly easy to discover x, but write a program instead.

6.5.13 A crypt-arithmetic puzzle consists of three words, containing no more than ten different letters, arranged thus:

$$FOUR$$
$$\underline{+\,FIVE}$$
$$NINE$$

The problem is solved by giving a mapping of letters to digits such that the result is a valid statement of arithmetic. For example, the above problem is solved by the mapping:

$$E \rightarrow 3;\ F \rightarrow 2;\ I \rightarrow 4;\ N \rightarrow 5;\ O \rightarrow 9;\ R \rightarrow 0;\ U \rightarrow 7;\ V \rightarrow 8$$

Design a program that solves crypt-arithmetic puzzles.

Chapter 7

Infinite Lists

Lists can be infinite as well as finite. In this chapter we shall describe some basic operations on infinite lists, show how they can be characterised as the limit of a sequence of approximations, and develop proof methods for reasoning about their properties, including a way to extend the principle of structural induction. We shall also give some illustrative applications. In particular, infinite lists can be used to model sequences of events ordered in time, so they provide a suitable framework in which to study interactive processes.

7.1 Infinite lists

Just as the finite list of integers from m to n is denoted by $[m \mathbin{..} n]$, the infinite list of all integers from m upwards is denoted by $[m \mathbin{..}]$. Thus, in a session one might have:

? $[1 \mathbin{..}]$
$[1, 2, 3, 4, 5, 6, 7, 8, 9, 10, 11, 12, 13, 14, 15, 16, \{interrupted\}$

?

Here, the user requested the computer to print the list of all integers starting from the number 1. Clearly it would take forever to print this list in full. After the first few elements of the list were printed the user got bored and hit the 'interrupt' key, which caused the computer to stop printing the list, type "$\{interrupted\}$" and wait for a new expression.

Infinite lists can be used just like any other lists in a program. A function can take an infinite list as an argument or return an infinite list as a result. For example, the following statements about infinite lists are all true:

$$
\begin{aligned}
\mathit{take}\, n\, [1 \mathbin{..}] &= [1 \mathbin{..} n] \\
[m \mathbin{..}]\,!\, n &= m + n \\
\mathit{map\ factorial}\, [1 \mathbin{..}] &= \mathit{scan}\, (\times)\, 1\, [1 \mathbin{..}]
\end{aligned}
$$

It is also possible to use infinite lists in list comprehensions. For example, the expression:

$$[x \char94 2 \mid x \leftarrow [1\,..];\; odd\ x]$$

denotes the list of all odd squares.

It is even possible to have an infinite list of infinite lists. For example, if we define:

$$powertable \;=\; [[m \char94 n \mid m \leftarrow [1\,..]] \mid n \leftarrow [2\,..]]$$

then *powertable* is an infinite list, each element of which is also an infinite list:

$$\begin{aligned} powertable \;=\; & [\,[1,4,9,16,25,\ldots], \\ & [1,8,27,64,125,\ldots], \\ & [1,16,81,256,625,\ldots], \\ & \ldots\,] \end{aligned}$$

Displaying a structure like *powertable* is problematic. If we type *powertable* in a session, then the computer will never get past trying to print the first row:

? powertable
$[[1,4,9,16,25,\{interrupted\}$

However, we can always see the second row by selecting it explicitly:

? powertable ! 1
$[1,8,27,64,125,\{interrupted\}$

The other rows of *powertable* can be displayed in a similar manner.

It is important *not* to assume that infinite lists in computing have the same kinds of properties as infinite sets do in conventional mathematics. For example, in set theory one might write:

$$\{x^2 \mid x \in \{1,2,3,4,\ldots\};\; x^2 < 10\}$$

to stand for the set of all squares that are less than 10, and this expression denotes the finite set $\{1,4,9\}$. However, if we type the corresponding list comprehension in a session then we get:

? $[x \char94 2 \mid x \leftarrow [1\,..];\; x \char94 2 < 10]$
$[1,4,9$

What has happened here is that the computer finds the first three elements and then goes into an infinite loop searching for some element in the infinite list $[4,5,6,\ldots]$ whose square is less than 10. Although it is reasonable to expect a mathematician to recognise that there is no such value, it is not reasonable to expect the same degree of sophistication from a computer program. In other words, we do not suppose that a mechanical evaluator is capable of conducting proofs, however trivial they might be. This does not mean that the behaviour of the computer is 'unmathematical', only that set theory is not the right theory for describing computations. A suitable theory will be presented later, and we shall see that we can give a precise value to the above expression without lapsing into informal explanations like 'and then it goes into an infinite loop'. In particular, the above expression has the precise value $1 : 4 : 9 : \perp$.

Incidentally, it is not difficult to modify the list comprehension so that it does return a proper list of all squares less than 10. Using the rules described in Chapter 3, we can can convert the comprehension into the equivalent form:

$$\textit{filter} \; (< 10) \; (\textit{map} \; (\hat{\;}2) \; [1 \mathinner{..}])$$

and changing the *filter* to *takewhile* yields the desired result:

? $\textit{takewhile} \; (< 10) \; (\textit{map} \; (\hat{\;}2) \; [1 \mathinner{..}])$
$[1, 4, 9]$

This works because *takewhile* stops scanning as soon as an element is found that does not satisfy the predicate, whereas *filter* scans the entire list. In effect, the mathematician's knowledge that one can stop looking as soon as the first square greater than 10 is encountered is here encoded in the choice to use *takewhile* to write the expression.

Exercises

7.1.1 Write a program that prints the infinite text:

1 sheep, 2 sheep, 3 sheep, 4 sheep, ...

as an aid for insomniacs.

7.1.2 Can every element of *powertable* be printed by first concatenating with *concat*? Define an infinite list *powerlist* that does return a list of all powers (greater than one) of all positive integers.

7.1.3 If:
$$\textit{cubes} = [i \hat{\;} 3 \mid i \leftarrow [1 \mathinner{..}]]$$
what are the values of $(64 \text{ in } \textit{cubes})$ and $(65 \text{ in } \textit{cubes})$?

7.2 Iterate

Recall that in mathematics, the notation f^n denotes a function composed with itself n times; thus $f^0 = id$, $f^1 = f$, $f^2 = f \cdot f$, $f^3 = f \cdot f \cdot f$, and so on, where *id* is the identity function. In our notation we will write f^n as (*power f n*). One way to define *power* is by the equations:

$$power\ f\ 0 \quad = \quad id$$
$$power\ f\ (n+1) \quad = \quad f \cdot power\ f\ n$$

Observe that f^n is similar in form to x^n, which denotes a number multiplied by itself n times, but one should be careful not to confuse the two.

The function *iterate* is defined informally as follows:

$$iterate\ f\ x \quad = \quad [x, f\ x, f^2 x, f^3 x, \ldots]$$

Thus *iterate* takes a function and a starting value and returns an infinite list. For example:

$$iterate\ (+1)\ 1 \quad = \quad [1,2,3,4,5,\ldots]$$
$$iterate\ (\times 2)\ 1 \quad = \quad [1,2,4,8,16,32,\ldots]$$
$$iterate\ (\mathbf{div}10)\ 2718 \quad = \quad [2718,271,27,2,0,0,\ldots]$$

We also have:

$$[m\ ..\ ] \quad = \quad iterate\ (+1)\ m$$
$$[m\ ..\ n] \quad = \quad takewhile\ (\leq n)\ (iterate\ (+1)\ m)$$

These equations provide one way of defining the notations $[m\ ..\ ]$ and $[m\ ..\ n]$. In the second equation, *takewhile* is used to truncate the infinite list to a finite list.

Here are some more examples of the use of *iterate*. First, the digits of a positive integer can be extracted by the function *digits* defined as follows:

$$digits \quad = \quad reverse \cdot map\ (\mathbf{mod}10) \cdot takewhile\ (\neq 0) \cdot iterate\ (\mathbf{div}10)$$

For example:

$$digits\ 2718$$
$$= \quad (reverse \cdot map\ (\mathbf{mod}10) \cdot takewhile\ (\neq 0))\ [2718,271,27,2,0,0,\ldots]$$
$$= \quad (reverse \cdot map\ (\mathbf{mod}10))\ [2718,271,27,2]$$
$$= \quad reverse\ [8,1,7,2]$$
$$= \quad [2,7,1,8]$$

Next, consider the function (*group n*) which breaks a list into segments of length n. We have:

$$group\ n \quad = \quad map\ (take\ n) \cdot takewhile\ (\neq [\ ]) \cdot iterate\ (drop\ n)$$

If the original list does not have a length which is evenly divisible by n, then the last segment will have length strictly less than n.

As the last two examples suggest, one often finds *map*, *takewhile*, and *iterate* composed together in sequence. Suppose we capture this pattern of computation as a generic function, *unfold* say, defined as follows:

$$unfold \ h \ p \ t \ = \ map \ h \cdot takewhile \ p \cdot iterate \ t$$

The key feature about *unfold* is that it is a general function for producing lists. Moreover, the functions h, t, and p correspond to simple operations on lists. We have:

$$\begin{aligned} hd \ (unfold \ h \ p \ t \ x) &= \ h \ x \\ tl \ (unfold \ h \ p \ t \ x) &= \ unfold \ h \ p \ t \ (t \ x) \\ nonnull \ (unfold \ h \ p \ t \ x) &= \ p \ x \end{aligned}$$

Thus, the first argument h of *unfold* is a function which corresponds to hd, the third function, t, corresponds to tl, and the second function, p, to a predicate which tests whether the list is empty or not.

A formal, recursive definition of *iterate* can be given in two ways. The first is a straightforward translation of the informal definition given above:

$$iterate \ f \ x \ = \ [power \ f \ i \ x \mid i \leftarrow [0 \, . \, .]]$$

This definition is rather inefficient, since it computes each of (*power f* 0 *x*), (*power f* 1 *x*), (*power f* 2 *x*), and so on, independently. Assuming that an application of f can be computed in a constant number of steps, computing (*power f i x*) requires a number of steps proportional to i. Hence, computing the first n elements of (*iterate f x*) requires a number of steps proportional to:

$$1 + 2 + \cdots + n = \frac{n(n+1)}{2}$$

that is, $O(n^2)$ steps.

The second way to define *iterate* is recursively, as follows:

$$iterate \ f \ x \ = \ x : iterate \ f \ (f \ x)$$

For example:

$$\begin{aligned} iterate \ (\times 2) \ 1 &= \ 1 : iterate \ (\times 2) \ ((\times 2) \ 1) \\ &= \ 1 : 2 : iterate \ (\times 2) \ ((\times 2) \ 2) \\ &= \ 1 : 2 : 4 : iterate \ (\times 2) \ ((\times 2) \ 4) \\ &= \ \cdots \end{aligned}$$

and so on. Here, each element of the result list is computed by applying f once to the previous element, and so the first n elements of (*iterate f x*) can be computed in $O(n)$ steps. The function *iterate* is useful largely because it can be computed in this efficient way. Incidentally, notice that *iterate* and *scan* are similar, in that both compute each element of the output list in terms of the preceding element.

Exercises

7.2.1 What is the value of:

$$map\ (3\times)\ [0\,..] = iterate\ (+3)\ 0$$

when '=' means denotational equality? What is its value when '=' means computable equality?

7.2.2 Use *iterate* to write an expression equivalent to $[a, b\,..\,c]$.

7.2.3 Define a function *showint* :: $num \rightarrow [char]$ that, given an integer, returns the string that denotes its value. For example, *showint* $42 = $ "42". (Don't use *show*, that would be cheating.)

7.2.4 Define the function *getint* :: $[char] \rightarrow num$ that is the inverse of *showint*. For example, *getint* "42" $= 42$. (This doesn't use infinite lists.)

7.3   Example: generating primes

The Greek mathematician Eratosthenes described essentially the following procedure for generating the list of all prime numbers:

1. Write down the list of numbers $2, 3, \ldots$;
2. Mark the first element p of this list as prime;
3. Delete all multiples of p from the list;
4. Return to step 2.

As a description of an algorithm, the above procedure appears highly unconventional: not only does the process as a whole not terminate, the first and third steps do not terminate either. It would seem that to implement Eratosthenes' method requires the creation of an infinite number of infinite processes.

Here is a diagram showing the first few steps of the algorithm:

```
 2   3   4   5   6   7   8   9  10  11  12  13  14  15  ···
     3       5       7       9      11      13      15  ···
             5       7              11      13          ···
                     7              11      13          ···
                             ⋮
```

In each line a bar has been drawn under every pth position, where p is the prime number that begins the line. One can think of these bars as forming an infinite 'sieve', which sifts the list of all numbers (poured into the top) until only primes are left. For this reason the method is usually called 'The Sieve of Eratosthenes'.

Eratosthenes' sieve is remarkably easy to describe as a functional program:

$$\begin{aligned} primes \quad &= \quad map\ hd\ (iterate\ sieve\ [2\mathbin{..}]) \\ sieve\ (p : xs) \quad &= \quad [x \mid x \leftarrow xs;\ x \bmod p \neq 0] \end{aligned}$$

This defines *primes* to be the infinite list of all prime numbers. The program is, more or less, a direct translation of the English description. Step 1 is represented by the term $[2\mathbin{..}]$, the cumulative effect of Step 2 by the term *map hd*, Step 3 by the function *sieve*, and Step 4 by the function *iterate*. Notice that the term $(iterate\ sieve\ [2\mathbin{..}])$ generates an infinite list of infinite lists.

Having defined *primes* as an infinite list, one can choose which portion of it to evaluate as a separate logical step. For instance, the first 100 primes will be generated by evaluating:

$$take\ 100\ primes$$

Similarly, we can obtain all the primes less than 100 by evaluating:

$$takewhile\ (< 100)\ primes$$

By freeing the generation of *primes* from the constraints of finiteness, we obtain a modular definition on which different 'boundary' conditions can be imposed in different situations.

It might appear that the construction of *primes* through the intermediary of an infinite list of infinite lists leads to a definition which is less efficient than it might otherwise be. Of course, these component lists are not computed in their entirety, but only in parts as and when evaluation demands. Well, let us try and improve the efficiency of the definition. Suppose we rewrite *primes* in the form:

$$\begin{aligned} primes \quad &= \quad rsieve\ [2\mathbin{..}] \\ rsieve\ xs \quad &= \quad map\ hd\ (iterate\ sieve\ xs) \end{aligned}$$

This is certainly no more efficient than the original version, but it serves as the starting point for a little massage. First, we have:

$$rsieve\ (p : xs) = map\ hd\ (iterate\ sieve\ (p : xs))$$

by instantiating $(p : xs)$ for xs in the definition of *rsieve*. Now, using the definition of *iterate*, the right-hand expression is equal to:

$$map\ hd\ ((p : xs) : iterate\ sieve\ (sieve\ (p : xs)))$$

Using the definition of *map* and *hd*, this expression is equal to:

$$p : map\ hd\ (iterate\ sieve\ (sieve\ (p : xs)))$$

and using the definition of *sieve*, it becomes:

$$p : map \; hd \; (iterate \; sieve \; [x \mid x \leftarrow xs; \; x \bmod p \neq 0])$$

Now comes the final, but crucial step. The second term in this expression is just another instance of *rsieve*, so the expression as a whole is equal to:

$$p : rsieve \; [x \mid x \leftarrow xs; \; x \bmod p \neq 0]$$

Essentially, what we have just accomplished is to show that:

$$rsieve \; (p : xs) = p : rsieve \; [x \mid x \leftarrow xs; \; x \bmod p \neq 0]$$

What is more, we can use this equation as a *new* definition of *rsieve*: both definitions produce a well-defined list, and the argument above shows that they must produce the same list. Starting with one definition of *rsieve* we have therefore synthesised another. Observe also that the synthesis proceeded by a chain of equational reasoning using only the definitions of the functions appearing in the definition. The second definition uses recursion explicitly, while the former does not. On the other hand, the new definition does not involve the creation of an infinite number of infinite lists, and is therefore slightly more efficient.

Exercises

7.3.1 Write a program to find the first prime number greater than 1000.

7.3.2 Consider the two functions:

$$
\begin{aligned}
sieve \; (p : xs) &= [x \mid x \leftarrow xs; \; x \bmod p \neq 0] \\
sieve' \; (p : xs) &= xs \; -\!- \; iterate \; (+p) \; 0
\end{aligned}
$$

Do they compute the same result? Compare the efficiency of the program for generating infinite lists of primes using the two definitions of *sieve*. (Hint: If *xs* is a list that contains *no* multiples of p, how many steps does it take to compute the first n elements of $sieve \; (p : xs)$ and $sieve' \; (p : xs)$?)

7.4 Infinite lists as limits

It has already been mentioned that some care is needed when dealing with infinite lists. In particular, we noted that the expression:

$$filter \; (< 10) \; (map \; (\hat{\;}2) \; [1 \mathinner{.\,.}])$$

does not have the value $[1, 4, 9]$, as one might expect, but rather the value $1 : 4 : 9 : \bot$. In order to understand more clearly why this is so, a theory of infinite lists is required, and that is what this section will provide, at least informally.

In mathematics, one way of dealing with infinite objects is by *limits*. An infinite object may be defined to be the limit of an infinite sequence of approximations. For example, the transcendental number π:

$$\pi = 3.14159265358979323846\cdots,$$

is an infinite object in this sense. It can be thought of as the limit of the infinite sequence of approximations:

$$3$$
$$3.1$$
$$3.14$$
$$3.141$$
$$3.1415$$
$$\vdots$$

The first element of the sequence, 3, is a fairly crude approximation to π. The next element, 3.1, is a little better; 3.14 is better still, and so on.

Similarly, an infinite list can also be regarded as the limit of a sequence of 'approximations'. For example, the infinite list $[1\,..\,]$ is a limit of the following sequence:

$$\perp$$
$$1 : \perp$$
$$1 : 2 : \perp$$
$$1 : 2 : 3 : \perp$$
$$\vdots$$

Again, the sequence consists of better and better approximations to the intended limit. The first term, $\perp$, is the undefined element, and thus a very crude approximation: it tells us nothing about the intended limit. The next term, $1 : \perp$ is a slightly better approximation: it tells us that the intended limit is a list whose first element is 1, but says nothing about the rest of the list. The following term, $1 : 2 : \perp$, is a little better still, and so on. Each successively better approximation is derived by replacing $\perp$ with a more defined value, and thus gives more information about the intended limit.

Any list ending in bottom, i.e. any list of the form $x_1 : x_2 : \cdots : x_n : \perp$, will be called a *partial list*. Every infinite list is the limit of an infinite sequence of partial lists. Thus, we have three kinds of lists: *finite* lists, which end in [] (such as $1 : 2 : 3 : []$, also written $[1,2,3]$); *partial* lists, which end in $\perp$, (such as $1 : 2 : 3 : \perp$); and *infinite* lists, which do not end at all (such as $[1,2,3,\ldots]$).

Now it turns out that if $xs_1,\ xs_2,\ xs_3,\ \ldots$ is an infinite sequence whose limit is xs, and f is a *computable* function, then $f\ xs_1,\ f\ xs_2,\ f\ xs_3,\ \ldots$ is an infinite sequence whose limit is $f\ xs$. This property, called *continuity*, is not true of arbitrary functions, but is true of all computable functions. For example, since $[1..]$ is the limit of the sequence given above, we can compute $map\ (\times 2)\ [1..]$ as follows:

$$
\begin{aligned}
map\ (\times 2)\ \perp &= \perp \\
map\ (\times 2)\ (1:\perp) &= 2:\perp \\
map\ (\times 2)\ (1:2:\perp) &= 2:4:\perp \\
map\ (\times 2)\ (1:2:3:\perp) &= 2:4:6:\perp \\
&\vdots
\end{aligned}
$$

The limit of this sequence is the infinite list $[2,4,6,8,\ldots]$ of positive even integers, just as we would expect.

A short word about applying functions to partial lists is in order here. No equation defining map matches $map\ (\times 2)\ \perp$ because $\perp$ does not match either $[\,]$ or $(x:xs)$. Thus $map\ (\times 2)\ \perp = \perp$ and we say this follows from *case exhaustion* on map. Thus we have:

$$
\begin{aligned}
map\ (\times 2)\ (1:\perp) &= (1\times 2):(map\ (\times 2)\ \perp) \quad (map.2) \\
&= 2:\perp \quad\quad\quad\quad\quad\quad\quad\quad (map.0)
\end{aligned}
$$

where we write $(map.0)$ to indicate case exhaustion on map. The rest of the sequence above is evaluated similarly.

As a second example, *filter even* $[1..]$ can be computed as follows:

$$
\begin{aligned}
filter\ even\ \perp &= \perp \\
filter\ even\ (1:\perp) &= \perp \\
filter\ even\ (1:2:\perp) &= 2:\perp \\
filter\ even\ (1:2:3:\perp) &= 2:\perp \\
filter\ even\ (1:2:3:4:\perp) &= 2:4:\perp \\
&\vdots
\end{aligned}
$$

Again, the limit is the infinite list $[2,4,6,\ldots]$, as expected. This gives a (simple) example of how an infinite list may be the limit of two different sequences.

Now consider the expression:

$$filter\ (<10)\ (map\ (\hat{\ }2)\ [1..])$$

mentioned earlier. By the method above, one can compute that $map(\hat{\ }2)[1..]$ is the limit of the infinite sequence that begins:

$$
\begin{aligned}
&\perp \\
&1:\perp \\
&1:4:\perp \\
&\vdots
\end{aligned}
$$

Applying *filter* (< 10) to this sequence gives the new sequence:

$$
\begin{array}{lcl}
filter\ (< 10)\ \bot & = & \bot \\
filter\ (< 10)\ (1 : \bot) & = & 1 : \bot \\
filter\ (< 10)\ (1 : 4 : \bot) & = & 1 : 4 : \bot \\
filter\ (< 10)\ (1 : 4 : 9 : \bot) & = & 1 : 4 : 9 : \bot \\
filter\ (< 10)\ (1 : 4 : 9 : 16 : \bot) & = & 1 : 4 : 9 : \bot \\
filter\ (< 10)\ (1 : 4 : 9 : 16 : 25 : \bot) & = & 1 : 4 : 9 : \bot \\
& \vdots &
\end{array}
$$

Here every element of the sequence after the third is equal to $1 : 4 : 9 : \bot$, and so that must also be the limit of the sequence. So we have shown:

$$filter\ (< 10)\ (map\ (\char`\~2)\ [1\mathbin{..}]) = 1 : 4 : 9 : \bot$$

as was asserted previously.

On the other hand, applying *takewhile* (< 10) to the first sequence above gives the sequence:

$$
\begin{array}{lcl}
takewhile\ (< 10)\ \bot & = & \bot \\
takewhile\ (< 10)\ (1 : \bot) & = & 1 : \bot \\
takewhile\ (< 10)\ (1 : 4 : \bot) & = & 1 : 4 : \bot \\
takewhile\ (< 10)\ (1 : 4 : 9 : \bot) & = & 1 : 4 : 9 : \bot \\
takewhile\ (< 10)\ (1 : 4 : 9 : 16 : \bot) & = & 1 : 4 : 9 : [\,] \\
takewhile\ (< 10)\ (1 : 4 : 9 : 16 : 25 : \bot) & = & 1 : 4 : 9 : [\,] \\
& \vdots &
\end{array}
$$

and the limit of this sequence is obviously $1 : 4 : 9 : [\,]$. This establishes:

$$takewhile\ (< 10)\ (map\ (\char`\~2)\ [1\mathbin{..}]) = 1 : 4 : 9 : [\,] = [1, 4, 9]$$

just as one would expect. These examples show that in addition to sequences whose limits are infinite lists, there are also 'degenerate' sequences whose limits are partial or finite lists.

One way to think of an infinite sequence of partial lists is as a description of the history of a computation. In these histories, $\bot$ stands for a part of a computation that has not yet been completed. As the computation proceeds, the approximations get better and $\bot$ is replaced by a more defined value. By running the computation long enough – that is, prolonging the sequence – one can compute as much of the list as may be required.

The utility of $\bot$ comes from the fact that it denotes a *completely undefined value*, and so one can use it in several ways. First, $\bot$ can denote the result of an illegal operation, such as (1 **div** 0) or *hd* [ ]. Second, $\bot$ can denote a computation that has not yet proceeded far enough to give an answer, but may (or may not) give more information later. This is the interpretation to

use in sequences of approximations as above. Third, $\bot$ can denote an infinite
loop. This is the interpretation to use if $\bot$ appears in the limit of an infinite
sequence, as in $1 : 4 : 9 : \bot$ in the filter example. The third interpretation is
really just a refinement of the second: it is the case where the computation
never does give more information.

7.5   Reasoning about infinite lists

Recall that the principle of induction over (finite) lists is as follows. To prove
by induction that $P(xs)$ holds for every finite list xs one must show two
things:

Case $[\,]$.   That $P([\,])$ holds; and

Case $(x : xs)$.   That if $P(xs)$ holds, then $P(x : xs)$ also holds for every x.

This is valid because every finite list has the form $x_1 : x_2 : \cdots : x_n : [\,]$, and
so can be built using just $(:)$ and $[\,]$.

How can we extend the induction principle to infinite lists? Well, as we
have just seen, every infinite list is the limit of an infinite sequence of partial
lists, so let us consider an induction principle for partial lists first.

It is easy to adapt the previous principle for partial lists. Just as every
finite list is built from $(:)$ and $[\,]$, every partial list has the form $x_1 : x_2 : \cdots :$
$x_n : \bot$, and so is built from $(:)$ and $\bot$. Thus, the same induction principle
works if we ignore the case for $[\,]$ above, and show instead:

Case $\bot$.   That $P(\bot)$ holds.

In fact, one can 'mix and match' cases as convenient: one can prove $P(xs)$
for any *finite* list by showing case $[\,]$ and case $(x : xs)$, for any *partial* list by
showing case $\bot$ and case $(x : xs)$, and for any *finite or partial* list by showing
case $\bot$, case $[\,]$, and case $(x : xs)$.

For example, here is a property that is true of partial lists but not of
finite lists. Observe that:

$$
\begin{aligned}
(1 : 2 : \bot) \,{+}\!\!{+}\, [3, 4] \;&=\; 1 : ((2 : \bot) \,{+}\!\!{+}\, [3, 4]) &&({+}\!\!{+}.2)\\
&=\; 1 : 2 : (\bot \,{+}\!\!{+}\, [3, 4]) &&({+}\!\!{+}.2)\\
&=\; 1 : 2 : \bot &&({+}\!\!{+}.0)
\end{aligned}
$$

In general we can prove:

$$
xs \,{+}\!\!{+}\, ys = xs
$$

for any partial list xs and any (partial, finite or infinite) list ys.

Proof. The proof is by induction on xs. Since xs is a partial list, the cases
are $\bot$ and $(x : xs)$.

Case $\perp$. We have:

$$\perp \mathbin{+\!\!\!+} ys \;=\; \perp \quad (+\!\!\!+.0)$$

which establishes the case.

Case $(x : xs)$. We have:

$$
\begin{aligned}
(x : xs) \mathbin{+\!\!\!+} ys &= x : (xs \mathbin{+\!\!\!+} ys) \quad (+\!\!\!+.2)\\
&= x : xs \qquad\qquad \text{(hypothesis)}
\end{aligned}
$$

which establishes the case. $\square$

So it is easy to extend induction to apply to partial lists. We can further extend it to apply to infinite lists as follows. An assertion P is said to be *chain complete* if whenever $ys_0, ys_1, ys_2, \ldots$ is an infinite sequence (or *chain*) with limit ys, and $P(ys_0), P(ys_1), P(ys_2), \ldots$ are all true, then $P(ys)$ is true also. Since every infinite list is the limit of a sequence of partial lists, it follows that if $P(xs)$ is true for every partial list xs and P is chain complete, then $P(xs)$ must also be true for every infinite list xs. Hence, the same induction principle as above can be used for infinite lists as well, so long as P is chain complete.

Fortunately, a wide range of predicates are chain complete. In particular, any equation $e_1 = e_2$ is a chain complete predicate in xs, where e_1 and e_2 are any computable expressions involving xs. Also, if $P_1(xs)$ and $P_2(xs)$ are chain complete predicates, then their conjunction $P_1(xs) \wedge P_2(xs)$ is also a chain complete predicate. Thus, most of the proofs in this book involve predicates that are chain complete, and so it suffices to use induction to demonstrate that the predicate holds for all partial lists, and it follows immediately that it holds for all infinite lists as well.

In particular, we have just shown that the equation $xs \mathbin{+\!\!\!+} ys = xs$ holds for all partial lists xs and arbitrary ys, and so it follows that it holds for infinite lists as well. This indeed matches our intuitions about computations. If we type $[1..] \mathbin{+\!\!\!+} [3, 4]$ in a session, we expect to get the same response as when we type $[1..]$, namely the infinite list $[1, 2, 3, \ldots]$.

Most of the laws proved previously hold for infinite lists as well as for finite lists. If we have proved a property for all finite lists xs by verifying the cases $[\,]$ and $(x : xs)$, then we can extend the proof to also cover infinite lists by simply verifying the additional case $\perp$. For example, one of the first laws we proved was that concatenation is associative, namely:

$$xs \mathbin{+\!\!\!+} (ys \mathbin{+\!\!\!+} zs) = (xs \mathbin{+\!\!\!+} ys) \mathbin{+\!\!\!+} zs$$

for every list xs, ys, and zs. The proof was by induction on xs, using the two cases $[\,]$ and $(x : xs)$, and so was valid only for finite list xs. However, we also have:

$$\perp \mathbin{+\!\!\!+} (ys \mathbin{+\!\!\!+} zs) = \perp = (\perp \mathbin{+\!\!\!+} ys) \mathbin{+\!\!\!+} zs$$

which establishes the case for $\perp$, and so the law holds for infinite lists xs as well. The original proof used no properties of ys or zs, and so is valid for infinite lists ys and zs also.

Of course, not all laws extend to infinite lists. For example, we previously proved that:

$$reverse\ (reverse\ xs) = xs$$

for all finite lists xs. Indeed, we even have that:

$$reverse\ (reverse\ \perp) = \perp$$

which seems to extend the law to infinite lists xs. However, a quick glance at the proof shows that it uses the auxiliary result:

$$reverse\ (ys \mathbin{+\!\!+} [x]) = x : reverse\ ys$$

for every x and finite list ys. We have:

$$reverse\ (\perp \mathbin{+\!\!+} [x]) = reverse\ \perp = \perp \neq x : \perp$$

and so the auxiliary result does *not* hold for infinite lists ys, and hence the main result does *not* hold for infinite lists xs. It is left as an exercise for the reader to show that $reverse\ xs = \perp$ for any infinite list xs, and hence $reverse\ (reverse\ xs) = \perp$ for any infinite list xs.

As a final word of caution, observe that there do exist predicates that are not chain complete. For example, if $P(xs)$ is the predicate 'xs is a partial list', and $ys_0, ys_1, ys_2, \ldots$ is a sequence of partial lists whose limit is the infinite list ys (for example, the sequence $\perp$, $1 : \perp$, $1 : 2 : \perp$, $\ldots$ whose limit is $[1, 2, 3, \ldots]$), then $P(ys_0), P(ys_1), P(ys_2), \ldots$ will all be true but $P(ys)$ will be false. For such predicates, induction can still be used to prove that the predicate holds for partial lists, but the proof will not necessarily extend to infinite lists.

7.5.1 The *take*-lemma

Unfortunately, the principle of induction introduced above is not always sufficient to establish every property of infinite lists we would like. Consider, for instance, the following assertion:

$$iterate\ f\ x = x : map\ f\ (iterate\ f\ x)$$

Here, *iterate* is the function:

$$iterate\ f\ x\ =\ x : iterate\ f\ (f\ x)$$

introduced in Section 7.2. Though true, the assertion cannot be proved by induction (at least not obviously so) because there is no appropriate argument of *iterate* to do the induction over. Indeed, what we would like to do is establish the assertion by induction over the structure of the *result* of applying *iterate*, not over either of its arguments.

Fortunately, there is a simple fact which captures what we want and can be used as the basis of an alternative proof technique. It stems from the observation that two lists, *xs* and *ys*, whether finite, infinite or partial, are equal just in the case that:

$$take\ n\ xs\ =\ take\ n\ ys$$

for all natural numbers *n*. We shall refer to this fact as the *take*-lemma.

In one direction the proof of the *take*-lemma is obvious: if *xs* = *ys*, then certainly *take n xs* = *take n ys* for any number *n*. To justify the result in the reverse direction, recall the definition of *take*:

$$
\begin{array}{lcl}
take\ 0\ xs & = & [\,] \\
take\ (n+1)\ [\,] & = & [\,] \\
take\ (n+1)\ (x:xs) & = & x:take\ n\ xs
\end{array}
$$

From these equations we can derive the following facts:

(i) $xs = \bot$ if and only if *take n xs* = $\bot$ for all positive *n*;

(ii) $xs = [\,]$ if and only if *take n xs* = $[\,]$ for all positive *n*;

(iii) $xs = x' : xs'$ for some *x'* and *xs'* if and only if:

$$take\ n\ xs\ =\ x' : take\ (n-1)\ xs'$$

for all positive *n*.

Proofs of these results are left as exercises for the reader.

Now suppose *xs* and *ys* are two lists such that *take n xs* = *take n ys* for all positive *n*. We shall argue that *xs* = *ys* by distinguishing three cases.

Case $xs = \bot$. Using fact (i) we have:

$$take\ n\ ys\ =\ take\ n\ xs\ =\ \bot$$

for all positive *n*. Using fact (i) a second time we obtain *ys* = $\bot$;

Case $xs = [\,]$. This is similar to the previous case, but uses fact (ii) twice;

Case $xs = x' : xs'$. Finally, if *xs* is of the form *x'* : *xs'*, then:

$$take\ n\ ys\ =\ x' : take\ (n-1)\ xs'$$

and so *ys* = *x'* : *xs'* = *xs* by fact (iii).

Hence in all three cases we have the desired conclusion that *xs* = *ys*.

The proof of the *take*-lemma may seem rather elaborate, for the result certainly appears intuitively obvious. However, intuition is not always a reliable guide in reasoning about non-finite lists. For example, the proposition that two lists *xs* and *ys* are equal just in the case that:

$$xs \mathbin! n = ys \mathbin! n$$

for all natural numbers *n* is false. As one counterexample, take $xs = \bot$ and $ys = [\bot]$. These lists are different but indexing with any natural number returns $\bot$ in all cases.

Let us now use the lemma to prove that:

$$iterate\, f\, x = x : map\, f\, (iterate\, f\, x)$$

for all *f* and *x*. Given the definition of *iterate*, an equivalent statement is that:

$$iterate\, f\, (f\, x) = map\, f\, (iterate\, f\, x)$$

By the *take*-lemma, this equation will follow if we can show:

$$take\, n\, (iterate\, f\, (f\, x)) = take\, n\, (map\, f\, (iterate\, f\, x))$$

for all natural numbers *n*.

Proof. The proof is by induction on *n*.

Case 0. Obvious, since $take\, 0\, xs = [\,]$ for any list *xs*.

Case $n + 1$.

$$
\begin{array}{lll}
take\,(n+1)\,(iterate\,f\,(f\,x)) & & \\
= & take\,(n+1)\,(f\,x : iterate\,f\,(f\,(f\,x))) & (iterate.1) \\
= & f\,x : take\,n\,(iterate\,f\,(f\,(f\,x))) & (take.3) \\
= & f\,x : take\,n\,(map\,f\,(iterate\,f\,(f\,x))) & (\text{hypothesis}) \\
= & take\,(n+1)\,(f\,x : map\,f\,(iterate\,f\,(f\,x))) & (take.3) \\
= & take\,(n+1)\,(map\,f\,(x : iterate\,f\,(f\,x))) & (map.2) \\
= & take\,(n+1)\,(map\,f\,(iterate\,f\,x)) & (iterate.1)
\end{array}
$$

as required. □

We shall give one further example of the *take*-lemma. Consider the infinite list *nats* defined by:

$$nats \;=\; 0 : map\,(+1)\,nats$$

We shall prove $nats = [0\,..]$ by showing that:

$$take\, n\, nats = [0\,..\,n-1]$$

for all natural numbers n. To do this, we need the useful subsidiary result that:

$$take\ n \cdot map\ f = map\ f \cdot take\ n$$

for all f and n. In other words, $take\ n$ commutes with $map\ f$. The proof is left as an exercise. The induction step for our assertion is:

$$
\begin{aligned}
&take\ (n+1)\ nats \\
&=\ take\ (n+1)\ (0 : map\ (+1)\ nats) &&(nats.1) \\
&=\ 0 : take\ n\ (map\ (+1)\ nats) &&(take.3) \\
&=\ 0 : map\ (+1)\ (take\ n\ nats) &&(map, take\ \text{comm.}) \\
&=\ 0 : map\ (+1)\ [0..n-1] &&(\text{hypothesis}) \\
&=\ 0 : [1..n] \\
&=\ [0..n]
\end{aligned}
$$

as required.

Exercises

7.5.1 Prove that:

$$iterate\ (+a)\ b = [(i \times a) + b \mid i \leftarrow [0..]]$$

7.5.2 Define:

$$
\begin{aligned}
loop1 &= loop1 \\
loop2 &= loop1 : loop2 \\
loop3 &= tl\ (1 : loop3)
\end{aligned}
$$

What are the values of $loop1$, $loop2$, and $loop3$? Give the infinite sequences that have these values as their limit.

7.5.3 Prove that $\#xs = \perp$ if xs is partial or infinite.

7.5.4 In Chapter 5 a proof was given that:

$$take\ n\ xs \mathbin{+\!\!+} drop\ n\ xs = xs$$

for all finite lists xs. Extend the proof to cover infinite lists xs.

7.5.5 Why does the proof of the second duality theorem in Chapter 5 not extend to infinite lists?

7.5.6 Prove that $drop\ n\ xs$ is a partial list whenever xs is a partial list. From this result, can we conclude that $drop\ n\ xs$ is infinite whenever xs is infinite?

7.5.7 Suppose we define:

$$fibs\ =\ 0 : 1 : [x + y \mid (x, y) \leftarrow zip\ (fibs, tl\ fibs)]$$

Prove that $fibs = map\ fib\ [0..]$, where fib is the Fibonacci function. State carefully any subsidiary results you use about the relationship of $take$ with zip.

7.6   Cyclic structures

Data structures, like functions, may be defined recursively. As a simple example, consider the definition:

$$ones \ = \ 1 : ones$$

We have:

$$
\begin{aligned}
ones \ &= \ 1 : ones \\
&= \ 1 : 1 : ones \\
&= \ 1 : 1 : 1 : ones \\
&\vdots
\end{aligned}
$$

and so *ones* is bound to the infinite list $[1, 1, 1, \ldots]$.

Recall that Section 6.2.2 discussed how expressions are represented as graphs inside the computer memory. The representation of *ones* as a graph is particularly interesting, as it involves a cyclic structure:

So in this case the entire infinite list may be represented within a fixed amount of space!

As a second example, consider the definition:

$$
\begin{aligned}
more \ &= \ \text{``More ''} \mathbin{+\!\!+} andmore \\
&\textbf{where} \ andmore = \text{``and more ''} \mathbin{+\!\!+} andmore
\end{aligned}
$$

The value of *more* is also an infinite list:

? *more*
More and more and more and more and more and m{*interrupted*}

After *more* has been evaluated, it will be represented by the graph:

'M' : 'o' : 'r' : 'e' : ' ' : 'a' : 'n' : 'd' : ' ' : 'm' : 'o' : 'r' : 'e' : ' ' :

which again involves a cycle.

We now consider three further examples of the use of cyclic structures.

7.6.1   Forever

Let *forever* be a function such that *forever x* is the infinite list $[x, x, x, \ldots]$, so the definition of *ones* above is equivalent to:

$$ones \ = \ forever \ 1$$

One way to define *forever* is:

$$forever\ x\ =\ x : forever\ x$$

This definition is correct, but does *not* create a cyclic structure. If *ones* and *forever* are defined as above, then after printing the first five elements, *ones* will be represented by the graph:

$$1 : 1 : 1 : 1 : 1 : forever\ 1$$

which is not cyclic. If the next element of the list is printed, the subterm *forever* 1 will be replaced by 1 : *forever* 1, and so the list of ones may grow longer without end. On the other hand, if the definition of *forever* is changed to:

$$forever\ x\ =\ zs$$
$$\textbf{where}\ zs = x : zs$$

then the definition of *ones* in terms of *forever* will produce the same cyclic structure as before.

7.6.2   Iterate

Here is a new definition of the function *iterate*, this time using a cyclic structure:

$$iterate\ f\ x\ =\ zs$$
$$\textbf{where}\ zs = x : map\ f\ zs$$

Consider the term *iterate* $(2\times)\,1$. The first few steps of evaluating this term are as follows:

$$iterate\ (2\times)\,1$$

$$\Rightarrow\quad \overline{1 : map\ (2\times)}$$

$$\Rightarrow\quad 1 : \overline{2 : map\ (2\times)}$$

$$\Rightarrow\quad 1 : 2 : \overline{4 : map\ (2\times)}$$

$$\vdots$$

Notice that if $f\ x$ can be computed in $O(1)$ steps then the first n elements of *iterate* $f\ x$ can be computed in $O(n)$ steps.

If we eliminate the where-clause from the above definition, we get yet another definition of *iterate*:

$$iterate\ f\ x\ =\ x : map\ f\ (iterate\ f\ x)$$

We showed in the previous section that *iterate* satisfies this equation. The new definition does not use cyclic lists, and turns out to be much less efficient than the previous definition. Considering again the term *iterate* $(2\times)\,1$, the first few steps of evaluating this term are:

$$iterate\,(2\times)\,1$$
$$\Rightarrow\quad 1 : map\,(2\times)\,(iterate\,(2\times)\,1)$$
$$\Rightarrow\quad 1 : 2 : map\,(2\times)\,(map\,(2\times)\,(iterate\,(2\times)\,1))$$
$$\Rightarrow\quad 1 : 2 : 4 : map\,(2\times)\,(map\,(2\times)\,(map\,(2\times)\,(iterate\,(2\times)\,1)))$$
$$\vdots$$

It can be seen that it now requires $O(n^2)$ steps to compute the first n elements of *iterate* $f\,x$. So in this example the use of cyclic structures is essential in achieving efficiency.

7.6.3   The Hamming problem

A well-known problem, due to the mathematician W.R. Hamming, is to write a program that produces an infinite list of numbers with the following properties:

 (i) The list is in ascending order, without duplicates.

 (ii) The list begins with the number 1.

 (iii) If the list contains the number x, then it also contains the numbers $2 \times x$, $3 \times x$, and $5 \times x$.

 (iv) The list contains no other numbers.

Thus, the required list begins with the numbers:

$$1, 2, 3, 4, 5, 6, 8, 9, 10, 12, 15, 16, \ldots$$

The Hamming problem is important, as it is typical of a class of questions known as *closure problems*. In general, a closure problem specifies a collection of *initial elements* and a class of *generator functions*. In this case, we are asked to find the closure of the initial element 1 under the generating functions $(2\times)$, $(3\times)$, and $(5\times)$. The Hamming problem has a particularly efficient solution because the generating functions are *monotonic*; for example, $(2\times)$ is monotonic because $x < y$ implies $2x < 2y$, and similarly for $(3\times)$ and $(5\times)$.

The key to the solution is to define a function *merge* that takes two lists of numbers in ascending order, and merges these into a single list of numbers in ascending order, containing exactly the numbers in the original lists with no duplications. This function may be defined as follows:

$$
\begin{aligned}
merge\,(x : xs)\,(y : ys) \;&=\; x : merge\,xs\,ys, & &\text{if } x = y\\
&=\; x : merge\,xs\,(y : ys), & &\text{if } x < y\\
&=\; y : merge\,(x : xs)\,ys, & &\text{if } y < x
\end{aligned}
$$

This definition is suitable only for merging infinite lists, and it is left as an exercise to extend it to be suitable for finite lists as well.

Given *merge* it is easy to define the required list, as follows:

$$hamming \;\; = \;\; 1 : merge \, (map \, (2\times) \, hamming)$$
$$(merge \, (map \, (3\times) \, hamming)$$
$$(map \, (5\times) \, hamming))$$

Initially, *hamming* will be represented by the following cyclic structure:

After the first seven elements of *hamming* have been printed, the above structure will have reduced to the following:

Note that first n elements of the list *hamming* can be computed in $O(n)$ steps.

An obvious generalisation of the Hamming problem is to replace the numbers 2, 3, and 5 by arbitrary positive numbers a, b, and c. We then have:

$$hamming' \, a \, b \, c \;\; = \;\; 1 : merge \, (map \, (a\times) \, (hamming' \, a \, b \, c))$$
$$(merge \, (map \, (b\times) \, (hamming' \, a \, b \, c))$$
$$(map \, (c\times) \, (hamming' \, a \, b \, c)))$$

This solution produces the correct answer, but does not form a cyclic structure, and so requires $O(n^2)$ steps to compute the first n elements of the result list. It is left as an exercise to modify *hamming'* so that it does form a cyclic structure.

Exercises

7.6.1 Draw the (degenerate) cyclic graphs that represent *loop1*, *loop2*, and *loop3* in Exercise 7.5.2.

7.6.2 Define *dither* by:

$$
\begin{aligned}
dither \;=\; & yes \\
\textbf{where}\; & yes & = & \quad \text{“Yes.”} + no \\
& no & = & \quad \text{“No!”} + maybe \\
& maybe & = & \quad \text{“Maybe?”} + yes
\end{aligned}
$$

What will be printed if *dither* is typed in a session? Draw the graph of the cyclic structure that represents this value.

7.6.3 Draw the four cyclic graphs that represent *hamming* after the first 1, 2, 3, and 4 elements have been printed.

7.6.4 Modify *hamming'* so that it forms a cyclic structure.

7.6.5 We can generalise the Hamming problem by replacing the multiples 2,3,5 with a list *as* of positive numbers. That is, we wish to find a list in ascending order that begins with 1 and such that if *x* is in the list and *a* is in *as*, then $a \times x$ is in the list. Write a program to solve the generalised Hamming problem.

7.6.6 We can also generalise the Hamming problem by replacing 1 with a list *bs* of positive numbers sorted in ascending order. That is, we now wish to find a list in ascending order such that every *b* in *bs* is in the list, and if *x* is in the list then $2x$, $3x$ and $5x$ are in the list. Write a program to solve this version of the Hamming problem.

7.7 Example: the paper–rock–scissors game

Our next example is instructive as well as entertaining. Not only does it introduce the idea of using infinite lists to model a sequence of interactions between processes, it also provides a concrete illustration of the necessity for formal analysis.

The paper–rock–scissors game is a familiar one to children, though it is known by different names in different places. The game is played by two people facing one another. Behind their backs, each player forms a hand in the shape of either a rock (a clenched fist), a piece of paper (a flat palm), or a pair of scissors (two fingers extended). At a given instant, both players bring their hidden hand forward. The winner is determined by the rule 'paper wraps rock, rock blunts scissors, and scissors cut paper'. Thus, if player 1 produces a rock and player 2 produces a pair of scissors, then player 1 wins because rock blunts scissors. If both players produce the same object, then the game is a tie and neither wins. The game continues in this fashion for a fixed number of rounds agreed in advance.

Our objective is to write a program to play and score the game. Suppose we represent a move by one of the strings "Paper", "Rock" and "Scissors", and define a round of the game to be a pair of moves, one for each player. It is convenient to introduce the synonyms:

$$move \quad == \quad [char]$$
$$round \quad == \quad (move, move)$$

(In the next chapter we shall see how moves can be denoted directly as values of a *new* type, rather than represented indirectly as lists of characters.)

In order to score a round, we need first to define the function *beats* which expresses the relative powers of the three objects. The definition is:

$$beats \text{ "Paper"} \quad = \quad \text{"Scissors"}$$
$$beats \text{ "Rock"} \quad = \quad \text{"Paper"}$$
$$beats \text{ "Scissors"} \quad = \quad \text{"Rock"}$$

Now we can define:

$$score\,(x,y) \quad = \quad (0,0), \quad \text{if } x = y$$
$$= \quad (1,0), \quad \text{if } x = beats\ y$$
$$= \quad (0,1), \quad \text{if } y = beats\ x$$

Each player in the game will be represented by a certain strategy. For instance, one simple strategy is, after the first round, always to produce what the opposing player showed in the previous round. This strategy will be called *reciprocate*, or *recip* for short. Another strategy, which we shall call *smart*, is to determine a move by counting the number of times the opponent has produced each of the three possible objects, and calculating the response appropriately.

We shall consider the details of particular strategies, and how they can be represented, later on. For the moment, suppose the type *strategy* is given in some way. The function *rounds* will have type:

$$rounds :: (strategy, strategy) \rightarrow [round]$$

This function takes a pair of strategies and returns the infinite list of rounds which ensue when each player follows his or her assigned strategy. Given *rounds* we can define a function *match*, with type:

$$match :: num \rightarrow (strategy, strategy) \rightarrow (num, num)$$

which determines the result of playing a fixed number of rounds of the game. The definition is:

$$match\ n \quad = \quad total \cdot map\ score \cdot take\ n \cdot rounds$$

The function *total* is defined by:

$$total\ scores \quad = \quad (sum\,(map\ fst\ scores), sum\,(map\ snd\ scores))$$

7.7.1 Representing strategies

In order to complete the model of the game, we must decide on how strategies are to be represented, and so supply the necessary definition of *rounds*. There are at least two possible methods for representing strategies and it is instructive to compare them in some detail. In the first, we take:

$$strategy \ == \ [move] \rightarrow move$$

Here, a strategy is a function which takes the (finite) list of moves made by the opponent so far and returns an appropriate reply. For example, the *recip* strategy can be programmed by:

$$
\begin{aligned}
recip \ xs \ &= \ \text{``Paper''}, \quad \textbf{if } xs = [\,] \\
&= \ last \ xs, \quad \textbf{otherwise}
\end{aligned}
$$

Here, "Paper" is an arbitrarily chosen first move, and *last* is the function which returns the last element of a non-empty list.

The second strategy *smart* can be defined by the equations:

$$
\begin{aligned}
smart \ xs \ &= \ \text{``Rock''}, && \textbf{if } xs = [\,] \\
&= \ choose \ (p, r, s), && \textbf{otherwise} \\
&\quad \textbf{where} \ p \ = \ count \ \text{``Paper''} \ xs \\
&\qquad\qquad\ q \ = \ count \ \text{``Rock''} \ xs \\
&\qquad\qquad\ r \ = \ count \ \text{``Scissors''} \ xs
\end{aligned}
$$

Here, "Rock" is again some arbitrarily fixed first move. The function *count* counts the number of times each object has been played; it is defined by:

$$count \ x \ xs \ = \ \#[y \mid y \leftarrow xs; \ x = y]$$

The function *choose* determines a move statistically. In order to define this function, suppose *rand* is a function which takes a number n and returns a 'random'' number a, depending on n, in the range $0 \le a < 1$. We can now write:

$$
\begin{aligned}
choose \ (p, r, s) \ &= \ \text{``Scissors''}, \quad \textbf{if } a < p \\
&= \ \text{``Paper''}, \quad \textbf{if } p \le a \wedge a < p + r \\
&= \ \text{``Rock''}, \quad \textbf{if } p + r \le a \wedge a < p + r + s \\
&\quad \textbf{where} \ a = (p + r + s) * rand(p + r + s)
\end{aligned}
$$

This function determines the appropriate move depending on whether a falls in the range $0 \le a < p$ or $p \le a < p + r$, or $p + r \le a < p + r + s$. For *choose* to be well-defined, at least one of p, r, or s must not be zero.

We can now define:

$$
\begin{aligned}
update \ (f, g) \ rs \ &= \ rs \ +\!\!+ \ [(f \ (map \ snd \ rs), g \ (map \ fst \ rs))] \\
rounds \ (f, g) \ &= \ map \ last \ (tl \ (iterate \ (update \ (f, g)) \ [\,]))
\end{aligned}
$$

The function *update* appends a new pair of moves to the list of existing rounds, and *rounds* generates the infinite list of rounds by repeatedly applying *update* to the initially empty list. The definition is somewhat clumsy. More importantly, it is not very efficient. Suppose a strategy takes time proportional to the length of the input to compute its result. It follows that *update* takes $O(n)$ steps to update a game of n rounds by a new one. Therefore, to compute a game of N rounds requires $O(N^2)$ steps.

An alternative representation.   For comparison, let us now consider another way we might reasonably represent strategies. This time we take:

$$strategy == [move] \rightarrow [move]$$

In the new representation, a strategy is a function which takes the infinite list of moves made by the opponent and returns the infinite list of replies. For example, the strategy *recip* is now implemented by the equation

$$recip\ ms\ =\ \text{``Paper''} : ms$$

This strategy returns "Paper" the first time, and thereafter returns just the move made by the opponent in the previous round. Observe that this version of *recip* produces each successive output with constant delay.

The strategy *smart* can be reprogrammed as follows:

$$
\begin{aligned}
smart\ xs\ &=\ \text{``Rock''} : map\ choose\ (counts\ xs) \\
counts\ &=\ tl \cdot scan\ (\oplus)\ (0,0,0) \\
&\textbf{where}\ (p,r,s) \oplus \text{``Paper''}\ =\ (p+1,r,s) \\
&\qquad\quad (p,r,s) \oplus \text{``Rock''}\ =\ (p,r+1,s) \\
&\qquad\quad (p,r,s) \oplus \text{``Scissors''}\ =\ (p,r,s+1)
\end{aligned}
$$

The value (*counts xs*) is the list of triples representing the running counts of the three move values. The *smart* strategy is also efficient in that it produces each successive output with constant delay.

With our new model of strategies we can redefine the function *rounds* in the following way:

$$
\begin{aligned}
rounds\ (f,g)\ &=\ zip\ (xs,ys) \\
&\textbf{where}\ xs\ =\ f\ ys \\
&\qquad\quad ys\ =\ g\ xs
\end{aligned}
$$

Here, *xs* is the list of replies computed by *f* in response to the list *ys* which, in turn, is the list of replies made by *g* in response to *xs*. To ensure that *rounds* (*f, g*) does generate an infinite list of well-defined moves, we require that the pair of mutually recursive definitions:

$$
\begin{aligned}
xs\ &=\ f\ ys \\
ys\ &=\ g\ xs
\end{aligned}
$$

generate infinite lists of well-defined elements. If f and g satisfy this condition, then the new definition of *rounds* computes the first n moves of the game in $O(n)$ steps, assuming that f and g compute each new move with constant delay. Thus, the second method for modelling strategies leads to a more efficient program than the earlier one.

7.7.2 Cheating

Unfortunately, however, there is a crucial flaw with the new method: it offers no protection against a strategy that cheats! Consider the strategy:

$$cheat \; xs \;\; = \;\; map \; beats \; xs$$

The first reply of *cheat* is the move guaranteed to beat the opponent's first move; similarly for subsequent moves. To see that *cheat* cannot be prevented from subverting the game, consider a match in which it is played against *recip*. Suppose:

$$xs \;\; = \;\; cheat \; ys$$
$$ys \;\; = \;\; recip \; xs$$

These equations have solutions xs and ys which are the limits of the sequence of approximations $xs_0, xs_1, \ldots$ and $ys_0, ys_1, \ldots$, respectively, where $xs_0 = ys_0 = \bot$ and:

$$xs_{n+1} \;\; = \;\; cheat \; ys_n$$
$$ys_{n+1} \;\; = \;\; recip \; xs_n$$

Now, we have:

$$xs_1 \;\; = \;\; cheat \; \bot = \bot$$
$$ys_1 \;\; = \;\; recip \; \bot = \text{``Paper''} : \bot$$

and so:

$$xs_2 \;\; = \;\; cheat \, (\text{``Paper''} : \bot) \;\; = \text{``Scissors''} : \bot$$
$$ys_2 \;\; = \;\; recip \; \bot \qquad\qquad = \text{``Paper''} : \bot$$

and so:

$$xs_3 \;\; = \;\; cheat \, (\text{``Paper''} : \bot) \quad = \text{``Scissors''} : \bot$$
$$ys_3 \;\; = \;\; recip \, (\text{``Scissors''} : \bot) \; = \text{``Paper''} : \text{``Scissors''} : \bot$$

Continuing in this way, we see that the limits of these sequences are indeed well-defined and, moreover, *cheat* always triumphs.

Can we find a way to protect against such a strategy? To answer this question, we need to take a closer look at what constitutes a fair strategy. Informally speaking, f is fair if it can determine its first move in the absence of any information about its opponent's first move, its second move only on the basis of the opponent's first move (at most), and so on. (Of course, it is not required that f take any account of the opponent's previous moves in order to compute a reply.)

More formally, f is fair if for all sequences $x_1, x_2, \ldots$ of opponent's moves, there exists moves $y_1, y_2, \ldots$ such that:

$$
\begin{aligned}
take\ 1\ (f\ \perp) &= [y_1] \\
take\ 2\ (f\ (x_1 : \perp)) &= [y_1, y_2] \\
take\ 3\ (f\ (x_1 : x_2 : \perp)) &= [y_1, y_2, y_3]
\end{aligned}
$$

and so on. In other words, we must have, for all infinite sequences of well-defined moves xs and for all $n \geq 0$, that:

$$
take\ (n+1)\ (f\ (prune\ n\ xs))
$$

is a list of $(n+1)$ well-defined moves, where *prune* is defined by the equations:

$$
\begin{aligned}
prune\ 0\ xs &= \perp \\
prune\ (n+1)\ (x : xs) &= x : prune\ n\ xs
\end{aligned}
$$

The *recip* strategy is fair in this sense because, using the fact that:

$$
take\ n\ (prune\ n\ xs) = take\ n\ xs
$$

for all n and xs, we have:

$$
\begin{aligned}
take\ (n+1)\ (recip\ (prune\ n\ xs)) &= take\ (n+1)\ (\text{"Paper"} : prune\ n\ xs) \\
&= \text{"Paper"} : take\ n\ (prune\ n\ xs) \\
&= \text{"Paper"} : take\ n\ xs
\end{aligned}
$$

The last expression is a list of $(n+1)$ well-defined moves, provided xs is an infinite list of well-defined moves.

The cheating strategy, on the other hand, is not fair. Since:

$$
\begin{aligned}
take\ 1\ (cheat\ (prune\ 0\ xs)) &= take\ 1\ (cheat\ \perp) \\
&= take\ 1\ \perp \\
&= \perp
\end{aligned}
$$

the fairness condition fails at the first step.

Now we need some way of ensuring that only fair strategies are admitted to the game. We can do this by defining a function *fair* so that $(fair\ f\ xs)$ returns an infinite list, equivalent to $(f\ xs)$, if f is a fair strategy, and returns a partial list otherwise. The function *fair* works by forcing f to return the first element of its output before it gives f the first element of its input. Similarly for the other elements. One definition of *fair* is:

$$
\begin{aligned}
fair\ f\ xs &= ys \\
&\mathbf{where}\ ys = f\ (synch\ ys\ xs) \\
synch\ (y : ys)\ (x : xs) &= x : synch\ ys\ xs, \ \mathbf{if}\ defined\ y
\end{aligned}
$$

Here, *defined* returns *True* if its argument is not $\bot$, and $\bot$ otherwise. In particular, we have

$$synch \, (\bot : ys) \, (x : xs) = \bot$$

We leave as an instructive exercise for the reader the proof that (*fair f xs*) returns an infinite list of well-defined moves if and only if f is a fair strategy.

It follows from the above analysis that to prevent cheating we must rewrite the definition of *rounds* as follows:

$$
\begin{aligned}
rounds \, (f, g) \;\; &= \;\; zip \, (xs, ys) \\
\textbf{where } xs \;\; &= \;\; fair \, f \, ys \\
ys \;\; &= \;\; fair \, g \, xs
\end{aligned}
$$

Exercises

7.7.1 Prove that:

$$prune \, n \, xs = take \, n \, xs \; \mathbin{+\!\!+} \; \bot$$

7.7.2 Give fair strategies in the paper-rock-scissors game that (i) never looks at the opponent's moves in calculating a reply; and (ii) looks only at every third move. Define a strategy which is fair for ten moves, but then cheats.

7.7.3 Prove that if f is a fair strategy, then *fair f xs = f xs*. Show that if f is not fair, then *fair f xs* is a partial list. What happens to the game in such a case?

7.7.4 Bearing in mind that *defined* is applied to strings, give a definition of *defined*.

7.8   Interactive programs

So far, all of our sessions with the computer have involved a uniform and simple pattern of interaction: the user types an expression to be evaluated at the keyboard, and then the value of this expression is printed on the screen. This style of interaction is suited for a wide range of purposes, but sometimes other forms of interaction are required. As a trivial example, we might wish that everything typed on the keyboard is 'echoed' on the screen, but with lower-case letters converted to upper-case. A more entertaining example would be a program to play the game of hangman. This section shows how interactive programs can be written in our functional programming notation.

An interactive program will be represented by a function f of type:

$$f :: [char] \rightarrow [char].$$

When f is run interactively, the input to f will be the sequence of characters typed at the keyboard, and the output of f will be the sequence of characters typed on the computer screen.

For example, the program that capitalises its input may be written as follows:

$$capitalises \quad = \quad map\ capitalise$$

$$capitalise\ x \quad = \quad decode\ (code\ x + offset),\quad \textbf{if}\ \text{'a'} \le x \wedge x \le \text{'z'}$$
$$= \quad x,\qquad\qquad\qquad\qquad \textbf{otherwise}$$
$$\textbf{where}\ offset = code\ \text{'A'} - code\ \text{'a'}$$

The function *capitalise* converts a lower-case letter to upper-case and leaves all other characters unchanged, and the function *capitalises* applies *capitalise* to each element of a list.

The type of *capitalises* is:

$$capitalises :: [char] \to [char]$$

and so it may be run as an interactive program. If we do so, then typing the sequence of keys:

Hello, world!

at the keyboard will cause the output:

HELLO, WORLD!

to appear on the computer screen. The program will be fully interactive. That is, as soon as 'H' is typed on the keyboard, an 'H' appears on the screen, and then when 'e' is typed an 'E' appears on the screen, and so on.

The program given above will run until the interrupt key is typed or the computer is turned off. One can also design an interactive program that terminates. For example, the program:

$$capitalises' \quad = \quad takewhile\ (\ne \text{'#'}) \cdot capitalises$$

behaves in the same way as *capitalises*, but terminates execution when the '#' character is typed. Notice that the '#' character will *not* be echoed on the screen.

7.8.1   Modelling interaction

What do interactive programs have to do with infinite lists? There is little in an interactive program that is infinite (except, perhaps, for the interminable wait when the computer is heavily loaded). However, we shall soon see that there are good reasons for considering the two topics together.

We can model interactive behaviour more precisely by considering sequences of partial lists. The behaviour of the *capitalises* program described above is modelled by the sequence:

$$
\begin{aligned}
capitalises \perp &= \perp \\
capitalises \ (\text{`H'} : \perp) &= \text{`H'} : \perp \\
capitalises \ (\text{`H'} : \text{`e'} : \perp) &= \text{`H'} : \text{`E'} : \perp \\
capitalises \ (\text{`H'} : \text{`e'} : \text{`l'} : \perp) &= \text{`H'} : \text{`E'} : \text{`L'} : \perp
\end{aligned}
$$

$$\vdots$$

This can be viewed as a history of the interactive session. When nothing has been typed at the keyboard, nothing has appeared on the screen. When an 'H' has been typed at the keyboard, an 'H' has appeared on the screen. When "He" has been typed at the keyboard, "HE" has appeared on the screen. And so on.

Just as earlier $\perp$ was used to denote a computation that has not yet completed, here $\perp$ is used to denote input that has not yet been typed at the keyboard, and output that has not yet appeared on the screen.

It was noted previously that a special case of a computation that has not yet completed is a computation that will never complete, that is, an infinite loop. Similarly, two special cases of input and output are the input that results when the keyboard is never touched again and the output that causes the screen never to be printed on again. These, too, are all denoted by $\perp$.

In short, exactly the same techniques used to model infinite lists are suitable for modelling interactive programs, and this is why the two topics are treated together.

7.8.2 Hangman

A simplified version of the game of hangman may be played as follows. First, one player enters a word. Then, the other player repeatedly guesses a letter. For each guess, the computer (which acts as mediator between the players) prints the word, with all of those letters *not* guessed so far replaced by a '−'. When all the letters in the word have been guessed, the process repeats. Thus, a typical session of hangman might begin like this:

```
Enter a word: -------
a    -a---a-
n    -an--an
t    -an--an
m    -an-man
h    han-man
g    hangman
Enter a word:
```

and now it is the other player's turn to enter a word. Notice that when a word to be guessed is entered, it is not printed but a '−' appears on the screen as each letter is typed on the keyboard.

The following program will play hangman, when the function *hangman* is run interactively:

$$hangman\ input$$
$$=\ \text{"Enter a word: "} + echo + \text{"}\gamma\text{"} + game\ word\ [\,]\ input'$$
where
$$echo\ =\ ['-'\mid w \leftarrow word]$$
$$word\ =\ before\ '\gamma'\ input$$
$$input'\ =\ after\ '\gamma'\ input$$

The function *game* is defined by:

$$game\ word\ guess\ (c:input)$$
$$=\ [c] + \text{"}\sqcup\text{"} + reveal + \text{"}\gamma\text{"} + rest$$
where
$$reveal\ =\ [dash\ w\mid w \leftarrow word]$$
$$dash\ w\ =\ w, \qquad\qquad\qquad \textbf{if } w \text{ in } (c:guess)$$
$$=\ '-', \qquad\qquad\qquad \textbf{otherwise}$$
$$rest\ =\ game\ word\ (c:guess)\ input,\ \textbf{if } '-' \text{ in } reveal$$
$$=\ hangman\ input, \qquad\qquad \textbf{otherwise}$$

The functions *before* and *after* are given by:

$$before\ x\ =\ takewhile\ (\neq x)$$
$$after\ x\ =\ tl \cdot dropwhile\ (\neq x)$$

In the above script, *word* is the word to be guessed, *guess* is the list of guesses so far, and *input* is the list of characters typed at the keyboard. Note that:

$$before\ '\gamma'\ \text{"hangman}\gamma\text{antmhg"}\ =\ \text{"hangman"}$$
$$after\ '\gamma'\ \text{"hangman}\gamma\text{antmhg"}\ =\ \text{"antmhg"}$$

and so *before* and *after* may be used to extract the word to be guessed and the remaining input.

Observe also that:

$$hangman\ \bot\ =\ \text{"Enter a word: "} + \bot$$
$$hangman\ ('h':\bot)\ =\ \text{"Enter a word: -"} + \bot$$
$$hangman\ ('h':'a':\bot)\ =\ \text{"Enter a word: --"} + \bot$$
$$\vdots$$

and so the prompt "Enter a word: " will be printed on the screen before any input is typed, and each character of the word will be echoed on the screen with a '-' as it is typed.

7.8.3   Utility functions

The process of writing interactive programs can be greatly aided by introducing a few utility functions. One such utility function is *read*, defined as
follows:

$$read \; msg \; g \; input \quad = \quad msg \mathbin{+\!\!+} line \mathbin{+\!\!+} \text{``}\Upsilon\text{''} \mathbin{+\!\!+} g \; line \; input'$$
$$\textbf{where} \; line \quad = \quad before \text{ `}\Upsilon\text{' } input$$
$$input' \quad = \quad after \text{ `}\Upsilon\text{' } input$$

The term (*read msg g*) denotes an interactive program (that is, a function of
type [*char*] → [*char*]) that prints the string *msg* on the screen, then reads
the next line *line* from the keyboard and echoes it on the screen as it is read,
and then behaves like the interactive program *g line* (so *g* must be such that
g line :: [*char*] → [*char*]).

For example, if we define:

$$hangman' \quad = \quad read \text{ ``Enter a word: '' } h$$
$$\textbf{where} \; h \; word = game \; word \text{ ``''}$$

then *hangman'* will be identical to *hangman*, except that when entering the
initial word each character will be echoed as itself (instead of each character
being echoed as a '–').

Another useful utility function is *read2*, which performs two read operations in sequence. It is defined as follows:

$$read2 \; (msg1, msg2) \; g \quad = \quad read \; msg1 \; g1$$
$$\textbf{where}$$
$$g1 \; line1 \quad = \quad read \; msg2 \; g2$$
$$\textbf{where}$$
$$g2 \; line2 \quad = \quad g \; (line1, line2)$$

The term *read2* (*msg1, msg2*) *g* denotes an interactive program that prints
the string *msg1*, reads and echoes a line *line1* from the keyboard, prints
the string *msg2*, reads and echoes a line *line2* from the keyboard, and then
behaves like the interactive program *g* (*line1, line2*).

The *read* function supports a particular style of interaction: input occurs
one line at a time and is always echoed. Utility functions to support other
styles of input can also be written, and some examples are given in the
exercises.

It is also convenient to introduce utility routines for output and for the
termination of an interactive session. These may be defined as follows:

$$write \; msg \; g \; input \quad = \quad msg \mathbin{+\!\!+} g \; input$$
$$end \; input \qquad\qquad = \quad \text{``''}$$

The term *write msg g* denotes an interactive program that prints the string
msg and then behaves like the interactive program *g*, and the term *end*
denotes the interactive program that terminates an interactive session.

It is easy to prove the following identities:

$$write\ (msg1\ \#\ msg2)\ g\ =\ write\ msg1\ (write\ msg2\ g)$$
$$read\ msg\ g\ =\ write\ msg\ (read\ ""\ g)$$

That is, writing the concatenation of two messages is equivalent to writing the first message followed by writing the second, and reading with a given message is equivalent to writing the message and then reading with an empty message.

As a trivial example, the infuriating program:

guess
$$=\ read\ \text{“Guess a word: ”}\ g$$
$$\textbf{where}$$
$$g\ word\ =\ write\ \text{“Right! Goodbye.}\text{\textbackslash"”}\ end,\quad \textbf{if}\ word = \text{“sheep”}$$
$$=\ read\ \text{“Wrong! Guess again: ”}\ g,\quad \textbf{otherwise}$$

forces the user to repeatedly guess a secret word (in this case, "sheep") and terminates when the word has been correctly guessed.

Utility functions are important because they allow interactive programs to be written at a higher level of abstraction. Notice that the *guess* program does not refer directly to the list of characters from the keyboard or the list of characters to the screen. All of the details of representing interactive programs as functions of type $[char] \rightarrow [char]$ have been hidden inside the implementation of the utility functions, and the users of such functions need not be concerned with these details.

7.8.4   Table lookup

This section presents a simple table lookup program as a further example of interaction and the use of utility functions.

A table associates *keys* with *values*, where keys and values are both strings. We will need three operations on tables:

(i)   *newtable* is a new table with no entries;

(ii)   (*enter k v t*) is identical to table *t* except the key *k* has value *v*;

(iii)   (*lookup t k*) is the value in table *t* associated with key *k*.

There are many possible ways to implement tables. For example, we could choose to represent tables as lists of (key,value) pairs, and implement the operations as follows:

$$newtable\ =\ [\,]$$
$$enter\ k\ v\ t\ =\ (k,v):t$$
$$lookup\ t\ k\ =\ hd\ vs,\qquad \textbf{if}\ vs \neq [\,]$$
$$=\ \text{“No entry”},\quad \textbf{otherwise}$$
$$\textbf{where}\ vs = [v'\ |\ (k',v') \leftarrow t;\ k' = k]$$

The following interactive program manipulates tables using only these three operations, so any other implementation of tables may easily be substituted for the above.

A simple interactive program for maintaining a table might behave as follows. First, the program requests a command, which must be either "enter" or "lookup" or "end". If the command is "enter", then a new key and value are requested and entered into the table. If the command is "lookup", then a key is request and its associated value in the table is printed. If the command is "end", then a suitable message is printed and the interactive session terminates.

The following program has the behaviour described above:

$$
\begin{array}{rcl}
table\ t & = & read\ \text{``Command: ''}\ tcommand \\
& & \textbf{where} \\
tcommand\ \text{``enter''} & = & read2\ (\text{``Key: ''}, \text{``Value: ''})\ tenter \\
tcommand\ \text{``lookup''} & = & read\ \text{``Key: ''}\ tlookup \\
tcommand\ \text{``end''} & = & write\ \text{``Exit program↓''}\ end \\[6pt]
tenter\ (k, v) & = & write\ \text{``↓↓''}\ (table\ (enter\ k\ v\ t)) \\
tlookup\ k & = & write\ (lookup\ t\ k\ \#\!\!+\ \text{``↓↓''})\ (table\ t)
\end{array}
$$

If *table newtable* is run interactively, then one might have the following session:

Command: <u>lookup</u>
Key: <u>exempli gratia</u>
No entry

Command: <u>enter</u>
Key: <u>exempli gratia</u>
Value: <u>For the sake of example</u>

Command: <u>enter</u>
Key: <u>id est</u>
Value: <u>That is to say</u>

Command: <u>lookup</u>
Key: <u>exempli gratia</u>
For the sake of example

Command: <u>end</u>
Exit program

For the program given here, the entries in the table are lost when the program exits. However, most functional languages also provide an interface to the file system of the computer, and this would allow the initial table to be read from a file and the final table to be stored in a file. The details of how this is done will not be discussed here.

This concludes a brief introduction to writing interactive programs in a functional notation. It is often supposed that functional programming languages are not suitable for expressing interactive programs, but it is hoped that the examples given here show that it is perfectly feasible to write interactive programs for a wide range of applications.

Exercises

7.8.1 Modify *hangman* to display a running total of the number of right and wrong guesses in a game.

7.8.2 What are the types of the utility functions *read*, *read2*, *write*, and *end*? (Hint: The types will be more meaningful if one writes *interactive* for the type $[char] \rightarrow [char]$.)

7.8.3 Write the utility function *read3*, which is like *read2* except it prompts for and reads three values.

7.8.4 Using *showint* and *getint* from Exercises 7.2.3 and 7.2.4, write utility functions *readint* and *writeint* to use in interactive programs that deal with integers.

7.8.5 When running the interactive program *table*, what happens if the command is not "enter", "lookup", or "end"? Is this behaviour acceptable? Modify *table* to be more robust.

7.8.6 The backspace character '⬅' when typed at the keyboard indicates that the previously typed character should be deleted, and when printed on the screen causes the cursor to be moved back one position. Write a utility function *readedit* that is similar to *read* except that '⬅' can be used to edit the input. For example, typing "goop⬅d" followed by a newline should cause the string "good" to be entered. (For echoing, note that a character already printed on the screen can be removed by printing "⬅␣⬅"; this backs over the character, writes a space in its place, and then moves the cursor back over the space.)

Chapter 8

New Types

So far we have seen three basic types, *num*, *bool* and *char*, and three ways of combining them to form new types. To recap, we can make use of (i) the function space operator → to form the type of functions from one given type to another; (ii) the tupling operator $(\alpha, \ldots, \beta)$ to form tuples of types; and (iii) the list construction operator $[\alpha]$ to form lists of values of a given type.

As well as using these three operators, we can also construct new types directly. How this is done is the subject of the present chapter. We shall describe a simple mechanism for introducing new types of values, illustrate how the mechanism is used in practice, and describe a little of its theoretical foundations.

8.1   Enumerated types

One simple way to define a new type is by explicit enumeration of its values. For example, suppose we are interested in a problem which deals with the days of the week. We can introduce a new type *day* by writing:

$$day ::= Sun \mid Mon \mid Tue \mid Wed \mid Thu \mid Fri \mid Sat$$

This is an example of a *type definition*. Notice the new sign ::= which serves to distinguish a type definition from a synonym declaration or a value definition. Notice also the vertical bars which separate what are called the *alternatives* of the type. The effect of the definition is to bind the name *day* to a new type which consists of eight distinct values, seven of which are represented by the new constants *Sun*, *Mon*, ..., *Sat*, and the eigthth by the ubiquitous ⊥ which is assumed to be a value of every type. The seven new constants are called the *constructors* of the type *day*. By convention, we shall distinguish constructor names from other kinds by beginning them with a capital letter. Thus, if an identifier begins with a capital letter, then it denotes a constructor; if it begins with a small letter, then it is a variable, defined value, or type name.

Here are some simple examples of the use of the type *day*. Firstly, values of type *day* can be printed and compared:

? *Mon*
Mon

? *Mon* = *Mon*
True

? *Mon* = *Fri*
False

However, a request to evaluate an expression such as *Mon* = "*Mon*" would cause the computer to signal a type error: the left-hand value has type *day*, while the right-hand value has type [*char*].

The values of an enumerated type are ordered by the position at which they appear in the enumeration. Hence we have:

? *Mon* < *Fri*
True

? *Sat* ≤ *Sun*
False

Like any other kind of value, the constructors of type *day* can appear in lists, tuples and function definitions. For example, we can define:

$$workday \quad :: \quad day \to bool$$
$$workday\ d \quad = \quad (Mon \le d) \land (d \le Fri)$$

$$weekend \quad :: \quad day \to bool$$
$$weekend\ d \quad = \quad (d = Sat) \lor (d = Sun)$$

It is also possible to use the new constructors as patterns in definitions. For example, the function *dayval* which converts days to numbers can be defined by the seven equations:

$$dayval\ Sun \quad = \quad 0$$
$$dayval\ Mon \quad = \quad 1$$
$$dayval\ Tue \quad = \quad 2$$

$$dayval\ Wed \quad = \quad 3$$
$$dayval\ Thu \quad = \quad 4$$
$$dayval\ Fri \quad = \quad 5$$
$$dayval\ Sat \quad = \quad 6$$

An alternative definition of *dayval* is:

$$dayval\ d \quad = \quad hd\ [k \mid (k, x) \leftarrow zip\ ([0\,..\,], days);\ x = d]$$
$$\textbf{where}\ days = [Sun, Mon, Tue, Wed, Thu, Fri, Sat]$$

The inverse function *valday* can be defined in a similar fashion. We can use *dayval*, together with *valday*, to define a function *dayafter* which returns the day after a given day:

$$dayafter\ d \quad = \quad valday\ ((dayval\ d + 1)\ \textbf{mod}\ 7)$$

Further examples. Recall from the previous chapter that we defined a move in the paper–rock–scissors game as being one of the strings: "Paper", "Rock" or "Scissors". Using an enumerated type definition, the type *move* can be defined directly by:

$$move \ ::= \ Paper \mid Rock \mid Scissors$$

This introduces three new constructors for the values of type *move*. The function *beats* of the previous chapter can now be defined by the equations:

$$
\begin{aligned}
beats\ Paper &= Scissors \\
beats\ Rock &= Paper \\
beats\ Scissors &= Rock
\end{aligned}
$$

Next, recall that in the description of the turtle-graphics program of Chapter 4 we used numerical or boolean codings for various quantities, such as directions and pen positions. With type enumerations we can write:

$$
\begin{aligned}
direction \ &::= \ North \mid East \mid South \mid West \\
pen \ &::= \ Up \mid Down
\end{aligned}
$$

These definitions are clearer than the coded versions because the names of the values are closely related to their roles. More importantly, they give an additional measure of security against misuse. For example, since a direction is no longer a number, the logical mistake of trying to add two directions numerically will be caught at the type-analysis stage of evaluation.

Given the mechanism of enumerated types, it should be clear that the type *bool* need not be considered as primitive. We simply define:

$$bool \ ::= \ False \mid True$$

Since *False* precedes *True* in the enumeration, it follows that $False < True$.

Similar remarks apply to the type *char*. We can define *char* as an enumerated type:

$$char ::= Ascii0 \mid Ascii1 \mid \ldots \mid Ascii127$$

consisting of 128 named constants. The only distinction between this definition of *char* and the built-in one is that, in the latter case, the naming and printing convention for constructors is non-standard (the same is true for numbers and lists).

8.2 Composite types

As well as defining a type by listing the names of its values, we can also define types whose values depend on those of other types. For example:

$$tag ::= Tagn\ num \mid Tagb\ bool$$

This defines a type *tag* whose values are denoted by expressions of the form (*Tagn n*), where *n* is an arbitrary number, and (*Tagb b*), where *b* is an arbitrary boolean value. There are also three additional values of *tag*: the value $\perp$, which is an element of every type, and the values (*Tagn* $\perp$) and (*Tagb* $\perp$). We shall consider these further below.

The names *Tagn* and *Tagb* introduce two constructors for building values of type *tag*. Each constructor denotes a function. The types of these functions are:

$$Tagn \quad :: \quad num \rightarrow tag$$
$$Tagb \quad :: \quad bool \rightarrow tag$$

There are two key properties that distinguish constructors such as *Tagn* and *Tagb* from other functions. First of all, an expression such as (*Tagn* 3) cannot be further simplified and is therefore a canonical expression. In other words, there are *no* definitions associated with constructor functions. Instead, constructors are regarded as primitive conversion functions whose role is just to change values of one type into another. In the present example, *Tagn* and *Tagb* take numbers and booleans and turn them into values of type *tag*.

The second property which makes *Tagn* and *Tagb* different from ordinary functions is that expressions of the form (*Tagn n*) and (*Tagb b*) can appear as patterns on the left-hand side of definitions. For example, we can recover the elements of the component types by defining the following 'selector' functions:

$$numval \quad :: \quad tag \rightarrow num$$
$$numval \,(\,Tagn\ n\,) \quad = \quad n$$

$$boolval \quad :: \quad tag \rightarrow bool$$
$$boolval \,(\,Tagb\ b\,) \quad = \quad b$$

Using pattern matching we can also define functions for discriminating between the alternatives of the type. For example, consider the predicate *isNum*, defined by:

$$isNum \,(\,Tagn\ n\,) \quad = \quad True$$
$$isNum \,(\,Tagb\ b\,) \quad = \quad False$$

This function has the property that:

$$isNum \perp \quad = \quad \perp$$
$$isNum \,(\,Tagn\ \perp\,) \quad = \quad True$$
$$isNum \,(\,Tagb\ \perp\,) \quad = \quad False$$

It follows that the three values $\perp$, *Tagn* $\perp$, and *Tagb* $\perp$ are all distinct, as we claimed earlier. The predicate *isBool* can be defined in a similar manner.

The values of *tag* are also ordered under the generic relation <. We have:

$$Tagn\ n < Tagn\ m \quad = \quad n < m$$
$$Tagn\ n < Tagb\ b \quad = \quad True$$
$$Tagb\ b < Tagn\ n \quad = \quad False$$
$$Tagb\ b < Tagb\ c \quad = \quad b < c$$

The second and third equations follow from the relative position of the alternatives in the definition of *tag*.

Further examples.   The right-hand side of the definition of *tag* contains two alternatives and involves two distinct component types, *num* and *bool*. In general, a type definition can contain one or more alternatives and zero or more component types. For example, the type:

$$temp ::= Celsius\ num \mid Fahrenheit\ num \mid Kelvin\ num$$

contains three alternatives yet only one component type, namely *num*. The type *temp* might be used to provide for multiple representations of temperatures. However, it is a fundamental property of all data types that distinct canonical expressions represent distinct values of the type, so we have:

? *Celsius* 0 = *Fahrenheit* 32
False

In order to compare temperatures in the expected way, we have to define an explicit equality test:

$$eqtemp :: temp \rightarrow temp \rightarrow bool$$

and use *eqtemp* instead of the built-in test (=). The appropriate definition of *eqtemp* is left as an exercise.

Another method for describing essentially the same information about temperatures is to define:

$$temp\ \ ==\ \ (tag, num)$$
$$tag\ \ \ \ ::=\ \ \ Celsius \mid Fahrenheit \mid Kelvin$$

Here, *temp* is not a new type but merely a synonym for a pair of values. Yet a third way is to write

$$temp\ \ ::=\ \ Temp\ tag\ num$$
$$tag\ \ \ ::=\ \ Celsius \mid Fahrenheit \mid Kelvin$$

Here, *temp* is a new type. Note that there is only one alternative in the definition of *temp*. Such types are called 'non-union' types in contrast to 'union' types which, by definition, contain at least two alternatives.

Here is another example of a type containing only one alternative:

$$file ::= File\ [record]$$

Values of type *file* take the form (*File rs*), where *rs* is a list of records. Since a file is *not* a list, we have to provide explicit functions for processing files. For example, to delete a record from a file, we can define a function:

$$delete\ \ \ \ \ \ \ \ \ \ ::\ \ record \rightarrow file \rightarrow file$$
$$delete\ r\ (File\ rs)\ \ =\ \ File\ (rs\ --\ [r])$$

Other useful file processing functions might include:

$$
\begin{array}{lll}
empty & :: & file \\
insert & :: & record \to file \to file \\
merge & :: & file \to file \to file
\end{array}
$$

One advantage of defining *file* as a special type, equipped with its own special set of operations, is an additional measure of security. With the synonym definition:

$$ file == [record] $$

every operation on lists is automatically valid for files and no protection against misuse is possible.

8.2.1 Polymorphic types

Type definitions can also be parameterised by type variables. For example, we can define:

$$ file\ \alpha ::= File\ [\alpha] $$

The previous type *file* now corresponds to the type (*file record*).

A revealing example of a polymorphic type definition is:

$$ pair\ \alpha\ \beta ::= Pair\ \alpha\ \beta $$

For example, we have:

$$
\begin{array}{lll}
Pair\ 3\ True & :: & pair\ num\ bool \\
Pair\ [3]\ 0 & :: & pair\ [num]\ num \\
Pair\ (Pair\ 1\ 2)\ 3 & :: & pair\ (pair\ num\ num)\ num
\end{array}
$$

Values of (*pair* $\alpha\ \beta$) can be put into one-to-one correspondence with values of (α, β). It follows that (α, β) need not be given as a primitive type. In just the same way, we can define versions of the tuple-type $(\alpha_1, \alpha_2, \ldots, \alpha_n)$ for any fixed n.

8.2.2 General form

We have now introduced all the essential features of type definitions. To summarise, a type $(t\ \alpha_1\ \alpha_2 \ldots \alpha_m)$ is defined by an equation:

$$ t\ \alpha_1\ \alpha_2 \ldots \alpha_m ::= C_1\ t_{11} \ldots t_{1k_1} \mid \ldots \mid C_n\ t_{n1} \ldots t_{nk_n} $$

where $m \geq 0$, $n \geq 1$ and $k_i \geq 0$ for $1 \leq i \leq n$. Furthermore, $C_1, \ldots, C_n$ are distinct constructor names, and each t_{ij} is a type expression.

The values of type t consist of $\bot$ and all expressions of the form

$$ C_i\ x_{i1} \ldots x_{ik_i} $$

where $1 \leq i \leq n$ and x_{ij} is an element of t_{ij} for $1 \leq j \leq k_i$. Thus, each possible way of building an expression in terms of constructors is valid and denotes a value of t. Furthermore, two values x and y of t are equal just in the cases that either:

(i) $x = y = \bot$; or

(ii) $x = C_i\, x_{i1} \ldots x_{ik_i}$ and $y = C_i\, y_{i1} \ldots y_{ik_i}$, where $1 \leq i \leq n$ and $x_{ij} = y_{ij}$ for $1 \leq j \leq k_i$.

Thus, every value is represented by a unique expression in terms of constructors.

Exercises

8.2.1 Give a one-line definition of the function *valday* described in Section 8.1.

8.2.2 Suggest a way of representing the type (α, β) by lists of length two. Generalise for arbitrary tuple-types.

8.2.3 Suppose a company keeps records of its personnel. Each record contains information about the person's name, sex, date of birth and date of appointment. Define a function that takes the current date and the file of personnel records and returns a list of names of those people who have served the company for twenty years or more. Supposing that employees hired before 1980 retire in the year in which they reach sixty-five, while employees hired after 1980 retire at sixty, define a function that calculates for a named employee the number of years before they retire. How would you organise the definitions so that they do not depend on the details of how personnel records are represented?

8.2.4 Suppose records have numeric keys. Define a function for merging two files whose records are in increasing order of key value.

8.2.5 Define functions for (i) testing the equality of two temperatures; and (ii) testing whether one temperature is colder than another.

8.3 Recursive types

Type definitions can also be recursive; in fact, much of the power of the type mechanism comes from the ability to define recursive types. To see what is involved, we consider three examples: natural numbers, lists and arithmetic expressions.

8.3.1 Natural numbers

The type *nat* of natural numbers is introduced by the definition:

$$nat ::= Zero \mid Succ\ nat$$

This definition says that *Zero* is a value of *nat*, and that (*Succ n*) is a value of *nat* whenever *n* is. For example, each of:

$$Zero$$
$$Succ\ Zero$$
$$Succ\ (Succ\ Zero)$$

are values of *nat*. In *nat*, the number 7 would be represented by the value:

$$Succ\ (Succ\ (Succ\ (Succ\ (Succ\ (Succ\ (Succ\ Zero))))))$$

In fact, every natural number is represented by a unique value of *nat*. On the other hand, not every value of *nat* represents a natural number. To start with, *nat* contains the value $\perp$ which does not correspond to a well-defined number. As we shall see, there are also other values in *nat* which do not represent numbers.

Many common arithmetic functions can be defined in terms of *nat* rather than *num*. For example, the operation $\oplus$ over *nat*, which corresponds to + over the natural numbers, is defined by:

$$n \oplus Zero \quad = \quad n$$
$$n \oplus (Succ\ m) \quad = \quad Succ\ (n \oplus m)$$

The number of reduction steps required to evaluate $(n \oplus m)$ is proportional to the *size* of *m*, where:

$$size\ Zero \quad = \quad 0$$
$$size\ (Succ\ n) \quad = \quad 1 + size\ n$$

To give one more, rather well-worn, example, consider:

$$fibnat\ Zero \quad = \quad Zero$$
$$fibnat\ (Succ\ Zero) \quad = \quad Succ\ Zero$$
$$fibnat\ (Succ\ (Succ\ n)) \quad = \quad fibnat\ (Succ\ n) \oplus fibnat\ n$$

This is, of course, the definition of the Fibonacci function expressed as a function over *nat*.

Notice the forms of the patterns involved in these two definitions. Each of the patterns *Zero* and (*Succ m*) is disjoint from the other and together they exhaust all possible forms for values of *nat*. The same holds true for the set of patterns *Zero*, (*Succ Zero*) and (*Succ (Succ n)*). The correspondence between *nat* and the natural numbers of *num* explains the restrictions on the forms of pattern matching permitted with *num*. The pattern $(n+1)$, of type *num*, corresponds to the pattern $(Succ\ n)$ of type *nat* and so n itself must match a natural number.

As with all type definitions, the ordering $<$ on *nat* is determined by the relative positions of the constructors in the declaration. Since *Zero* precedes *Succ* we have:

$$
\begin{aligned}
Zero < Zero &= False \\
Zero < Succ\ n &= True \\
Succ\ m < Zero &= False \\
Succ\ m < Succ\ n &= m < n
\end{aligned}
$$

This ordering corresponds to the normal interpretation of $<$ on natural numbers.

Now let us return to the point about there being 'extra' values in *nat*. The values:

$$\bot,\quad Succ\ \bot,\quad Succ\ (Succ\ \bot),\ \ldots$$

are all different and each is an element of *nat*. To see that they are different, consider the relation $\ll$ defined by:

$$
\begin{aligned}
\ll &&::\ \ &num \rightarrow nat \rightarrow bool \\
0 \ll (Succ\ n) &&=\ \ &True \\
(k+1) \ll (Succ\ n) &&=\ \ &k \ll n
\end{aligned}
$$

Informally, $(k \ll n)$ takes the value *True* if the natural number k is less than the number represented by the element n of *nat*, and $\bot$ otherwise. Since:

$$
\begin{aligned}
0 \ll \bot &= \bot \\
0 \ll (Succ\ \bot) &= True
\end{aligned}
$$

we have $Succ\ \bot \neq \bot$. In other words, *Succ* is not a strict function. More generally, we have for $m < n$ that:

$$
\begin{aligned}
m \ll (Succ^m\ \bot) &= \bot \\
m \ll (Succ^n\ \bot) &= True
\end{aligned}
$$

where f^n means f iterated n times, and so $Succ^m\ \bot \neq Succ^n\ \bot$.

There is also one further value of *nat*, namely the 'infinite' number:

$$Succ\ (Succ\ (Succ\ldots))$$

If we define:

$$inf\ =\ Succ\ inf$$

then *inf* denotes this value of *nat*. It is left as an exercise to show that *inf* is distinct from any other given element of *nat*.

To summarise what we have learnt about *nat*, we can divide the values of *nat* into three classes: (i) the *finite* numbers which correspond to well-defined natural numbers; (ii) the *partial* numbers, $\perp$, $(Succ \perp)$, and so on; and (iii) a single *infinite* number. This last value represents, in a sense that can be made quite precise, the unique 'limit' of the partial numbers. We have encountered a similar classification for the case of lists in the previous chapter and we shall see that it holds true of *all* recursive types. There will be the *finite* elements of the type; the *partial* elements, and the *infinite* elements. As in the case of lists, there will in general be more than one infinite element, but each such value will be the limit of the sequence of partial elements which approximate it.

Structural induction. In order to reason about the properties of elements of a recursive type, we can appeal to the principle of structural induction. The principle of induction for *nat* is as follows. In order to show that a property $P(n)$ holds for each finite element n of *nat*, it is only sufficient to show that:

Case *Zero.* That $P(0)$ holds;

Case *(Succ n).* That if $P(n)$ holds, then $P(Succ\ n)$ holds also.

We have seen many examples of the corresponding induction principle for 'ordinary' natural numbers in previous chapters, so we shall not give any new ones here. The induction method can be justified by the same kind of reasoning as was presented in Chapter 5. One important point to absorb is that the method only suffices to show that property P holds for every *finite* number. If, somewhat perversely, we want to show that it also holds for every partial number, then we have to prove more, namely that $P(\perp)$ holds as well. However, there are very few properties that hold for all finite and partial numbers. In a sense, the partial numbers are irrelevant members of *nat* since they contribute little that is essential to the structure.

The integers. Having dealt with the natural numbers, let us briefly see how to model the positive and negative integers. It is instructive to consider first an approach that does not give quite what is wanted. Suppose we define the type:

$$int ::= Zero \mid Succ\ int \mid Pred\ int$$

The intention here is that the number 1 is represented by *Succ Zero*, the number -2 is represented by *Pred(Pred Zero)*, and so on. Unfortunately, *int* contains many more 'integers' than intended. For example:

? *Succ (Pred Zero)* = *Pred (Succ Zero)*
False

and so *Succ (Pred Zero)* is distinct from *Pred (Succ Zero)*.

Although it is possible to use the above definition of *int* as a basis for modelling the positive and negative integers, a better method is to base the definition of *int* on *nat* and define:

$$int ::= Pos\ nat\ |\ Neg\ nat$$

Every non-zero integer can now be represented uniquely as a member of *int*. The number 0 has two representations, (*Pos Zero*) and (*Neg Zero*). It is left as an exercise to give a definition of *int* in which 0 is also represented uniquely.

8.3.2   Lists as a recursive type

Lists can also be introduced by a recursive type definition:

$$list\ \alpha ::= Nil\ |\ Cons\ \alpha\ (list\ \alpha)$$

This definition says that *Nil* is a value of (*list α*), and (*Cons x xs*) is a value of (*list α*) whenever *x* is a value of *α* and *xs* is a value of (*list α*). For example:

$$\bot$$
$$Nil$$
$$Cons \perp Nil$$
$$Cons\ 1 \perp$$
$$Cons\ 1\ (Cons\ 2\ Nil)$$

all denote distinct values of type (*list num*).

Values of type (*list α*) can be put into one-to-one correspondence with values of type [*α*]. It follows that lists need not be provided as a primitive type. It also follows that the properties of (*list α*) are just the same as have already been described for ordinary lists in previous chapters. For example, there are values of (*list α*) which represent partial and infinite lists. Consider the sequence of expressions:

$$\bot$$
$$Cons\ 1 \perp$$
$$Cons\ 1\ (Cons\ 2 \perp)$$
$$Cons\ 1\ (Cons\ 2\ (Cons\ 3 \perp))$$
$$\vdots$$

Each term in the above sequence denotes a different value of (*list num*). Moreover, each term is obtained from its predecessor by replacing ⊥ by an expression of the form (*Cons n* ⊥). Each term is therefore 'more defined' than its predecessor, and is an approximation to the infinite list:

$$Cons\ 1\ (Cons\ 2\ (Cons\ 3\ldots))$$

The type *list num* contains an infinite number of infinite lists; nevertheless, each is the limit of the sequence of its partial approximations.

Structural induction. The principle of structural induction for type (*list* α) is as follows. In order to show that a property $P(xs)$ holds for all finite elements xs of type (*list* α) it is necessary to show that:

Case *Nil*. That $P(Nil)$ holds;

Case (*Cons x xs*). That if $P(xs)$ holds, then $P(Cons\ x\ xs)$ also holds for all x of type α.

We have already seen many examples of the corresponding principle for ordinary lists, so we shall give no new ones here. In order to show that P holds for partial lists as well, we have to add an extra case and show that

Case $\perp$. That $P(\perp)$ holds.

Provided P is chain-complete, proof of these three cases is sufficient to show that P holds for all finite, partial and infinite lists.

8.3.3 Arithmetic expressions as a recursive type

Finally, we show how to model the syntactic structure of arithmetic expressions by a recursive type. This type is different from previous examples in that it is *non-linear*. Non-linear types are also called *trees* and will be discussed further in the following chapter.

For present purposes, we assume that an arithmetic expression is built out of numbers and the four operations $+, -, \times$ and $/$. The structure of an arithmetic expression is revealed by the following description: if e is an arithmetic expression, then either:

(i) e is a number; or

(ii) e is an expression of the form $e_1 \oplus e_2$, where e_1 and e_2 are arithmetic expressions, and $\oplus$ is one of $+, -, \times$ or $/$.

This recursive description can be translated directly into a type definition:

$$aexp \quad ::= \quad Num\ num \mid Exp\ aexp\ aop\ aexp$$
$$aop \quad ::= \quad Add \mid Sub \mid Mul \mid Div$$

The type *aexp* has two constructors, *Num* and *Exp*, corresponding to the two clauses of the above description. The type *aexp* is non-linear because *aexp* appears in two places in the second alternative of the definition. The enumerated type *aop* consists of four constructors, one for each arithmetic operation.

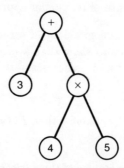

Figure 8.1 An arithmetic expression.

Here are some simple examples of elements of *aexp*. The expression (3+4) is represented in *aexp* by the value:

$$Exp\ (Num\ 3)\ Add\ (Num\ 4)$$

Similarly, the expression $3 + 4 \times 5$ is represented by the value:

$$Exp\ (Num\ 3)\ Add\ (Exp\ (Num\ 4)\ Mul\ (Num\ 5))$$

The structure of this expression is pictured as a tree in Figure 8.1.

We can convert values of type *aexp* to numbers by means of an evaluation function *eval* defined as follows:

$$
\begin{array}{lll}
eval & :: & aexp \to num \\
eval\ (Num\ n) & = & n \\
eval\ (Exp\ e1\ op\ e2) & = & apply\ op\ (eval\ e1)\ (eval\ e2)
\end{array}
$$

The subsidiary function *apply* is defined by cases:

$$
\begin{array}{lll}
apply\ Add & = & (+) \\
apply\ Sub & = & (-) \\
apply\ Mul & = & (\times) \\
apply\ Div & = & (/)
\end{array}
$$

Each operator in *aop* is therefore mapped directly to the associated arithmetic operator. Thus, to evaluate an expression that is not a number, we evaluate its two subexpressions and apply the associated operator.

For the purposes of comparison, here are two other possible ways of representing arithmetic expressions as a recursive type. First, consider:

$$
\begin{array}{lll}
aexp1 & ::= & Num\ num \mid Add\ aexp1\ aexp1 \mid Sub\ aexp1\ aexp1 \\
& & \mid Mul\ aexp1\ aexp1 \mid Div\ aexp1\ aexp1
\end{array}
$$

In this version, the arithmetic operators have been identified as individual constructors of *aexp1*.

Second, consider:

$$aexp2 \quad ::= \quad Num\ num \mid Exp\ aexp2\ aop\ aexp2$$
$$aop \quad == \quad (num \rightarrow num \rightarrow num)$$

In this version of *aexp*, the arithmetic operators appear directly as functions. For example, $(3 + 4)$ is represented as the element:

$$Exp\ (Num\ 3)\ (+)\ (Num\ 4)$$

of *aexp2* and the evaluation function *eval2* is defined by:

$$eval2\ (Num\ n) \quad = \quad n$$
$$eval2\ (Exp\ e1\ op\ e2) \quad = \quad op\ (eval2\ e1)\ (eval2\ e2)$$

Of the three versions of *aexp*, the first is arguably the simplest. To emphasise this point, consider the problem of determining whether an arithmetic expression is a sum, i.e. contains only addition operations. Given the first definition of *aexp*, we can write:

$$isasum\ e \quad = \quad and\ [op = Add \mid op \leftarrow ops\ e]$$

$$ops\ (Num\ n) \quad = \quad []$$
$$ops\ (Exp\ e1\ op\ e2) \quad = \quad [op] +\!\!+ ops\ e1 +\!\!+ ops\ e2$$

Given the second definition of *aexp* we have to write something like:

$$isasum\ (Num\ n) \quad = \quad True$$
$$isasum\ (Add\ e1\ e2) \quad = \quad isasum\ e1 \wedge isasum\ e2$$
$$isasum\ (Sub\ e1\ e2) \quad = \quad False$$
$$isasum\ (Mul\ e1\ e2) \quad = \quad False$$
$$isasum\ (Div\ e1\ e2) \quad = \quad False$$

The second definition involves more equations since there are more constructors of the type.

Finally, given the third definition of *aexp*, the problem of defining *isasum* cannot be solved. We cannot compare functions, so there is no way we can determine whether an operator of *aexp* denotes addition.

Structural induction. Finally, we look at the principle of structural induction as applied to *aexp*. This says that in order to prove that a property $P(e)$ holds for every finite expression e it is sufficient to show that:

Case *(Num n)*. That $P(Num\ n)$ holds for every n;

Case *(Exp e1 op e2)*. That if $P(e1)$ and $P(e2)$ hold, then $P(Exp\ e1\ op\ e2)$ also holds for every operation *op*.

We shall give two examples to illustrate this particular form of structural induction. For the first, define *numcount* and *opcount* by:

$$numcount\,(Num\;n) \quad\;\; = \;\; 1$$
$$numcount\,(Exp\;e1\;op\;e2) \;\; = \;\; numcount\;e1 + numcount\;e2$$

$$opcount\,(Num\;n) \quad\;\; = \;\; 0$$
$$opcount\,(Exp\;e1\;op\;e2) \quad = \;\; 1 + opcount\;e1 + opcount\;e2$$

We show that:

$$numcount\;e = 1 + opcount\;e$$

for all finite expressions *e*.

Proof. The proof is by induction on *e*.

Case (*Num n*). We have:

$numcount\,(Num\;n)$	$=\;\;1$	(*numcount*.1)
	$=\;\;1+0$	(arithmetic)
	$=\;\;1 + opcount\,(Num\;n)$	(*opcount*.1)

as required.

Case (*Exp e1 op e2*). We have:

$numcount\,(Exp\;e1\;op\;e2)$

$=$	$numcount\;e1 + numcount\;e2$	(*numcount*.2)
$=$	$1 + opcount\;e1 + 1 + opcount\;e2$	(hypothesis)
$=$	$1 + (1 + opcount\;e1 + opcount\;e2)$	(arithmetic)
$=$	$1 + opcount\,(Exp\;e1\;op\;e2)$	(*opcount*.2)

as required. □

The second example of structural induction concerns the proof of correctness of a simple compiler for arithmetic expressions. Imagine a simple computer for evaluating arithmetic expressions. This computer has a 'stack' and can execute 'instructions' which change the value of the stack. The class of possible instructions is defined by the type declaration:

$$instr ::= Load\;num \mid Apply\;aop$$

A stack value is just a list of numbers, so we define:

$$stack == [num]$$

The effect of executing an instruction in *instr* is defined by:

execute	$::$	$instr \rightarrow stack \rightarrow stack$
$execute\,(Load\;x)\;xs$	$=$	$x : xs$
$execute\,(Apply\;op)\,(x1 : x2 : xs)$	$=$	$apply\;op\;x2\;x1 : xs$

In words, (*Load x*) inserts x as a new element at the front of the stack, and (*Apply op*) applies the arithmetic operation op to the second and first numbers of the stack, leaving the result on the stack.

A sequence of instructions is executed by the function *run* defined by:

$$
\begin{aligned}
run \qquad &::\ [instr] \rightarrow stack \rightarrow stack \\
run\ [\,]\ xs \quad &=\ xs \\
run\ (in : ins)\ xs\ &=\ run\ ins\ (execute\ in\ xs)
\end{aligned}
$$

An alternative definition of *run* can be based on *foldl* (see Exercise 8.3.7.)

An expression can be translated (or *compiled*) into a list of instructions by the function *compile*, defined by:

$$
\begin{aligned}
compile \qquad\qquad &::\ aexp \rightarrow [instr] \\
compile\ (Num\ n) \quad &=\ [Load\ n] \\
compile\ (Exp\ e1\ op\ e2)\ &=\ compile\ e1 + \!\!+ compile\ e2 + \!\!+ [Apply\ op]
\end{aligned}
$$

We shall now prove the following assertion:

$$run\ (compile\ e)\ xs = eval\ e : xs$$

for all finite expressions e and stores xs. The proof is by structural induction over *aexp*.

Case (*Num n*). We have:

$$
\begin{aligned}
run\ (compile\ (Num\ n))\ xs\ &=\ run\ [Load\ n]\ xs & (compile.1) \\
&=\ run\ [\,]\ (execute\ (Load\ n)\ xs) & (run.2) \\
&=\ execute\ (Load\ n)\ xs & (run.1) \\
&=\ n : xs & (execute.1) \\
&=\ eval\ (Num\ n) : xs & (eval.1)
\end{aligned}
$$

as required.

Case (*Exp e1 op e2*). To establish this case, we need a subsidiary lemma about *run*. The lemma says that:

$$run\ (ins1 + \!\!+ ins2)\ xs = run\ ins2\ (run\ ins1\ xs)$$

for all *ins1*, *ins2*, and stores *xs*. The proof is left as an exercise.

Now we have:

$$
\begin{aligned}
&run\ (compile\ (Exp\ e1\ op\ e2))\ xs) \\
=\ &run\ (compile\ e1 + \!\!+ compile\ e2 + \!\!+ [Apply\ op])\ xs & (compile.2) \\
=\ &run\ [Apply\ op]\ (run\ (compile\ e2)\ (run\ (compile\ e1)\ xs)) & (lemma) \\
=\ &run\ [Apply\ op]\ (run\ (compile\ e2)\ (eval\ e1 : xs)) & (hyp.) \\
=\ &run\ [Apply\ op]\ (eval\ e2 : eval\ e1 : xs) & (hyp.) \\
=\ &run\ [\,]\ (execute\ (Apply\ op)\ (eval\ e2 : eval\ e1 : xs)) & (run.2) \\
=\ &execute\ (Apply\ op)\ (eval\ e2 : eval\ e1 : xs) & (run.1) \\
=\ &apply\ op\ (eval\ e1)\ (eval\ e2) : xs & (execute.2) \\
=\ &eval\ (Exp\ e1\ op\ e2) : xs & (eval.2)
\end{aligned}
$$

as required. □

Exercises

8.3.1 Suppose *inf* = *Succ inf*. Show that *inf* is distinct from any other element of *nat*.

8.3.2 Define multiplication and exponentiation as operations on *nat*.

8.3.3 Devise a representation of integers by a type *int* in which each integer is represented uniquely.

8.3.4 Devise a function *unparse* :: *aexp* → [*char*] that prints an arithmetic expression; for example:

? *unparse* (*Exp* (*Num* 3) *Add* (*num* 4))
(3+4)

As a more difficult exercise, define a function *parse* which takes a string describing a fully parenthesised arithmetic expression and produces its representation as an element of *aexp*.

8.3.5 Consider, by analogy with the function *fold* on lists, the function *foldexp* which has type:

$$foldexp :: (num \to \alpha) \to (\alpha \to aop \to \alpha \to \alpha) \to aexp \to \alpha$$

and is defined by the equations:

foldexp f g (*Num x*) = *f x*
foldexp f g (*Exp e1 op e2*) = *g* (*foldexp f g e1*) *op* (*foldexp f g e2*)

Using *foldexp* define the functions:

$$
\begin{aligned}
eval \quad &:: \quad aexp \to num \\
size \quad &:: \quad aexp \to num \\
unparse \quad &:: \quad aexp \to [char]
\end{aligned}
$$

8.3.6 The function *unparse* produces the conventional form of writing arithmetic expressions in which binary operators appear between their arguments. We can also write expressions with operators coming before or after their arguments. For example, the expression 3 + 4 × 5 can be written as:

+3 × 4 5   (preorder listing)
3 4 5 × +   (postorder listing)

Define functions *preorder*, and *postorder*, each having the type *aexp* → [*val*], where:

$$val ::= Nval\ num \mid Oval\ aop$$

8.3.7 Define the function *run* using *foldl* rather than an explicit recursion. Using the law

$$foldl\ (\oplus)\ a\ (xs \mathbin{+\!\!+} ys) = foldl\ (\oplus)\ (foldl\ (\oplus)\ a\ xs)\ ys$$

deduce that

$$run\ (ins1 \mathbin{+\!\!+} ins2)\ xs = run\ ins2\ (run\ ins1\ xs)$$

for all sequences of instructions *ins1* and *ins2*.

8.3.8 Explain why the proof of correctness of the arithmetic expression compiler does not extend to infinite expressions.

8.3.9 Modify the definition of *aexp* to handle unary minus. Give the modified *eval* function.

8.3.10 Modify the definition of *aexp* to include numeric variables. By definition, an *environment* is a function that associates each variable with a numeric value. Define a function *eval* which takes an environment and an element of *aexp* and returns its value. How would you extend the definition of *aexp* and represent environments so that expressions of the form '*e1* where $x = e2$' can be included?

8.3.11 Consider a language of propositional expressions based on the connectives $\lor$, $\land$ and $\neg$ and variables $p0, p1, \ldots$. Design a representation *pexp* for propositional expressions and define a function that returns a list of the distinct variables appearing in an expression. Define a function that determines whether an expression is a tautology. (*Hint:* Test an expression under all assignments of truth-values to variables.)

8.4 Abstract types

When we use the mechanism of type definitions to introduce a new type, we are in effect naming its values. With the exception of functions, each value of a type is described by a unique expression in terms of constructors. Using definition by pattern matching as a basis, these expressions can be generated, modified and inspected in various ways. It follows that there is no need to name the operations associated with the type. Types in which the values are prescribed, but the operations are not, are called 'concrete' types.

The situation is just the reverse with so-called 'abstract' types. An abstract type is defined not by naming its values, but by naming its operations. How values are represented is therefore less important than what operations are provided for manipulating them. Of course, the meaning of each operation has to be described. One approach, called *algebraic specification*, is to state the relationships between the operations as a set of algebraic laws.

Examples of this approach are given below. Another method is to describe
each operation in terms of the most abstract representation (or *model*) possible. This model can involve general mathematical structures such as sets
and functions.

In order to implement an abstract type, the programmer has to provide a
representation of its values, define the operations of the type in terms of this
representation, and show that the implemented operations satisfy the prescribed relationships. Apart from these obligations, the programmer is free
to choose between different representations on the grounds of efficiency or
simplicity. Some programming languages provide mechanisms for hiding the
implementation of an abstract type so that reference to the concrete representation is not permitted elsewhere in the program. Such 'abstraction barriers'
are useful in the design of large programs; in particular, a representation can
be changed without affecting the validity of the rest of the program.

It is beyond the scope of this book to describe specific mechanisms for
handling abstract types. Instead, we shall content ourselves with a few examples of the general idea of viewing a type in terms of its operations rather
than its values. In particular, we shall discuss alternative implementations
of the same set of abstract operations in order to compare their advantages
and disadvantages. First of all, though, we need to consider the notion of
representation in more detail.

8.4.1   Abstraction functions

In order to formalise the notion of representing one class of values by another,
we introduce the idea of an 'abstraction' function *abstr*. Suppose A denotes
the class of values to be represented and B denotes the representing type.
The function *abstr* has type:

$$abstr :: B \to A$$

If $abstr\, b = a$, then b is said to *represent* the value a. The minimal reasonable
requirement on *abstr* is that it should be surjective, that is, every value a
in A should have at least one representation b for which $abstr\, b = a$. If, in
addition, *abstr* is a bijective function, then each value in A is represented by
a unique value in B. However, we do not require that *abstr* be bijective, nor
even that it be a total function. If *abstr* is total, then every element of B
will represent some value in A; if not, then only certain elements of B will
be 'valid' representations. This point is discussed further below.

A simple example of a bijective abstraction function is one that describes the correspondence between $[\alpha]$ and the type $(list\ \alpha)$ discussed in
Section 8.3.2:

$$
\begin{aligned}
abstr & :: & (list\ \alpha) \to [\alpha] \\
abstr\ Nil & = & [\,] \\
abstr\ (Cons\ x\ xs) & = & x : abstr\ xs
\end{aligned}
$$

On the other hand, the function:

$$
\begin{aligned}
abstr \quad && :: \quad & nat \to num \\
abstr\ Zero \quad && = \quad & 0 \\
abstr\ (Succ\ x) \quad && = \quad & abstr\ x + 1
\end{aligned}
$$

which formalises the correspondence between nat and the natural numbers is not bijective: every partial element of nat is mapped to $\bot$. However, every natural number is associated with a unique finite element of nat.

The above examples of abstraction functions are all definable within our programming notation but this will not be the case in general. The function $abstr$ belongs to the wider class of general mathematical functions and must be understood in this sense. To illustrate this point, consider the problem of representing sets in our programming language. In mathematical notation, the empty set is denoted by $\{\,\}$, a singleton set containing just the value x is denoted by $\{x\}$, and the union of two sets X and Y is denoted by $X \cup Y$. The abstraction function:

$$
\begin{aligned}
abstr \quad && :: \quad & [\alpha] \to set\ \alpha \\
abstr\ [\,] \quad && = \quad & \{\,\} \\
abstr\ (x : xs) \quad && = \quad & \{x\} \cup abstr\ xs
\end{aligned}
$$

describes a representation of sets by lists. In effect, it says that a set is represented by listing its elements in some order, possibly with duplicates. For instance, the set $\{1, 2, 3\}$ is represented by the lists $[1, 2, 3]$, $[3, 2, 2, 1]$ and $[1, 1, 2, 2, 3]$, as well as many others. Mathematical sets are not provided as primitive, so $abstr$ is not a legal definition in our programming notation.

8.4.2 Valid representations

Suitably formulated, the function $abstr :: B \to A$ gives complete information about how elements of A are represented by elements of B. In particular, if $(abstr\ b)$ is well-defined, then b is said to be a *valid* representation. It is sometimes convenient to introduce an explicit predicate, *valid* say, that determines what representations are valid. The intention is that arguments to $abstr$ are considered to be restricted to those x for which $(valid\ x)$ is true.

To illustrate, suppose we want to represent sets of values by lists. Consider again the abstraction function:

$$
\begin{aligned}
abstr \quad && :: \quad & [\alpha] \to set\ \alpha \\
abstr\ [\,] \quad && = \quad & \{\,\} \\
abstr\ (x : xs) \quad && = \quad & \{x\} \cup abstr\ xs
\end{aligned}
$$

and the following three definitions of a valid representation:

$$
\begin{aligned}
valid1\ xs \quad && = \quad & True \\
valid2\ xs \quad && = \quad & nodups\ xs \\
valid3\ xs \quad && = \quad & nondec\ xs
\end{aligned}
$$

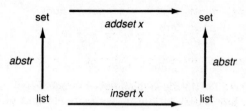

Figure 8.2 Commuting diagrams.

Here (*nodups xs*) is the condition that *xs* contains no duplicate elements and (*nondec xs*) is the condition that *xs* is a list in non-decreasing order. The pairs (*abstr, valid1*), (*abstr, valid2*) and (*abstr, valid3*) describe three different representations of finite sets in terms of lists. In the first representation, every (finite) list is a valid representation of some set; in the second only lists that do not contain duplicates are valid, while in the third only lists in non-decreasing order are considered valid representations.

8.4.3 Specifying operations

As well as formalising the correspondence between values of A and B, the abstraction function *abstr* :: $B \rightarrow A$ can also be used to specify corresponding operations. For example, consider the operation:

$$addset \quad :: \quad \alpha \rightarrow set\ \alpha \rightarrow set\ \alpha$$
$$addset\ x\ s \quad = \quad \{x\} \cup s$$

that adds an element x to a set s. The function:

$$insert \quad :: \quad \alpha \rightarrow [\alpha] \rightarrow [\alpha]$$

which implements this operation in terms of lists is specified by the equation

$$abstr\ (insert\ x\ xs) = addset\ x\ (abstr\ xs)$$

Such specifications are often pictured as so-called 'commuting diagrams'. In Figure 8.2, the class of values to be represented is placed above the representing type and the abstraction function is drawn as an arrowed line. Corresponding operations are drawn in a similar way. A diagram is said to commute if both ways of following the arrows lead to the same result. This means we require

$$abstr \cdot (insert\ x) \quad = \quad (addset\ x) \cdot abstr$$

Here are three possible implementations of *insert*:

$$insert1 \; x \; xs \;\; = \;\; [x] \mathbin{+\!\!+} xs$$

$$insert2 \; x \; xs \;\; = \;\; [x] \mathbin{+\!\!+} [y \mid y \leftarrow xs; \; x \neq y]$$

$$insert3 \; x \; xs \;\; = \;\; takewhile \, (< x) \, xs \mathbin{+\!\!+} [x] \mathbin{+\!\!+} dropwhile \, (\leq x) \, xs$$

The function *insert1* is a valid implementation of *addset* under the abstraction mapping (*abstr*, *valid1*). Since (*insert2* x xs) is a non-duplicated list if xs is, *insert2* is a valid implementation for (*abstr*, *valid2*). Finally, since (*insert3* x xs) is in non-decreasing order if xs is, we have that *insert3* is valid for the abstraction mapping (*abstr*, *valid3*). We leave the proof of these claims to the reader.

8.4.4 Queues

We shall now illustrate the ideas introduced above by considering some examples of abstract types, starting with queues. Informally, a queue is a list of values which are processed in a special way. Suppose (*queue* α) denotes some collection of values of type α on which the following operations are defined:

$$
\begin{array}{lll}
start & :: & queue \; \alpha \\
join & :: & queue \; \alpha \to \alpha \to queue \; \alpha \\
front & :: & queue \; \alpha \to \alpha \\
reduce & :: & queue \; \alpha \to queue \; \alpha
\end{array}
$$

The informal interpretation of these operations is as follows: *start* generates, or 'starts', an empty queue; (*join* q x) returns a queue which is identical to q except that x has 'joined' as a new last member; (*front* q) is the value at the 'front' of the (non-empty) queue q; and (*reduce* q) is q 'reduced' by the removal of the front element.

We can express the intended relationships between the various operations by the following equations:

$$
\begin{array}{lcl}
front \, (join \; start \; x) & = & x \\
front \, (join \, (join \; q \; x) \; y) & = & front \, (join \; q \; x) \\
reduce \, (join \; start \; x) & = & start \\
reduce \, (join \, (join \; q \; x) \; y) & = & join \, (reduce \, (join \; q \; x)) \; y
\end{array}
$$

These equations constitute what is called an *algebraic specification* of the abstract type (*queue* α). Although they look like formal definitions of *front* and *reduce* in terms of a data type based on the constructors *start* and *join*, they should be understood only as expressing certain algebraic laws that the four operations must satisfy. On the other hand, it is certainly possible to base the representation of queues on the type:

$$repqueue \; \alpha ::= Start \mid Join \, (repqueue \; \alpha) \; \alpha$$

under the abstraction function:

$$\begin{array}{lcl} abstr & :: & repqueue\ \alpha \rightarrow queue\ \alpha \\ abstr\ Start & = & start \\ abstr\ (Join\ q\ x) & = & join\ (abstr\ q)\ x \end{array}$$

With minor notational changes, the above equations can then be interpreted as formal definitions of the functions *front'* and *reduce'* which implement the operations *front* and *reduce*. The essential characteristic of this particular representation is that evaluating $(join\ q\ x)$ requires constant time, while reducing a queue and determining the front element each require time proportional to the number of elements in the queue.

An obvious alternative representation of queues is to use lists. We shall leave details as an exercise. A third representation of queues is to use balanced trees, a data structure we will describe in Chapter 9. In this representation all of the operations can be carried out in only $O(\log n)$ steps, where n is the number of elements in the queue.

8.4.5 Arrays

A second example of an abstract type is provided by arrays. Basically, an array is a finite list whose elements may be modified and inspected, but the number of elements in the list does not change. Suppose $(array\ \alpha)$ denotes the abstract type defined by the following four operations:

$$\begin{array}{lcl} mkarray & :: & [\alpha] \rightarrow array\ \alpha \\ length & :: & array\ \alpha \rightarrow num \\ lookup & :: & array\ \alpha \rightarrow num \rightarrow \alpha \\ update & :: & array\ \alpha \rightarrow num \rightarrow \alpha \rightarrow array\ \alpha \end{array}$$

Informally, $(mkarray\ xs)$ creates an array from a given list xs; the value $(length\ A)$ is the number of elements in the array; $(lookup\ A\ k)$ returns the kth element of A, counting from 0; and $(update\ A\ k\ x)$ returns an array that is identical to A except that its kth element is now x.

We can express the relationships between the operations by the following equations:

$$\begin{array}{lcl} length\ (mkarray\ xs) & = & \#xs \\ length\ (update\ A\ k\ x) & = & length\ A \\ \\ lookup\ (mkarray\ xs)\ k & = & xs\ !\ k \\ lookup\ (update\ A\ j\ x)\ k & = & x, \qquad\qquad \text{if } j = k \\ & = & lookup\ A\ k, \quad \textbf{otherwise} \end{array}$$

One way to represent arrays is by a pair of values, a list and a number giving the length of the list. Suppose we set:

$$reparray\ \alpha\ ==\ ([\alpha], num)$$

and define:

$$
\begin{array}{lll}
valid & :: & reparray\ \alpha \to bool \\
valid\ (xs, n) & = & (\#xs = n)
\end{array}
$$

$$
\begin{array}{lll}
abstr & :: & reparray\ \alpha \to array\ \alpha \\
abstr\ (xs, n) & = & mkarray\ xs
\end{array}
$$

The array operations can be implemented by the definitions:

$$
\begin{array}{lll}
mkarray'\ xs & = & (xs, \#xs) \\
length'\ (xs, n) & = & n \\
lookup'\ (xs, n)\ k & = & xs\ !\ k \\
update'\ (xs, n)\ k\ x & = & (ys, n), \quad \textbf{if}\ k < n \\
& & \textbf{where}\ ys = take\ k\ xs \mathbin{+\!\!\!+} [x] \mathbin{+\!\!\!+} \\
& & \qquad\qquad drop\ (k + 1)\ xs
\end{array}
$$

Under this representation, the cost of either accessing or modifying an array element is $O(n)$ steps, where n is the length of the array. In particular, evaluating:

$$lookup'\ (update'\ (xs, n)\ k\ x)\ k$$

requires $O(n)$ steps.

A second representation of arrays is obtained by replacing the list in the first representation by a function defined on an initial segment of the natural numbers. Define:

$$reparray\ \alpha == (num \to \alpha, num)$$

and the abstraction function:

$$
\begin{array}{lll}
abstr & :: & reparray\ \alpha \to array\ \alpha \\
abstr\ (f, n) & = & mkarray\ (map\ f\ [0 .. n - 1])
\end{array}
$$

The array operations are then implemented by the functions:

$$
\begin{array}{lll}
mkarray'\ xs & = & (f, \#xs) \\
& & \textbf{where}\ f\ k = xs\ !\ k \\
length'\ (f, n) & = & n \\
lookup'\ (f, n)\ k & = & f\ k \\
update'\ (f, n)\ k\ x & = & (g, n), \quad \textbf{if}\ 0 \le k \wedge k < n \\
& & \textbf{where}\ g\ j = x, \quad \textbf{if}\ j = k \\
& & \qquad\qquad\ \ = f\ j, \quad \textbf{otherwise}
\end{array}
$$

With this representation, the cost of evaluating an array lookup depends on the history of updates. For example, evaluating:

$$lookup'\ (update'\ (xs, n)\ k\ x)\ k$$

requires only constant time.

In the next chapter we shall describe a third representation of arrays in which the cost of computing $lookup$ or $update$ is proportional to $O(\log n)$ steps, where n is the length of the array.

8.4.6 Sets

The primary example of an abstract type is the notion of a set. In fact, all of mathematics can be explained in terms of the theory of sets. Sets can be represented by lists, lists with no duplicates, ordered lists, trees, boolean functions, and so on, but no representation is more fundamental than any other. The programmer is therefore free to choose between them on the grounds of what set operations are required and how efficiently they can be implemented.

Suppose we are interested in the abstract type $set\ \alpha$ which consists of the following six operations:

$$
\begin{array}{lll}
empty & :: & set\ \alpha \\
unit & :: & \alpha \to set\ \alpha \\
union & :: & set\ \alpha \to set\ \alpha \to set\ \alpha \\
inter & :: & set\ \alpha \to set\ \alpha \to set\ \alpha \\
differ & :: & set\ \alpha \to set\ \alpha \to set\ \alpha \\
member & :: & \alpha \to set\ \alpha \to bool
\end{array}
$$

The meanings of these operations can be explained informally as follows.

1. The constant $empty$ denotes the empty set; this set is also denoted by the special symbol $\{\ \}$.

2. The function $unit$ takes an element x of type α and returns a singleton set containing x; in mathematical notation we write $unit\ x = \{x\}$.

3. The function $union$ takes two sets S and T and returns the set which contains all the elements of S and T; in mathematical notation we write $union\ S\ T = S \cup T$.

4. The function $inter$ computes the intersection of two sets. The result of $(inter\ S\ T)$ is the set consisting of the common members of S and T. The mathematical notation for this operation is $\cap$; thus $inter\ S\ T = S \cap T$.

5. The function $differ$ computes the difference of two sets. The result of $(differ\ S\ T)$ is the set which contains all the elements of S that are not in T. In mathematical notation we write $differ\ S\ T = S \setminus T$.

6. The predicate $member$ takes a value x and a set S and returns $True$ or $False$ depending on whether x is a member of S. In mathematical notation, $(member\ x\ S)$ is written as $x \in S$.

In many applications the operations:

$$
\begin{array}{rcl}
insert\ x\ S & = & S \cup \{x\} \\
delete\ x\ S & = & S \setminus \{x\}
\end{array}
$$

together with *empty* and *member*, are the only ones required. A type based
on these four operations is often called a 'dictionary'.

The crucial operation on sets is the test for membership. It satisfies the
following laws:

$$
\begin{aligned}
x \in \{\,\} &= \textit{False} \\
x \in \{y\} &= (x = y) \\
x \in (A \cup B) &= (x \in A) \vee (x \in B) \\
x \in (A \cap B) &= (x \in A) \wedge (x \in B) \\
x \in (A \setminus B) &= (x \in A) \wedge \neg(x \in B)
\end{aligned}
$$

for all values of x. In addition, two sets are defined to be equal if and only
if they have the same members. From these facts we can derive a number of
laws about $\cup$, $\cap$ and $\setminus$. In particular,

$$
\begin{aligned}
A \cup (B \cup C) &= (A \cup B) \cup C & \text{(associativity)} \\
A \cup B &= B \cup A & \text{(commutativity)} \\
A \cup A &= A & \text{(idempotence)} \\
A \cup \{\,\} &= A & \text{(identity)}
\end{aligned}
$$

Thus, $\cup$ is like $+\!\!+$ except that it is commutative and idempotent as well as
associative.

We have already seen how to represent finite sets by arbitrary lists, lists with
no duplicates, and ordered lists. It is interesting to compare the efficiency
of the various set operations under these three representations. For brevity,
we consider only the implementations of $\cup$ and $\setminus$. Using unrestricted lists we
can define:

$$
\begin{aligned}
union\ xs\ ys &= xs +\!\!+ ys \\
differ\ xs\ ys &= [x \mid x \leftarrow xs;\ \neg member\ x\ ys]
\end{aligned}
$$

One suitable definition of *member* is:

$$
\begin{aligned}
member\ x\ [\,] &= \textit{False} \\
member\ x\ (y : xs) &= (x = y) \vee member\ x\ xs
\end{aligned}
$$

Suppose xs has length n and represents a set of N elements. Thus, N is
the number of distinct elements in xs. Let m and M be the analogous
values for ys. Then evaluating $(union\ xs\ ys)$ takes $O(n)$ steps, and evaluating
$(differ\ xs\ ys)$ takes $O(n \times m)$ steps. On the other hand, n can be arbitrarily
larger than N; similarly for m and M.

Using non-duplicated lists, we have to change the definition of *union* to
read:

$$
union\ xs\ ys = xs +\!\!+ [y \mid y \leftarrow ys;\ \neg member\ y\ xs]
$$

Both $(union\ xs\ ys)$ and $(differ\ xs\ ys)$ now require only $O(N \times M)$ steps.

Finally, using ordered lists we can define:

$$
\begin{aligned}
union\,[\,]\,ys &= ys \\
union\,(x:xs)\,[\,] &= x:xs \\
union\,(x:xs)\,(y:ys) &= x:union\,xs\,(y:ys), &&\textbf{if } x < y \\
&= x:union\,xs\,ys, &&\textbf{if } x = y \\
&= y:union\,(x:xs)\,ys, &&\textbf{if } x > y
\end{aligned}
$$

$$
\begin{aligned}
differ\,[\,]\,ys &= [\,] \\
differ\,(x:xs)\,[\,] &= x:xs \\
differ\,(x:xs)\,(y:ys) &= x:differ\,xs\,(y:ys), &&\textbf{if } x < y \\
&= differ\,xs\,ys, &&\textbf{if } x = y \\
&= differ\,(x:xs)\,ys, &&\textbf{if } x > y
\end{aligned}
$$

With this representation, evaluating ($union\ xs\ ys$) and ($differ\ xs\ ys$) requires only $O(N + M)$ steps each.

Of the three representations, it therefore appears that the one using ordered lists is the best. The union, intersection and difference of two sets can be evaluated in time proportional to the sum of the sizes of the sets. On the other hand, the test for set membership and the two dictionary operations:

$$
\begin{aligned}
insert\ x\ xs &= union\,(unit\ x)\,xs \\
delete\ x\ xs &= differ\ xs\,(unit\ x)
\end{aligned}
$$

each require linear time. In Chapter 9 we shall describe a representation for sets in which each of *member*, *insert* and *delete* can be computed in $O(\log n)$ steps, where n is the size of the given set.

8.4.7   Infinite sets

The representations discussed above only work for finite sets. More precisely, consider the infinite list $[1\,..]$ representing the infinite set of positive integers and the test:

$$member\ 0\ [1\,..]$$

Since 0 is not in the set of positive integers, we require that the above expression evaluates to *False*. Instead, it evaluates to $\bot$. The process of searching an infinite list for a value that is not present never terminates.

We can go some way to solving this problem by choosing a different representation. Suppose we represent a set by a function that tests for membership. The abstraction function here is:

$$
\begin{aligned}
abstr\quad &::\quad (\alpha \rightarrow bool) \rightarrow set\ \alpha \\
abstr\ p\quad &=\quad \{x \mid p\ x = True\}
\end{aligned}
$$

Under this representation, the infinite set of positive integers is represented by the function:

$$positive\ x\ =\ x > 0 \wedge integer\ x$$

The given set operations are implemented by the definitions:

$$
\begin{aligned}
\textit{empty} \quad &= \quad \textit{const False} \\
\textit{unit } x \quad &= \quad (= x) \\
\textit{union } p\, q \quad &= \quad r \quad \textbf{where } r\, x = p\, x \lor q\, x \\
\textit{inter } p\, q \quad &= \quad r \quad \textbf{where } r\, x = p\, x \land q\, x \\
\textit{differ } p\, q \quad &= \quad r \quad \textbf{where } r\, x = p\, x \land \neg q\, x \\
\textit{member } x\, p \quad &= \quad p\, x
\end{aligned}
$$

On the other hand, with this representation there is no way to test the equality of two sets, or even to list the elements of a finite set. If we are representing just sets of positive integers (say), then the function:

$$\textit{enumerate } p \quad = \quad [\, x \mid x \leftarrow [1\,..];\ p\, x\,]$$

will return a list of the elements of the set represented by the predicate p, but this list will always be infinite or partial.

Exercises

8.4.1 Prove that each of *insert1*, *insert2* and *insert3* satisfies the specification for inserting a value into a set.

8.4.2 Consider the following representation of queues:

$$\textit{queue } \alpha == (\textit{num} \to \alpha, \textit{num})$$

The abstraction function is:

$$
\begin{aligned}
\textit{abstr}\,(f, 0) \quad &= \quad \textit{start} \\
\textit{abstr}\,(f, n + 1) \quad &= \quad \textit{join}\,(\textit{abstr}\,(f, n))\,(f\,(n + 1))
\end{aligned}
$$

Implement the queue operations and show they satisfy their algebraic specifications.

8.4.3 It is possible to represent lists by functions (from lists to lists) under the abstraction and representation functions:

$$
\begin{aligned}
\textit{abstr} \quad &::\quad ([\alpha] \to [\alpha]) \to [\alpha] \\
\textit{abstr } f \quad &=\quad f\,[\,] \\
\\
\textit{reprn} \quad &::\quad [\alpha] \to ([\alpha] \to [\alpha]) \\
\textit{reprn } xs \quad &=\quad (xs \mathbin{+\!\!+})
\end{aligned}
$$

Thus a list xs is represented by a function f such that $f\,[\,] = xs$.

Construct definitions of the functions *cons* and *cat* satisfying:

$$
\begin{aligned}
\textit{abstr}\,(\textit{cons } x\, f) \quad &=\quad x : \textit{abstr } f \\
\textit{abstr}\,(\textit{cat } f\, g) \quad &=\quad \textit{abstr } f \mathbin{+\!\!+} \textit{abstr } g
\end{aligned}
$$

Synthesise a function *rev* such that:

$$abstr \cdot rev \cdot reprn = reverse$$

and hence derive yet another definition of list reversal which works in linear time.

8.4.4 Consider the following type for representing lists:

$$seq\ \alpha ::= Nil \mid Unit\ \alpha \mid Cat\ (seq\ \alpha)\ (seq\ \alpha)$$

Give the definition of a suitable abstraction function *abstr* :: $seq\ \alpha \rightarrow [\alpha]$. Write down the specification of the function *tailseq* which corresponds to *tl* on lists. Give an implementation of *tailseq* and show that it meets the specification. In general, what are the advantages and disadvantages of representing lists in this way?

8.4.5 Consider the problem of describing a simple line editor. Suppose a *line* is a sequence of characters $c_1 c_2 \ldots c_n$ together with a position p, where $0 \le p \le n$, called the *cursor*.

The following operations on lines are required:

$$
\begin{array}{rcl}
newline & :: & line \\
movestart & :: & line \rightarrow line \\
moveend & :: & line \rightarrow line \\
moveleft & :: & line \rightarrow line \\
moveright & :: & line \rightarrow line \\
insert & :: & char \rightarrow line \rightarrow line \\
delete & :: & line \rightarrow line
\end{array}
$$

The informal description of these operations is as follows: (i) the constant *newline* denotes an empty line; (ii) *moveleft* moves the cursor one position to the left (if possible); similarly for *moveright*; (iii) *movestart* places the cursor at the beginning of the line; similarly, *moveend* places the cursor at the end of the line; (iv) *delete* deletes the character at the cursor position; and finally (v) (*insert x*) inserts a new character at the cursor position. Give formal specifications for these operations, either algebraically or by a suitable abstract model. Suggest a suitable representation for *line*, implement the given operations, and show that they meet their specifications.

Chapter 9

Trees

Any data-type which exhibits a non-linear (or 'branching') structure is generically called a *tree*. Trees serve as natural representations for any form of hierarchically organised data. One example was given in the last chapter, where the syntactic structure of arithmetic expressions was modelled as a tree. As we shall see, trees are also useful for the efficient implementation of functions concerned with search and retrieval.

There are numerous species and subspecies of tree. They can be classified according to the precise form of the branching structure, the location of information within the tree, and the nature of the relationships between the information in different parts of the tree. In the present chapter we shall study two or three of the most common species, describe a little of the basic terminology associated with trees, and outline some of the more important applications.

9.1 Binary trees

As its name implies, a binary tree is a tree with a simple two-way branching structure. This structure is captured by the following type declaration:

$$btree \; \alpha ::= \; Tip \; \alpha \mid Bin \; (btree \; \alpha) \; (btree \; \alpha)$$

A value of ($btree \; \alpha$) is therefore either a 'tip' (indicated by the constructor Tip), which contains a value of type α, or a binary 'node' (indicated by the constructor Bin), which consists of two further trees called the *left* and *right* subtrees of the node. For example, the tree:

$$Bin \; (Tip \; 1)$$
$$(Bin \; (Tip \; 2) \; (Tip \; 3))$$

consists of a binary node with a left subtree ($Tip \; 1$), and a right subtree ($Bin \; (Tip \; 2) \; (Tip \; 3)$) which, in turn, has a left subtree ($Tip \; 2$) and a right

233

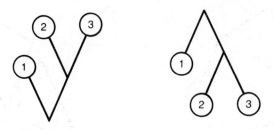

Figure 9.1 Upward and downward trees.

subtree (*Tip* 3). Compare this element of (*btree num*) with the tree:

$$Bin\,(Bin\,(Tip\,1)\,(Tip\,2))$$
$$(Tip\,3)$$

Although the second tree contains the same sequence of numbers in its tips as the first, the way the information is organised is quite different and the two expressions denote distinct values.

A tree can be pictured in one of two basic ways, growing upwards or growing downwards. Both orientations are illustrated in Figure 9.1. The downward pointing orientation is the one normally preferred in computing, and this is reflected in some of the basic terminology of trees. For instance, we talk about the 'depth' of a tree rather than its 'height'. The depth of a tree is defined below.

9.1.1   Measures on trees

There are two important measures on binary trees, size and depth. The *size* of a tree is the number of tips it contains. Hence:

$$size\,(Tip\,x) \quad = \quad 1$$
$$size\,(Bin\,t1\,t2) \quad = \quad size\,t1 + size\,t2$$

The function *size* plays the same role for trees as (#) does for lists. In particular, a tree is finite if and only if it has a well-defined size.

There is a simple, but important, relationship between the number of tips and the number of nodes in a finite tree: the former is always one more than the latter. If we count the number of nodes by the function *nsize*, where:

$$nsize\,(Tip\,x) \quad = \quad 0$$
$$nsize\,(Bin\,t1\,t2) \quad = \quad 1 + nsize\,t1 + nsize\,t2$$

then we have:

$$size\,t = 1 + nsize\,t$$

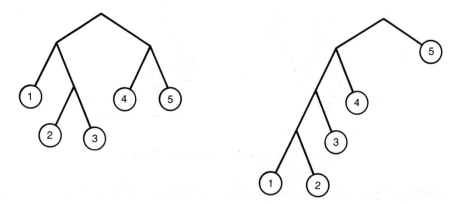

Figure 9.2 Trees of depth 3 and 4.

for all binary trees t. The result can be proved by structural induction and is left as an exercise. It also holds, by default, in the case of infinite trees, since both sides of the above equation reduce to $\bot$.

The second useful measure on trees is the notion of depth. The depth of a finite tree is defined as follows:

$$
\begin{aligned}
depth\,(\mathit{Tip}\ x) &= 0 \\
depth\,(\mathit{Bin}\ t1\ t2) &= 1 + (depth\ t1)\,\mathbf{max}\,(depth\ t2) \quad,
\end{aligned}
$$

In words, the depth of a tree consisting of a single tip is 0; otherwise it is one more than the greater of the heights of its two subtrees. For example, the tree on the left in Figure 9.2 has depth 3, while the one on the right has depth 4. Notice these trees have the same size and, indeed, exactly the same sequence of tip values. The notion of depth is important because it is a measure of the time required to retrieve a tip value from a tree.

Although two trees of the same size need not have the same depth, the two measures are not independent. The following result is one of the most important facts about binary trees. It says that:

$$
size\ t \leq 2\,\widehat{\ }\ depth\ t
$$

for all (finite) trees t. We shall prove this inequality by structural induction on t.

Case $(\mathit{Tip}\ x)$. We have:

$$
\begin{aligned}
size\,(\mathit{Tip}\ x) &= 1 & (size.1) \\
&= 2\,\widehat{\ }\,0 & (\widehat{\ }.1) \\
&= 2\,\widehat{\ }\,depth\,(\mathit{Tip}\ x) & (depth.1)
\end{aligned}
$$

as required.

Case (*Bin t1 t2*).   Assume, by way of induction, that:

$$size\ t1 \leq 2 \char`^\ depth\ t1$$
$$size\ t2 \leq 2 \char`^\ depth\ t2$$

and let:

$$d = (depth\ t1)\ \mathbf{max}\ (depth\ t2)$$

We now have:

$$
\begin{aligned}
size\ (Bin\ t1\ t2) \ &= \ size\ t1 + size\ t2 &&(size.2)\\
&\leq \ 2 \char`^ (depth\ t1) + 2 \char`^ (depth\ t2) &&\text{(hypothesis)}\\
&\leq \ 2 \char`^ d + 2 \char`^ d &&\text{(monotonicity of \char`^)}\\
&= \ 2 \char`^ (1 + d) &&\text{(arithmetic)}\\
&= \ 2 \char`^ (depth\ (Bin\ t1\ t2)) &&(depth.2)
\end{aligned}
$$

as required. $\square$

By taking logarithms (to base 2), we can restate the result in the following equivalent form:

$$depth\ t \geq \log_2 (size\ t)$$

for all finite trees t.

Given any positive integer n, it is always possible to construct a tree of size n with depth d satisfying:

$$d = \lceil \log_2 n \rceil$$

where $\lceil x \rceil$ denotes the smallest integer $k \geq x$. Such trees are said to be *minimal*. In general, there will be more than one minimal tree of a given size. Minimal trees are useful because, by making a tree minimal, we can ensure that the cost of retrieving tip values is as small as possible.

9.1.2   Map and fold over trees

The generic functions *map* and *fold* for lists have analogues *mapbtree* and *foldbtree* for binary trees. They are defined as follows:

$$
\begin{aligned}
mapbtree &\ ::\ (\alpha \rightarrow \beta) \rightarrow btree\ \alpha \rightarrow btree\ \beta\\
mapbtree\ f\ (Tip\ x) &\ =\ Tip\ (f\ x)\\
mapbtree\ f\ (Bin\ t1\ t2) &\ =\ Bin\ (mapbtree\ f\ t1)\ (mapbtree\ f\ t2)
\end{aligned}
$$

$$
\begin{aligned}
foldbtree &\ ::\ (\alpha \rightarrow \alpha \rightarrow \alpha) \rightarrow btree\ \alpha \rightarrow \alpha\\
foldbtree\ (\oplus)\ (Tip\ x) &\ =\ x\\
foldbtree\ (\oplus)\ (Bin\ t1\ t2) &\ =\ (foldbtree\ (\oplus)\ t1) \oplus (foldbtree\ (\oplus)\ t2)
\end{aligned}
$$

Many operations on trees can be defined in terms of these functions. For example, the sum of the tips in a tree of numbers can be defined by:

$$sumtips = foldbtree\ (+)$$

The size of a tree is defined by:

$$size = foldbtree \ (+) \cdot mapbtree \ (const \ 1)$$

and the depth of a tree is defined by:

$$
\begin{aligned}
depth \ &= \ foldbtree \ (\oplus) \cdot mapbtree \ (const \ 0) \\
&\textbf{where} \ \ d1 \oplus d2 = 1 + (d1 \ \textbf{max} \ d2)
\end{aligned}
$$

Finally, the function *tips* for listing the tip values of a tree in left to right order can be defined by:

$$
\begin{aligned}
tips \ &= \ foldbtree \ (+\!\!+) \cdot mapbtree \ unit \\
&\textbf{where} \ \ unit \ x = [x]
\end{aligned}
$$

The function *mapbtree* satisfies laws similar to the function *map*. In particular, we have:

$$mapbtree \ f \cdot mapbtree \ g \ = \ mapbtree \ (f \cdot g)$$

for any functions f and g. We also have the identity:

$$map \ f \cdot tips = tips \cdot mapbtree \ f$$

which relates *map*, *tips* and *mapbtree*.

There is also a law relating *foldbtree* and *foldr1* (or, equally, *foldl1*). It says that if $\oplus$ is associative, then:

$$
\begin{aligned}
foldbtree \ (\oplus) \ &= \ foldr1 \ (\oplus) \cdot tips \\
&= \ foldl1 \ (\oplus) \cdot tips
\end{aligned}
$$

(Note that *tips* always returns a non-empty list.) All of the above identities can be proved by structural induction.

Like *map* and *fold* with lists, we can use *foldbtree* and *mapbtree* to define many functions over trees without using recursion explicitly. Since the resulting definitions are shorter, this is certainly a good idea in any application where a number of tree processing functions are required. On the other hand, a direct recursive definition is just as good in simple situations. Unlike lists, there is a natural recursive decomposition of trees in terms of their subtrees, so a definition which exhibits the same kind of recursive decomposition is often simplest.

9.1.3 Labelled binary trees

Finally, we introduce a slight variation on the basic structure of binary trees. By definition, a *labelled* binary tree is a value of the following type:

$$lbtree \ \alpha \ \beta ::= Tip \ \alpha \mid Bin \ \beta \ (lbtree \ \alpha \ \beta) \ (lbtree \ \alpha \ \beta)$$

Here, binary nodes are 'labelled' with values of a second type β. Apart from these additional values, a labelled binary tree has exactly the same structure as the earlier kind. Because extra information is available, many operations on binary trees can be implemented efficiently in terms of labelled binary trees. We shall see examples of this idea in subsequent sections.

Exercises

9.1.1 Prove that the number of tips in a binary tree is always one more than the number of internal nodes.

9.1.2 The subtrees of a binary tree t can be defined by:

$$\begin{aligned} subtrees\,(Tip\ x) &= [Tip\ x] \\ subtrees\,(Bin\ t1\ t2) &= subtrees\ t1 \mathbin{+\!\!+} subtrees\ t2 \mathbin{+\!\!+} [Bin\ t1\ t2] \end{aligned}$$

State and prove a relationship between $\#(subtrees\ t)$ and $size\ t$.

9.1.3 Show that:

$$depth\ t \leq size\ t - 1$$

for all finite binary trees.

9.1.4 Prove that if xs is a list of 2^n values, then there is a unique minimal tree t such that $tips\ t = xs$.

9.1.5 Prove that a minimal tree of size n has depth $\lceil \log_2 n \rceil$.

9.1.6 Design a function that takes a non-empty list xs into a minimal tree t such that $tips\ t = xs$.

9.1.7 Prove the laws:

$$\begin{aligned} mapbtree\ f \cdot mapbtree\ g &= mapbtree\ (f \cdot g) \\ map\ f \cdot tips &= tips \cdot mapbtree\ f \\ foldbtree\ (\oplus) &= foldr1\ (\oplus) \cdot tips \end{aligned}$$

where, in the last law, $\oplus$ is associative.

9.1.8 Suppose $f = foldbtree(\oplus)$, where $\oplus$ is associative with identity element e. Prove that $f\ t = fm\ t\ e$, where:

$$fm = foldbtree\ (\cdot) \cdot mapbtree\ (\oplus)$$

Using this result and the fact that:

$$\begin{aligned} tips &= foldbtree\ (\mathbin{+\!\!+}) \cdot mapbtree\ unit \\ &\mathbf{where}\ unit\ x = [x] \end{aligned}$$

derive the equation:

$$tips \; t = mtips \; t \; [\,]$$

where

$$mtips = foldbtree \; (\cdot) \cdot mapbtree \; (:)$$

Compare the costs of computing ($tips \; t$) by the two definitions. (*Hint:* Recall that the cost of computing $xs \; +\!\!+ \; ys$ is proportional to $\#xs$.)

9.2   Huffman coding trees

As a first example of the use of binary trees, we shall consider the problem of coding data efficiently. As many computer users know only too well, it is often necessary to store files of information as compactly as possible in order to free precious space for other, more urgent, purposes. Suppose the information to be stored is a text consisting of a sequence of characters. The ASCII standard code uses seven bits to represent each of $2^7 = 128$ possible different characters, so a text of n characters contains $7n$ bits of information. For example, the letters 't', 'e', and 'x' are represented in ASCII by the codes:

$$
\begin{array}{rcl}
t & \longrightarrow & 1110100 \\
e & \longrightarrow & 1100101 \\
x & \longrightarrow & 1111000
\end{array}
$$

In particular, the text "text" is coded in ASCII as the sequence:

$$1110100110010111110001110100$$

of 28 bits. As ASCII is a fixed-length code, the original text can be recovered by decoding each successive group of seven bits.

One idea for reducing the total number of bits required to code a text is to abandon the notion of fixed-length codes, and seek instead a coding scheme based on the relative frequency of occurrence of the characters in the text. The basic idea is to take a sample piece of text, estimate the number of times each character appears, and choose short codes for the more frequent characters and longer codes for the rarer ones. For example, if we take the codes:

$$
\begin{array}{rcl}
t & \longrightarrow & 0 \\
e & \longrightarrow & 10 \\
x & \longrightarrow & 11
\end{array}
$$

then "text" can be coded as the bit sequence 010110 of length 6.

It is important to realise that codes must be chosen in such a way as to ensure that the coded text can be deciphered uniquely. To illustrate, suppose the codes had been:

$$
\begin{array}{rcl}
t & \longrightarrow & 0 \\
e & \longrightarrow & 10 \\
x & \longrightarrow & 1
\end{array}
$$

Under this scheme, "text" would be coded as the sequence 01010 of length 5. However, the string "tee" would be coded by exactly the same sequence, and this is obviously not what is wanted. The simplest way to prevent this happening is to choose codes so that no code is a proper initial segment (or *prefix*) of any other.

As well as requiring unique decipherability, we also want the coding scheme to be optimal. An optimal coding scheme is one which minimises the expected length of the coded text. More precisely, if characters c_j, for $1 \leq j \leq n$, have probabilities of occurrence p_j, then we want to choose codes with lengths l_j such that

$$\sum_{j=1}^{n} p_j l_j$$

is as small as possible.

One method for constructing an optimal code satisfying the prefix property is called Huffman coding (after its inventor, David Huffman). Each character is stored as a tip of a binary tree, the structure of which is determined by the computed frequencies. The code for a character c is a sequence of binary values describing the path in the tree to the tip containing c. Such a scheme guarantees that no code is a prefix of any other. We can define a path formally by:

$$
\begin{array}{lll}
step & ::= & Left \mid Right \\
path & == & [step]
\end{array}
$$

A path is therefore a sequence of steps, each of which is one of the two values *Left* or *Right*. A path can be traced by the function *trace*, defined by:

$$
\begin{array}{lll}
trace\ (Tip\ x)\ [\,] & = & x \\
trace\ (Bin\ t1\ t2)\ (Left : ps) & = & trace\ t1\ ps \\
trace\ (Bin\ t1\ t2)\ (Right : ps) & = & trace\ t2\ ps
\end{array}
$$

If ps is a path in t leading to a tip, then $(trace\ t\ ps)$ is the value associated with the tip; otherwise $trace\ t\ ps = \perp$.

To illustrate the idea, consider the tree:

$$
\begin{array}{c}
Bin\ (Bin\ (Tip\ \text{'x'})\ (Tip\ \text{'e'})) \\
(Tip\ \text{'t'})
\end{array}
$$

In this tree the character 'x' is coded by the path $[Left, Left]$, character 'e' by $[Left, Right]$, and character 't' by $[Right]$. So 't' is coded by one bit of information, while the others require two bits. For example, the string "text" is encoded by the sequence:

$$[Right, Left, Right, Left, Left, Right]$$

which is the same as 010110 when *Right* is replaced by 0 and *Left* by 1.

There are three aspects to the problem of implementing Huffman coding: (i) building a binary tree; (ii) coding a sequence of characters; and (iii) decoding a coded sequence. We shall deal with these stages in reverse order.

Decoding.   Suppose ps is a sequence of steps representing a sequence xs of characters with respect to a given tree t. The function $decodexs$, where $decodexs\ t\ ps = xs$, can be defined in the following way:

$$
\begin{aligned}
decodexs\ t\ ps & = & traces\ t\ t\ ps \\
traces\ t\ (\textit{Tip}\ x)\ [\,] & = & [x] \\
traces\ t\ (\textit{Tip}\ x)\ (p:ps) & = & [x] +\!\!\!+ traces\ t\ t\ (p:ps) \\
traces\ t\ (\textit{Bin}\ t1\ t2)\ (\textit{Left}:ps) & = & traces\ t\ t1\ ps \\
traces\ t\ (\textit{Bin}\ t1\ t2)\ (\textit{Right}:ps) & = & traces\ t\ t2\ ps
\end{aligned}
$$

The first argument of $traces$ is the given tree, while the second argument is the subtree currently being traversed. Each time a tip is reached, the associated character is produced and t is regenerated in order to process the remaining paths, if any. The time for decoding is clearly linear in the length of ps. Notice that if ps does not correspond to a legal sequence of paths, then $(decodexs\ t\ ps)$ will be a partial list.

Coding.   Next, let us deal with step (ii), the coding phase. Here, the input is a sequence of characters and the output is a sequence of steps. We can define:

$$codexs\ t = concat \cdot map\ (codex\ t)$$

so the problem reduces to how to code a single character. The following definition of $codex$ is straightforward, but leads to an inefficient algorithm:

$$
\begin{aligned}
codex\ (\textit{Tip}\ y)\ x & = & [\,], & \quad \textbf{if } x = y \\
codex\ (\textit{Bin}\ t1\ t2)\ x & = & \textit{Left}:codex\ t1\ x, & \quad \textbf{if } member\ t1\ x \\
& = & \textit{Right}:codex\ t2\ x, & \quad \textbf{if } member\ t2\ x
\end{aligned}
$$

The formal definition of $member$ is:

$$
\begin{aligned}
member\ (\textit{Tip}\ y)\ x & = & (x = y) \\
member\ (\textit{Bin}\ t1\ t2)\ x & = & member\ t1\ x \lor member\ t2\ x
\end{aligned}
$$

Note that if x is not a tip value in t, then $codex\ t\ x = \bot$.

The trouble with the definition of $codex$ lies in the many costly calculations of $member$. Since the time to calculate $(member\ t\ x)$ is $O(n)$ steps, where $n = size\ t$, the time $T(n)$ required to compute $(codex\ t\ x)$ in the worst possible case satisfies:

$$T(n) = T(n-1) + O(n)$$

and so $T(n) = O(n^2)$. The worst possible case arises, for instance, when every left subtree has size 1, and x appears as the rightmost tip value. It also arises when every right subtree has size 1, and x appears as the leftmost tip value.

One way to improve this unacceptable quadratic behaviour is to define:

$$
\begin{aligned}
codex\ t\ x &= hd\ (codesx\ t\ x) \\
codesx\ (Tip\ y)\ x &= [[\,]], && \textbf{if } x = y \\
&= [\,], && \textbf{otherwise} \\
codesx\ (Bin\ t1\ t2)\ x &= map\ (Left:)\ (codesx\ t1\ x)\,+\!\!+ \\
&\quad\ map\ (Right:)\ (codesx\ t2\ x)
\end{aligned}
$$

This is an example of the list of successes technique described in Chapter 6. The value $(codesx\ t\ x)$ is a list of *all* paths in t which lead to a tip containing x. If t is a tip, then the list is either empty (if the characters do not match), or is a singleton list containing the empty path. If t is not a tip, then the final list is the concatenation of the list of paths through the left subtree with the list of paths through the right subtree. If t contains exactly one occurrence of x, then $(codesx\ t\ x)$ will be a singleton list containing the desired path. We shall leave as an exercise the proof that this version of $codex$ requires only $O(n)$ steps.

Constructing a Huffman tree. Now we must deal with the most interesting part, building a coding tree. Let us suppose that the relative frequencies of the characters have been computed from the sample, so we are given a list of pairs:

$$[(c_1, w_1), (c_2, w_2), \ldots, (c_n, w_n)]$$

where $c_1, c_2, \ldots, c_n$ are the characters and $w_1, w_2, \ldots, w_n$ are numbers, called *weights*, indicating the frequencies. The probability of character c_j occurring is therefore w_j/W, where $W = \sum w_j$. Without loss of generality, we shall also suppose that the weights satisfy $w_1 \leq w_2 \leq \cdots \leq w_n$, so the characters are listed in increasing order of likelihood.

The procedure for building a Huffman tree is as follows. The first step is to convert the list of character-weight pairs into a list of trees by applying $(map\ Tip)$. Each tip will contain a pair (x, w), where x is a character and w its associated weight. This list of trees is then reduced to a single tree by repeatedly applying a function which combines two trees into one, until just a single tree is left. Thus:

$$build\ =\ until\ single\ (combine \cdot map\ Tip)$$

Here, $(until\ p\ f)$ is the function that repeatedly applies f until p becomes true, and *single* is the test for a singleton list.

The effect of *combine* on a list ts of trees is to combine two trees in ts with the lightest weights, where:

$$
\begin{aligned}
weight\ (Tip\ (x, w)) &= w \\
weight\ (Bin\ t1\ t2) &= weight\ t1 + weight\ t2
\end{aligned}
$$

Thus, the weight of a tree is the sum of the weights in its tip nodes.

In order to determine at each stage which are the lightest trees, we simply keep the trees in increasing order of weight. Thus:

$$combine\,(t1 : t2 : ts) \quad = \quad insert\,(Bin\ t1\ t2)\ ts$$

where:

$$
\begin{aligned}
insert\ u\ [\,] \quad &= \quad [u] \\
insert\ u\ (t : ts) \quad &= \quad u : t : ts, \qquad \text{if } weight\ u \le weight\ t \\
&= \quad t : insert\ u\ ts, \quad \textbf{otherwise}
\end{aligned}
$$

Although this definition of *combine* is adequate, it leads to an inefficient algorithm as tree weights are constantly recomputed. A better solution is to store the weights in the tree as labels, and this is where the idea of using a labelled binary tree comes in. Consider the type:

$$htree ::= Leaf\ num\ char \mid Node\ num\ htree\ htree$$

Here, a tip node is indicated by a new constructor *Leaf* that takes two arguments: a number and a character. A binary node is indicated by the new constructor *Node*. The numeric label is a value w satisfying:

$$w = weight\,(Node\ w\ t1\ t2)$$

where:

$$
\begin{aligned}
weight\,(Leaf\ w\ x) \quad &= \quad w \\
weight\,(Node\ w\ t1\ t2) \quad &= \quad weight\ t1 + weight\ t2
\end{aligned}
$$

By maintaining this relationship we can avoid recomputing weights.

To implement the change, we redefine:

$$
\begin{aligned}
build \quad &= \quad unlabel \cdot (until\ single\ combine) \cdot map\ leaf \\
leaf\,(x, w) \quad &= \quad Leaf\ w\ x
\end{aligned}
$$

where *unlabel* throws away the labels after they have served their purpose:

$$
\begin{aligned}
unlabel\,(Leaf\ w\ x) \quad &= \quad Tip\ x \\
unlabel\,(Node\ w\ t1\ t2) \quad &= \quad Bin\,(unlabel\ t1)\,(unlabel\ t2)
\end{aligned}
$$

We must also modify the definition of *combine*:

$$
\begin{aligned}
combine\,(t1 : t2 : ts) \quad &= \quad insert\,(Node\ w\ t1\ t2)\ ts \\
&\qquad \textbf{where } w = wt\ t1 + wt\ t2
\end{aligned}
$$

$$
\begin{aligned}
wt\,(Leaf\ w\ x) \quad &= \quad w \\
wt\,(Node\ w\ t1\ t2) \quad &= \quad w
\end{aligned}
$$

The modification of *insert* is left as an exercise.

Let us see this algorithm at work on an example. Consider the sequence:

$$[(`G', 8), (`R', 9), (`A', 11), (`T', 13), (`E', 17)]$$

of characters and their weights. The first step is to convert this into the list:

$$[Leaf\ 8\ `G', Leaf\ 9\ `R', Leaf\ 11\ `A', Leaf\ 13\ `T', Leaf\ 17\ `E']$$

of leaf trees. The next step is to combine the first two trees and rearrange the resulting trees in increasing order of weight. Thus we obtain:

$$[Leaf\ 11\ `A',$$
$$Leaf\ 13\ `T',$$
$$Node\ 17\ (Leaf\ 8\ `G')\ (Leaf\ 9\ `R'),$$
$$Leaf\ 17\ `E']$$

The result of the second step is the list:

$$[Node\ 17\ (Leaf\ 8\ G)\ (Leaf\ 9\ `R'),$$
$$Leaf\ 17\ `E',$$
$$Node\ 24\ (Leaf\ 11\ `A')\ (Leaf\ 13\ `T')]$$

The third step gives:

$$[Node\ 24\ (Leaf\ 11\ `A')\ (Leaf\ 13\ `T'),$$
$$Node\ 34\ (Node\ 17\ (Leaf\ 8\ `G')\ (Leaf\ 9\ `R'))$$
$$(Leaf\ 17\ `E')]$$

so the final tree is:

$$Node\ 58\ (Node\ 24\ (Leaf\ 11\ `A')\ (Leaf\ 13\ `T'))$$
$$(Node\ 34\ (Node\ 17\ (Leaf\ 8\ `G')\ (Leaf\ 9\ `R'))$$
$$(Leaf\ 17\ `E'))$$

In this tree, which is pictured in Figure 9.3, the characters 'A', 'T' and 'E' are coded by two-bit sequences and 'G' and 'R' by three-bit sequences.

The average, or expected, length of a character code is:

$$\sum w_j l_j / \sum w_j$$

where l_j is the number of bits assigned to character c_j. In the above example this value is:

$$((11 + 13 + 17) \times 2 + (8 + 9) \times 3)/(8 + 9 + 11 + 13 + 17)$$

or approximately 2.29. The crucial property of a Huffman code is that it minimises expected length. Putting it another way, a Huffman tree has the property that it is a binary tree, over tip values $w_1, w_2, \ldots, w_n$, which minimises the sum of the "weighted" path lengths $w_j l_j$ for $1 \leq j \leq n$. For a proof of this fact, the reader should consult Knuth [3] or Standish [11].

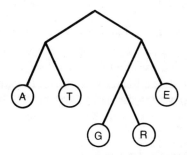

Figure 9.3 A Huffman coding tree.

Exercises

9.2.1 Explain why a Huffman code has the prefix property.

9.2.2 Construct a code which does not satisfy the prefix property, but which nevertheless is such that every text can be uniquely decoded.

9.2.3 Consider the functions $(codes\ t)$ and $(decodes\ t)$ for coding and decoding sequences of characters with Huffman's method. Show that:

$$decodes\ t\ (codes\ t\ xs) = xs$$

for all finite sequences xs.

9.2.4 Suppose $U(n)$ denotes the worst case cost of calculating $(codes\ t\ x)$ for a tree t of size n, under the assumption that this list is empty. Show that

$$U(n) = O(1) + \max\{U(m) + U(n - m)|1 \leq m < n\}$$

for $n > 1$, and hence prove that $U(n) = O(n)$.

Now suppose $S(n)$ is the time required to compute the head of $(codes\ t\ x)$, assuming that this list is not empty. Show that:

$$S(n) = O(1) + \max\{S(m)\max(U(m) + S(n - m))|1 \leq m < n\}$$

for $n > 1$, and hence prove that $S(n) = O(n)$.

9.2.5 Suppose we define:

$$codemem\ t\ x\quad =\quad (codex\ t\ x, member\ t\ x)$$

Synthesise a new definition of $codemem$ which does not depend on $codex$. Redefine $codex$ in terms of $codemem$. What is the cost of calculating $(codex\ t\ x)$ with the new definition?

9.2.6 Modify the definition of *insert* in the tree combining part of Huffman's algorithm to use the weight-labelled representation of Huffman trees.

9.2.7 In the coding phase of Huffman's algorithm, the function *codex* is applied to every occurrence of every character in the text. But all we really need do is to compute (*codex t x*) just once for each character x, store this information in a table, and use the table for subsequent retrieval. This table can itself be implemented as a binary tree. Write functions for implementing this idea, and hence show that the cost of coding characters can be brought down to $O(\log n)$, where n is the number of characters.

9.3 Binary search trees

In this section we shall study a variety of tree, called a binary search tree, that is useful for representing values of the abstract type (*set* α) in which the only set operations allowed are:

$$
\begin{array}{lll}
empty & :: & set\ \alpha \\
insert & :: & \alpha \to set\ \alpha \to set\ \alpha \\
delete & :: & \alpha \to set\ \alpha \to set\ \alpha \\
member & :: & \alpha \to set\ \alpha \to bool
\end{array}
$$

These operations are defined as follows:

$$
\begin{array}{lll}
empty   & = & \{\,\} \\
insert\ x\ s & = & s \cup \{x\} \\
delete\ x\ s & = & s \setminus \{x\} \\
member\ x\ s & = & x \in s
\end{array}
$$

We shall first introduce binary search trees as another example of labelled binary trees. Later on, we shall revise the definition slightly. Suppose t is a binary tree whose tip values are in increasing order when read from left to right. Label each subtree s of t with the rightmost tip value in the left subtree of s. Because the tips are sorted, this value will be the largest value in the left subtree of s. The result is a binary search tree. Note that a binary search tree is a tree of type (*lbtree* α α).

Here is how the information at the labels is used. Consider the function *member* which determines whether a value x appears as a tip value somewhere in a tree t. If x is less than the label of t, then x can only appear in the left subtree of t; similarly, if x is greater than the label of t, it can only appear in the right subtree. Finally, if x equals the label of t, then x must be a tip value. We can therefore define *member* in the following way:

$$
\begin{array}{llll}
member\ x\ (Tip\ y)   & = & (x = y) & \\
member\ x\ (Bin\ y\ t1\ t2) & = & member\ x\ t1, & \text{if } x < y \\
                         & = & True, & \text{if } x = y \\
                         & = & member\ x\ t2, & \text{if } x > y
\end{array}
$$

In the worst case, the time taken to compute ($member\ t\ x$) is proportional to the depth of t. If t is minimal, then the time required is at most $O(\log n)$ steps, where $n = size\ t$.

The trouble with the given definition of binary search trees is that information is duplicated. With one exception, every value appears twice in the tree, once as a tip and once as a label. More precisely, suppose we define the functions:

$$
\begin{array}{lcl}
labels\,(\,Tip\ x\,) & = & [\,] \\
labels\,(\,Bin\ x\ t1\ t2\,) & = & labels\ t1 \,+\!\!\!+\, [x] \,+\!\!\!+\, labels\ t2 \\
\\
tips\,(\,Tip\ x\,) & = & [x] \\
tips\,(\,Bin\ x\ t1\ t2\,) & = & tips\ t1 \,+\!\!\!+\, tips\ t2
\end{array}
$$

for listing the labels and tips of a tree. Then we have:

$$
labels\ t = init\,(\,tips\ t\,)
$$

whenever t is a finite binary search tree. The proof is a simple exercise in structural induction. Notice also that ($labels\ t$) is a list in increasing order if ($tips\ t$) is.

In order to avoid storing redundant information, suppose we throw away the tip values. This idea leads to a new type:

$$
bstree\ \alpha ::= Nil\ |\ Bin\ \alpha\,(\,bstree\ \alpha\,)\,(\,bstree\ \alpha\,)
$$

in which the constructor Tip is replaced by a constant Nil. We now define an element t of ($bstree\ \alpha$) to be a binary search tree if ($labels\ t$) is a list in increasing order, where:

$$
\begin{array}{lcl}
labels\ Nil & = & [\,] \\
labels\,(\,Bin\ x\ t1\ t2\,) & = & labels\ t1 \,+\!\!\!+\, [x] \,+\!\!\!+\, labels\ t2
\end{array}
$$

From now on, we shall use the revised definition of binary search trees. The revised definition of $member$ is straightforward and is left as an exercise.

Finite sets can be represented by binary search trees under the abstraction function $abstr$ and valid representation predicate $valid$ defined by:

$$
\begin{array}{lcl}
abstr\ t & = & set\,(\,labels\ t\,) \\
valid\ t & = & ordered\,(\,labels\ t\,)
\end{array}
$$

where set is the function that converts a list into a set of its values. The operations $empty$, $insert$, $delete$ and $member$ on trees are specified by the equations:

$$
\begin{array}{lcl}
abstr\ empty & = & \{\,\} \\
abstr\,(\,insert\ x\ t\,) & = & (\,abstr\ t\,) \cup \{x\} \\
abstr\,(\,delete\ x\ t\,) & = & (\,abstr\ t\,) \setminus \{x\} \\
abstr\,(\,member\ x\ t\,) & = & x\epsilon(\,abstr\ t\,)
\end{array}
$$

The implementation of *empty* as the empty tree *Nil* is immediate, and the definition of *member* requires only a minor change to the one given above. This leaves us with *insert* and *delete*. The implementation of *insert* can be synthesised from its specification and the result is the following definition:

$$
\begin{aligned}
insert\ x\ Nil &= Bin\ x\ Nil\ Nil \\
insert\ x\ (Bin\ y\ t1\ t2) &= Bin\ y\ (insert\ x\ t1)\ t2, &&\textbf{if }x < y \\
&= Bin\ y\ t1\ t2, &&\textbf{if }x = y \\
&= Bin\ y\ t1\ (insert\ x\ t2), &&\textbf{if }x > y
\end{aligned}
$$

We shall synthesise *delete*, leaving *insert* as an exercise.

9.3.1   Tree deletion

In this section we are going to synthesise the following definition of *delete*:

$$
\begin{aligned}
delete\ x\ Nil &= Nil \\
delete\ x\ (Bin\ y\ t1\ t2) &= Bin\ y\ (delete\ x\ t1)\ t2, &&\textbf{if }x < y \\
&= join\ t1\ t2, &&\textbf{if }x = y \\
&= Bin\ y\ t1\ (delete\ x\ t2), &&\textbf{if }x > y \\[2mm]
join\ t1\ t2 &= t2, &&\textbf{if }t1 = Nil \\
&= Bin\ x\ t\ t2, &&\textbf{otherwise} \\
&\textbf{where }(x, t) = split\ t1 \\[2mm]
split\ (Bin\ x\ t1\ t2) &= (x, t1), &&\textbf{if }t2 = Nil \\
&= (y, Bin\ x\ t1\ t), &&\textbf{otherwise} \\
&\textbf{where }(y, t) = split\ t2
\end{aligned}
$$

The synthesis is a good illustration of the interaction between program design and program proof and, for the interested reader, merits careful attention. It is fairly detailed, so some readers may care to skip the rest of the section.

The specification of *delete* is:

$$abstr\ (delete\ x\ t) = (abstr\ t) \setminus \{x\}$$

where $abstr = set \cdot labels$. It is left as an exercise to show that any function *delete* satisfying the equation:

$$labels\ (delete\ x\ t) = (labels\ t) -- [x]$$

will also satisfy the original specification. Using this second equation as a starting point, we shall now synthesise a constructive definition of *delete*.

The synthesis is organised into cases, depending on the value of t.

Case *Nil*.   Here we have:

$$
\begin{aligned}
labels\ (delete\ x\ Nil) &= (labels\ Nil) -- [x] &&\text{(spec)} \\
&= [\,] -- [x] &&(labels.1) \\
&= [\,] &&(--.1) \\
&= labels\ Nil &&(labels.1)
\end{aligned}
$$

Hence a satisfactory definition of (*delete x Nil*) is to take:

$$delete \ x \ Nil = Nil$$

Case (*Bin y t1 t2*). Here we have:

$$
\begin{aligned}
&labels \ (delete \ x \ (Bin \ y \ t1 \ t2)) \\
&= \ (labels \ (Bin \ y \ t1 \ t2)) -- [x] \qquad \text{(spec)} \\
&= \ (labels \ t1 \mathbin{+\!\!+} [y] \mathbin{+\!\!+} labels \ t2) -- [x] \quad (labels.2)
\end{aligned}
$$

In order to continue with the derivation, we need a lemma about $(--)$. This lemma says that if $(xs \mathbin{+\!\!+} [y] \mathbin{+\!\!+} ys)$ is in increasing order, then:

$$
\begin{aligned}
(xs \mathbin{+\!\!+} [y] \mathbin{+\!\!+} ys) -- [x] \ &= \ (xs -- [x]) \mathbin{+\!\!+} [y] \mathbin{+\!\!+} ys, \quad \text{if } x < y \\
&= \ xs \mathbin{+\!\!+} ys, \qquad\qquad\qquad\quad \text{if } x = y \\
&= \ xs \mathbin{+\!\!+} [y] \mathbin{+\!\!+} (ys -- [x]), \quad \text{if } x > y
\end{aligned}
$$

Proof of this result is left to the reader.

To return to the derivation, we now need to identify three subcases.

Subcase $x < y$. Here we have:

$$
\begin{aligned}
&labels \ (delete \ x \ (Bin \ y \ t1 \ t2)) \\
&= \ (labels \ t1 \mathbin{+\!\!+} [y] \mathbin{+\!\!+} labels \ t2) -- [x] \\
&= \ (labels \ t1 -- [x]) \mathbin{+\!\!+} [y] \mathbin{+\!\!+} labels \ t2 \quad \text{(lemma)} \\
&= \ labels \ (delete \ x \ t1) \mathbin{+\!\!+} [y] \mathbin{+\!\!+} labels \ t2 \quad \text{(spec)} \\
&= \ labels \ (Bin \ y \ (delete \ x \ t1) \ t2) \qquad\qquad (labels.2)
\end{aligned}
$$

Hence we can take:

$$delete \ x \ (Bin \ y \ t1 \ t2) \ = \ Bin \ y \ (delete \ x \ t1) \ t2, \ \text{if } x < y$$

Subcase $x > y$. This case is similar and we obtain:

$$delete \ x \ (Bin \ y \ t1 \ t2) \ = \ Bin \ y \ t1 \ (delete \ x \ t2), \ \text{if } x > y$$

Subcase $x = y$. In this case we get:

$$labels \ (delete \ x \ (Bin \ y \ t1 \ t2)) = labels \ t1 \mathbin{+\!\!+} labels \ t2$$

In order to make further progress, we now need to invent a second function, *join* say, satisfying:

$$labels \ (join \ t1 \ t2) = labels \ t1 \mathbin{+\!\!+} labels \ t2$$

Given *join*, we can take:

$$delete \ x \ (Bin \ y \ t1 \ t2) \ = \ join \ t1 \ t2, \ \text{if } x = y$$

Let us now write down the complete definition of *delete*:

$$
\begin{aligned}
delete\ x\ Nil\ &=\ Nil \\
delete\ x\ (Bin\ y\ t1\ t2)\ &=\ Bin\ y\ (delete\ x\ t1)\ t2, & \text{if } x < y \\
&=\ join\ t1\ t2, & \text{if } x = y \\
&=\ Bin\ y\ t1\ (delete\ x\ t2), & \text{if } x > y
\end{aligned}
$$

The result of the synthesis so far is to replace one problem by another: how to define *join*. We shall give two versions of *join*. The first is simple but unsatisfactory, while the second is more complicated but superior.

Recall that the specification of *join* reads:

$$
labels\ (join\ t1\ t2) = labels\ t1 \mathbin{+\!\!+} labels\ t2
$$

The first synthesis of $(join\ t1\ t2)$ proceeds by case analysis on $t1$.

Case *Nil*. We have:

$$
\begin{aligned}
labels\ (join\ Nil\ t2)\ &=\ labels\ Nil \mathbin{+\!\!+} labels\ t2 & \text{(spec)} \\
&=\ [\ ] \mathbin{+\!\!+} labels\ t2 & (labels.1) \\
&=\ labels\ t2
\end{aligned}
$$

Hence we can define:

$$
join\ Nil\ t2 = t2
$$

Case $(Bin\ x\ u1\ u2)$. Here we get:

$$
\begin{aligned}
labels\ (join\ (Bin\ x\ u1\ u2)\ t2) & \\
=\ labels\ (Bin\ x\ t1\ t2) \mathbin{+\!\!+} labels\ t2 & \text{(spec)} \\
=\ labels\ u1 \mathbin{+\!\!+} [x] \mathbin{+\!\!+} labels\ u2 \mathbin{+\!\!+} labels\ t2 & (labels.2) \\
=\ labels\ u1 \mathbin{+\!\!+} [x] \mathbin{+\!\!+} labels\ (join\ u2\ t2) & \text{(spec)} \\
=\ labels\ (Bin\ x\ u1\ (join\ u2\ t2)) & (labels.2)
\end{aligned}
$$

Hence we can define:

$$
join\ (Bin\ x\ u1\ u2)\ t2 = Bin\ x\ u1\ (join\ u2\ t2)
$$

The result of this synthesis is the following definition of *join*:

$$
\begin{aligned}
join\ Nil\ t2\ &=\ t2 \\
join\ (Bin\ x\ u1\ u2)\ t2\ &=\ Bin\ x\ u1\ (join\ u2\ t2)
\end{aligned}
$$

While this definition of *join* is perfectly correct, it is unsatisfactory because the depth of the resulting tree can be quite large. In effect, the second tree *t2* is appended as a new subtree at the bottom right of *t1*. The result is a tree whose depth is the sum of the depths of *t1* and *t2*. As we have seen, the efficiency of tree insertion and membership depends critically on the depth of the tree and we would like to ensure that, when joining trees, we keep the depth as small as is reasonably possible. Hence we reject this definition of *join* and try and look for a better one.

The second attempt at a synthesis of *join* from its specification involves the step of rewriting:

$$labels\ t1 + \!\!+\ labels\ t2 = init\ (labels\ t1) + \!\!+\ [last\ (labels\ t1)] + \!\!+\ (labels\ t2)$$

This step is valid provided *labels t1* $\neq$ []. Furthermore, let us introduce the functions *initree* and *lastlab* satisfying the equations:

$$\begin{aligned}
labels\ (initree\ t) &=\ init\ (labels\ t) \\
lastlab\ t &=\ last\ (labels\ t)
\end{aligned}$$

The case *t1 = Nil* for the new synthesis of *join* is the same as before. The remaining case is as follows.

Case *t1* $\neq$ *Nil*. We have:

$$\begin{aligned}
labels\ &(join\ t1\ t2) \\
=\ &labels\ t1 + \!\!+\ labels\ t2 &&\text{(spec)} \\
=\ &init\ (labels\ t1) + \!\!+\ [last\ (labels\ t1)] + \!\!+\ labels\ t2 &&\text{(above)} \\
=\ &labels\ (initree\ t1) + \!\!+\ [lastlab\ t1] + \!\!+\ labels\ t2 &&\text{(above)} \\
=\ &labels\ (Bin\ (lastlab\ t1)\ (initree\ t1)\ t2) &&(labels.2)
\end{aligned}$$

Hence we can define:

$$\begin{aligned}
join\ t1\ t2 &=\ Bin\ x\ u1\ t2, \quad \textbf{if}\ t1 \neq Nil \\
\textbf{where}\ x &=\ lastlab\ t1 \\
u1 &=\ initree\ t1
\end{aligned}$$

The synthesis of a constructive definition of *initree* and an efficient version of *lastlab* will be left to the reader. These functions can be combined into a function *split* satisfying:

$$split\ t = (lastlab\ t, initree\ t)$$

and the definition of *join* can be written in the form:

$$\begin{aligned}
join\ t1\ t2 &=\ t2, &&\textbf{if}\ t1 = Nil \\
&=\ Bin\ x\ t\ t2, &&\textbf{otherwise} \\
\textbf{where}\ &(x,t) = split\ t1
\end{aligned}$$

This definition of *join* is better than the earlier one because, in general, it results in a tree with a smaller depth. The situation can be summarised in the following way. Suppose a binary search tree *t* of size *n* has been constructed by a sequence of insertions and deletions of 'random' elements. On average, we can expect the depth of *t* to be $O(\log n)$, and so a further insertion or deletion will take $O(\log n)$ steps. For a proof of this fact, see Knuth [10].

Finally, it is important to bear in mind that *join* is not a general function for joining two arbitrary binary search trees. The specification of (*join t1 t2*) entails the condition:

$$max\ (labels\ t1) \leq min\ (labels\ t2)$$

In fact, there is no simple method for joining two arbitrary trees; the best approach is to build the new tree from scratch. It follows that binary search trees are not particularly efficient for the implementation of other set operations, such as set union or set difference. If these are the crucial operations in a given application, then a representation of sets by ordered lists is the most appropriate.

Exercises

9.3.1 Prove that:

$$labels\ t = init\ (tips\ t)$$

9.3.2 The function *initree*, used in the synthesis of binary search tree deletion, is specified by the equation:

$$labels\ (initree\ t) = init\ (labels\ t)$$

Synthesise a constructive definition of *initree*.

9.3.3 Derive an efficient version of *lastlab*, where:

$$lastlab\ t = last\ (labels\ t)$$

9.3.4 Show that any function *delete* satisfying the equation:

$$labels\ (delete\ x\ t) = (labels\ t) -\!\!-\ [x]$$

will satisfy the original specification of *delete*.

9.3.5 Synthesise the definition of *insert* for inserting a new value into a binary search tree. Also, synthesise a version of *delete* which uses the rule

$$labels\ t1 +\!\!\!+\ labels\ t2 = labels\ t1 +\!\!\!+\ [hd\ (labels\ t2)] +\!\!\!+\ tl\ (labels\ t2)$$

instead of the one given in the text.

9.4 Balanced trees

The tree insertion and deletion operations studied in the last section suffer from the disadvantage that they are efficient only on average. Although a sequence of insertions and deletions of random elements can be expected to produce a tree whose depth is reasonably small in relation to its size, there is always the possibility that a very unbalanced tree will emerge. In this section we will outline a technique which guarantees that both insertion and deletion can be performed in logarithmic time.

The idea is to impose an extra condition on binary search trees, namely that they should be *balanced*. A binary tree t is said to be (depth-) balanced if $(depthbal\ t)$ holds, where:

$$depthbal\ Nil \quad = \quad True$$
$$depthbal\ (Bin\ x\ t1\ t2) \quad = \quad abs\ (depth\ t1 - depth\ t2) \le 1 \wedge$$
$$depthbal\ t1 \wedge depthbal\ t2$$

In words, a balanced tree is a tree with the property that the depth of the left and right subtrees of each node differ by at most one. A balanced tree may not be minimal, but its depth is always reasonably small in comparison to its size. The precise relationship between depth and size in a balanced tree is analysed below.

Let us consider how to rebalance a tree after an insertion or deletion. Define the *slope* of a tree by:

$$slope\ Nil \quad = \quad 0$$
$$slope\ (Bin\ x\ t1\ t2) \quad = \quad depth\ t1 - depth\ t2$$

A tree t is therefore balanced if $abs\ (slope\ s) \le 1$ for every subtree s of t. Since a single insertion or deletion can alter the depth of any subtree by at most one, rebalancing is needed when $slope\ t = 2$ or $slope\ t = -2$. The two situations are symmetrical, so we shall study only the case $slope\ t = 2$.

Suppose then that $t = Bin\ x\ t1\ t2$, where $t1$ and $t2$ are balanced trees, but $slope\ t = 2$. There are two cases to consider:

(i) If the left subtree $t1$ of t has slope 1 or 0, then t can be rebalanced by a simple 'rotation' to the right. This operation is pictured in Figure 9.4, where the depths of the various subtrees appear as labels. It can be seen from the picture that the rotation operation restores the balance of t, without destroying the binary search tree condition.

(ii) On the other hand, if $slope\ t1 = -1$, then we first have to rotate $t1$ to the left before rotating t to the right. This initial rotation left is pictured in Figure 9.5.

The various rebalancing operations can be expressed as functions in a fairly direct fashion. First, the main function *rebal* for rebalancing a tree,

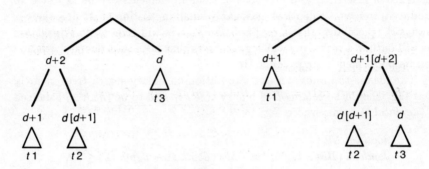

Figure 9.4 Simple rotation right.

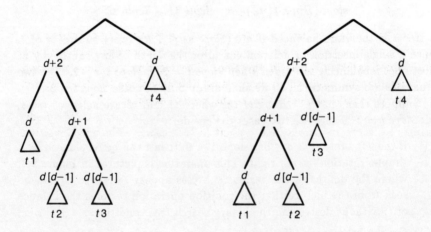

Figure 9.5 Initial rotation left.

assuming its subtrees are themselves balanced, is defined by:

$$
\begin{aligned}
rebal\ t &= shiftr\ t, &&\textbf{if }\ slope\ t = 2 \\
&= shiftl\ t, &&\textbf{if }\ slope\ t = -2 \\
&= t, &&\textbf{otherwise}
\end{aligned}
$$

The functions *shiftr* and *shiftl* are used to distinguish the kinds of rotation necessary. The operation *shiftr* has been described above, and *shiftl* deals with the symmetrical case when the right subtree has become too large. They are defined formally as follows:

$$
\begin{aligned}
shiftr\ (Bin\ x\ t1\ t2) &= rotr\ (Bin\ x\ (rotl\ t1)\ t2), &&\textbf{if }\ slope\ t1 = -1 \\
&= rotr\ (Bin\ x\ t1\ t2), &&\textbf{otherwise}
\end{aligned}
$$

$$
\begin{aligned}
shiftl\ (Bin\ x\ t1\ t2) &= rotl\ (Bin\ x\ t1\ (rotr\ t2)), &&\textbf{if }\ slope\ t2 = 1 \\
&= rotl\ (Bin\ x\ t1\ t2), &&\textbf{otherwise}
\end{aligned}
$$

Finally, the rotations *rotr* and *rotl* for rotating a tree to the right or left are defined by the equations:

$$
\begin{aligned}
rotr\ (Bin\ x\ (Bin\ y\ t1\ t2)\ t3) &= Bin\ y\ t1\ (Bin\ x\ t2\ t3) \\
rotl\ (Bin\ x\ t1\ (Bin\ y\ t2\ t3)) &= Bin\ y\ (Bin\ x\ t1\ t2)\ t3
\end{aligned}
$$

It is left as an exercise for the reader to show formally that:

$$
\begin{aligned}
labels\ (rotr\ t) &= labels\ t \\
labels\ (rotl\ t) &= labels\ t
\end{aligned}
$$

and hence that:

$$
labels\ (rebal\ t) = labels\ t
$$

Ignoring the cost of computing *slope*, a single rebalancing operation can be carried out in constant time. Slope calculations can be avoided by storing slope values as extra labels in the tree. The rotation functions *rotr* and *rotl* must then be modified to ensure that the new slope labels are stored correctly. We shall leave details as an instructive exercise.

Now let us see how the definition of *insert* has to be changed (the modifications to *delete* are similar and are left to the reader). The new definition is:

$$
\begin{aligned}
insert\ x\ Nil &= Bin\ x\ Nil\ Nil \\
insert\ x\ (Bin\ y\ t1\ t2) &= rebal\ (Bin\ y\ (insert\ x\ t1)\ t2), &&\textbf{if }\ x < y \\
&= Bin\ y\ t1\ t2, &&\textbf{if }\ x = y \\
&= rebal\ (Bin\ y\ t1\ (insert\ x\ t2)), &&\textbf{if }\ x > y
\end{aligned}
$$

Thus *rebal* is applied to every tree along the path to the newly inserted node. In fact, it can be shown that at most one tree actually requires rebalancing as a result of an insert operation, but this can occur anywhere along the path. Since *rebal* requires constant time, the cost of computing *insert* is $O(\log n)$ steps, where n is the size of the tree.

9.4.1   Analysis of depth

Finally, let us determine the relationship between size and depth in a balanced
tree. The idea is to construct, for each natural number d, a balanced tree
of depth d with the minimum possible size. Call this size $S(d)$. Once we
know $S(d)$, we can estimate the depth d in terms of the size n by solving the
relation $S(d) \le n$.

Since *Nil* is the only tree of depth 0, we have $S(0) = 0$. Similarly, the
only tree of depth 1 is of the form (*Bin x Nil Nil*) so we have $S(1) = 1$. In
general, it should be clear that the smallest possible balanced tree with depth
$(d+2)$ is of the form (*Bin x t1 t2*), where one of *t1* or *t2* is a balanced tree
of depth $d + 1$ and the other is a balanced tree of depth d. It follows from
this argument that:

$$\begin{aligned} S(0) &= 0 \\ S(1) &= 1 \\ S(d+2) &= 1 + S(d) + S(d+1) \end{aligned}$$

This definition is similar to that of the Fibonacci function *fib*. A simple
induction argument shows that:

$$S(d) = \mathit{fib}\,(d+2) - 1$$

Furthermore, we know from the discussion of Fibonacci numbers in Chapter
5 that:

$$\mathit{fib}\,(d) = \frac{1}{\sqrt{5}}(\phi^d - \widehat{\phi}^d)$$

where:

$$\phi = \frac{1 + \sqrt{5}}{2} \quad \text{and} \quad \widehat{\phi} = \frac{1 - \sqrt{5}}{2}$$

Since $|\widehat{\phi}| < 1$, it follows that:

$$S(d) = \frac{1}{\sqrt{5}}(\phi^{d+2} - \widehat{\phi}^{d+2}) - 1 > \frac{1}{\sqrt{5}}\phi^{d+2} - 2$$

Hence, if $S(d) \le n$, we have:

$$n > \frac{1}{\sqrt{5}}\phi^{d+2} - 2$$

Equivalently, taking logarithms to base 2, we have:

$$d < (\log_\phi 2)\log_2(n+2) + (\log_\phi \sqrt{5} - 2)$$

Finally, since $\log_\phi 2 = 1.4404\ldots$ it follows that the depth of a balanced tree
is never more than about 45 per cent worse than the theoretical minimum.

Exercises

9.4.1 Consider the functions *rotr* and *rotl* for carrying out rotations on balanced trees. Show that:

$$\begin{aligned} labels\,(rotr\;t) &= labels\;t \\ labels\,(rotl\;t) &= labels\;t \end{aligned}$$

and so:

$$labels\,(rebal\;t) = labels\;t$$

9.4.2 Slope calculations in balancing binary search trees can be avoided by storing slope values as extra labels in the tree. Give the appropriate type definitions and show how to modify the rotation functions *rotl* and *rotr* to maintain this information.

9.4.3 Why does at most one tree actually require rebalancing after an *insert* operation on balanced trees?

9.4.4 Give the definition of *delete* for deleting a value from a balanced tree.

9.4.5 Implement sets using ordered lists, binary search trees, and balanced binary search trees. Asymptotic analysis tells us that for sufficiently large sets, balanced trees will be the best implementation. Experiment to determine for what size of set each representation is most appropriate.

9.5 Arrays

As a final illustration of the use of binary trees, we shall consider the problem of implementing arrays efficiently. Recall from Section 8.5 the abstract type $(array\;\alpha)$ defined by the following four operations:

$$\begin{aligned} mkarray &\;::\; [\alpha] \rightarrow array\;\alpha \\ length &\;::\; array\;\alpha \rightarrow num \\ lookup &\;::\; array\;\alpha \rightarrow num \rightarrow \alpha \\ update &\;::\; array\;\alpha \rightarrow num \rightarrow \alpha \rightarrow array\;\alpha \end{aligned}$$

An element of $(array\;\alpha)$ is essentially a finite list whose elements may be modified and inspected, but whose length does not change. A representation of arrays by finite lists was given in Section 8.5; with this method, the cost of each array operation is linear in n, the length of the array. By representing arrays as binary trees, we can reduce the cost of each operation to $O(\log n)$ steps.

The basic idea is to represent an array by a *size-balanced* binary tree. A tree t is a size-balanced tree if $(sizebal\;t)$ holds, where:

$$\begin{aligned} sizebal\,(Tip\;x) &= True \\ sizebal\,(Bin\;t1\;t2) &= abs\,(size\;t1 - size\;t2) \leq 1 \wedge \\ &\quad\; sizebal\;t1 \wedge sizebal\;t2 \end{aligned}$$

The definition of a size-balanced tree is therefore similar to that of a depth-balanced one. Unlike depth-balanced trees, a size-balanced tree is necessarily minimal. The proof of this fact is left as an exercise for the reader.

Building a tree. We shall represent an array (with length greater than zero) by a size-balanced tree whose tip values, in left to right order, are the array elements. We therefore require:

$$tips \, (mkarray \; xs) = xs$$

where *tips* is the function for listing the tip values in left to right order. Given that we want *mkarray* to return a size-balanced tree, the following definition should be straightforward:

$$
\begin{aligned}
mkarray \; xs \;\; &= \;\; Tip \, (hd \; xs), && \textbf{if } \; n = 1 \\
&= \;\; Bin \, (mkarray \; ys) \, (mkarray \; zs), && \textbf{if } \; n > 1 \\
&\textbf{where} \;\; n \;\; = \;\; \#xs \\
&\phantom{\textbf{where}} \;\; ys \;\; = \;\; take \; (n \; \textbf{div} \; 2) \; xs \\
&\phantom{\textbf{where}} \;\; zs \;\; = \;\; drop \; (n \; \textbf{div} \; 2) \; xs
\end{aligned}
$$

Since $(n \; \textbf{div} \; 2)$ and $(n - n \; \textbf{div} \; 2)$ differ by at most 1, it should be clear that *mkarray* returns a size-balanced tree. The time $T(n)$ required by *mkarray* to build a tree of size n is the sum of the time needed to split the list, which is $O(n)$ steps, and the time to construct two subtrees, which is approximately $2T(n/2)$ steps. Hence T satisfies the recurrence equation:

$$T(n) = 2T(n/2) + O(n)$$

for $n > 1$, and so:

$$T(n) = O(n \log n)$$

It follows that it takes $O(n \log n)$ steps to build a size-balanced tree by *mkarray*. This time can be reduced to $O(n)$ steps (see Exercise 9.5.4).

Accessing the tips. To implement *lookup*, we use information about tree sizes to control the search. The formal definition of *lookup* can be synthesised from the equation:

$$lookup \; t \; k = (tips \; t) \; ! \; k$$

and is given by:

$$
\begin{aligned}
lookup \, (Tip \; x) \; 0 \;\; &= \;\; x \\
lookup \, (Bin \; t1 \; t2) \; k \;\; &= \;\; lookup \; t1 \; k, && \textbf{if } \; k < m \\
&= \;\; lookup \; t2 \; (k - m), && \textbf{otherwise} \\
&\textbf{where} \;\; m = size \; t1
\end{aligned}
$$

The essential point here is that if k is less than m, the size of the left subtree $t1$ of t, then the tip at position k will be found at the same position in $t1$. If, on the other hand, $k \geq m$, then the kth tip will be the tip at position $(k - m)$ in the right subtree. Ignoring the cost of computing *size* for the moment, it follows that retrieving the kth tip will require $O(\log n)$ steps whenever t is a minimal tree of size n.

The way to avoid costly recomputations of *size* is, once again, to use labelled binary trees. Each tree is labelled with the size of its left subtree. The necessary modification to *mkarray* is straightforward:

$$
\begin{array}{lll}
mkarray & :: & [\alpha] \to lbtree\ \alpha\ num \\
mkarray\ xs & = & Tip\ x, & \textbf{if}\ n = 1 \\
& = & Bin\ m\ (mkarray\ ys)\ (mkarray\ zs), & \textbf{if}\ n > 1 \\
& & \textbf{where}\ n\ =\ \#xs \\
& & \qquad\quad m\ =\ n\ \textbf{div}\ 2 \\
& & \qquad\quad ys\ =\ take\ m\ xs \\
& & \qquad\quad zs\ =\ drop\ m\ xs
\end{array}
$$

We can now rewrite the definition of *lookup* as:

$$
\begin{array}{lll}
lookup\ (Tip\ x)\ 0 & = & x \\
lookup\ (Bin\ m\ t1\ t2)\ k & = & lookup\ t1\ k, & \textbf{if}\ k < m \\
& = & lookup\ t2\ (k - m), & \textbf{otherwise}
\end{array}
$$

With the new definition, the time required to compute *lookup* is $O(\log n)$ steps. Notice that the price paid for this improvement is the extra space needed to store information about tree sizes.

The definition of *update* is equally simple:

$$
\begin{array}{lll}
update\ (Tip\ y)\ 0\ x & = & Tip\ x \\
update\ (Bin\ m\ t1\ t2)\ k\ x \\
& = & Bin\ m\ (update\ t1\ k\ x)\ t2, & \textbf{if}\ k < m \\
& = & Bin\ m\ t1\ (update\ t2\ (k - m)\ x), & \textbf{otherwise}
\end{array}
$$

Observe that if k does not lie in the range $0 \leq k < size\ t$, then $update\ t\ k\ x = \bot$.

Finally, to complete the repertoire of array operations, the function *length* for determining the number of elements in the array is defined by:

$$
\begin{array}{lll}
length\ (Tip\ x) & = & 1 \\
length\ (Bin\ m\ t1\ t2) & = & m + length\ t2
\end{array}
$$

Here, *length* is the same function as *size*.

The reason we can successfully represent arrays by size-balanced trees is that the trees do not change shape, so rebalancing is never required. Rebalancing a tree to restore the size condition is more time consuming than rebalancing to restore the depth condition.

Exercises

9.5.1 Show that a size-balanced tree is minimal.

9.5.2 Prove that *lookup* satisfies its specification, i.e:

$$lookup\ t\ k = (tips\ t)\,!\,k$$

9.5.3 Prove that *mkarray* returns a size-balanced tree.

9.5.4 Generalise *mkarray* to a function *mkarray2* satisfying:

$$mkarray2\ n\ xs = (mkarray\ (take\ n\ xs), drop\ n\ xs)$$

Using this equation as a starting point, synthesise the following new definition of *mkarray2*:

$$
\begin{aligned}
mkarray2\ n\ xs \quad &= \quad (Tip\,(hd\ xs), tl\ xs), \quad \textbf{if } n = 1 \\
&= \quad (Bin\ t1\ t2, zs), \qquad \textbf{if } n > 1 \\
\textbf{where}\ (t1, ys) \quad &= \quad mkarray2\ m\ xs \\
(t2, zs) \quad &= \quad mkarray2\ (n - m)\ ys \\
m \quad &= \quad n\ \textbf{div}\ 2
\end{aligned}
$$

Write down the recurrence relation for $T(n)$, the time required to evaluate (*mkarray2 n xs*), and hence show that the new definition leads to a more efficient computation.

9.5.5 Suppose t is the minimal binary tree of size 2^n. Define a function (*binary n*) so that:

$$lookup\ t\ k = trace\ t\ (binary\ n\ k)$$

where *trace* was defined in Section 9.2 This idea leads to an alternative method for efficient list indexing. Extend a list xs with as many $\perp$ values as necessary to ensure that its length is a power of two. Build the minimal binary tree from the new list, and use the above definition of *lookup*. Does this method use more or less space than the labelled tree approach?

9.5.6 Write functions similar to *mkarray* for building a labelled binary tree in which (i) the label of a tree is the maximum tip value; (ii) the label of a tree is its depth.

9.5.7 Construct suitable definitions of *mktree* and *revtree* so that:

$$reverse = tips \cdot revtree \cdot mktree$$

Estimate the time-complexity of this version of list reversal.

9.5.8 Repeat Exercise 9.4.5 by implementing arrays by lists, binary search trees, depth balanced binary search trees, and size balanced trees. Experiment to determine for what length of array each representation is most appropriate.

9.5.9 What other common list-processing functions are made more efficient by representing lists as binary trees?

9.6 General trees

Now let us turn to trees with a multiway branching structure. Consider the type declaration:

$$gtree\ \alpha ::= Node\ \alpha\ [gtree\ \alpha]$$

An element of $(gtree\ \alpha)$ thus consists of a labelled node together with a list of subtrees. For example, $(Node\ 0\ [\,])$ is an element of $(gtree\ num)$, and so is:

$$Node\ 0\ [Node\ 1\ [\,], Node\ 2\ [\,], Node\ 3\ [\,]]$$

It is even possible to have trees with an infinite number of immediate subtrees; for example:

$$Node\ 0\ [Node\ n\ [\,]\ |\ n \leftarrow [1\,..]]$$

is also an element of $(gtree\ num)$. A tree t is said to be *finitary* if every node of t has a finite number of immediate subtrees; in other words, if ts is a finite list in every subexpression $(Node\ x\ ts)$ of t. The above tree is therefore not finitary.

The notions of size and depth extend to general trees:

$$
\begin{aligned}
size\,(Node\ x\ ts) &= 1 + sum\,(map\ size\ ts) \\
depth\,(Node\ x\ ts) &= 0, & &\text{if } ts = [\,] \\
&= 1 + max\,(map\ depth\ ts), & &\textbf{otherwise}
\end{aligned}
$$

A tree is *finite* if it has a well-defined size. Note that a tree can be finitary without being finite. Unlike the case of binary trees, the size of a general tree can be arbitrarily larger than its depth.

General trees have numerous applications and arise naturally whenever a hierarchical classification is discussed. For example, this book is organised as a tree structure as the method for numbering chapters and sections shows. The departmental structure of many large organisations is also usually expressed as a tree. We shall consider one application of general trees below, and another in the next section.

9.6.1 Expression trees

We implicitly describe a tree structure whenever we write down a bracketed expression. Consider, for example, the expression:

$$f\left(g\left(x,y\right),z,h\left(u\right)\right)$$

This expression can be represented by the general tree:

Node f [Node g [Node x [ ], Node y [ ]], Node z [ ], Node h [Node u [ ]]]

It is easy to see that every expression can be written as a tree in this way. In particular, the representation of:

$$f\left(e_1, e_2, \ldots, e_n\right)$$

is a tree:

Node f [t₁, t₂, ..., tₙ]

where t_j is the representation of e_j. Conversely, every (finite) tree can be written as a linear expression involving label values, brackets and commas.

Functional programmers often prefer to curry their expressions, and the above example can also be written in the, by now familiar, following form:

$$f\left(g \; x \; y\right) z \left(h \; u\right)$$

This expression can be represented by the binary tree pictured in Figure 9.6. The rule here is that an application $(e_1 \; e_2)$ is represented by a tree $(Bin \; t_1 \; t_2)$, where t_j is the representation of e_j, and a constant x is represented by $(Tip \; x)$. Conversely, every finite binary tree can be represented in the form of a curried expression. Since general expressions and curried expressions are interconvertible, it must be the case that each (finite) general tree can be translated into a unique binary tree, and vice versa. So, let us construct functions that implement this translation.

We can convert an element of $(gtree \; \alpha)$ into an element of $(btree \; \alpha)$, where:

$$btree \; \alpha ::= \; Tip \; \alpha \mid Bin \; (btree \; \alpha) \; (btree \; \alpha)$$

by applying a function $curry :: gtree \; \alpha \rightarrow btree \; \alpha$ defined by:

$$curry \; (Node \; x \; ts) = foldl \; Bin \; (Tip \; x) \; (map \; curry \; ts)$$

In words, to convert a general tree we convert all its subtrees, and then combine them into a binary tree whose structure follows the left association order of application. For example:

$$
\begin{aligned}
curry \; (Node \; x \; [\,]) \;\; &= \;\; foldl \; Bin \; (Tip \; x) \; (map \; curry \; [\,]) \\
&= \;\; foldl \; Bin \; (Tip \; x) \; [\,] \\
&= \;\; Tip \; x
\end{aligned}
$$

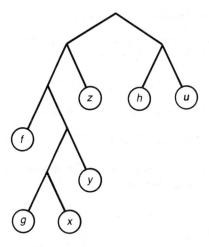

Figure 9.6 A curried expression.

and:

$$curry\ (Node\ f\ [t1, t2])$$
$$= \quad foldl\ Bin\ (Tip\ f)\ (map\ curry\ [t1, t2])$$
$$= \quad foldl\ Bin\ (Tip\ f)\ [curry\ t1, curry\ t2]$$
$$= \quad foldl\ Bin\ (Bin\ (Tip\ f)\ (curry\ t1))\ [curry\ t2]$$
$$= \quad Bin\ (Bin\ (Tip\ f)\ (curry\ t1))\ (curry\ t2)$$

It is left as an exercise for the reader to show that $(curry\ t)$ returns a well-defined binary tree if t is a finitary tree; however, the correspondence breaks down if t is non-finitary.

Let us now construct the inverse correspondence:

$$uncurry :: btree\ \alpha \rightarrow gtree\ \alpha$$

We are going to synthesise $uncurry$ from the specification:

$$uncurry\ (curry\ t) = t$$

for all (finitary) general trees t. The synthesis is by cases.

Case $(Tip\ x)$. To synthesize a value for $uncurry\ (Tip\ x)$, we reason that:

$$Tip\ x \quad = \quad foldl\ Bin\ (Tip\ x)\ [] \qquad (foldl.1)$$
$$= \quad foldl\ Bin\ (Tip\ x)\ (map\ curry\ []) \quad (map.1)$$
$$= \quad curry\ (Node\ x\ []) \qquad (curry.1)$$

Hence:

$$uncurry\ (Tip\ x) \quad = \quad uncurry\ (curry\ (Node\ x\ [])$$
$$= \quad Node\ x\ [] \qquad (spec.)$$

Case (*Bin b1 b2*). To construct a value for *uncurry* (*Bin b1 b2*), we suppose that:

$$b1 \;=\; curry\,(Node\;x\;ts) \qquad (b1.1)$$
$$b2 \;=\; curry\;t \qquad\qquad\quad (b2.1)$$

It follows from the first equation and the definition of *curry* that:

$$b1 \;=\; foldl\;Bin\,(Tip\;x)\,(map\;curry\;ts) \qquad (b1.2)$$

We also need the law:

$$foldl\,(\oplus)\,(foldl\,(\oplus)\,a\;xs)\;ys \;=\; foldl\,(\oplus)\,a\,(xs \mathbin{+\!\!+} ys) \quad (\text{law})$$

Now we reason:

$$
\begin{aligned}
&Bin\;b1\;b2\\
=\;& foldl\;Bin\;b1\;[b2] &(foldl.1, foldl.2)\\
=\;& foldl\;Bin\,(foldl\;Bin\,(Tip\;x)\,(map\;curry\;ts))\,[b2] &(b1.2)\\
=\;& foldl\;Bin\,(Tip\;x)\,(map\;curry\;ts \mathbin{+\!\!+} [b2]) &(\text{law})\\
=\;& foldl\;Bin\,(Tip\;x)\,(map\;curry\;ts \mathbin{+\!\!+} [curry\;t]) &(b2.1)\\
=\;& foldl\;Bin\,(Tip\;x)\,(map\;curry\,(ts \mathbin{+\!\!+} [t])) &(map, +\!\!+)\\
=\;& curry\,(Node\;x\,(ts \mathbin{+\!\!+} [t])) &(curry.1)
\end{aligned}
$$

Hence we have:

$$
\begin{aligned}
uncurry\,(Bin\;b1\;b2) \;&=\; uncurry\,(curry\,(Node\,(ts \mathbin{+\!\!+} [t])))\\
&=\; Node\;x\,(ts \mathbin{+\!\!+} [t]) \qquad (\text{spec.})
\end{aligned}
$$

We have therefore shown that:

$$
\begin{aligned}
uncurry\,(Tip\;x) \;&=\; Node\;x\;[\,]\\
uncurry\,(Bin\;b1\;b2) \;&=\; Node\;x\,(ts \mathbin{+\!\!+} [t])\\
&\quad \textbf{where }\; Node\;x\;ts \;=\; uncurry\;b1\\
&\qquad\qquad\qquad t \;=\; uncurry\;b2
\end{aligned}
$$

It is possible to improve the efficiency of *uncurry*; details are left as an exercise.

9.6.2 Example: pattern matching

Let us now consider an important application that exploits the representation of expressions by general trees. Informally, a *pattern matcher* is a program that tests whether some given expression e, called the *target*, fits a specified expression p, called the *pattern*. For instance, suppose the pattern is the expression:

$$(x, [y])$$

where x and y denote variables. This pattern matches the target:

$$(3, [True])$$

under the substitution $\{x \rightarrow 3, y \rightarrow \mathit{True}\}$ in which x is replaced by 3 and y by True. However, the same pattern does not match the target:

$$(3, (\mathit{True}, \mathit{Nil}))$$

because pairs and lists are not comparable. More precisely, the constructor $(,)$ for pairs is distinct from the constructor $(:)$ for lists. As another example, consider the pattern:

$$(x, [x])$$

This pattern matches the target $(3, [3])$, but does not match $(3, [\mathit{True}])$ since 3 and True are non-equal constants.

Given a pattern p composed of constructors and variables, and a target expression e composed of constructors only, we want to define a function *match* so that $(\mathit{match}\ p\ e)$ is the substitution, if it exists, under which p matches e.

The first job is to specify the problem more precisely, and for this we need to give a formal definition of the class of expressions. We take:

$$exp ::= Var\ var \mid Con\ con\ [exp]$$

where:

$$
\begin{aligned}
var &== string \\
con &== string
\end{aligned}
$$

The only difference between *exp* and the form of a general tree introduced above is the presence of the additional 'tip' nodes (*Var var*) for representing variables. For example, the pattern $(0, [y])$ can be expressed as the following element of *exp*:

$$Con\ \text{``Pair''}\ [Con\ \text{``0''}\ [\,], Con\ \text{``Cons''}\ [Var\ \text{``y''}, Con\ \text{``Nil''}\ [\,]]]$$

Here, $(\mathit{Pair}\ x\ y)$ corresponds to (x, y), and $(\mathit{Cons}\ x\ xs)$ to $x : xs$. Note that the constants 0 and *Nil* are represented as constructors of no arguments. We assume that each constructor c is associated with a fixed number, *arity c*, of arguments, so that $(\mathit{Con}\ c\ es)$ is only well-formed if $\#es = \mathit{arity}\ c$.

By definition, a pattern is an arbitrary element of *exp*, while a constant expression is an element of *exp* that does not contain variables. For convenience, we introduce the type synonyms:

$$
\begin{aligned}
pattern &== exp \\
conexp &== exp
\end{aligned}
$$

Substitutions. Next we need to formalise the notion of a substitution. In general, a substitution is a function that maps variables to expressions:

$$subst == var \rightarrow exp$$

However, the substitutions that arise in pattern matching satisfy an important restriction: they return constant expressions only. In other words, if
substitution s is defined for a variable x, then $(s\ x)$ is a constant expression.
It is convenient to consider substitutions as total functions, so we shall allow
the exception $s\ x = Var\ x$ to the above rule, if no other value for x is defined.

Since we want to set up the algebra of substitutions in a particular way,
we shall describe them as an abstract data type. This means we can postpone
committing ourselves to a particular representation of substitutions, whether
as functions or in some other way.

The abstract type $subst$ has five basic operations:

$$
\begin{array}{rcl}
(\star) & :: & subst \rightarrow var \rightarrow exp \\
iden & :: & subst \\
unit & :: & var \rightarrow exp \rightarrow subst \\
(\oplus) & :: & subst \rightarrow subst \rightarrow subst \\
dom & :: & subst \rightarrow set\ var
\end{array}
$$

The operation $(\star)$ corresponds to functional application under the interpretation of substitutions as functions: if s is a substitution and x an element
of var, then $s \star x$ is the expression to be substituted for x. Using $(\star)$ we can
define the result of applying a substitution to an arbitrary pattern:

$$
\begin{array}{rcl}
apply & :: & subst \rightarrow pattern \rightarrow exp \\
apply\ s\ (Var\ x) & = & s \star x \\
apply\ s\ (Con\ c\ ps) & = & Con\ c\ (map\ (apply\ s)\ ps)
\end{array}
$$

The substitution $iden$ (short for 'identity') maps every variable x to the
expression $(Var\ x)$; thus:

$$ iden \star x = Var\ x $$

for all x in var. In particular, we have:

$$ apply\ iden\ e = e $$

for all expressions e.

The substitution $(unit\ x\ e)$ has the property that:

$$
\begin{array}{rcll}
(unit\ x\ e) \star y & = & e, & \text{if } x = y \\
& = & Var\ y, & \textbf{otherwise}
\end{array}
$$

Thus, the function $apply\ (unit\ x\ e)$ takes an expression and replaces every
occurrence of $(Var\ x)$ by e, but leaves other variables unchanged.

The function dom returns the 'essential' variables of a substitution. It is
defined abstractly by the equation:

$$ dom\ s = \{x \mid s \star x \neq Var\ x\} $$

In particular:

$$dom\ iden\ \ \ \ \ =\ \{\,\}$$
$$dom\,(unit\ x\ e)\ =\ \{x\},\ \ (\text{if}\ e \neq Var\ x)$$

The function *dom* is needed below.

Finally, the operation (⊕) combines two substitutions. This is a partial operation which is defined only if the substitutions are compatible. Two substitutions are compatible if they return the same results on all essential variables. We define:

$$compatible\ s1\ s2\ =\ all\ \{s1 \star x = s2 \star x \mid x \,\epsilon\, dom\ s1 \cap dom\ s2\}$$

For example, (*unit x e1*) and (*unit x e2*) are compatible if *e1* = *e2*. Note that *iden* is compatible with all substitutions since its *dom* value is empty.

If *s1* and *s2* are compatible, then we define:

$$(s1 \oplus s2) \star x\ =\ s1 \star x,\ \ \text{if}\ x \,\epsilon\, dom\ s1$$
$$=\ s2 \star x,\ \ \text{if}\ x \,\epsilon\, dom\ s2$$
$$=\ Var\ x,\ \ \textbf{otherwise}$$

It follows that:

$$s1 \oplus s2 = s2 \oplus s1$$

for all compatible *s1* and *s2*.

The algebra of substitutions under ⊕ is similar to the algebra of sets under ∪. In particular:

$$
\begin{array}{lll}
s1 \oplus iden & =\ s1 & \text{(identity)} \\
s1 \oplus s2 & =\ s2 \oplus s1 & \text{(commutativity)} \\
s1 \oplus s1 & =\ s1 & \text{(idempotency)} \\
s1 \oplus (s2 \oplus s3) & =\ (s1 \oplus s2) \oplus s3 & \text{(associativity)}
\end{array}
$$

However, unlike ∪, the operation ⊕ is partial; for example, the associative law only holds if *s1*, *s2* and *s3* are pairwise compatible because only in this case is either side defined.

Since it is inconvenient to work with partial algebras, let us turn ⊕ into a total operation. The way to do this is to 'lift' the class of substitutions by including an extra element, called *Fail*, to denote the inconsistent substitution. In general, we can define the type:

$$lift\ \alpha\ ::=\ Fail \mid Ok\ \alpha$$

for lifting a type α by including one extra element. We then have:

$$lsubst\ ==\ lift\ subst$$

where *subst* is the type that represents substitutions.

We can now define the lifted version $\otimes$ of $\oplus$ by:

$$
\begin{array}{lll}
\textit{Fail} \otimes \textit{as} & = & \textit{Fail} \\
(\textit{Ok } s) \otimes \textit{Fail} & = & \textit{Fail} \\
(\textit{Ok } s1) \otimes (\textit{Ok } s2) & = & \textit{Ok } (s1 \oplus s2), \quad \text{if } \textit{compatible } s1 \; s2 \\
& = & \textit{Fail}, \qquad\qquad\quad \textbf{otherwise}
\end{array}
$$

It is left to the reader to check that $\otimes$ is an associative, commutative and idempotent operation, with identity element ($\textit{Ok iden}$) and zero element $\textit{Fail}$.

The pattern matcher. We have now erected enough machinery both to specify the function $\textit{match}$ and to implement it. Given finite elements p and e of $\textit{exp}$, where e does not contain variables and neither p nor e contain $\bot$, the value of ($\textit{match } p \; e$) is an augmented substitution $\textit{as}$ such that either:

1. $\textit{as} = \textit{Ok } s$ and $\textit{apply } s \; p = e$; or

2. $\textit{as} = \textit{Fail}$ and $\textit{apply } s \; p \neq e$ for all s.

The most straightforward implementation of $\textit{match}$ is as follows:

$$
\begin{array}{lll}
\textit{match} & :: & \textit{pattern} \rightarrow \textit{conexp} \rightarrow \textit{lsubst} \\
\textit{match} \,(\textit{Var } x)\, e & = & \textit{Ok } (\textit{unit } x \; e) \\
\textit{match} \,(\textit{Con } c \; ps)\,(\textit{Con } d \; es) & & \\
& = & \textit{combine} \,(\textit{zipwith match ps es}), \quad \text{if } c = d \\
& = & \textit{Fail}, \qquad\qquad\qquad\qquad\qquad\quad \textbf{otherwise} \\
\textit{combine} & = & \textit{foldr} \,(\otimes)\,(\textit{Ok iden})
\end{array}
$$

The function $\textit{zipwith}$ is defined by:

$$
\textit{zipwith } f \; xs \; ys \;\; = \;\; [f \; x \; y \mid (x, y) \leftarrow \textit{zip} \,(xs, ys)]
$$

Since $\otimes$ and ($\textit{Ok iden}$) form a monoid, we could also define $\textit{combine}$ by:

$$
\textit{combine} = \textit{foldl} \,(\otimes)\,(\textit{Ok iden})
$$

The definition of $\textit{match}$ can be explained as follows. If the pattern consists of a single variable x, then the match succeeds with the unit substitution $\{x \rightarrow e\}$, where e is the target. Otherwise, if the pattern and target begin with the same constructor, then corresponding subexpressions are matched, and the resulting substitutions are combined. If any two of these resulting substitutions are incompatible, or if the pattern and target begin with different constructors, then the result is failure. We shall leave the proof that the implementation of $\textit{match}$ meets its specification as an instructive exercise.

Although the given definition of $\textit{match}$ is reasonably simple, it does not lead to the most efficient algorithm. Testing two substitutions for compatiblity involves computing intersections of the $\textit{dom}$ values of substitutions. A superior algorithm can be based on the idea of testing $s1$ and $s2$ for compatibility only when one of them is a unit substitution. Consider the function:

$$
\begin{aligned}
match1 \qquad\qquad &::\quad lsubst \rightarrow (pattern, exp) \rightarrow lsubst \\
match1 \; as\,(p,e) \;\; &=\quad as \otimes match\; p\; e
\end{aligned}
$$

Since $(Ok\;iden)$ is the identity element of $\otimes$, we have:

$$
match\; p\; e = match1\;(Ok\;iden)\,(p,e)
$$

and so $match$ can be defined in terms of $match1$. Starting with the given definition of $match1$, it is possible to derive the following alternative definition:

$$
\begin{aligned}
match1\; Fail\,(p,e) \;\; &=\quad Fail \\
match1\;(Ok\;s)\,(Var\;x,e) & \\
&=\quad Ok\,(extend\;s\;x\;e), && \textbf{if } s \star x = Var\;x \\
&=\quad Ok\;s, && \textbf{if } s \star x = e \\
&=\quad Fail, && \textbf{otherwise} \\
match1\;(Ok\;s)\,(Con\;c\;ps, Con\;d\;es) & \\
&=\quad foldl\; match1\;(Ok\;s)\,(zip\;ps\;es), && \textbf{if } c = d \\
&=\quad Fail, && \textbf{otherwise}
\end{aligned}
$$

The subsidiary function $extend$ satisfies:

$$
\begin{aligned}
(extend\;s\;x\;e) \star y \;\; &=\quad e, && \textbf{if } x = y \\
&=\quad s \star y, && \textbf{otherwise}
\end{aligned}
$$

We shall leave the pleasure of synthesising the above definition to the reader. The revised definition of $match$, in terms of $match1$, has one very useful feature: apart from $iden$, the only abstract operation on substitutions appearing in the definition is $\star$! Since we no longer have to compute dom values, we can implement substitutions directly as functions. Specifically, we take:

$$
subst == var \rightarrow exp
$$

replace $\star$ by functional application, and define:

$$
iden\; x = Var\; x
$$

Exercises

9.6.1 Give a definition of $mapgtree$ that is the analogue of map for general trees.

9.6.2 Show that:
$$
uncurry\,(curry\; t) = t
$$
for all finitary trees t. Give an example of a non-finitary tree for which the above equation fails to hold.

9.6.3 Define a function *foldlgtree* that is the analogue of *foldl* on general trees, and show that:

$$foldlgtree\ (\oplus) = foldbtree\ (\oplus) \cdot curry$$

9.6.4 Consider the synthesis of *uncurry* from *curry*. Suppose we look for a constructive definition of *uncurry* of the form:

$$uncurry = foldbtree\ (\oplus) \cdot mapbtree\ f$$

Calculate the functions $\oplus$ and f.

9.6.5 Define the function *curry1* by:

$$
\begin{array}{lll}
curry1 & :: & gtree\ \alpha \rightarrow btree\ \alpha \rightarrow gtree\ \alpha \\
curry1\ ts\ b & = & Node\ x\ (fs +\!\!+ ts) \\
& & \textbf{where}\ Node\ x\ fs = uncurry\ b
\end{array}
$$

Express *uncurry* in terms of *curry1*. Synthesise an alternative definition of *curry1*, and estimate the potential gains in efficiency.

9.6.6 Consider the abstract data type of substitutions. Show that $\oplus$ is associative, commutative and idempotent. Show that *iden* is the identity element of $\oplus$. Similarly, show that $\otimes$ is associative, commutative and idempotent, with identity element (*Ok iden*) and zero element *Fail*.

9.6.7 Show that substitutions s and (*unit x e*) (where $e \neq Var\ x$) are compatible just in the case that:

$$(s \star x = Var\ x) \vee (s \star x = e)$$

Hence show that, if s and (*unit x e*) are compatible, then:

$$
\begin{array}{llll}
(s \oplus unit\ x\ e) \star y & = & e, & \textbf{if}\ x = y \\
& = & Var\ y, & \textbf{otherwise}
\end{array}
$$

9.6.8 Prove that, if *s1* and *s2* are compatible, then:

$$s1 \oplus s2 = (apply\ s1) \cdot (s2\star)$$

9.6.9 Prove that the pattern matching function *match* meets its specification.

9.6.10 Synthesise the alternative definition of *match1*.

9.7 Game trees

An interesting application of general trees is to the problem of programming a two-person game like Chess or Tic-Tac-Toe. Such games are defined by a set of values, called *positions*, and a function *move* that determines for each possible position the set of new positions that can arise. Starting from a given initial position, two players move alternately until some position is reached in which no further moves are possible. Depending on the rules, the game either ends in a draw or one player is designated the winner. Usually the winner is the player who makes the last legal move. At each step of the game, players will attempt to choose the move that maximises their chances of winning. This is the situation we are going to model as a functional program.

Suppose we are given some type *position* and a function:

$$moves :: position \rightarrow [position]$$

for computing new positions. We can study the progression of a game by representing it as a tree. The nodes of the tree are labelled with positions, so we introduce the type:

$$gtree ::= Node\ position\ [gtree]$$

We can build a game tree from a given position by:

$$
\begin{aligned}
gametree &\quad :: \quad position \rightarrow gtree \\
gametree\ p &\quad = \quad reptree\ moves\ p \\
reptree\ f\ x &\quad = \quad Node\ x\ (map\ (reptree\ f)\ (f\ x))
\end{aligned}
$$

In practice, the tree (*gametree p*) will often be very large and, for some games, it may actually be infinite. A tree can be pruned to a fixed depth by the function *prune* defined by:

$$
\begin{aligned}
prune\ 0\ (Node\ x\ ts) &\quad = \quad Node\ x\ [\,] \\
prune\ (n+1)\ (Node\ x\ ts) &\quad = \quad Node\ x\ (map\ (prune\ n)\ ts)
\end{aligned}
$$

Applying (*prune n*) to a tree will therefore cut off all nodes further than n steps away from the root. Note the similarity between *prune* and *take*.

In order to select a move in a given position, an intelligent player will look ahead a certain amount to see whether the game will develop favourably or unfavourably as a consequence of the move. Except for trivial games, it is not feasible to explore the complete tree when analysing positions, so the player will first prune the tree to some fixed depth. After pruning, the player makes a rough estimate, called *static evaluation*, of the possible end positions. The result of static evaluation of a position p is a numerical measure of the worth of p. We shall suppose that the description of a position contains information about whose turn it is to move and that the worth of a position is always as

it appears to the moving player. We also suppose that if a position is worth
w to one player, then it is worth $(-w)$ to the other player. Such games
are called *zero-sum* games because the sum of the worths to each player of
any position is always zero; in particular, when one player wins, the other
player loses. Having computed static estimates, a player will then choose a
move which leads to the best possible end position, bearing in mind that the
opposing player will try and do the same.

Here is a simple example. The tree in Figure 9.7 represents a game tree
that has been pruned to a depth two by one of the players, say player A, in an
attempt to find the best move. The tips of this tree are labelled with the static
estimates of the end positions as a measure of worth to player A (because it
is As turn to move in these positions). The best of these has value 65. If,
however, player A chooses the move that leads to this position, then player
B will counter by choosing the move that leads to the position with worth
(-40). In fact, the best that A can do is to arrive at the position with worth
20. This value is called the *minimax* value of the tree. In Figure 9.7, internal
nodes of the tree are labelled with their minimax values. These values can be
calculated in the following way. If position p has next positions $p_1, p_2, \ldots, p_n$
with worths $w_1, w_2, \ldots, w_n$, then the minimax value of p is given: by

$$max\ [-w_1, -w_2, \ldots, -w_n]$$

or, equivalently, by:

$$-min\ [w_1, w_2, \ldots, w_n]$$

(Remember, the worth of a position is always calculated as it appears to
the player to move in the position.) Assuming that trees are labelled with
numerical estimates of positions, rather than the positions themselves, we
can define *minimax* by:

$$minimax\ (Node\ x\ ts)\ =\ x, \qquad\qquad\qquad \textbf{if } ts = [\,]$$
$$=\ -min\ (map\ minimax\ ts), \quad \textbf{otherwise}$$

Notice that only the numerical estimates attached to end positions are used
by *minimax*.

To compute the minimax value of a position, we define:

$$dynamic\ n\ =\ minimax \cdot mapgtree\ static \cdot prune\ n \cdot gametree$$

The function $(dynamic\ n)$ takes a position, generates a game tree, prunes
the tree to a given depth n, converts the tree into a tree of static estimates
(with the help of some given function $static :: position \to num$), and finally
computes its minimax value. Although *static* is applied to every position
of the tree, and not just terminal positions, only the static estimates of
terminal positions are needed. Under lazy evaluation, the static estimates of
non-terminal positions will never be computed.

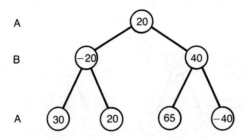

Figure 9.7 A game tree.

We have shown how to calculate the minimax value of a position p, but not how to use it to select a move. Clearly, the required move is one which leads to a position with value $(-v)$, where v is the minimax value of p. The problem is to avoid computing minimax values twice. One solution is to use additional labels to remember position values. We shall leave details as an exercise.

9.7.1   The alpha–beta algorithm

When exploring large game trees it is important to do as little work as possible. In this respect, the given method for computing *minimax* is not optimal. Consider the tree in Figure 9.8. The tips marked ? represent positions whose static values are not known. This means that y is not known either. However, we do know that $y \geq 30$ and this information is sufficient to determine x:

$$x = -min\,[20, y] = -20$$

Putting it another way, the minimax value of the left subtree puts an upper bound on the usefulness of calculating y exactly. Once it is established that the value of y must exceed this bound, even if y is not known exactly, further calculation of y can be abandoned. Since exploration of the tree below y only serves to give lower bounds to y, we can therefore stop computing y whenever the two bounds cross.

This idea leads to an improvement, called *alpha–beta pruning*, on the minimaxing procedure. The key to the optimisation is to consider a bounded version, *bmx* say, of the function *minimax*. We specify *bmx* by the equation:

$$bmx\ a\ b\ t = a \textbf{ max}\ (minimax\ t)\ \textbf{min}\ b$$

where a and b are numbers (the 'alpha' and 'beta' values) such that $a \leq b$. Since:

$$(a \textbf{ max } x) \textbf{ min } b = a \textbf{ max } (x \textbf{ min } b)$$

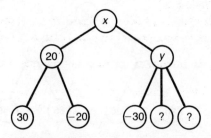

Figure 9.8 An incomplete tree.

whenever $a \le b$, brackets can be omitted from the right-hand expression without fear of ambiguity.

The function bmx can be used to compute $minimax$ provided some constant $m > 0$ is given such that:

$$-m \le static\ p \le m$$

for all positions p. We then have:

$$minimax\ t = bmx\ (-m)\ m\ t$$

Although the specification of bmx refers to the value $(minimax\ t)$, this value is not required to determine bmx when $a = b$. We have:

$$bmx\ a\ a\ t = a$$

and so evaluation of $(minimax\ t)$ is not required. This is the basis of alpha–beta pruning. Put simply, the bounded evaluation of a tree is carried out sequentially in some order, and the estimates a and b are improved as evaluation unfolds. If and when the bounds coincide, the minimax value can be returned without exploring any more of the tree.

As a final exercise in program synthesis, let us now derive an alternative definition of bmx that implements the alpha–beta algorithm. We start with the specification:

$$bmx\ a\ b\ (Node\ x\ ts) = a\ \textbf{max}\ (minimax\ (Node\ x\ ts))\ \textbf{min}\ b$$

where $a \le b$ and consider two cases. (For brevity, we write mmx for $minimax$.)

Case $ts = [\,]$. Here we have:

$$
\begin{aligned}
&bmx\ a\ b\ (Node\ x\ [\,]) \\
&= \quad a\ \textbf{max}\ (mmx\ (Node\ x\ [\,]))\ \textbf{min}\ b \quad \text{(spec.)} \\
&= \quad a\ \textbf{max}\ x\ \textbf{min}\ b \quad\quad\quad\quad\quad\quad (minimax.1)
\end{aligned}
$$

Case $ts \neq [\,]$. Here we have:

$bmx \; a \; b \; (Node \; x \; ts)$
$= \; a \, \textbf{max} \, (mmx \, (Node \; x \; ts)) \, \textbf{min} \; b \qquad (\text{spec.})$
$= \; a \, \textbf{max} \, (-min \, (map \; mmx \; ts)) \, \textbf{min} \; b \qquad (minimax.1)$

In order to proceed, we introduce a new function cmx, satisfying:

$$cmx \; a \; b \; ts = a \, \textbf{max} \, (-min \, (map \; mmx \; ts)) \, \textbf{min} \; b$$

where $a \leq b$. We can now write:

$$bmx \; a \; b \; (Node \; x \; ts) \;\; = \;\; cmx \; a \; b \; ts, \;\; \text{if} \;\; ts \neq [\,]$$

The remaining steps are directed towards obtaining a recursive definition of cmx that does not involve mmx. There are two cases to consider, depending on whether $ts = [\,]$ or not. For the second, we shall need the following law of negation:

$$-(x \, \textbf{min} \; y) = (-x) \, \textbf{max} \, (-y)$$

Case $[\,]$. Here we have:

$cmx \; a \; b \; [\,]$
$= \; a \, \textbf{max} \, (-min \, (map \; mmx \; [\,])) \, \textbf{min} \; b \quad (\text{spec}:cmx)$
$= \; a \, \textbf{max} \, (-min \, [\,]) \, \textbf{min} \; b \qquad\qquad (map.1)$
$= \; a \, \textbf{max} \, (-\infty) \, \textbf{min} \; b$
$= \; a$

Case $(t : ts)$. Here we have:

$cmx \; a \; b \; (t : ts)$
$= \; a \, \textbf{max} \, (-min \, (map \; mmx \, (t : ts))) \, \textbf{min} \; b \qquad\qquad (\text{spec}: cmx)$
$= \; a \, \textbf{max} \, (-((mmx \; t) \, \textbf{min} \, (min \, (map \; mmx \; ts)))) \, \textbf{min} \; b$

using laws of map and min. To improve readability, let us introduce the abbreviations:
$$x \;\; = \;\; mmx \; t$$
$$y \;\; = \;\; min \, (map \; mmx \; ts)$$

so the last expression is:

$a \, \textbf{max} \, (-(x \, \textbf{min} \; y)) \, \textbf{min} \; b$
$= \; a \, \textbf{max} \, ((-x) \, \textbf{max} \, (-y)) \, \textbf{min} \; b \qquad (\text{negation})$
$= \; (a \, \textbf{max} \, (-x) \, \textbf{max} \, (-y)) \, \textbf{min} \; b \qquad (\text{assoc}:\textbf{max})$
$= \; (a \, \textbf{max} \, (-x) \, \textbf{min} \; b) \, \textbf{max} \, (-y) \, \textbf{min} \; b$

using the distributive laws of **max** and **min**. Expanding out the abbreviations x and y, the last expression is just $(cmx \; a' \; b \; ts)$, where:

$$a' = a \, \textbf{max} \, (-mmx \; t) \, \textbf{min} \; b$$

Finally, by applying negation twice we obtain:

$$
\begin{aligned}
a' &= a \max (-mmx\ t) \min b \\
&= -((-a) \min (mmx\ t) \max (-b)) \\
&= -bmx\ (-b)\ (-a)\ t
\end{aligned}
$$

We have therefore obtained that:

$$
\begin{aligned}
cmx\ a\ b\ [\,] \quad &= \quad a \\
cmx\ a\ b\ (t : ts) \quad &= \quad cmx\ a'\ b\ ts \\
&\qquad \textbf{where}\ \ a' = -bmx\ (-b)\ (-a)\ t
\end{aligned}
$$

As a final step, we make use of the fact that:

$$
cmx\ a\ a\ ts = a
$$

and so, when the bounds a and b are equal, further exploration of ts is unnecessary. The right-hand side of the definition of cmx is changed to read:

$$
\begin{aligned}
cmx\ a\ b\ (t : ts) \quad &= \quad a', &&\textbf{if}\ a' = b \\
&= \quad cmx\ a'\ b\ ts, &&\textbf{otherwise} \\
&\qquad \textbf{where}\ \ a' = -bmx\ (-b)\ (-a)\ t
\end{aligned}
$$

Let us conclude by writing out the complete definition of bmx:

$$
\begin{aligned}
bmx\ a\ b\ (Node\ x\ ts) \quad &= \quad a \max x \min b, &&\textbf{if}\ ts = [\,] \\
&= \quad cmx\ a\ b\ ts, &&\textbf{otherwise} \\[1em]
cmx\ a\ b\ [\,] \quad &= \quad a \\
cmx\ a\ b\ (t : ts) \quad &= \quad a', &&\textbf{if}\ a' = b \\
&= \quad cmx\ a'\ b\ ts, &&\textbf{otherwise} \\
&\qquad \textbf{where}\ \ a' = -bmx\ (-b)\ (-a)\ t
\end{aligned}
$$

Exercises

9.7.1 If *prune* is analogous to *take*, suggest a function analogous to *drop*.

9.7.2 Design a function that takes a positive integer n and a game tree gt, and returns a game tree ngt such that (i) ngt is a subtree of gt; (ii) ngt contains the position estimated by (*dynamic n*) to be the best end position achievable.

9.7.3 Design a program to play Noughts and Crosses (also called Tic-Tac-Toe). Make the program interactive.

Appendix A

The ASCII Character Set

The table on the following page gives the numerical codes of the characters in the ASCII character set. The primitive function:

$$code :: char \rightarrow num$$

converts a character to its ASCII code number (in the range 0 to 127), and:

$$decode :: num \rightarrow char$$

does the reverse. In particular, the newline character '⤶' in strings has code 10, and the space character '␣' has code 32.

0	NUL	32	SP	64	@	96	'
1	SOH	33	!	65	A	97	a
2	STX	34	"	66	B	98	b
3	ETX	35	#	67	C	99	c
4	EOT	36	$	68	D	100	d
5	ENQ	37	%	69	E	101	e
6	ACK	38	&	70	F	102	f
7	BEL	39	'	71	G	103	g
8	BS	40	(	72	H	104	h
9	HT	41	)	73	I	105	i
10	LF	42	*	74	J	106	j
11	VT	43	+	75	K	107	k
12	FF	44	,	76	L	108	l
13	CR	45	−	77	M	109	m
14	SO	46	.	78	N	110	n
15	SI	47	/	79	O	111	o
16	DLE	48	0	80	P	112	p
17	DC1	49	1	81	Q	113	q
18	DC2	50	2	82	R	114	r
19	DC3	51	3	83	S	115	s
20	DC4	52	4	84	T	116	t
21	NAK	53	5	85	U	117	u
22	SYN	54	6	86	V	118	v
23	ETB	55	7	87	W	119	w
24	CAN	56	8	88	X	120	x
25	EM	57	9	89	Y	121	y
26	SUB	58	:	90	Z	122	z
27	ESC	59	;	91	[	123	{
28	FS	60	<	92	\	124	|
29	GS	61	=	93	]	125	}
30	RS	62	>	94	^	126	~
31	US	63	?	95	_	127	DEL

Appendix B

Some Standard Functions

Below, arranged in alphabetical order, is a summary of the most commonly used functions, together with their definitions.

1. *and.* Returns the logical conjunction of a list of booleans:

$$
\begin{aligned}
and \quad &:: \quad [bool] \to bool \\
and \quad &= \quad foldr\ (\land)\ True
\end{aligned}
$$

2. (+\!+). Concatenates two lists:

$$
\begin{aligned}
(+\!+) \qquad\qquad &:: \quad [\alpha] \to [\alpha] \to [\alpha] \\
[\,]+\!+ys \qquad &= \quad ys \\
(x:xs)+\!+ys \quad &= \quad x:(xs+\!+ys)
\end{aligned}
$$

3. *concat.* Concatenates a list of lists:

$$
\begin{aligned}
concat \quad &:: \quad [[\alpha]] \to [\alpha] \\
concat \quad &= \quad foldr\ (+\!+)\ [\,]
\end{aligned}
$$

4. *const.* Creates a constant-valued function:

$$
\begin{aligned}
const \quad &:: \quad \alpha \to \beta \to \alpha \\
const\ k\ x \quad &= \quad k
\end{aligned}
$$

5. *drop.* Selects a final segment of a list:

$$
\begin{aligned}
drop \qquad\qquad\quad &:: \quad num \to [\alpha] \to [\alpha] \\
drop\ 0\ xs \qquad\quad &= \quad xs \\
drop\ (n+1)\ [\,] \quad &= \quad [\,] \\
drop\ (n+1)\ (x:xs) \quad &= \quad drop\ n\ xs
\end{aligned}
$$

6. *dropwhile*. Removes the longest initial segment of a list all of whose elements satisfy a given predicate:

$$
\begin{aligned}
&dropwhile &&:: &&(\alpha \rightarrow bool) \rightarrow [\alpha] \rightarrow [\alpha] \\
&dropwhile\ p\ [\,] &&= &&[\,] \\
&dropwhile\ p\ (x:xs) &&= &&dropwhile\ p\ xs, &&\text{if } p\ x \\
& &&= &&x:xs, &&\text{otherwise}
\end{aligned}
$$

7. *filter*. Filters a list with a predicate:

$$
\begin{aligned}
&filter &&:: &&(\alpha \rightarrow bool) \rightarrow [\alpha] \rightarrow [\alpha] \\
&filter\ p\ [\,] &&= &&[\,] \\
&filter\ p\ (x:xs) &&= &&x:filter\ p\ xs, &&\text{if } p\ x \\
& &&= &&filter\ p\ xs, &&\text{otherwise}
\end{aligned}
$$

8. *foldl*. Fold-left:

$$
\begin{aligned}
&foldl &&:: &&(\alpha \rightarrow \beta \rightarrow \alpha) \rightarrow \alpha \rightarrow [\beta] \rightarrow \alpha \\
&foldl\ f\ a\ [\,] &&= &&a \\
&foldl\ f\ a\ (x:xs) &&= &&strict\ (foldl\ f)\ (f\ a\ x)\ xs
\end{aligned}
$$

9. *foldl1*. Fold-left over non-empty lists:

$$
\begin{aligned}
&foldl1 &&:: &&(\alpha \rightarrow \alpha \rightarrow \alpha) \rightarrow [\alpha] \rightarrow \alpha \\
&foldl1\ f\ (x:xs) &&= &&foldl\ f\ x\ xs
\end{aligned}
$$

10. *foldr*. Fold-right:

$$
\begin{aligned}
&foldr &&:: &&(\alpha \rightarrow \beta \rightarrow \beta) \rightarrow \beta \rightarrow [\alpha] \rightarrow \beta \\
&foldr\ f\ a\ [\,] &&= &&a \\
&foldr\ f\ a\ (x:xs) &&= &&f\ x\ (foldr\ f\ a\ xs)
\end{aligned}
$$

11. *foldr1*. Fold-right over non-empty lists:

$$
\begin{aligned}
&foldr1 &&:: &&(\alpha \rightarrow \alpha \rightarrow \alpha) \rightarrow [\alpha] \rightarrow \alpha \\
&foldr1\ f\ [x] &&= &&x \\
&foldr1\ f\ (x:y:xs) &&= &&f\ x\ (foldr1\ f\ (y:xs))
\end{aligned}
$$

12. *fst*. Selects the first component of a pair:

$$
\begin{aligned}
&fst &&:: &&(\alpha, \beta) \rightarrow \alpha \\
&fst\ (x, y) &&= &&x
\end{aligned}
$$

13. *hd*. Returns the first element of a non-empty list:

$$
\begin{aligned}
&hd &&:: &&[\alpha] \rightarrow \alpha \\
&hd\ (x:xs) &&= &&x
\end{aligned}
$$

14. *id*. The identity function:

$$id \quad :: \quad \alpha \to \alpha$$
$$id \; x \;\; = \;\; x$$

15. *init*. Returns a list without its last element:

$$init \qquad :: \quad [\alpha] \to [\alpha]$$
$$init \, (x : xs) \;\; = \;\; [\,], \qquad \qquad \text{if } xs = [\,]$$
$$= \;\; x : init \; xs, \;\; \textbf{otherwise}$$

16. *iterate*. Produces an infinite list of iterated applications of a function to a value:

$$iterate \qquad :: \quad (\alpha \to \alpha) \to \alpha \to [\alpha]$$
$$iterate \, f \, x \;\; = \;\; x : iterate \, f \, (f \, x)$$

17. *last*. Returns the last element of a non-empty list:

$$last \qquad :: \quad [\alpha] \to \alpha$$
$$last \, (x : xs) \;\; = \;\; x, \qquad \qquad \text{if } xs = [\,]$$
$$= \;\; last \; xs, \;\; \textbf{otherwise}$$

18. (#). Returns the length of a list:

$$(\#) \qquad \qquad :: \quad [\alpha] \to num$$
$$\#[\,] \qquad \qquad = \;\; 0$$
$$\#(x : xs) \qquad = \;\; 1 + \#xs$$

19. (−−). List-difference: $(xs -- ys)$ is the list that results when, for each element y in ys, the first occurrence (if any) of y is removed from xs:

$$(--) \qquad \qquad :: \quad [\alpha] \to [\alpha] \to [\alpha]$$
$$xs -- [\,] \qquad \;\; = \;\; xs$$
$$xs -- (y : ys) \;\; = \;\; remove \; xs \; y \; -- \; ys$$
$$\textbf{where}$$
$$remove \, [\,] \, y \qquad \;\; = \;\; [\,]$$
$$remove \, (x : xs) \, y \;\; = \;\; xs, \qquad \qquad \text{if } x = y$$
$$= \;\; x : remove \; xs \; y \quad \textbf{otherwise}$$

20. (!). List-index: $(xs \, ! \, n)$ returns the nth element of xs:

$$(!) \qquad \qquad \qquad :: \quad [\alpha] \to num \to \alpha$$
$$(x : xs) \, ! \, 0 \qquad \;\; = \;\; x$$
$$(x : xs) \, ! \, (n + 1) \;\; = \;\; xs \, ! \, n$$

21. ($\wedge$). Logical conjunction:

$$
\begin{aligned}
(\wedge) \quad &:: \quad bool \rightarrow bool \rightarrow bool \\
True \wedge y \ &= \ y \\
False \wedge y \ &= \ False
\end{aligned}
$$

22. ($\vee$). Logical disjunction:

$$
\begin{aligned}
(\vee) \quad &:: \quad bool \rightarrow bool \rightarrow bool \\
True \vee y \ &= \ True \\
False \vee y \ &= \ y
\end{aligned}
$$

23. ($\neg$). Logical negation:

$$
\begin{aligned}
(\neg) \quad &:: \quad bool \rightarrow bool \\
\neg\, True \ &= \ False \\
\neg\, False \ &= \ True
\end{aligned}
$$

24. *map*. Applies a function to every element of a list:

$$
\begin{aligned}
map \quad &:: \quad (\alpha \rightarrow \beta) \rightarrow [\alpha] \rightarrow [\beta] \\
map\ f\ [] \ &= \ [] \\
map\ f\ (x : xs) \ &= \ f\ x : map\ f\ xs
\end{aligned}
$$

25. *max*. Returns the maximum value in a non-empty list:

$$
\begin{aligned}
max \quad &:: \quad [\alpha] \rightarrow \alpha \\
max \ &= \ foldl1\ (\mathbf{max})
\end{aligned}
$$

26. *min*. Returns the minimum value in a non-empty list:

$$
\begin{aligned}
min \quad &:: \quad [\alpha] \rightarrow \alpha \\
min \ &= \ foldl1\ (\mathbf{min})
\end{aligned}
$$

27. *or*. Returns the logical disjunction of a list of booleans:

$$
\begin{aligned}
or \quad &:: \quad [bool] \rightarrow bool \\
or \ &= \ foldr\ (\vee)\ False
\end{aligned}
$$

28. *product*. Returns the product of a list of numbers:

$$
\begin{aligned}
product \quad &:: \quad [num] \rightarrow num \\
product \ &= \ foldl\ (\times)\ 1
\end{aligned}
$$

29. *reverse.* Reverses a finite list:

$$reverse \quad :: \quad [\alpha] \to [\alpha]$$
$$reverse \quad = \quad foldl \, prefix \, [\,]$$
$$\textbf{where} \; prefix \, xs \, x = x : xs$$

30. *scan.* Applies *foldl* to every initial segment of a list:

$$scan \qquad :: \quad (\alpha \to \beta \to \alpha) \to \alpha \to [\beta] \to [\alpha]$$
$$scan \, f \, a \, xs \quad = \quad a : scan' \, f \, a \, xs$$
$$\textbf{where} \; scan' \, f \, a \, [\,] \qquad = \quad [\,]$$
$$scan' \, f \, a \, (x : xs) \quad = \quad scan \, f \, (f \, a \, x) \, xs$$

31. *snd.* Selects the second component of a pair:

$$snd \qquad :: \quad (\alpha, \beta) \to \beta$$
$$snd \, (x, y) \quad = \quad y$$

32. *sort.* Sorts a finite list into non-decreasing order (using *quicksort*):

$$sort \qquad :: \quad [\alpha] \to [\alpha]$$
$$sort \, [\,] \qquad = \quad [\,]$$
$$sort \, (x : xs) \quad = \quad sort \, [u \mid u \leftarrow xs; \; u < x]$$
$$+\!\!\!+ [x]$$
$$+\!\!\!+ sort \, [u \mid u \leftarrow xs; \; u \geq x]$$

33. *sum.* Returns the sum of a list of numbers:

$$sum \quad :: \quad [num] \to num$$
$$sum \quad = \quad foldl \, (+) \, 0$$

34. *tl.* Removes the first element of a non-empty list:

$$tl \qquad :: \quad [\alpha] \to [\alpha]$$
$$tl \, (x : xs) \quad = \quad xs$$

35. *take.* Selects an initial segment of a list:

$$take \qquad\qquad :: \quad num \to [\alpha] \to [\alpha]$$
$$take \, 0 \, xs \qquad\quad = \quad [\,]$$
$$take \, (n+1) \, [\,] \qquad = \quad [\,]$$
$$take \, (n+1) \, (x : xs) \quad = \quad x : take \, n \, xs$$

36. *takewhile.* Selects the longest initial segment of a list all of whose elements satisfy a given predicate:

$$takewhile \qquad\qquad :: \quad (\alpha \to bool) \to [\alpha] \to [\alpha]$$
$$takewhile \, p \, [\,] \qquad = \quad [\,]$$
$$takewhile \, p \, (x : xs) \quad = \quad x : takewhile \, p \, xs, \qquad \textbf{if } p \, x$$
$$= \quad [\,], \qquad\qquad\qquad\quad \textbf{otherwise}$$

37. *until*. Applied to a predicate, a function and a value, returns the result of applying the function to the value the smallest number of times in order to satisfy the predicate:

$$
\begin{aligned}
until \quad &:: \quad (\alpha \to bool) \to (\alpha \to \alpha) \to \alpha \to \alpha \\
until\ p\ f\ x \ &= \quad x, \qquad\qquad\qquad \text{if } p\ x \\
&= \quad until\ p\ f\ (f\ x), \quad \text{otherwise}
\end{aligned}
$$

38. *zip*. Takes a pair of lists into a list of pairs of corresponding elements:

$$
\begin{aligned}
zip \qquad\qquad\qquad &:: \quad ([\alpha],[\beta]) \to [(\alpha,\beta)] \\
zip\,([\,],ys) \qquad\quad &= \quad [\,] \\
zip\,((x:xs),[\,]) \qquad &= \quad [\,] \\
zip\,((x:xs),(y:ys)) &= \quad (x,y) : zip\,(xs,ys)
\end{aligned}
$$

Appendix C

Programming in Miranda

Although we have not used the specific syntax of a particular programming language in this book, the notation is – apart from typographical issues – very close to a subset of the functional language Miranda[1]. In this Appendix we give a quick and informal description of how to translate the notation used in the book into Miranda. Readers are advised that what follows does not constitute a definition of Miranda; in particular, there are many features of Miranda that we have not introduced into our notation, and certain conventions and restrictions that followed in the book may not be enforced by Miranda. For a more detailed discussion of Miranda, see David Turner's article: *An Overview of Miranda*, SIGPLAN Notices, December 1986.[2]

Conditional equations. Perhaps the main difference in writing definitions in Miranda is that the particular keyword **if** is omitted before guards in functions defined by cases. For example the definition:

$$
\begin{aligned}
strep\ xs\quad &=\quad [0], &&\textbf{if }\ ys = [\,] \\
&=\quad ys, &&\textbf{otherwise} \\
&\textbf{where}\ \ ys = dropwhile\ (= 0)\ xs
\end{aligned}
$$

is translated into Miranda as follows:

```
strep xs = [0],   ys = []
         = ys,    otherwise
         where ys = dropwhile (=0) xs
```

Note that `otherwise` and `where` are reserved words in Miranda.

Typography. The Miranda syntax for the mathematical and other symbols used in the book is described under four headings as follows.

---

[1] Miranda is a trade-mark of Research Software Ltd.

[2] Further information about the Miranda system and its availability for various computers may be obtained from Research Software Ltd, 23 St Augustines Road, Canterbury CT1 1XP, England, or from the following electronic mail address - "mira-request@ukc.ac.uk".

Basic operators.
These are translated according to the table:

Book	/	div	mod	×	++	∧	∨	¬	≠	≥	≤
Miranda	/	div	mod	*	++	&	\/	~	~=	>=	<=

Ascii characters.
In common with many languages, Miranda uses an "escape" convention for denoting certain characters inside character and string constants: this involves prefixing another character by a backslash \. The most common instance is the newline character '↵', which is translated as '\n'. Also, the backslash, the single-quote, and the double-quote character are translated as '\\', '\'', and '\"' respectively.

User defined operators.
In Miranda all user defined infix operators are written as normal identifiers preceded by a $ character. Taking our picture processing operators (see Chapter 4) as examples, **above** becomes $above and **below** becomes $below. Thus, the function:

$$lframe\ (m, n)\ p\ =\ (p\ \textbf{beside}\ empty\ (h, n - w))$$
$$\textbf{above}\ empty\ (m - h, n)$$
$$\textbf{where}\ h\ =\ height\ p$$
$$w\ =\ width\ p$$

would be written in Miranda as:

```
lframe (m,n) p = (p $beside empty(h,n-w))
                 $above empty (m-h,n)
                 where  h = height p
                        w = width p
```

Type variables.
Generic type variables for which in this book we have used the greek letters α, β, γ, and so on, are written in Miranda *, **, ***, and so on. For example, the type of the function map is expressed in Miranda as follows:

```
map :: (* -> **) -> [*] -> [**]
```

Standard functions.   The Miranda standard environment provides a library of useful functions, many of which have been used in this book. However, there are some differences with the list given in Appendix B, the most important of which are as follows:

(i) The function *foldl* is given a different type and definition in Miranda. In Miranda the definition of *foldl* is essentially as follows:

```
foldl :: (* -> ** -> **) -> ** -> [*] -> **
foldl f a [] = a
foldl f a (x:xs) = foldl f (f x a) xs
```

In particular, `foldl` has the same type as `foldr`. Moreover, `foldl` is not made strict in its second argument.

For example, in Miranda we can write:

```
reverse = foldl (:) []
```

In the notation used in this book, we have

$$reverse \ = \ foldl \ snoc \ [\,]$$
$$\textbf{where} \ \ snoc \ xs \ x = x : xs$$

(ii) The function *zip* is provided in Miranda, but as a curried function `zip2`, with the definition:

```
zip2 :: [*] -> [**] -> [*,**]
zip2 (a:as) (b:bs) = (a,b):zip2 as bs
zip2 as bs = []
```

Miranda also defines `zip3`, `zip4`, and so on (up to 6) for zipping triples and other tuples.

(iii) The following functions are not (currently) provided in the Miranda standard environment:

foldl1   *foldr1*   *scan*   *fst*   *snd*

(iv) The infix operators **max** and **min** are not provided in Miranda. Instead one uses the listwise functions `max` and `min`. So, where in this book we write (a **max** b), the Miranda programmer would write `max[a,b]`.

Bibliography

[1] Marvin Minsky (1967) *Computation: Finite and Infinite Machines.* Prentice Hall Inc., Englewood Cliffs, NJ.

[2] Donald E. Knuth (1969) *The Art of Computer Programming, Volume 2: Seminumerical Algorithms.* Addison-Wesley, Reading, Mass.

[3] Donald E. Knuth (1968) *The Art of Computer Programming, Volume 1: Fundamental Algorithms.* Addison-Wesley, Reading, Mass.

[4] Robert S. Boyer and J. Strother Moore (1979) *A Computational Logic.* Academic Press, London.

[5] M. J. Gordon, R. Milner, and C. P. Wadsworth (1979) *Edinburgh LCF. Lecture Notes in Computer Science 78*, Springer-Verlag, Berlin.

[6] Larry Paulson (1983) Rewriting in *Cambridge LCF. Science of Computer Programming*, **3**:119–149.

[7] Simon L. Peyton Jones and Philip Wadler. The semantics of pattern-matching and efficient implementation of pattern-matching. Chapters 4 and 5 of reference [8].

[8] Simon L. Peyton Jones (1987) *The Implementation of Functional Programming Languages.* Prentice Hall International, Hemel Hempstead.

[9] Peter Henderson (1980) *Functional Programming: Application and Implementation.* Prentice Hall International, Hemel Hempstead.

[10] Donald E. Knuth (1973) *The Art of Computer Programming, Volume 3: Sorting and Searching.* Addison-Wesley, Reading, Mass.

[11] Thomas A. Standish (1980) *Data Structure Techniques.* Addison-Wesley, Reading, Mass.

Index